——————— THE TEXAS SUPREME COURT ———————

TEXAS LEGAL STUDIES SERIES
Texas Supreme Court Historical Society

*Texas's rich legal heritage spans more than three centuries and has
roots in both Spanish law and the English common law, but this dimension
of the state's history is relatively unexplored. Books in the Texas Legal Studies
Series examine a range of topics, including state-specific studies and
those with a regional or national focus.*

THE TEXAS
SUPREME COURT

A Narrative History, 1836–1986

JAMES L. HALEY

UNIVERSITY OF TEXAS PRESS
Austin

Requests for permission to reproduce material
from this work should be sent to:
Permissions
University of Texas Press
P.O. Box 7819
Austin, TX 78713-7819
http://utpress.utexas.edu/about/book-permissions

∞ The paper used in this book meets the minimum requirements of
ANSI/NISO Z39.48-1992 (R1997) (Permanence of Paper).

Library of Congress Cataloging-in-Publication Data
Haley, James L.
The Texas Supreme Court : a narrative history, 1836–1986 /
by James L. Haley. — 1st ed.
p.   cm. — (Texas legal studies series)
Includes bibliographical references and index.
ISBN 978-0-292-74458-5 (cloth : alk. paper)
1. Texas. Supreme Court—History.   2. Courts of last resort—
Texas—History.   3. Law—Texas—History.   I. Title.
KFT1712.H35   2013
347.764′03509—dc23
2012026733

doi:10.7560/744585

Nothing so bespeaks a people as their notions of justice. Their jurisprudence . . . is the supreme expression of their moral convictions. In it their very character is indelibly written, and hence by it they are to be truly judged.

NELSON PHILLIPS
CHIEF JUSTICE (1915–1921)
SUPREME COURT OF TEXAS

CONTENTS

FOREWORD

"There's nothing entertaining about a state court. It's legal drudgery." I was told this by a respected historian when the Texas Supreme Court Historical Society was sizing up the task of writing the present volume. I disagreed then, and continued to disagree over the years, yet had only my theatrical predisposition to see dramatic conflict in the most casual interactions to buttress my opinion. But as soon as the manuscript chapters for the first book-length history of the Texas Supreme Court since 1917 began rolling off Jim Haley's printer in 2010, I had the proof I needed. Filling the pages were story after story, rich in character, thick with tension, and as compelling to read as a mystery novel. Buried beneath the dry legalities of Texas judicial history lay a narrative stream that Haley located with the art and certainty of a seasoned dowser. The dream of the society for the past thirteen years was finally coming to pass.

That dream began in the summer of 1997 during a board of trustees meeting that concentrated largely on how to increase the historical society's archival holdings of court-related material. Toward the end of the meeting, former justice Will R. Wilson expressed his hope that "the society would sponsor a published history of the Supreme Court." And he added, parenthetically, that he would be willing to "contribute money toward such a project." A few minutes later, as one of the final decisions of the day, the board selected Southern Methodist University School of Law professor Joseph W. McKnight, who was, as you might suspect, absent from this particular meeting, for the task of considering Judge Wilson's offer and submitting a proposal.

That which you hold in your hand differs from the book proposed by Professor McKnight. The subject is the same, of course, and the time frame similar, even if a bit longer, but the board's decision to rely on a single author's point of view, to commission a historian who had attended law school but who was not a lawyer, to concentrate as much on stories as on cases, to include judicial biographies in the main text, and to appeal to the largest possible audience draws this book more in line with the first history of the Court, the one Harbert Davenport wrote almost a century ago, and closer to the handful of other state court histories—those for Tennessee and Missouri, for example—that were on the market when this book was begun. The degree to which this approach altered the initial concept for this book probably disappointed those who came to the task with a grand vision for the final product. Committee members charged with the society's history book project originally sought a masterwork in three volumes—a chronicle of the Court that included an in-depth study of all the important cases and judicial trends in one volume, with a second volume set aside for biographies, and a third for short articles on court-related topics. More than a judicial history of the Court, the boxed set of books would serve as a reference work written by attorneys for use by attorneys, and would become an invaluable resource for the legal community—a bold reach for the definitive edition.

The book that James Haley was asked to write in 2009, however, was never meant to survey all the cases, sort through all the events, or even mention all the justices who sat on the Court. Though smaller in scope, Haley's book had a far more challenging task: it had to change people's attitudes about Texas judicial history, remove the perception of "legal drudgery," and capture the attention of everyone from the appellate lawyer to the history buff, the middle school teacher to the law school professor, along with all those folks who live outside Texas. Most importantly, Haley had to convince attorneys, especially the younger crop of law school graduates, that as a field of study, civil litigation in Texas is worthy of their time and effort, and quite possibly a career.

Compared to cases laid before the United States Supreme Court, where practically every petition amounts to a confrontation with the Constitution, the civil appeals that reach the Texas Supreme Court, shorn of the pathos and intrigue of criminal conduct and largely devoid of state constitutional concerns—certainly the civil rights issues so often seen at the federal level—present a dismal picture for the legal historian wishing to captivate the general public. This perception is especially true of the twentieth century, the period for which in-depth research in the state's judicial history is most needed. Whenever legal scholars, who regularly tromped about the Republic era plowing up rustic cases and colorful characters, surveyed the wide, unbroken fields of the subsequent century, they would balk. Across that fence lay one hundred years of lawsuits and civil appeals over contracts, patents, insurance, interest payments, royalties—an exponentially increasing number of cases resting on an ever-narrower set of issues. Almost to a person, the scholars turned away. They didn't see it as a chance to lay claim to the field for themselves; rather they perceived the subject as one filled with arid legal issues that would be of interest only to a legal specialist. Besides, no one had surveyed the ground; there was no map to give them the lay of the land. Venturing into the twentieth century meant breaking some very hard soil. They would need to spend months of tedious spadework preparing case studies, trend analyses, inquiries on procedural rules, and shifts in judicial philosophy. And after all the facts were gathered, they would still have to sift through the documents to find compelling stories. The prospect of teasing a coherent story line, much less an entertaining one, from a mountain of civil lawsuits was a task they would rather avoid. And they did. Everyone did, pretty much right up until the history book project began.

Contributing authors, nevertheless, took to the field in 2000 with enthusiasm and high aspirations. Organizing chapter assignments, time frames, and research requirements, the volunteer team of authors outlined the first of the three-volume history. The nineteenth century would sort itself out, of course—plenty of solid research from which to draw, some penned as early as the 1890s, the best published in the last thirty years, much of it written by the contributing authors themselves. But the twentieth century? They had only the vaguest notion what they might find after 1900. They undertook their work in their spare time, on weekends and holidays, without compensation, aided by an occasional college student but largely dependent on their own research skills. And those recruited to make sense of the twentieth century labored under especially disheartening conditions. After a point, it became clear they needed more time to develop the important cases within their time frames. But in truth it would probably have required a barnful of historians concentrating on large and small projects across a whole range of issues to satisfactorily consolidate the judicial history of the last century. Contributing authors punched holes in the soil, producing solid, substantive work in specific regions. Despite their efforts, however, no one writing about the twentieth century, except Professor Michael Ariens, managed to traverse his entire time frame. It was inexpressibly daunting. And while Ariens uncovered a fascinating story hidden within his decade, 1911–1921, he would no doubt be the first to admit that he could have written three more papers of the same length on those very same years.

James Haley's task, then, was to pull together the valuable work accomplished by the contributing authors, find enough narrative sustenance in each decade to feed the current group of readers—attorneys and laypeople—and, if possible, to water the ground for a new crop of legal historians. Haley went drilling for water and struck a geyser. We are all the beneficiaries of his success.

William S. Pugsley
Executive Director
Texas Supreme Court Historical Society

PREFACE

The last book-length history of the Texas Supreme Court was published almost a century ago. Harbert Davenport's *The History of the Supreme Court of the State of Texas* appeared in 1917, the year the United States entered World War I. As a paradigm for his treatment, Davenport drew on the example of James D. Lynch's *The Bench and Bar of Texas*, published in 1885. Both books were products of their times, leaden in style and uncritical in their approach. With a few important exceptions, all the justices were described as profound in their scholarship, farseeing in their written opinions, wise, kind, universally beloved, and pillars of their communities. The exceptions were, of course, those justices imposed on the state by the U.S. military during Reconstruction, who were characterized as venal, wicked, and prejudiced. In Davenport's words, "In the judicial annals of no other country has there been a more lamentable, shameless prostitution of a court of justice to the interest of lawless political conspirators against constitutional government."

The passage of time and the mountain of legal history that have accumulated since Davenport's day, not to mention his Civil War–forged blinders, would by themselves justify revisiting the Texas Court's history. Add to these the fact that the genuinely significant, even monumental, achievements of Texas jurisprudence were stories left largely untold even then, and the case for such a book becomes overwhelming. In addition to devising simplified forms of pleading that could be the envy of any jurisdiction, Texas jurists of the nineteenth century, in the words of legal historian James Paulsen, "invented the homestead, implemented the concept of universal jury trial, and accomplished the first successful merger of law and equity." "Moreover," he added, "when Texas entered the Union as a community property state, it did so as the first American jurisdiction to provide constitutional recognition for married women's property rights."

Then, too, much of this legacy was handed down from a frontier full of danger and uncertainty. One justice was kidnapped by an invading Mexican army, another was assassinated by rampaging feudists, others participated in shootouts with hostile Indians, and more than one was carried off by yellow fever. The story therefore contains a considerable element of drama. The early Court met during different terms in different towns, rivers would rise and mail be lost, and often the records they received from lower courts were incomplete, not to say (as they sometimes noted in their opinions) a mess. In fact, the survival of a written record of the state's early cases was, from the beginning, never assured. Had not the Republic's eager-beaver reporter James W. Dallam made collating and printing those early rulings his life's work (a venture undertaken at his own expense—and reward, once his volume of Republic of Texas–era decisions began selling), there is no guarantee that much would have survived at all.

Scholarly interest in the Texas Supreme Court has never lain fallow, by any means. Justices of earlier years such as Oran Milo Roberts (1857–1862, 1864–1866, 1874–1878) and Reuben Reid Gaines (1886–1911) were fascinated by the legacy of the high bench to which they ascended, and wrote able articles on its history and their predecessors. That tradition was continued in later years by such justices as Few Brewster (1945–1957), Joe R. Greenhill (1957–1982), James R. Norvell (1957–1968), and others.

In addition, a number of legal scholars have worked their way into becoming nationally known authorities on certain eras and facets of the Court's history: Joseph McKnight on the jurisprudence of the Spanish and Mexican eras and on matrimonial law; James W. Paulsen on the Court and justices during the Republic of Texas and antebellum periods; Hans Baade on the Reconstruction Courts and other elements of nineteenth-century law; Michael Ariens on broad legal trends, including the evolution of women's rights and the issue of Court productivity and pendency; and former chief justice Thomas R. Phillips on judicial elections and reform. Others have written important articles that illuminate particular eras of Court history: William Chriss on the Gilded Age and the Court's important rulings on the railroad and insurance giants of that time; and Judge Mark Davidson on the Court in the World War II and postwar eras. This volume stands on all of their shoulders, and the willingness of several of them to read and comment on the manuscript has been both an immense benefit to the book and a testament to their generosity of spirit.

The notion of a history of the Texas Supreme Court—what such a history should contain, how it should be structured, what it should convey—will strike different people differently. The first thought might be that it should be a history of Texas law, and doubtless there are a few scholars of Texas's legal arcana who, when they first learned that such a title was forthcoming, anticipated a monograph detailing the evolution of the legal system. Actually, such a book has already been written: Michael Ariens's *Lone Star Law*, published after work on this book was completed, ably fills that gap.

In contrast, the goal of the present volume is to broaden public interest in the state's highest tribunal beyond those people directly connected with the Court. In so many clauses of the social contract, Texas spent its first 150 years trying to catch up to a modern understanding of things. Few people realize that in the area of law, Texas began its American journey far ahead of most of the rest of the country, far more enlightened on such subjects as women's rights and the protection of debtors. It is a fascinating story populated by fascinating people, and if the goal is to give general readers an appreciation of their unique judicial heritage, then the approach mandated is that of narrative history: to unfold the story as a tale told.

Certainly legal theory must be discussed and cases cited, but within the context of developing a narrative as uniquely Texan as longhorn cattle. Texans will be surprised at the symbiotic relationship between themselves and their Supreme Court, how over the past century and a half they have shaped it even as it has shaped their society. Therefore, this is a history not of the law but of the Court, of the men and women who ascended to it, and of how their rulings have been woven into the tapestry of Texas history.

ACKNOWLEDGMENTS

More than thirty years ago, I entered the University of Texas School of Law, enamored of the U.S. Constitution and Americans' broad notion of "justice." Two years later, I departed to follow a still keener love of history. Thus, when Bill Pugsley, executive director of the Texas Supreme Court Historical Society, first approached me about writing a narrative history of that Court, I thought I had died and gone to heaven. I will always be in his debt for seeking me out and managing the business end of making the book happen.

The greatest challenge from my side, which threatened to turn the process into something of a "reality show," was that the society needed a manuscript in a year. This necessitated working with a consulting editor who could bring me up to speed on key issues, supply me with source material that I would otherwise have to locate on my own, and generally take care of the sorts of things that in earlier years necessitated my taking fifteen years to write *Sam Houston* and seven years to write *Passionate Nation*. This consulting editor was Marilyn Duncan, already in the society's employ and formerly the longtime publications director for the Lyndon B. Johnson School of Public Affairs. In my career of over a dozen books, I have worked with some good editors, but never one who combined the editorial eye and instinct with an almost Germanic efficiency in finding key materials, and such empathy and understanding of the writing process. Working with her has been a revelation, and all I need say of her modesty is that she declined to assume coauthor status, which I offered and which she surely deserves.

In the real world of book publishing, even as it changes beneath our feet, such an effort as this would have been impossible without a financial commitment from key members of the historical society, which includes some of the most prominent members of the Texas bench and bar. Under the fundraising leadership of Larry McNeill, support for this book has been abundant and gratifying.

Equally so has been the generosity of the legal scholars outlined by Bill below, who so kindly made their own research available to me and in many cases consented to read and comment on the manuscript. I was left in awe of their mastery of their subjects, and I hope I merit their approval for the way I have sought to interpret the Texas Supreme Court's history for a broader audience.

James L. Haley

With a history book such as this, whose roots and inspiration reach back decades, before the decision to write was ever made or the author chosen, the task of acknowledging everyone who contributed in some way to its successful completion would require a chapter unto itself, and the possibility of overlooking someone whose assistance substantially improved the manuscript during those long years is too easy to contemplate.

This book arose from the love of judicial history held by the founders of the Texas Supreme Court Historical Society, especially chief justices Robert Calvert, Joe R. Greenhill, and Jack Pope, each of whom studied and wrote about the Supreme Court's history, collected invaluable photographs and memorabilia, and then in 1990 signed the articles of incorporation that created the historical society. Chief Justice Pope saved hundreds of original prints and negatives collected by Judge Ocie Speer from certain destruction when he purchased them from Steck Publishing and donated them to the Tarlton Law Library Special Collections Department at the University of Texas. Justice Jack Hightower, the society's first president, shepherded the organization through the first eight years of its existence, gathering important historical material from the Hemphill family, from former chief justices Hickman, Calvert, and Greenhill, and from many others.

The lifeblood of any project is money. Judge Will R. Wilson not only suggested the idea for a history book in 1997, but also contributed $5,000 as seed money the same year. Judge William L. Garwood quickly added another $10,000 on top of that through his family's foundation. These contributions to the initial history book project were followed by donations over the years from dozens of members too numerous to record here. Both the Garwood Foundation and Judge Garwood made additional contributions, listed below, once James Haley was signed as the author. John Crain aided the society in obtaining a grant from the Summerlee Foundation in 2003, for which $6,000 was set aside to digitize material in the Greenhill collection and another

$10,000 to support the original history book project. The Summerlee Foundation tops the list of donors with the largest cumulative contribution toward the book in all its permutations, a total of $26,000.

Professor Joseph W. McKnight, the doyen of Texas legal history and author of dozens of works on the Spanish antecedents to Texas jurisprudence, persuaded a cadre of talented judges, attorneys, and law professors to volunteer their time to research and write on specific periods of the Court's history, and their research manuscripts served as the core material from which Jim Haley drew his ideas. Barry Bishop, Robert Dabney, Jr., the Honorable Sarah B. Duncan, Professor Paul Kens, Alfred Mackenzie, and Professor L. Wayne Scott were among the contributing authors who conducted research early on in the project. Special acknowledgment goes to Chief Justice James T. Worthen of the Twelfth Court of Appeals, who downloaded every Supreme Court case from 1923 to 1935 and placed copies in twelve white binders arranged by year. He had just finished reading and annotating every single case when he was called to early duty as chair of the Council of Chief Justices and had to leave the project.

Dallas attorney Roger Button conducted two video interviews with Judge Will Wilson and wrote an important paper on the *Motl v. Boyd* water rights case; Harris County district judge Mark Davidson, a trailblazer in twentieth-century Texas legal history, wrote articles with Kent Rutter on the female briefing attorneys during World War II, on the 1944 Critz-Simpson race, and on the 1958 Greenhill-Hughes race, as well as a case study that was included in the society-sponsored book on slave laws in antebellum Texas; and Dallas attorney Jeffrey D. Dunn, who remains a leader in Republic-era research, particularly on the Battle of San Jacinto, stepped out of his usual time frame to write a myth-shattering paper on Governor Pat Neff's appointment of the three-woman Court in 1925. All three gentlemen made presentations at the society's sessions at Texas State Historical Association's annual meetings.

University of Texas Law School professor Hans Baade also stepped beyond his usual time period when he tackled the turbulent post–Civil War period and Reconstruction, submitted the first research paper produced by the group of contributing authors, and subsequently published a version of it in the *St. Mary's Law Journal*. Professor Mark Steiner, of the South Texas College of Law, cracked the numbers on the so-called Consensus Court of the early twentieth century and presented his paper, along with that of Professor Baade, at the 2004 meeting of the American Society of Legal History.

St. Mary's Law School professor Michael Ariens made a presentation at the 2004 Texas State Historical Association meeting on women's legal status at the turn of the century, then uncovered the person on the Court responsible for the backlog of cases in the 1910s that led to the creation of the Commission of Appeals in 1918 and quite possibly motivated Harbert Davenport to produce his 1917 history of the Supreme Court. Ariens's research was the first paper sponsored by society to be published in the *St. Mary's Law Journal*. He went on to write a thoroughly researched book on Texas legal history titled *Lone Star Law*, which was published after our manuscript was prepared. William Chriss, an Austin attorney and member of the society's board of trustees, wrote two insightful papers on the closing decades of the nineteenth century and published them online. He is writing a biographical essay on Judge Jack Pope that will be included in the first book the society plans to publish under its own banner.

Professor James Paulsen of the South Texas College of Law offered advice, guidance, and encouragement to fellow contributing authors in the original history book project, and later to James Haley. Paulsen's trio of articles for a 1986 issue of the *Texas Law Review* continues to be the starting point for anyone researching the Republic-era Court. His knowledge of the "Old Court" of Hemphill, Lipscomb, and Wheeler is encyclopedic, which he will freely share with anyone who asks. We look forward to someday reading his magisterial and, we dare say, earth-shaking study on the first three Supreme Court justices for the State of Texas, the product of more than two decades of research.

Behind every good legal historian is an industrious researcher, digging through archival files, scrolling through microfilm, and photocopying law review articles. A file cabinet in the society's office is crammed with material collected over the years, with an equal number of files packed away in boxes. Of the dozens of researchers hired by the contributing authors over the years, several stand out. Keely Hennig, Stephen Melendi, Deborah Meleski, Elizabeth Pugliese, Kathryn Ann Ritcheske, Alice Shukalo, and Meredith Strutton aided our contributing authors in the early years. Kathleen Bachus, Christine Hortick, and Matthew Willis gave able support to Professor Ariens in his efforts; Dolph Briscoe IV (yes, very much related) assisted Alfred Mackenzie with research in the Texas Collection at Baylor University; and Andrew Dowdy, Tyler James, Steven Qualls, Travis Richins, and Peter Wahbi worked with Professor McKnight in Dallas. Kathleen Rice conducted tedious research in the Legislative Reference Library.

Susan Serio left behind history and a law degree to pursue a more tranquil career as a psychiatric nurse, but not before she plumbed the depths for information on the three-woman Court and submitted a highly detailed report of her findings to Jeff Dunn. Carissa Peterson wrangled a small herd of researchers hired by Robert Dabney, culling the stock down to the most efficient and productive one—herself—a fact to which I can attest from the diverse research requests which she handled for me with alacrity.

The very talented Jim Cullen interviewed and wrote superb biographical sketches of former chief justices Pope and Greenhill. Claudia Jenks toiled away in her basement office on weekends, transcribing the handwritten minutes books for the Court's administrative actions and turning fluid script into searchable spreadsheets. The late Jay Harrison, who came within a jot of being a nationally certified genealogist, devoted long hours, many on his own time, digging for the absolute *certain* proof of the vital dates, names, and facts that form the raw data of a judicial biography.

We turn now to the book at hand, and to those who brought it to fruition. The society began negotiating with James L. Haley to write this book in June 2009 during the swirling vortex of a crashing economy. Just at that moment we were given a once-in-a-lifetime opportunity to retain an award-winning historian to write a narrative history of the Texas Supreme Court. Board president Larry McNeill insisted, and rightly so, that the society had to have the money in hand before the author was commissioned.

A tanking economy, a narrow window of opportunity, and a crying need for $100,000 fast—who do you call? Harry Reasoner of Vinson & Elkins. Unruffled by the gloomy economy, Mr. Reasoner assured Judge Jack Pope and Larry McNeill that the project was worthwhile and the goal achievable. He immediately turned to his friend, Joe Jamail, who matched the $10,000 donation from Vinson & Elkins with an equal contribution of his own. Reasoner then wrote a raft of letters to friends and associates, exhorting them to contribute toward the book. At the same time, McNeill sent letters, made telephone calls, and held one-on-one meetings with board trustees, managing partners, and community leaders around the state. When all was said and done, the team of Reasoner and McNeill had surpassed the fund-raising objective by a comfortable margin, raising more money in ten months than had been raised for any other project in the society's twenty-year history. A complete list of the donors to the book written by James Haley appears below.

Successful completion of the book depended on the society's ability to weather the financial crisis with its administrative structure intact. Judge Craig T. Enoch, who was instrumental in kick-starting the society's publication series with *The Laws of Slavery in Texas*, continued the organization's momentum as board president. With the arrival of board president Lynne Liberato and president-elect Warren Harris in 2011, the society surpassed fund-raising benchmarks that had been reached before the economic downturn, making it possible to confidently plan new book projects well into the future.

Photography can make history come alive. For their generous assistance under a tight deadline, we must thank Alexandra Myers of the State Bar Archives, Elizabeth Haluska-Rausch of Tarlton Law Library Special Collections, John Anderson of the Texas State Library and Archives Commission, and Daniel Alonzo of the Austin History Center, all of whom helped us dive into their collections and find the perfect images. We also extend warm thanks to Angela Phillips Pringos Box for contributing a rare image of her distinguished relative Chief Justice Nelson Phillips.

Thanks are also due Dale Propp and his able staff at the Texas State Law Library for patiently guiding us through their extraordinary and wonderfully accessible collection. A special note of appreciation goes to Leslie Prather-Forbes for finding and forwarding arcane law review articles, legislative amendments, and Supreme Court decisions, saving us time and travel, and for helping with the fact-checking.

Former chief justice Tom Phillips produced a catalog of every judicial primary, general election, and runoff from 1851 to the present, listing each contender and the final tally of votes. He offered this astounding trove of data as a possible appendix, but as a consequence of word-count restrictions on the present volume, his comprehensive study and commentary will be published by the society as a separate work. Judge Phillips also reviewed early drafts of the manuscript, giving wise counsel that steered the narrative away from rough shoals that could have sunk a project such as this. He continued to offer valuable suggestions right up to the final submission.

Retired administrative chief of the court Bill Willis read and corrected an early draft, and took time away from his morning coffee to regale me with stories about the Court. Professor Jim Paulsen provided substantive comments on the Republic and antebellum chapters, and Professor Gordon Bakken, of California State University, Fullerton, offered valuable suggestions for source materials in his review of our manuscript for the University of Texas Press.

Not only did our acquisitions editor, Bill Bishel, guide our first book with the University of Texas Press through the publication maze, it was he who originally tipped us off that James Haley might be available to write our history book. He has remained our friend and champion, even though the work of escorting the present book fell to his associate, Allison Faust. Allison was joined in her efforts to produce this volume by Lynne Chapman, Kaila Wyllys, Regina Fuentes, and Nancy Bryan.

ACKNOWLEDGMENTS

Just as Larry McNeill coordinated the fund-raising for this book, Marilyn Duncan, the society's consulting editor, took charge of manuscript production. For my part, I merely stood aside and let Haley and Duncan work their magic. And in the case of Marilyn, that magic went well beyond the usual editorial contributions. Not only was she the single person in direct and continual contact with Haley throughout the writing process, but she also wrote the book proposal, created the budget, set the production schedule, and compiled the materials distributed to potential donors. She gathered the needed source material, supervised research by Susan Burneson, and conducted much of it herself. The chronology of the Court's history found at the back of the book is her creation entirely. Appendix materials started by other hands were pulled together by Marilyn and put in a shape and sequence most beneficial for this book. Photo research, clearance of rights, and drafting the captions—all her work. She guided the direction and tone of Haley's early chapters with tact and finesse. Then, once the final manuscript chapters arrived, she took up her pen and began to edit. Along with grammar and punctuation, she cross-checked the facts against the sources, catching errors large and small, not only in Haley's manuscript, but in the source material itself. Her contribution to the book, its clarity and accuracy—and to the recorded history of the Court in general—is significant, yet wondrously imperceptible to anyone not familiar with the earlier drafts.

I close these acknowledgments with grateful thanks to James L. Haley, who shouldered an enormous task under trying conditions and a tortuous deadline with good humor, patience, and harmonious collaboration. He has a gift for storytelling, fluid prose, and a dramatic energy that can make the act of reading judicial history a thoroughgoing pleasure, with knowledge and appreciation of the Court tagging along for the fun of it. You can't help but learn something new, any more than you can keep from turning the page to find out what happens next. That was the objective of this book, first and foremost. And I believe Marilyn and Larry would join me in saying that Jim Haley pulled it off magnificently.

William S. Pugsley
Executive Director
Texas Supreme Court Historical Society
February 8, 2012

xxiii

DONORS TO THIS BOOK

$10,000

Vinson & Elkins LLP

Joseph D. Jamail, Jr.

*

Haynes and Boone, LLP

Baker Botts

Bracewell & Giuliani LLP

The Summerlee Foundation

Fulbright & Jaworski LLP

$5,000

Clark, Thomas & Winters, PC

Winstead PC

Locke Lord LLP

Hon. Jack Pope, Chief Justice (Ret.)

Kelly Hart & Hallman LLP

ECG Foundation

McKool Smith

$2,500

Judge William L. Garwood

Yetter Coleman LLP

Beck, Redden & Secrest, LLP

$1,000

Beirne, Maynard & Parsons, LLP

Skadden, Arps, Slate, Meagher & Flom LLP

Greer, Herz & Adams, LLP

Harris, Finley & Bogel, PC

Scott, Douglass & McConnico, LLP

Ogletree, Deakins, Nash, Smoak & Stewart, PC

Graves, Dougherty, Hearon & Moody, PC

Morgan, Lewis & Bockius LLP

Don Davis

Sprouse Shrader Smith PC

Barron & Newburger, PC
Bob Black

Dykema Gossett PLLC
Alexander Dubose & Townsend
LLP

$500

Almanza, Blackburn & Dickie LLP
Atlas, Hall & Rodriguez LLP
Larry McNeill
C. Andrew Weber
S. Shawn Stephens

W. Frank Newton
Justice Jeff Brown
William S. Pugsley
Alfred Mackenzie

THE TEXAS SUPREME COURT

PROLOGUE

$\mathbf{W}$hen Texas voters line up at the polls every other November, they do so to choose not just their statewide executive officials and the next legislature, but also that portion of their judiciary standing for election. Included on the ballot are candidates for the Texas Supreme Court, the Court of Criminal Appeals, and the fourteen regional Courts of Appeals. The judges elected to serve on those appellate benches join a vast judicial system that also includes more than 450 state district court judges, 500 county court judges, 800 justices of the peace, and 1,500 municipal court judges.[1]

Very few of the voters who cast their ballots have any awareness that many of the rights that they take most for granted, including preservation of their homesteads from seizure for debt, or the right to adopt children, or, most especially, the right of married women to community property, do not stem from Texas's association with the United States or from America's adoption of the English common law.

This lack of understanding is not surprising, for it dates almost from the time of Texas's admission as the twenty-eighth state in 1845. In the realm of women's rights, the misinformation began with the publication of the monumental *History of Woman Suffrage*, edited by suffragist pioneers Elizabeth Cady Stanton, Matilda Joslyn Gage, and Susan B. Anthony. "New York," they declared, "was the first state to emancipate wives from the slavery of the old common law of England, and to secure to them equal property rights. This occurred in 1848."[2] In point of fact, Texas had joined the Union three years earlier than that with a community-property provision enshrined in its state constitution (thanks to strong support from the Republic-era judiciary), but that fact was not widely publicized in the North because it was thought unseemly to acknowledge such a progressive stance coming from a southern, slaveholding state. In fact, so far from being as progressive as Texas, New York debated a community-property provision at its own constitutional convention in 1846, and turned it down.[3]

The state of Texas is now more than one and a half centuries old, but the roots of many of its most basic legal features predate its association with the United States by some three and a half centuries—and are part of a legal heritage vastly different from that adopted by England and America: that of Spain. And indeed, its recognition of the legal equality of women reaches back to the fifteenth-century monarch who was the first to insist upon that station for herself: Queen Isabella of Castile.

When Christopher Columbus arrived in the New World in October 1492, he was just past forty years old and had already experienced a life of high adventure and cruel disappointment.[4] He was Genoese, an Italian, sailing in service of the joint monarchs of a newly unified Spain, Ferdinand of Aragon and Isabella of Castile.

Both Italy and Spain, as countries of the western Mediterranean, had inherited the intellectual legacy of ancient Rome. Their languages, cultures, and customs were similar; they adhered to the Roman Catholic religion; and their legal systems were based on the Roman civil law. There were aspects of Ferdinand and Isabella's regime, such as the persecution and expulsion of the Jews, for which history has held them—but particularly Isabella—to more or less strict account. But other aspects of their government were remarkable for their forward thinking. In the law of debtor and creditor, their joint decree was that debts should be enforced, but that collection should not impair the ability of the debtor to make a living. This was in stark contrast to the theory of debt under the English common law, which embraced even the imprisonment of debtors until they could think of some way to pay what they owed.

Other aspects of Spanish law reflected equally sound common sense. Most of Iberia was semiarid, and the purchase of land did not include the right to adjoining or even through-flowing water unless that right was specifically included in the purchase. This was the polar opposite of the corresponding practice under the Anglo-Saxon common law, where in rainy England the right to use the abundant water was assumed without question. The Spanish civil law also recognized the concept of adoption, by which children other than legitimate "heirs of the body" could be legally included in families, again an idea unknown to the common law. But the greatest difference between the two dominant Western legal systems was in the standing of women before the law.

In England, a woman's identity became subsumed in that of her husband when she married; property that was hers before marriage became his; she could not enter into contracts—her station was roughly equivalent to that of a child or a mental incompetent. Under the civil law, the vastly different state of things was embodied by Isabella herself, who as a young princess had been so used as a pawn in the games of powerful men that when she married, she refused a crown matrimonial. It was she herself who chose Ferdinand of Aragon as her husband, insisted on taking her throne as Ferdinand's equal in power, and squeezed a prenuptial agreement out of him.[5]

All these areas of Spanish jurisprudence would come to have enormous implications for the land we would know as Texas. It was Isabella who took the lead in outfitting Columbus's expedition, and her gamble paid off: his discovery of the New World, and then the successes of the conquistadores, Pizarro in Peru and Cortés in Mexico, made Spain the dominant power in Europe and opened the floodgates of looted native wealth. Within two generations, Spanish cities in the New World became cultural centers in their own right, with writers and composers, cathedrals and universities, and the complex, arcane system of laws whose enforcement descended from viceroy down to governor and further down to commandants civil and military.

The return of conquistadores to Spain with wealth and status inflamed the ambitions of others who were keen to make a name for themselves before the New World was completely divided up. Minor nobles with little prospect of advancement at home attached themselves to older conquering relatives, got fitted for armor, and sailed west. All were acutely aware of their places in the hierarchy of the nobility. They knew exactly whom they could abuse and exactly whose hands they had to kiss.

The first to set foot on territory that later became Texas, on November 6, 1528, was Álvar Núñez Cabeza de Vaca, a minor grandee who, given a choice, took his mother's name because it carried higher rank than his father's. (An ancestor of his mother once marked a strategic pass with a cow's skull—"Cabeza de Vaca"—which resulted in a Spanish military victory.)[6] Cabeza de Vaca lurked about the court of Spain's young King Carlos, grandson of Ferdinand and Isabella, until he gained favorable notice. He then attached himself to Pánfilo de Narváez, the erstwhile lieutenant governor of Cuba, who had been sent to Mexico to arrest Cortés for exceeding his commission, but whom Cortés defeated in battle and sent packing. Back in Spain, Narváez obtained the king's approval to explore Florida. He returned to Cuba early in 1528 with Cabeza de Vaca as his treasurer, and reached Florida in April with three hundred men. Within a short time, Narváez got his men lost, provoked the natives to murderous hostility, lost contact with his ships, and had his survivors build five barges to float along the coast west to the Mexican settlements and safety. He greatly underestimated the size of the Gulf of Mexico, and it took a month just to cross the discharge of the Mississippi.

On the morning of November 6, with the survivors in the last barge freezing cold and nearly starved, a heavy surf cast them onto the beach of either Galveston or a neighboring island. Quickly discovered by a tribe of tall, tattooed Indians called Karankawas, the Spaniards were helpless to defend themselves, as "it would have been difficult to find six that could rise from the ground."[7] Gathering their strength, the Spanish presented hawkbells and beads to the natives, and in return were fed, warmed, housed, and otherwise treated as honored guests.

Within a few months the hospitality waned, for about half of the Karankawas died of European diseases to which they had no immunity, such as smallpox. Assembling a kind of court that they called a *mitote*, the Indians debated whether they should kill the remaining Spaniards and, hopefully, save themselves from their evil magic. The warrior who had become more or less the Europeans' keeper made a keen observation and argument. If the strange men from the sea had the power to hex people to death, they no doubt would use that power to save themselves. Yet sixty-five of the eighty men who washed ashore had died, so it was clear that they were as much victims as the Karankawas themselves. After due consideration, the decision of the mitote was that the castaways would be allowed to live. Texas, it seemed, had a system of justice already, and the unknown Karankawa warrior who argued for sparing the lives of the Spaniards has a claim to be recognized as Texas's first legal advocate in recorded history.

ONE

ANCIENT HERITAGE,
NEW CIRCUMSTANCE

With three other last survivors of the Narváez expedition, Álvar Núñez Cabeza de Vaca dwelled in Texas for seven years before making his way to colonial civilization and then back to Spain. Organized entradas of exploration and imperial claim soon followed, most prominently by Francisco Vásquez de Coronado in 1540 and Luis de Moscoso de Alvarado in 1542. The explorations sought two commodities: gold to finance the empire, and native souls for the glory of the Catholic Church.[1] In practice, the second goal finished a poor second to the first; not until 1582 did an expedition under Antonio de Espejo enter Texas with the design of proselytizing the natives. Little came of it, and for the next century Texas lay as the Empty Quarter of New Spain. In 1685, word of a French interloper, the Sieur de la Salle, in Spanish Texas spurred the empire to action. Internal dissension and attacks by the Karankawas ended the French incursion, whose last victims were given Christian burial by the Spanish expedition that finally discovered the wrecked Fort St. Louis (near present-day Inez) in 1689.[2] By then, the French had a solid claim to the Mississippi, dividing New Spain from Florida.

Bowing to the necessity of commencing settlement, the Spanish sent priests under Father Dámian Massanet to establish a mission for the Tejas Indians in 1690. Massanet was a Franciscan; he had arrived in Mexico from Spain seven years earlier to found the College of Santa Cruz de Querétaro. But it was the military who selected the general location of the mission, and in a challenge to French ambitions, they planted it on the Neches River, some two hundred miles east of Fort St. Louis. Massanet and his missionaries were warmly received by the natives. "It was at no time necessary for the safety of the priests to leave soldiers among the Tejas," he wrote, "for from the very first they welcomed us with so much affection . . . that they could hardly do enough to please us."[3] Whether suspicious of the Indians or wary of French ambitions, the commander left behind an intimidating military garrison that neither the priests nor the Indians wanted.

Given that the missions and padres were governed by canon law, and the troops by military law, legal confusion was bound to reign in the area. The priests, who were sincere in their ministry to the natives, and the soldiers, often crude and violent and with an eye on the native women, could not abide one another. Massanet himself characterized the officer of his guard as an "incapable and undeserving old man."[4] This first mission failed within three years, but when the priests and soldiers came back in 1716, they established what they claimed to be a provincial capital at Los Adaes, east even of the Sabine River and in French territory, even farther from central control. Supreme justice in Texas at this time often consisted of what an abusive and dictatorial officer or provincial governor could get away with, knowing that redress was hundreds of miles and many months away.

The most egregious example seems to have been Governor Jacinto Barrios, a hard-bitten Indian fighter who nonetheless made a fortune collecting furs from natives and selling them to the French. He was duped by Apaches into opening the San Saba Mission, which was sacked by Comanches owing to some Apache trickery. Finding Barrios a hard man to work for, his civilian secretary, Manuel Antonio de Soto, sought to quit his job in 1753, but Barrios refused to give him permission to leave the province. Soto escaped to Natchitoches, in French Louisiana, for which Barrios falsely accused him of desertion (nonmilitary personnel could not desert the military). It took Soto a whole decade to clear his name.[5]

After more than a generation of establishing and withdrawing missions and presidios, the viceregal administration realized that the key to holding Texas was to plant a permanent civilian settlement. Los Adaes was becoming increasingly untenable, and in 1718 the Eastern Provinces' ablest governor, the Marqués de Aguayo, established a new town, San Fernando de Béxar, on the San Antonio River at the eastern edge of a range of limestone hills, about halfway across the breadth of Texas. The accompanying mission quickly expanded to four, and the villa of San Fernando, often referred to as Béxar and then San Antonio, became the locus of settlement in Texas. However, given the vast distance from the Mexican interior, in a province roamed by Apaches in the west, Comanches on the plains, and Karankawas along the coast, very few citizens of the empire could be induced to join such a venture. Spain therefore recruited settlers from another of its territories, the Canary Islands, off the west coast of Africa.[6] At first, the government's ambition was to round up four hundred; it was an unrealistic goal, but by the time the plan was abandoned, fifty-five pioneers representing fifteen families from the Canary Islands had made the trek to Béxar in 1731, led by Juan Leal Goráz.[7]

The arrival of civilians in Texas complicated the legal picture. Organized settlement made Béxar the only town in what would become Texas to be governed by an *ayuntamiento* (town council), which consisted of four *regidors* (aldermen) presided over by two alcaldes (an office that embraced functions roughly equivalent to those of mayor and justice of the peace).[8] This form of government came to be the standard in Spanish Texas, and the development added civil law to canon and military law, and resort to it was quick. The Canary Islanders had come, enticed by the promise of land, but more importantly to them, they were also promised the title and station of hidalgos, or gentlemen, which in their experience excused them from performing physical labor.[9] On the frontier, of course, no one was excused from working, and although the Canary Islanders became the founders of San Antonio's upper society, disputes among them were frequent and nasty.

None of them, however, were lawyers, or knew how to prepare and file a suit. Thus it fell to the villa's *notario*, or secretary to the ayuntamiento, himself an islander appointed the same year as their arrival, to devise a system to prepare cases for legal process. Francisco de Arocha had few preceding documents to draw on as examples, and the traditional story is that he had been given the job only because of the legibility of his hand.[10] Thrown upon his own invention, Arocha required that a plaintiff who came to court set down who he was, what wrong had been done him and by whom, and what redress he sought. The defendant was then sought out to make answer, and the case could proceed. This was shorter by many steps than what was required under the common law of the English-speaking world, a simple and effective form of pleading a case that has led to Arocha's being called Texas's first lawyer.[11]

Fathering fifteen children, many of whom married into the families that became prominent landholders, Arocha became an important man to cultivate a friendship with. So too did his good friend the *alguacil mayor* (chief constable), Don Vicente Álvarez Travieso. With land at the root of family ambitions, disputes over land could become bitter and protracted; one suit between the Hernández and Menchaca families filed in 1757 was kept active for a century.[12] Even more hot tempered were land disputes between the settlers and the missions, which controlled large acreages and cattle herds for the benefit of the native Indians who had enrolled at the missions. The priests, one suit charged, "looking out for their Indians, protected by the King's laws for that purpose," had deliberately made improvements on lands to keep the settlers from being able to claim them.[13] Constable Travieso spent much of his time shuttling back and forth to Mexico City (about 1,700 miles round trip) with petitions aimed over the heads of local authorities.

Despite the predilection of leading Bexareños to file suit on one another, the law came to favor voluntary settlement, amicable when possible, rather than pursue litigation to its lengthy and expensive conclusion. The rancorous land suit between the Menchaca and Hernández families resulted in a compromise settlement arranged by the viceroy himself in 1759, two years after it began. (It was only later revived by heirs.)[14] Juan Leal Goráz, who led the Canary Islanders into Texas, also became notorious for his frequent resort to the courts. In one case he sued another resident over ownership of a mule, but the two parties were persuaded to auction the animal and donate the proceeds to the building fund of a new church.[15] Goráz further stirred up legal discontent during his term as Béxar's first alcalde when he followed the example of previous local authorities in throwing his weight around. Once, he clapped into prison three other local officials who had neglected to fence their fields according to the relevant ordinance, and then he denied them bond to remain free while pursuing appeals. It took an act of the viceroy to release them, and in subsequent years an alcalde's power to act in such a way was diluted by giving concurrent jurisdiction to both alcaldes.[16]

For the eighty years from the founding of San Antonio to the close of the eighteenth century, Texas stagnated, strong enough to maintain itself against the wilderness and hostile Indians, but dangerous and remote enough to discourage active emigration from the Mexican interior. And during those decades, the Spanish empire itself declined, too large and expensive to maintain as Spain lost her preeminence to England. And there was revolution in the world. Both the United States and France had overthrown monarchical yokes, and many of the educated class in New Spain began to share that dream. For all the books written on the broad topic of Texas and its origins, one context that is seldom acknowledged is that Latin America, of which Tejas was a minor component, began pursuing its own vision of independent democracy a generation before Texas won its separate existence in 1836.

In fact, Mexico's first broad uprising against royal Spanish rule, instigated by Padre Miguel Hidalgo y Costilla's famous *grito* of September 16, 1810 (still celebrated as Mexican Independence Day), was contemporaneous with the insurrection of Simón Bolivar in Venezuela and actually predated a similar movement by José de San Martín in Peru and Chile. While the American Revolution was widely admired throughout Latin America, in that strip where New Spain bordered the United States the perspective was quite different. Political factions within the United States saw the possibility of taking advantage of Latin unrest and Spanish instability, which had included the rise and fall of a Bonaparte pretender on the Spanish throne during the Napoleonic Wars. After about 1800, Spanish governors in Texas had to contend with a series of American interlopers (known as "filibusters") who kept crossing the border with the intention of setting up tinpot personal empires on Spanish soil.[17]

Most filibusters came to murky and violent ends, but for the most part, officials of the Spanish government in Texas were faithful to their constitution and laws.[18] This was especially true in the case of one American, Moses Austin, who appeared in the provincial capital of San Antonio de Béxar shortly before Christmas 1820 with a proposal to settle Anglo-American colonists from the United States in the vacant wilderness of Texas. Neither the governor, Antonio María Martínez, who had been chasing American filibusters since taking office four years before, nor the military commandant, Joaquín de Arredondo, who had slaughtered hundreds of antiroyalist insurgents after the abortive "Green Flag" rebellion of 1812, were favorably disposed. However, Austin hung his petition on a clause of the liberal Spanish Constitution that accompanied the Bourbon restoration, which provided that former subjects of the Spanish crown who sought readmission to the country be allowed to do so. Austin's case was squarely on point: he had removed from Virginia to Missouri (then part of Louisiana) and operated a lead mine for the government during that brief period when Louisiana belonged to Spain, and from which the crown had profited considerably.[19]

The Spanish were keenly aware of their failure to populate the empty province; a census undertaken in 1783 descried only 2,819 subjects north of the Rio Grande, not much to show for 250 years of ownership.[20] If Austin could bring in Catholic Americans who would swear allegiance to Spain, they could serve as a barrier to hostile Indian tribes and might even make the province productive. Austin's colony was approved, but he died shortly after returning to the United States to organize the immigration. The project was taken over by his son, Stephen F. Austin, who after an agreeable meeting with Governor Martínez began introducing American colonists in 1821.

Ironically, when Mexico launched a second and more determined campaign for independence, it originated not among Hidalgo's oppressed peonage, but among wealthy, upper-class *peninsulares* (those born in Spain) and *criollos* (those born in Mexico but of pure Spanish descent). They were moved to act by the renewal of the liberal constitution in Spain (Ferdinand VII had been able to suppress it, but only for a time), which they feared might give the lower-class mestizos (those of mixed Spanish and Indian heritage) pretensions to social place and privilege. This revolution succeeded in 1821, and the transfer of power happened amicably in Texas, thanks in large part to the pragmatic Martínez.[21] Austin's colonization contract was in jeopardy, however, having been approved by the Spanish crown but then disallowed by the new Mexican Congress. Stephen Austin marshaled what resources he could and journeyed to Mexico City to try to rescue the scheme.

What he found there was a city, and government, "in an unsettled State," he wrote, "the whole people and Country still agitated by the revolutionary Convulsion . . . public opinion vacillating as to the form of Government which ought to be adopted . . . Party spirit raging."[22] The revolution's emergent strongman, Agustín de Iturbide, was made emperor, then deposed; Austin no sooner gained the favor of one minister responsible for colonization than he was replaced by another minister. He lobbied his colonization bill through one Congress, only to have it be dissolved. Enough months of this and he concluded, "These people will not do for a Republic."[23]

Eventually, he was able to return to his Texas colonists with a firm contract in hand, and on terms far more liberal than he had originally thought possible. The new regime recognized that it would, for the near future, be too occupied with its own survival to give much attention to the new American colony. The government could not effectively provide courts or magistrates. Young Austin, however, had so impressed those in power with his perfect manners, his command of the Spanish language, his sincere desire to bring civilization to the wilderness, and his manifest honesty, that he was given a free hand to administer justice in his domain. To his colonists, his word would be the law—except in capital cases, which would be referred to the capital.

Austin quickly found that his judicial functions, if he performed them all himself, would be overwhelming, and he had more important business than to settle "little neighborhood disputes about cows and calves."[24] He vested trial jurisdiction in the alcaldes of his settlements, and when still badgered by appeals in which the disputed value was more than $25, he created an appeals court composed of the alcaldes sitting en banc.[25]

The aftershocks of revolution looked as though they might be quieted when Mexico adopted the Constitution of 1824, a progressive document authored by Miguel Ramos Arizpe, a congressional deputy and native Coahuilan. Austin had earlier shown Arizpe a draft of his own guidelines for a national government, on which Arizpe made marginal notes, but Arizpe's reputation as a legal scholar and the author of Spain's 1812 Constitution made Austin's hope that he had influenced the course of Mexican democracy somewhat overblown.[26] Nevertheless, the new country took its first steps toward self-government, all of them provisional. After the fall of Iturbide, the Congress, in the absence of a constitution, declared a reorganization of the government on January 31, 1824, and it shared general similarities with Austin's template. It was essentially federalist in its outlook, relinquishing some meaningful power to the several states of the Mexican confederation. At first, Texas and its Anglo-American colonies were attached to Coahuila and Nuevo León as the Internal State of the East, but only three months later, Nuevo León was detached, leaving Texas as the junior partner of the dual state of Coahuila y Tejas.[27] On August 13 of that year, the state congress—the equivalent of what Americans would know as a legislature—inaugurated itself, again provisionally, in the absence of a state constitution.

One responsibility left to the states was the establishment of courts of law. The judicial power of Coahuila y Tejas, "for the present," was vested in the existing courts, which were admonished not to contravene the new and more democratic order.[28] But while the government became more democratic in form, the legal system remained rooted in the ancient Roman or civil law of Spain. With the adoption of the Mexican Constitution in October 1824 and of the state constitution of Coahuila y Tejas in March 1827, the power of the judiciary was brutally circumscribed, walled off from exercising anything like the power wielded by courts in the Anglo-Saxon system. The state constitution provided for three "halls" of justice under the governance of a supreme tribunal. But the function of those courts was limited to merely "applying" the laws—they "shall never interpret the same, or suspend their execution."[29] The existence of a strong judiciary as a check on legislative or executive power, which was a fundamental tenet of the English common law familiar to Austin and his American colonists, was not part of the Mexican vision. With so little to actually do, it is not surprising that there is little record of activity of state courts of Coahuila y Tejas under this framework.[30]

The weakness of the new constitutional system, from the standpoint of the American colonists now in Mexican Texas, was that the entire legal infrastructure was located in Coahuila. The only justice that could be obtained within Texas was what was dispensed by local alcaldes, which was often deficient, but no appellate recourse was closer than the capital, Saltillo, some four hundred miles and several weeks distant. And Texas needed a functioning judicial system with increasing urgency. Mexico's need to populate Texas was answered so well by the system of contracting with colonial *empresarios* that within a few years of Austin's arrival, Texas was divided into a patchwork of more than two dozen colonies licensed to settle some eight thousand families, all but a handful of them American. At first, Austin handpicked his settlers and so was able to vouch for their character and industrious habits, as his contract required. Other empresarios, reaching further to fill their contracts, were less scrupulous. Even worse, the lure of easy land in Mexican Texas brought a surreptitious slough of debtors, vagrants, and fugitives sneaking across the boundary to squat on vacant land until they could make themselves legal or blend into the population.

Many of these derelicts, whom Austin referred to with contemptuous humor as his "leatherstockings," shared none of the loyalty that Austin and his early colonists had sworn to Mexico. Indeed, some of them, spiritual heirs of the American filibusters from early in the century, came with the design to split Texas away from Mexico and add it to the United States. This culminated as early as January 1827 in the abortive "Fredonian Rebellion," centered on Nacogdoches, against Mexican rule. Austin hastily rounded up a militia and aided Mexican troops in crushing the uprising, but alarm bells rang deep within Mexico.[31]

In 1828, the government dispatched one of its ablest officers, General Don Manuel de Mier y Terán, to make a tour of inspection in Texas and report on conditions. The document he filed was astonishing, both for the keenness with which he grasped the social and political situation, and for the frankness with which he conceded that the Anglo colonists had legitimate grievances that merited attention. Mexican officials slighted and abused the American newcomers, and Mexico's court system was too distant for the colonists to practicably seek redress. "I have witnessed grave occurrences," wrote Mier y Terán, "both political and judicial. . . . The colonists find it unendurable that they must go three hundred leagues to lodge a complaint against the petty pickpocketing that they suffer from a venal and ignorant alcalde," who in fact had little or no knowledge of the complex new colonization laws, but who had "a chance to come out with some money" by finding in favor of Tejano land claimants over the American settlers.[32] (Around this time, the term "Tejano" came to be used for Texas residents of Mexican descent.) While Mier y Terán was sympathetic to the problems of the American colonists, his first concern was for the welfare of Mexico, and in Texas he beheld a province that was increasingly dominated by foreign residents indifferent or even hostile to the national interest. Among his recommendations was a ban on further emigration from the United States, which was adopted in the *ley* (law) of April 6, 1830, an act that alarmed even the most loyal of the settlers.

Complicating matters further was the more or less continuous struggle for power in Mexico itself. The competing interests that had fueled a decade of revolution had hardened into hostile political factions: centralists (backed by the church, the military, and the wealthy upper class), who envisioned a Mexico united under a strong central government and leader; and federalists (composed of liberals and intellectuals operating on behalf of the vast lower class), who contended for a system in which power would be shared with the several states. The first decade of Mexico's existence was a confusion of coups, countercoups, and insurgencies. During that decade, Stephen F. Austin managed to navigate between the two factions without committing himself or his colony, dealing earnestly with whoever was in power; his goal always was for the law to be interpreted in a way that would benefit Texas's economic progress. By 1832, however, unrest in Texas, along with Austin's diminishing influence over the colonies, had led to a second abortive rebellion.

The American colonies in Mexico began life with an exemption from paying taxes until they could get an economy established. That exemption now expired, and their reaction to Mexico's installation of a collector of port duties at the settlement of Anahuac not only demonstrated their general distaste for taxation, but also highlighted conditions that were taken for granted in Mexico—such as the quartering of troops in private homes—but were anathema to the Americans. Disputes arose also over slavery, which, though illegal in Mexico, the authorities tacitly condoned in Texas in order to foster development of the economy, which centered on growing cotton. In Anahuac, shooting erupted when the new Mexican commandant sheltered runaway slaves in the garrison. The colonists involved in the brief insurrection escaped punishment by declaring their loyalty to the latest contender for the Mexican presidency, General Antonio López de Santa Anna.[33]

Wearied of Texas's insignificance as a province attached to the state of Coahuila, Texans gathered in San Felipe de Austin for the Convention of 1833, and dispatched Austin to Mexico City with the draft of a Texas constitution and a proposal for separate statehood within Mexico. As soon as Santa Anna took power, however, he took leaves of absence until he could determine which way the political winds were blowing in the capital. Austin, having all but concluded that he would fail in his mission, was surprised when Santa Anna, after returning the second time, awarded Texans a number of the concessions they had sought. Anglo colonists would be allowed to start retail businesses, and the ban on further immigration—the most hated provision of the *ley* of April 6, 1830—was suspended. Equally meaningful and welcome was the creation of a separate judicial circuit specifically for Texas; it consisted of a superior judicial court that met in the capitals of three separate districts—Béxar, Brazos, and Nacogdoches—and was presided over by a superior judge.

The law went into surprising specifics on the formalities to be observed by Texas courts, from the dress of the superior judge—"black or dark blue, and a white sash with gold tassels, and this dress shall be used on all solemn occasions"—to the requirement that he open court "by pronouncing a discourse analogous to the circumstances."[34] Less showy, but treated as a major concession by the Mexican authorities, was the granting of trial by jury in criminal cases, long and vociferously pleaded for by the Americans, for whom jury trials were a benchmark of political liberty.

In actuality, the provision of jury trials had already been envisioned, admittedly in a cautious and tentative way, in the Constitution of Coahuila y Tejas, which in 1827 directed the state congress to move toward "the trial by jury in criminal cases, to extend the same gradually, and even to adopt it in civil cases in proportion as the advantages of this valuable institution become practically known."[35] This constitutional provision was implemented by decree in 1830, but the notion of "jury" it enshrined was not one that American settlers recognized or wanted.[36] Reflecting the government's reluctance to diverge from the traditions inherited from New Spain, one jury was elected to serve for an entire year, hearing all cases, rather like a judicial incarnation of the *cabildo* (municipal council). Composed of seven men, juries had the authority to examine the parties to a case, needed only a simple majority to reach a decision, and determined the severity of the punishment. While there was, indeed, less opportunity for judicial abuse under this system than in hearings before an alcalde, it so little resembled the form of jury trial expected by the American colonists that it became part of the cultural misunderstanding that contributed to the eventual revolution: the Americans complained that little had been done to address their needs, even as the Mexicans believed they had done all that could be expected of them and felt that the Americans were a nest of ingrates.

Nevertheless, Texas was now served by its own judicial circuit, and a candidate for superior judge was required to be a lawyer, at least twenty-five years old and of unimpaired citizenship, who was also a man "of probity and science."[37] Once nominated by the governor and appointed by the legislature, he could not be removed from office except for legally established cause. His compensation was to be three thousand dollars a year, but in acknowledgment of the state's dearth of cash, the sum could be paid in land for the first year, at the rate of one *sitio* (or league, equaling 4,428 acres) of land per hundred dollars.[38]

The selection of the superior judge was an issue of great moment, and the governor picked an American émigré, Thomas Jefferson Chambers.[39] He was thirty-two, a unique choice with unique abilities. After the establishment of Austin's colony and its many counterparts in Texas, nearly all the immigrants came into the granted lands either legally under agreements with the empresarios or as illegal squatters. Chambers, by contrast, had left the United States directly for Mexico City, arriving in 1826, and there he had devoted three years to studying the language and law of his new country and immersing himself in the culture by boarding with a Mexican family. It was understandable that Chambers would seek a new life. Born into poverty in Virginia, the last of twenty children of a father who left an estate of only five hundred dollars, he cultivated mentors who sponsored him in reading for the law in Kentucky, then removed to Alabama to escape debt before relocating to Mexico to seek his fortune.

Once he worked himself into the circles of power, Chambers moved to Saltillo as the protégé of Vice Governor Victor Blanco, and was made surveyor general of Texas almost as soon as he gained his certification. It was a post for which he was paid the staggering personal empire of eleven leagues of land—more than 48,000 acres, which he took in five widely separated parcels. It was a base from which he, in partnership with Texas land commissioner Juan Antonio Padilla, opened ambitious land speculations. Casting an eye back to his poverty-stricken origins, Chambers began using all the influence he could muster to amass the greatest fortune he could grasp. He became a Mexican citizen in 1830, and through some energetic pulling of strings became the only American lawyer in Coahuila at the time Texas was granted a judicial circuit. He was an obvious choice for superior judge.[40]

Thus, by appointment and confirmation, Chambers lay claim to being recognized as the first chief justice of a supreme court in Texas. His claim would be stronger had he ever been able to actually sit as a judge under that appointment, but he was not. Having contended so earnestly for a federalist form of government in which significant power was reserved to the states, politicians within Coahuila y Tejas then fell upon each other in squabbles to elevate their own respective locales to preeminence. Their rivalries led to violence, the state capital was removed at least nominally from Saltillo to the smaller mountain town of Monclova, more than a hundred miles to the north, and competing governors commanded militias and issued orders as though there were no other claimants. All this made it impossible for Chambers to organize the court system in Texas.

He did, however, manage to win issuance of a decree modifying the earlier provision for jury trials. Known as the Chambers Jury Law, enacted April 17, 1834, it attempted to bridge the chasm between the common law jury and the Mexican hybrid, but crossed the bridge only halfway: juries were increased in size to twelve members, were empowered to hear both criminal and civil cases, required a supermajority of eight to reach a decision, and were given the right to overrule a judge's instructions. Their findings of fact were to be final unless the jury had been corrupted, and jurors not agreeing with the verdict could issue written dissents.[41]

Whether the Chambers Jury Law could have eventually won over the restive colonists became a moot point, however, for the political chaos became too great to overcome. In addition to the animosity between Saltillo and Monclova, the congress when it acted did so usually for the benefit of the Mexican population, not of Texas, which had only two representatives in that body.[42] Having witnessed the self-destruction of the state government in Coahuila, Chambers, superior judge of a nonexistent court, along with Texas's two representatives in the legislature, published a broadside on November 1, 1834, calling for a meeting of Texas citizens in San Antonio de Béxar in mid-November to decide how to respond to the crisis, even to the point of contemplating formation of a provisional government. Chambers thus was among the first to foresee Texas's eventual separation from Mexico.[43]

Revolution in Texas was rendered inevitable when Santa Anna, abandoning his earlier stance as a federalist, abrogated the Constitution of 1824 and replaced it with the Siete Leyes, under which, while preserving the form of democracy with a congress and executive departments, he assumed personal rule in all but the name. During the subsequent seven months of war, Chambers contributed materially and monetarily to the success of the struggle for independence. He used his own money and credit to dispatch volunteers from the United States, albeit the fight was over by the time they arrived, but he did not find Texans grateful for his sacrifices. Out of all his vast land holdings, he settled in southeast Texas, in Chambers County, to promote his new town of Chambersia. His ego and the rapacity of his land dealings, however, up to and including the eviction of longtime residents from land to which he managed to gain title, led to his being lavishly despised. Under the Republic and then under statehood, Chambers ran for high office half a dozen times, but was never elected; eventually he was assassinated, shotgunned through the window of his home, probably by a litigant in one of his blizzard of lawsuits over land.[44]

The failure of Mexico to establish a functioning court system in Texas was less the end of the Hispanic story there than it seems. For nearly a century and a half, since the arrival of Father Massanet in 1690, people in Texas had been granted land, had married, and had entered into contracts, all while living under and relying upon Spanish law. For a decade and a half, American immigrants had done the same, and the legal affairs of all carried over from one national regime to another. The accent of this Spanish heritage would color Texas's legal history and require accommodation by subsequent Texas Supreme Courts, during both the Republic and statehood, to a degree that is unique within the American union.

TWO

GOOD INTENTIONS,
FITFUL BEGINNINGS

The Republic of Texas maintained its independence by force of arms and international recognition for nine years and ten months, from March 2, 1836, to December 31, 1845, although executive power did not transfer to the United States for a further six weeks. During that decade, four presidents in Texas (five if Sam Houston's two terms are counted separately) wielded executive authority, including nominating candidates for chief justice and associate judges of the Supreme Court. The provisional president, David G. Burnet (in office from March 16 to October 22, 1836), and more particularly the second elected president, Mirabeau B. Lamar (December 10, 1838, to December 13, 1841), saw the country as a nation among nations, envisioned Texas as the third power in North America, and were little interested in annexation by the United States. The first and third elected president and dominant political force of the era, Sam Houston (October 22, 1836, to December 10, 1838, and December 13, 1841, to December 9, 1844) exercised all his guile to euchre a largely unwilling United States into accepting Texas as the twenty-eighth state, and then exulted in being the bête noire who savaged both the plans and the happiness of Burnet and Lamar, whose hatred for him was virtually bottomless.[1] The last president, Anson Jones (December 9, 1844, to February 19, 1846), was widely believed to favor annexation but was elected without declaring his views on the subject.[2]

After the storm of revolution, the first national capital was established at a village called Columbia, in Brazoria County, mostly because the Mexican army had bypassed it, and therefore not burned it. It had a tavern, Fitchett and Gill, and the busiest boardinghouse in town was a great spreading live oak tree, where merchants and officials alike spread their bedrolls. The two houses of Congress met in separate frame buildings; the larger one, for the House of Representatives, had an attic and eave sheds.[3] Constitutional government in Texas commenced when the First Congress was gaveled to order on October 3, 1836, with fourteen senators and thirty members of the House.

As the judiciary was initially organized, there were four judicial districts covering the original twenty-two counties. Under the judiciary article of the constitution, each district judge would hold court in various towns along his circuit, and each was ex officio an associate judge of the Supreme Court.[4] When they sat together, en banc, presided over by the chief justice who had no circuit of his own, they were the Supreme Court. Importantly, a majority of the district judges had to be present for a session to take place. Judiciary acts passed by the Republic Congress specified various times and places for the district courts to meet, and called for the Supreme Court to convene for a single session each year. Those acts, however, did not reckon with the distances involved, transportation difficulties, fragile health, the changing meeting times provided for in subsequent legislation regarding the judiciary, or other complications that, taken together, allowed years to pass without the Supreme Court of Texas ever actually meeting. In fact, although Congress elected the first chief justice and associate judges in December 1836, the Supreme Court did not hold its first session until January 1840.[5]

Frontier conditions presented a not inconsiderable spectrum of obstacles to the establishment of a functioning judiciary. Indeed, just an introductory overview of the personnel of the Supreme Court of the Texas Republic, postponing consideration of jurisprudential development, will speak volumes about the judges' backgrounds and experience, the obstacles and sometimes dangers they faced. Life itself in Texas during the decade from 1836 to 1845 — from its extraordinary social mobility, which allowed outsiders to arrive and reinvent themselves into whatever they needed to be, to the stunning fragility of life, by which disease or violence could lay low the highest prospects or proudest ambitions — is illuminated by the profiles of the men who served in the judiciary.

Throughout the life of the Republic, there were four chief justices, and no fewer than twenty-five men served as district judges and therefore, at least nominally, as associate judges of the Texas Supreme Court. Even with such divergent national aspirations and political needs, and with unsettled conditions in much of the country and frontier mortality being what it was, it still seems a surprisingly large number. They varied widely in age, origin, and judicial experience. Somewhat fewer than half were Masons, and while that affiliation provided some unity of basic principles and beliefs, it probably did not alter the course of Texas jurisprudence.[6]

Even more surprising is the fact that such a gallery of educated and experienced jurists could be found in the rude, bump-and-rumble Republic.

Sam Houston was elected president in September 1836, to be inaugurated in December, but Burnet resigned the ad interim presidency on October 22 over his inability to control the willful and defiant army. Thus, when the Congress selected James T. Collinsworth as the first chief justice of the Texas Supreme Court on December 16, it was no surprise that he was a Houston ally.[7] He was only thirty; like Houston, he was a Tennesseean and protégé of Andrew Jackson, and had already worked for five years as U.S. district attorney in Tennessee's Western District. In the Texas revolutionary government known as the Permanent Council, he chaired the Military Affairs Committee and nominated Houston as commander in chief of Texas forces. A signer of both the Declaration of Independence and the Constitution of the Republic of Texas, he joined Houston's staff as aide-de-camp and fought at the Battle of San Jacinto. Like Houston, he loved books and had a library of some 175 volumes, mostly law. But also like Houston, he had a propensity for excesses of drink and melancholy. Collinsworth was not, however, the polarizing figure that the older Houston was, and actually served briefly as ad interim secretary of state to Burnet.[8] This tenure ended when he was elected to the Senate in November 1836, a seat that he resigned two weeks later to become chief justice. Truly, few governments could offer the chance for such rapid advancement.

And he might have risen higher. In June 1838, Collinsworth allowed his name to be entered (for in that day it was not considered dignified to campaign for, or even appear to seek, office) in the contest for the presidency of the Republic. He was Houston's choice as his successor, running against Mirabeau B. Lamar, who, after the revolution, had succeeded Burnet as Houston's archenemy. The contest was bitter; Houston's followers were divided, some preferring Texan diplomat Peter Grayson. Calumnies of the most appalling sort were hurled. Collinsworth, either by accident or in drunken despair, disappeared over the side of a boat while crossing Galveston Bay in July, and drowned. Early Texas financier Thomas McKinney was not surprised. "Collinsworth went exactly as you . . . presumed," he wrote a friend. "I was here and had been with him . . . and he was under the influence of Ardent Spirits for a week before hand."[9] Grayson also had committed suicide in Tennessee two days before, and Lamar won the presidency without opposition.

Houston, now a lame duck, appointed the attorney general of the Republic, John Birdsall, to replace Collinsworth as interim chief justice. Birdsall, of uncertain age but about forty-eight, was highly educated and able, a former New York circuit judge (appointed by Governor DeWitt Clinton when Birdsall was only about twenty) and three-term New York state senator. His appointment was made on August 10, but with both of Houston's presidential candidates dead, Lamar swept into power with a majority in the Congress, and Birdsall's interim appointment was not confirmed. After fierce and divisive debate, Congress chose instead Thomas Jefferson Rusk, a onetime Houston ally who was moving to establish his own profile in the government.[10] With both Houston and Birdsall out of a job, they formed a partnership to enter law practice in January 1839, but Birdsall, who had a history of delicate health, died of yellow fever the following July.[11]

In Rusk, the Congress chose a man who, as secretary of war during the revolution, had saved the cause by letting Sam Houston fight his own way and not following through on Burnet's orders to force Houston to fight in circumstances that would have been premature and doomed to defeat. Rusk was plainspoken, and his papers from his arrival in Texas in 1834 are full of misspellings and grammatical errors, but they show continual improvement through the next few years, and he built an impressive library.[12] He had read for the law in his native South Carolina (sponsored by John C. Calhoun) and had practiced in Georgia. Nonetheless, he was not distinguished in the law when he was elected chief justice on December 12, 1838, at age thirty-five. With no Court to convene at that time,[13] Rusk engaged in civic pursuits and commanded the Nacogdoches militia in President Lamar's war to expel the Cherokees from the country—an act that alienated him from Houston for many years. It was under Rusk's gavel that the Texas Supreme Court first convened, on January 13, 1840. In Rusk's only term to conduct the Court's business, he authored five opinions, which were rather mundane. As one writer noted, Rusk's lackluster performance was perhaps a reflection of the times: "It can not be said of Judge Rusk that he was a learned judge or a profound lawyer. . . . But his knowledge of law was equal to the circumstances which surrounded him. If his opinions are apparently arbitrary and sententious in their brevity, it must be borne in mind that it would have been absurd to quote precedents and authorities from systems of law which had not been adopted by the republic."[14] Rusk resigned on June 30, 1840, to go into private practice. His replacement, John Hemphill, finally brought stability and deeper legal thinking to the Court.

Like Rusk, Hemphill was from South Carolina; unlike Rusk, he was destined to be a protean force in Texas jurisprudence over the next two decades. He was thirty-six when elected chief justice, the son of a minister and a minister's daughter but estranged from his parents; he was a lonely bachelor but a formidable legal scholar. He had graduated second in his class from Jefferson College in Pennsylvania, where he was particularly noted for his facility with languages. He returned to South Carolina and taught school for a couple of years before reading for the law beginning in the spring of 1829 and being admitted to practice the following November, a remarkably rapid course of study. His status as a southern gentleman required some military pretense, and in 1836, as Texas was in the throes of revolution, Hemphill served as a lieutenant of volunteers in suppressing the Seminole rebellion in Florida. There he was stricken with malaria, and with his health thus imperiled, he immigrated to Texas in 1838.[15]

Washington-on-the-Brazos, where independence had been declared and the constitution adopted, had been supplanted as the capital first by Columbia and then by Houston, but it was still a leading town, and its elevated prairie was considered drier and more healthful than Houston or Columbia for con-valescents such as Hemphill. He opened a practice there in September 1838; immediately alert to the importance of Spanish law in Texas's affairs, he made it his first order of business to apply himself to the language and to amassing a withering library of texts on the Spanish system of civil law. It was likely this expertise that gained him the Fourth District judgeship, from which he oversaw the largely Latino affairs in West Texas, and he relocated to San Antonio, where he quickly earned a reputation as one of the Republic's most learned and capable judges. Hemphill served as Fourth District judge until his elevation to chief justice following the resignation of Thomas Jefferson Rusk. As chief justice of the Republic from December 1840 until annexation, and then for thirteen years more under the state government, Hemphill was a central figure in the developing of Texas's jurisprudence and deserved the honorific later given him as the "John Marshall of Texas."[16]

The fitful beginnings of Texas justice are seen more clearly in the tenures of the district judges, many of whose careers were cut short by yellow fever, invasion, investigation, or simply higher ambition, and many of whom never actually participated in a session of the Supreme Court.[17] The First Judicial District went through six judges in ten years, although it started off with some promise of stability when Shelby Corzine was elected its first judge in December 1836. He was forty-three, had been in Texas less than two years, and settled in San Augustine with his wife and seven children. Like Collins-worth, he boasted a strong Sam Houston connection: they were the same age, and both had been wounded fighting Creek Indians under Jackson at the Battle of Horseshoe Bend, Alabama, in 1814. During his two-year tenure as district judge, Corzine presided over the treason trial resulting from the abortive Córdova Rebellion (an attempt by some residents of Nacogdoches to take up arms against the Republic in favor of Mexico), and served on the commission to settle the Texas–United States boundary. Had the Supreme

Court ever met during Corzine's tenure, he could have done good work, but it did not, and he remained among those who were associate judges in name only.[18]

When Corzine died at age forty-five on February 8, 1839, Lamar had been president for only two months, and he used the vacancy to demonstrate that he had protégés no less ready and able than Houston's. He selected as an interim appointee Ezekiel Wimberly Cullen; only twenty-five, and without judicial experience, he was a judge's son from Georgia, where he had known Lamar during the latter's days as a newspaper editor. Young Cullen served in the Third Congress of the Republic as chairman of the education committee, where he managed Lamar's bill to use some of Texas's vast, vacant domain to support public schooling, thus helping Lamar gain his nickname as the "Father of Texas Education."

Congress did not concur with Cullen's interim appointment, and replaced him in November 1839 with Anthony Shelby of Galveston, who served out the remaining two years of the deceased Corzine's term. In January 1841, Congress elected Thomas Johnson to replace him, but Shelby, noting the constitution's mandate for four-year terms, refused to leave the post. Neither man backed down, throwing legal affairs in the First District into confusion and prompting passage of a public resolution condemning both as "obnoxious . . . and as properly to be regarded as vampyres upon the public purse."[19] Attempts at mediation failed, and ultimately both men resigned the post. Each subsequently submitted claims to be paid for their services, and ultimately Congress agreed to pay them both.[20]

In September 1841, the First District bench finally found some stability in twenty-six-year-old Richard Morris, a Virginian who had established a practice in Galveston. He held the post for three years, sat en banc as an associate judge during the 1842, 1843, and 1844 terms, and earned his elders' respect for the thoughtfully reasoned opinions that he authored. His promising legal career was cut short by yellow fever in Galveston in August 1844.

Replacing Morris on the First District bench was John Baker Jones, forty-three, a native of South Carolina who had settled in Galveston before the revolution and then served in the Republic Congress. Jones served on the Supreme Court in its final session before annexation—beginning December 15, 1845—and authored five opinions. Two of those played their role in the evolution of Texas jurisprudence—particularly in overturning a jury verdict and denying relief to a plaintiff, a creditor seeking payment, by construing that the creditor's suit had not been continued on remand, but was a new action, and therefore the statute of limitations had run.[21] Texas courts by the end of the Republic had come to a sympathetic view of debtors in their struggles with creditors, and what might seem like a stretch to find relief for the debtor was midstream for Texas judicial philosophy of the day.

In the Second Judicial District, affairs looked like they might start on a more certain footing when one of President Houston's San Jacinto veterans, Benjamin Cromwell Franklin, was elected judge on December 20, 1836. Like Collinsworth, Franklin managed to navigate the dangerous currents between Houston and Burnet and keep the good opinion of both. Franklin was thirty-one, a Georgian admitted to that state's bar at twenty-two. His first activity upon arriving in Texas in 1835 was Indian fighting, and in affairs with Mexico he right away became identified with the "war party" that favored immediate independence. When war came, President Burnet commissioned him a captain, but lacking his own company he fought gamely as a lowly private at San Jacinto. After Houston's crushing victory in the battle, it was Franklin and his company captain, Robert Calder, who were sent to Burnet with the news.[22]

Of all the jurists in the first generation of district judges, Franklin was the only one who had already held a judicial commission for the country. On April 3, 1836, sailors of the Texas warship *Invincible* had boarded and seized an American-flagged brig, the *Pocket*, near the mouth of the Rio Grande. The *Invincible*'s captain had been apprised that the *Pocket* carried Mexican naval officers and war materiel from the United States to supply Santa Anna's army. The contraband was impounded and the vessel taken as a prize to Galveston before the *Invincible* sailed on to New Orleans for supplies. American business interests who profited from trade with Mexico, and their insurers, were not sympathetic to the Texas Revolution, and caused the *Invincible*'s crew to be arrested for piracy. Although the case was ultimately settled, the Texas government, realizing that it had not officially declared a blockade, hurriedly created a special judicial district with jurisdiction over admiralty cases, and thus empowered to rule on the incident.[23] Franklin was appointed by President Burnet to preside over the case, which made him the first judge to hear a case in the name of the Republic of Texas; he ruled that the *Pocket* was taken as a lawful prize. Burnet's choice of Franklin was vindicated when Congress elected him district judge, and he heard his first case in that capacity in Brazoria on March 27, 1837. He resigned the bench two and a half years later to open a private practice in Galveston.[24]

The Lamar government replaced him with Henry Whiting Fontaine, a Kentuckian whose wife, the mother of their twelve children, had died on the road to Texas. Once in the new country, he married a widow with ten children of her own, with whom he had four more, and settled down to practice law in the new town of Houston, which was founded in the spring of 1837. Appointed in August 1839 to succeed Franklin, Fontaine resigned in September, citing financial reasons, and died very soon thereafter aged only thirty-two.[25] He was replaced by a highly qualified John Scott, formerly solicitor general of North Carolina. When doubts were raised whether the appointment was legal, he resigned, and then made a bid for election to the post in November.[26] He lost that election to thirty-year-old William Jefferson Jones, who steadied the bench during a five-year tenure. A well-traveled Virginian who had worked for President Lamar's Georgia newspaper, Jones had subsequently run his own paper in Mobile, Alabama, before joining Lamar in Texas. He served as Lamar's campaign manager in his successful bid for the presidency in 1838, and warmed Lamar's heart even further by fighting in his war to expel Texas Cherokees from the country. Jones's term as an associate judge carried into the years that the Supreme Court actually functioned, and he authored seventeen opinions during various terms from 1840 to 1845. One of his opinions cemented the practice that the Texas Supreme Court would not disturb jury verdicts unless there were findings to necessitate doing so.[27]

The six counties of the Third Judicial District presented a challenge to the Texas Congress. Located in the densest part of the Piney Woods along the Louisiana border, the area's reputation for lawlessness dated back to the Neutral Ground agreement of 1806. After purchasing Louisiana from France, the United States could not agree with Spain on which stream constituted the boundary between them, and each country sent an army to bolster its claims. The two commanders, however, declined to risk bloodshed until an agreement could be reached, and each pulled his troops back to agreed positions. Since then, even though sovereignty passed to the United States in 1819 under the Adams-Onís Treaty, which renounced the U.S. claim to Texas, the Piney Woods had been a no-man's-land harboring fugitives and cutthroats of all descriptions.[28]

Into this lawless hell the First Congress dispatched perhaps the one frontier lawyer who was equal to the task, the redoubtable Robert McAlpin Williamson, the Patrick Henry of Texas, so called for his early and ardent advocacy for independence from Mexico. A native of Georgia born in 1804, he had spent much of his life conquering adversity. At fifteen he was laid low by an attack of "white swelling," a frontier diagnosis probably of juvenile tuberculous arthritis, which confined him to bed for two years—time that he used to master languages and mathematics. When he emerged, his right leg was drawn back at the knee, necessitating use of a prosthesis and giving him his lifelong sobriquet "Three-Legged Willie." He was admitted to the Georgia bar by twenty-one, about the time that an ill-defined scandal propelled him to a new life in Texas.

Personally popular, convivial, an accomplished storyteller, a banjo player and folk percussionist at "pattin' juba," and a celebrated dancer—wooden leg notwithstanding—Williamson undertook his judicial circuit in 1837 with a will. In Columbus, a town that had not been rebuilt since being burned by the Mexican army, he held court under an oak tree. Further into the depths of East Texas, one incident occurred that made its way into frontier legend. In Shelby County, where a bloody feud known as the Regulator-Moderator War had broken out, one partisan declared that the proceedings would not go forward. (The "war" started as a dispute over land fraud, but quickly degenerated into a series of vendettas.) Perhaps thinking to overawe a judge who was visibly a cripple, he struck his Bowie knife into Williamson's bench and declared, "This, sir, is the law of Shelby County!" Undaunted, Williamson drew his pistol, laid it on the table beside the knife with the muzzle pointed at the challenger, and declared, "Then this, sir, is the constitution that overrules your law."[29] The case proceeded without further disturbance.

Williamson wed in 1837, and in January 1839 resigned from his bench and relocated to Washington County, which he soon represented in Congress. A somewhat pacified Third District then passed to John T. Mills, an Irishman who was only twenty-one. Mills resigned in December 1840, having participated in one session of the Supreme Court. His judicial career was renewed in January 1842 when he was elected to the newly created Seventh District.

In the Third District, Mills was replaced in January 1841 by the remarkable R. E. B. (Robert Emmett Bledsoe) Baylor, who had served in the state legislatures of his native Kentucky and adopted Alabama. He moved to Texas after a religious conversion, and by the time he had settled in Washington County he was more famous as a Baptist preacher. In 1840 he performed the marriage of Sam Houston, then in his interregnum, to Baylor's relative by marriage, Margaret Lea of Alabama. A gentleman scholar and bachelor, Baylor was elected to the Third District bench in 1841, when he was deeply involved in organizing a Baptist college in the town of Independence, an institution that would soon be known as Baylor University.[30]

Since Baylor kept the bench to the end of the Republic, he participated en banc as an associate judge of the Supreme Court from the January 1841 term through the December 1845 term. He wrote fifteen opinions during the Republic, of which one contemporary commentator noted, "like those of his associates at that period, they are terse and seemingly without much reference to precedents, [but] they manifest an earnest search for truth, and a conscientious dispensation of justice."[31] Baylor continued to serve as district judge after annexation, stepping down only when the courts stopped functioning in 1863.[32]

Even as the Third District showcased the challenges of homegrown lawlessness, the Fourth Judicial District, centered on San Antonio and covering areas to the west, presented challenges no less daunting—the potential of Indian attack and fresh invasion by Mexico. The first judge elected to this district was James W. Robinson. At forty-six, he was one of the oldest men assigned a bench under the Republic, but he was a man hardened to disagreeable circumstances. He was a native of Indiana, where he had been a law partner of future president William Henry Harrison. It was a life he forfeited when he abandoned his wife and five children to relocate to Arkansas and then Texas. He served as lieutenant governor in the provisional government in place before Texas's declaration of independence. Indeed it was the disastrous inability of members of that government to work together that led to the Convention of 1836, which declared independence, and when the ad hoc legislature impeached the governor, Henry Smith, Robinson was putative head of the revolutionary government for a short time. He soon put off such airs, however, and fought as a private at San Jacinto.

Robinson served as judge for three years before resigning under threat of impeachment in January 1840 on the strength of a petition charging him with a long catalog of "crimes of the deepest and darkest dye . . . overlooked on account of his station."[33] Although later vindicated, Robinson had collected a long roster of enemies, and purportedly resigned because he felt his judicial effectiveness was over.

Robinson relocated to start private practice in Austin, a new city founded the year before to serve as the national capital. Austin lay eighty miles northeast of San Antonio in territory still strongly claimed by Comanche Indians, who had been clashing more frequently and more violently with the Anglo Texans as they spread west into their domain. Robinson, however, did not have to travel to Austin to meet the Comanche threat. Several weeks after he resigned in 1840, several score Comanches, including women and children, entered San Antonio under a truce to discuss peace terms. Their chiefs had agreed to repatriate captives that they had taken, but it was soon apparent that they had brought only one with them, an adolescent girl named Matilda Lockhart, who showed plain evidence that she had been shockingly tortured. When Lockhart informed the Texas commissioners that the Comanches held as many as fifteen whites, but had determined to bring them in one at a time in order to get the highest price for each, the chiefs were told that they would be held hostage until all prisoners were returned.

James Robinson attended the meeting in the Council House, accompanied by John Hemphill, his replacement on the Fourth District bench. (After holding court in San Antonio that day, Hemphill had adjourned the session to allow the courtroom to be used for the meeting.) The Comanches, unwilling to be taken hostage, made a break for freedom, lashing out with knives and stringing their bows. The Texan guard opened fire inside the Council House, and Comanches outside who attempted to flee were intercepted by other military units. When the fighting stopped, all twelve Comanche chiefs were dead, as well as eighteen warriors, three women, and two children. Twenty-nine were captured and jailed; only one escaped. Six Anglos and one Latino were dead, and several injured, including a stunned John Hemphill, who had gutted an Indian warrior with his Bowie knife after being attacked and suffering a slight wound himself.[34]

The Council House Fight was a stark introduction to West Texas for Hemphill, but as noted earlier, he went on to distinguish himself in the Fourth District as a judge of rare ability. He served less than a year before being elected chief justice of the Supreme Court in December 1840. His position in the Fourth District was taken up in early 1841 by forty-three-year-old Anderson Hutchinson. A thorough southerner, Hutchinson was born in Virginia, had been admitted to the bar in Tennessee, and had practiced there as well as in Alabama and Mississippi. Before relocating to Texas in 1840, he published a tour de force compendium of the laws of Mississippi, with commentaries. The legislature of that state was so undone by this accomplishment that it purchased two thousand copies, some of which, along with his reputation, undoubtedly preceded him to Texas.[35] Few other men in Texas were as qualified to unpack and become a judge. The new national capital of Austin was part of his circuit in the Fourth District, and one of the first cases he heard gave him as much insight into Texas domestic conditions as it did into international relations.

After five years of independence, Texas had finally started winning diplomatic recognition from the European powers, including France, which dispatched a quarrelsome journeyman representative in Alphonse DuBois, Comte de Saligny, to serve as chargé d'affaires. (Texas was still not an important enough country to rate a full ambassador.) While waiting for the construction of his residence on a hill east of Austin, DuBois ensconced himself at Bullock's Hotel at Congress Avenue and Pecan Street, running up a sizeable bill for himself and his chef, Eugene Pluyette. It was the practice in Austin for residents who raised hogs not to pen them, but to let them forage at large through the town. Some of these free roamers — they may have belonged to Bullock the innkeeper — broke into the Comte de Saligny's room and ate some linen and some diplomatic dispatches.

The ensuing dispute between Bullock and DuBois deteriorated after Pluyette dispatched one of the hogs and served it to the count for dinner. DuBois refused to pay his hotel bill, which he said was padded, and Bullock socked the Comte de Saligny in the nose. The case wound up before Hutchinson as a simple assault, but DuBois insisted that the dignity of France had been offended and that harsher measures be taken against Bullock. Unable to obtain satisfaction under the law, DuBois stormed off to New Orleans, leaving the new "French Legation" unoccupied, as Austin residents cracked jokes about the "No-Account de Saligny."[36]

Nor was the "Pig War" the strangest occurrence that Anderson Hutchinson witnessed from the bench of the Fourth District. While holding court in San Antonio in September 1842, the proceedings were shattered when the courtroom was stormed by Mexican troops. Six years after the end of the Texas Revolution, Santa Anna decided to renew his claim to the renegade province, and sent a fast-moving column of fourteen hundred troops under General Adrian Woll to seize San Antonio. The entirety of the Fourth District Court—judge, jury, counsel, and witnesses—were taken hostage, marched all the way to Mexico City, and locked in Perote Castle. There they stayed until spring of 1843, when American diplomats secured their freedom.[37] This finally convinced Hutchinson that frontier judging was more than he had bargained for, and he returned to the sanity of Mississippi in 1843. Still, Hutchinson's tenure as judge included sitting on the Supreme Court en banc during the 1841 and 1842 terms. He wrote fifteen opinions, the largest number per term of any member of the Court during the Republic period.[38]

Ironically, Hutchinson's replacement had also been one of the Perote prisoners. William Early Jones was a former Georgia legislator and more recently a Texas congressman, of unknown age but about thirty-five, known by the nickname "Fiery." Jones wrote nine opinions during his tenure on the Supreme Court in the 1844 and 1845 terms.[39]

As Texas began to grow into its vast geography, new judicial districts were created to supplement the original four. The Fifth Judicial District was set in the turbulent East Texas of the Neutral Ground. First to be elected district judge by the Congress was E. T. Branch in 1838, probably the only justice who arrived in Texas by being put ashore by the pirates who had robbed him and taken his vessel. He taught school in the new town of Liberty; when revolution came he joined the army, fought at San Jacinto, and then represented Liberty County in the early Congresses. He served as Fifth District judge for nine months.

Appointed to replace him was George W. Terrell, thirty-seven, witty, urbane, and highly qualified, having been attorney general of Tennessee before coming to Texas. In Terrell, however, the rivalry between Houston and Lamar reached a high pitch, for the Tennessee governor Terrell had served more than a decade before was none other than Sam Houston, and Lamar's appointment of Terrell as district judge was meant to drive a wedge between them. At this Lamar succeeded—for a time. Houston counseled Terrell not to take the job, but did not stand in his way when he accepted. A few months later, Terrell repented and wrote Houston, "I recollect you said to me that Burnett offered me the appointment . . . for the purpose of bribing me, that if I accepted it I would not hold it a month—that he would require of me such partisan subserviency that I would resine the office in a fit of indignation—and that if I did not accept he would be my enemy always. This at the time I attributed to your prejudice against the man, which prevented you from doing him justice. . . . You knew the man better than I did."[40] Terrell did serve long enough to sit at a meeting of the Supreme Court, and wrote five opinions.[41]

In 1842 the Texas Congress elected to the Fifth District judgeship William Beck Ochiltree, a North Carolinian of meager education who had practiced law in Alabama before moving to Texas in 1839. Despite his lack of learning, Ochiltree established himself in Nacogdoches, a town with a number of able attorneys, and built a successful practice. He sat on the Supreme Court during the 1842, 1843, and 1844 terms, writing eighteen opinions, an unusually large number. He was the presiding district judge when Shelby County broke out in the Regulator-Moderator War, and he got to see mob passions at their height. Informed during a court session that one of the factions had trained a cannon on the courthouse, Ochiltree, in the spirit of Three-Legged Willie before him, "laid a brace of pistols on the table before him, . . . ordered the sheriff to remove the cannon and arrest anyone who dared to resist."[42] His other interests and political ambitions led him to leave the bench in 1844 to serve as secretary of the treasury, attorney general, and then adjutant general of the Republic.

Ochiltree's replacement, Royall T. Wheeler, offered a strong contrast in background: a Vermont Yankee with a classical education. He was admitted to the bar in Ohio before moving south, to Arkansas, where he went into partnership with an ardent exponent of the Southern slavocracy, Williamson S. Oldham. In 1839 Wheeler relocated to San Augustine, Texas, where he went into practice with Republic congressman Kenneth L. Anderson. Wheeler was elected judge of the Fifth District in 1844 after serving two years as district attorney. With so little time left in the life of the Republic, he might have become one more minor entry in the list of associate judges, but his force of argument and his opinions—especially in dissent—led to his retention on the district court after statehood and to a twenty-year career on the Supreme Court, including seven years as chief justice.[43]

The first judge elected to the Sixth District was Richardson Scurry, on January 20, 1840. A Tennesseean educated by private tutors, he had come to

Texas with a volunteer company and arrived in time to fight at San Jacinto. During his brief tenure as district judge, he served on the Supreme Court's January 1841 term, writing three opinions. He became a political ally of Sam Houston, and when he resigned his judgeship to become district attorney for the Fifth District, it paved the way to his becoming a congressman of the Republic and then Speaker of the House, where he was an effective advocate for Houston's policies.

Scurry was replaced by Patrick Churchill Jack, who had been a firebrand along with his law partner, William Barret Travis, in the Anahuac Disturbances of 1832. He was still only thirty-three, and occupied the bench for three years before succumbing to yellow fever in 1844. During those three terms of the Supreme Court, however, he authored eleven opinions, some of them remarkably forward-looking. The last judge of the Sixth District before annexation was Milford Phillips Norton, born in Maine and resided in Massachusetts before immigrating, at forty-five, to Texas, where he practiced law in Galveston. He wrote three opinions for the Republic Court's final session.

In the Seventh Judicial District, created in 1840, John M. Hansford was the first judge, serving until 1842. A Kentuckian of unknown age, he soon became enmeshed in a reinvigorated Regulator-Moderator War. In an environment in which no one was allowed to remain neutral, Hansford chose the Moderators, but then presided over a trial of Charles W. Jackson, a founder of the Regulators. His conduct of the trial, which may have been geared to his own survival, led to his impeachment and resignation. He was then assassinated anyway by vengeful Regulators. Elected to replace Hansford was John T. Mills, who had previously served in the Third District. He remained in this post until annexation.

They were a potent gallery of frontier Texas manhood: some sickened and died, some were killed, some survived, some fell victim to political animosities, and some dared outlaws to do their worst. The wonder is not that the early Texas judiciary could be confused and uncertain; the wonder is that they accomplished as much as they did.

THREE

A FUNCTIONING JUDICIARY

Frontier mayhem notwithstanding, the Texas courts set to their business with a kind of order that quickly became familiar to both bench and bar. Each district judge traveled in a circuit to hold court in the various counties of his jurisdiction twice a year. The necessity for this travel from court to court consumed large amounts of time, but at least the journeys were not lonely. Since attorneys commonly represented clients in more than one town on a judge's circuit, they would ride with him for company and, considering frontier conditions, safety. Oran Roberts, whom President Houston appointed district attorney for San Augustine in 1844, noted that "it was not unusual to see a dozen or more lawyers and the judge mount their horses, with saddle-bags, blankets, and tie ropes; and, thus equipped, start on their journey around the district. . . . As some of them would drop out of the company at different points others would fill their places, so that about an equal number of traveling lawyers in addition to the local bar, would be found in attendance at nearly every court."[1] Roberts, who went on to serve three separate tenures on the Supreme Court, noted that district judges traveled with their legal retinues until after the Civil War, when legal practice became more localized.

Fraternization between lawyers and judges was common and not hidden, especially as it became apparent that all of them were to some extent trapped together in Texas's monetary confusion. Then as now, lawyers with a good practice found it no financial blessing to be named to the bench, especially since a district judge's initial salary of $3,000 a year was in 1842 reduced to $1,750, and this was when the value of the currency was collapsing under the Lamar administration. At that time James Pinckney Henderson, formerly Texas minister to the United States, rejoiced at inheriting a law practice worth $10,000 a year from a lawyer who had been named district judge.[2]

Two years later, in 1844, the salary was reduced to only $1,500, and even that pay was often uncollectible.[3] This was the depth of the "retrenchment" era of Sam Houston's second term; not even the president was able to redeem his pay vouchers, nor were the secretary of state, the minister to the United States, or the land commissioner, for there was simply no money in the treasury.[4] In December 1841, Hemphill and another of the country's most distinguished judges, R. E. B. Baylor, conveyed memorials to the Congress, asking to be paid what was owed them. Hemphill had received only $625 of $6,000 due him, and that was not enough even to pay his creditors for expenses incurred since ascending the bench.[5]

Toward the closing days of the Republic, former chief justice Rusk, who had resigned years before to make a better living for himself, complained that the surfeit of lawyers was driving down their earnings as well. Many in the legal profession, judges and counsel alike, had to earn other income to make ends meet. Many of course were planters, but two enterprising law partners formed a second business as barbers, prompting them to post a notice that in their new practice, they would continue to "clip" the public.[6]

Frontier conditions being what they were, and with no functioning Supreme Court during the first three years of the Republic to give unity or guidance, the ad hoc nature of Texas justice did not escape notice in the United States. An Ohio literary monthly called the *Hesperian* regularly published the observations of a Texas correspondent (whose name regrettably was never subscribed in a byline) in whose view Texas courts represented "confusion and uncertainty that almost amounts to chaos. . . . [Each] lawyer in Texas has his own system of practice; and each judge his own rule of decision and it is a matter of little consequence whether the first is consistent with common sense, to say nothing of accuracy, or whether the latter is at war with the most obvious principles of justice."[7]

Like its American model, the Constitution of the Republic of Texas framed only the broadest outline of a judicial branch. These general provisions were that the Congress would create from three to eight judicial districts, each with a judge who would also be an associate judge of the Supreme Court and who would have to reside in that district. The chief justice rode no circuit and thus had no residency requirement. The chief justice and the district judges would be elected by both houses of Congress by joint ballot, their terms fixed at four years; they would be eligible for reelection, and their salaries could not be altered during their term of office. The Supreme Court's jurisdiction would be strictly appellate, both civil and criminal, and the Congress was mandated to, "as early as practicable, introduce, by statute, the common law of England" as the decisive authority.[8] There followed, however, a critical loophole: the Congress could, "in their judgment," substitute other bodies of law as controlling when Texas's unique interests made it desirable (except in the realm of criminal law, which was to remain under the common law in all cases). Given Texas's historic ties to the civil law system of Spain, this was a portentous concession.

In a number of important respects, the Constitution failed to provide a workable court structure for the emerging Republic. By making the Supreme Court a part-time temporary committee rather than a permanent governmental body, by giving that temporary committee full appellate jurisdiction, and by placing no limits on the right to appeal, the Constitution essentially guaranteed that the Court would face an avalanche of cases during its single session each year.[9]

The First Congress had been in its second session of the year for about ten weeks when the first act relating to the judiciary was approved, on December 15, 1836, fleshing out the provisions of the Constitution.[10] In addition to setting the judges' salaries, the Congress set the term of the Supreme Court to begin annually on the first Monday in December and be held at the seat of government—which proved to be no little adventure, because the capital of the Republic, located at Columbia when the act was passed, moved to Houston in 1837, to Austin in 1839, to Washington-on-the-Brazos in 1842, and subsequently back to Austin.

A second act relating to the judiciary followed a week after the first, on December 22, in which the Congress settled on establishing four judicial districts.[11] The First District was an irregular wedge of northern and eastern Texas, along the Red River from Louisiana west to the Indian frontier, and south along the Sabine almost to the coast; the Second was a much smaller block in the more thickly settled counties along the coast in the heart of the original Anglo colonies; the Third lay interior to the second and stretched northwest to the Indian frontier; and the Fourth consisted of the coastal bend and brush country from San Antonio to the Rio Grande. Under Mexican rule, the municipal alcaldes' courts were the tribunals of first resort, and after independence, their dockets were transferred to the district courts.[12]

The Supreme Court may have been slow to convene its first session, but the various district courts handled crowded dockets from the beginning, with the district judges traveling their multicounty circuits twice a year to hear daunting numbers of cases. The burden was so arduous, in fact, that some of the judges apparently found it impossible to make the journey to the capital to take their seats on the Supreme Court. The first scheduled session of the Court, in Houston on December 1837, was canceled when a quorum was not met. Representative Patrick Jack was sufficiently incensed that he called for the impeachment of the absent judges, but Congress instead passed a law imposing a $1,000 fine for such absenteeism.[13]

Perhaps in an effort to improve the judges' attendance at Court, in May 1838 Congress moved the annual meeting date from the first Monday in December to the second Monday in January. Even that tactic failed to have its desired effect, however, since the January 1839 session had to be canceled because of the absence of the new chief justice, Thomas J. Rusk, who didn't learn of his election by the Congress until two weeks after the session was scheduled to begin. Rusk accepted the appointment, but with reservations; by the next Christmas, he had indicated to President Lamar that he was willing to get the Court started but intended to resign immediately after.[14]

The first session of the Supreme Court finally met on January 13, 1840, in the home of Republic treasurer Asa Brigham, in the new national capital of Austin, alert for Indian attack. Chief Justice Rusk presided, with associate judges Anthony Shelby, William J. Jones, John T. Mills, and perhaps E. T. Branch in attendance.[15] Judge James Robinson also attended, but he resigned the following week under threat of impeachment, and was immediately replaced by Hemphill, who became the only man during the Republic period to serve as both associate and chief.[16]

Once convened under Rusk, the Supreme Court set a tone of conservative deference to the other branches of government.[17] The opportunity to set an important precedent came in a suit challenging the constitutionality of electing county-level chief justices, an office not described in the Texas Constitution. It was unusual in that the question was submitted by the parties to solicit the Court's opinion, not as an appeal from an adverse judgment, so from that standpoint, the Court did assume an expanded role for itself. Almost giving away his native Irish lilt, the young justice John T. Mills wrote of the judicial article of the Constitution, "'Tis true . . . 'there shall be in each County a County Court,'—but does this create the office of Chief Justice? Does the office live in the Court, or in the judge who presides?"[18] Mills held that the power accorded the Congress to organize the judiciary was sufficient to find the offices "strictly constitutional." Moreover, the president was within the power of his office to have refused to answer a summons to appear in the case, and therefore could not be held in contempt of the original court.

The Rusk Court thus showed its disinclination to interfere in the powers constitutionally awarded to the other branches of government. Its narrow holding in *Harvey v. Patterson* (1840) showed equally clearly its hesitation to interpret a statute so as to enlarge the Congress's intention. The Harveys, free persons of color, lost a suit in a lower court. The law provided that appellants had to post a bond to secure the further costs of counsel, but it made an exception for those who had not the means to do so. Section 15 permitted them upon their oath to proceed without posting a bond for legal fees. Mary

Harvey had declared herself "too poor to pay the fees, and too friendless and humble to give any Bond," and she offered to take the oath as provided by law.[19] The trial court declined to hear her oath, on the grounds that persons of color were barred, by section 26 of the same act, from swearing them.

In a deceptively clever opinion, the Fourth District's John Hemphill avoided choosing between sections 15 and 26—doing so might have defined the rights of black people in Texas courts. He ruled instead that section 15 relieved poor persons of the obligation to post bond for counsel's fees, but not of the payment of court costs. If Mary Harvey wished to have her appeal heard, she would have to find a way to post a bond to cover at least that amount. To relieve her of this obligation, and enlarge section 15 to include court costs, would require a "looseness of construction" that would amount to an unwarranted assumption of congressional intent.[20] Even while the ruling deferred to the Congress's legislative power, however, the fact that the Court allowed Mary Harvey to petition it without filing notice of appeal or posting a bond, and then heard her cause, staked out a role for the newly operational Court that seemed to go beyond its constitutional limitation to be purely appellate in its jurisdiction. (It also, not coincidentally, began a long line of cases in which the Supreme Court stretched its own rules to allow court access to impoverished persons of color.)

Perhaps the Rusk Court's shrewdest decision—or its most disingenuous, from the loser's point of view—was in *Board of Land Commissioners of Milam County v. Bell* (1840).[21] William W. Bell had arrived in Texas in October 1836, six months after independence was won at the Battle of San Jacinto, and about the same time as the establishment of constitutional (as opposed to ad interim) government. The First Congress met, and Sam Houston was inaugurated, on October 22. Settling in Milam County, Bell claimed the right to a league and labor of land (4,605 acres; a league was a Spanish unit of land equal to 4,428 acres, and a labor was 177) under the colonization law of Coahuila y Tejas. That county's board of land commissioners refused him, but the district court found in Bell's favor and issued a writ of mandamus to compel the commissioners to patent him the land. The commissioners appealed to the Supreme Court.

In the omnibus provisions of the Act of January 1840, the Texas Congress extended continuing legality to the colonization laws of Coahuila, under which vast tracts of land had been granted to settlers. The popular mood among Texans in the years after the revolution, however, was to sever as many ties to the previous government as they could. Holding for Bell could well have precipitated a flood of suits for land grants based on the old Coahuila framework. Faced with the Congress's intent to give continued effect to the

Coahuila colonization laws, Rusk found a way to hold against Bell for the league and labor: he found that the Coahuila legislature itself had, through its subsequent acts and decrees, effectively repealed its earlier colonization laws. That might have been sufficient to dispose of the matter, but sensing the import of the case, Rusk clarified his decision: the district court should not have issued the writ of mandamus until after it had ordered the commissioners to patent the land, and then only if they had refused to do so. Further, Bell was entitled to a Republic headright of 1,280 acres from the land board, and Rusk remanded the case back to the district court "in order that appellee may obtain his certificate for the twelve hundred and eighty acres of Land according to law."[22] Rusk's opinion, punctilious as to procedure and discerning in its logic to a calculated effect, was a long chalk from the rough letters of the lawyer who had arrived in Texas in 1834 on the trail of embezzlers.

Judge William J. Jones of the Second District concurred in the result, but voiced the view prevalent in Texas that independence had severed obligations made under Mexican laws as surely as it had ended Mexican sovereignty.

One researcher has noted that, while the Rusk Court proceeded with a kind of leaden, mainstream body of work, it was that very conservatism that placed the Texas Supreme Court on a credible footing with the rest of the government. Things were about to change, dramatically, but the quantum leap of influence of the Supreme Court under Hemphill might not have been possible without Rusk's having achieved acceptance of the Court's place at the national table.[23]

The constitutionally required statute recognizing the precedents of the English common law as binding in Texas was enacted on January 20, 1840, the same date that John Hemphill was elected judge of the Fourth District and was immediately seated as an associate judge of the Supreme Court.[24] The establishment of the common law as the basis for Texas jurisprudence was rather ironic for Hemphill, because after amassing a large civil law library and making a thorough study of it, he found much to admire. In the vast majority of the American states, and especially in the original thirteen, legal development was hidebound by their citizens' descent from the English common law that had governed them as British subjects for generations.[25] Texans, however, finding themselves in the position to choose between the respective merits of the common law versus civil law, opened the Republic's legal history with a question as sensible as it was fundamental: which serves better? Especially after he was elevated to chief justice, Hemphill often chose the civil law as the basis for his decisions.

The Court was very frank about it: "Our courts have either adhered to their former practice, or have adopted such rules of their own as seemed dictated by considerations of policy and convenience, rather than pursue the common law practice, where the rule which it afforded was found to be unsuited to our system, or inconvenient of application."[26]

Even as the Texas Constitution charged the Congress with establishing the judiciary, it also mandated that the Supreme Court promulgate a fair procedure for its workings. The main issue of judicial housekeeping that had to be gotten in hand was pleadings—the formal process by which an aggrieved party gained a court's ear, and by which the party accused of injury made answer. Under the Anglo-American common law, pleadings were a baroque exchange of declaration, plea, replication, rejoinder, surrejoinder, rebutter, and surrebutter, each step of which had particular requirements. In Texas, ever since 1731, when San Antonio's town secretary Francisco de Arocha had scrounged for a simple, effective mechanism to get parties to state their business, pleadings had consisted simply of petition and answer: the first from a plaintiff, laying out who he was, what injury had been done him and by whom, and what relief he wanted, the second from the defendant, responding to the accusation.

In one of its early cases, *Fowler v. Poor*, decided in the January term of 1841 (Hemphill's first as chief), the Texas Supreme Court opted for the Spanish model. Noting that the Texas Congress had expressly allowed that the mandated deference to the common law did not extend to pleadings, the Court admitted that "our system of proceedings in civil suits differs from that known in England, and adopted in most of the States of the United States."[27] The simplicity of petition and answer had served the people so well that business in the lower courts "shall be conducted in the same manner for the future."[28]

The issue surfaced again three years later in the case of *Hamilton v. Blank*. In a longer exposition, the Hemphill Court noted that owing to the ingenuity of lawyers, pleading "had become so refined in its subtleties as to substitute in many instances the shadow for the substance."[29] But the object of the statute on pleadings, the Court insisted, was "to simplify as much as possible" the basic process of getting into court. It was clear that Texas had jettisoned the common law's "technicalities and useless forms" and required "only a full and fair statement of the facts upon which the party relied, and the relief sought . . . to enable the court to act intelligently."[30]

Hemphill's preference was predictable, and in the case of *Scott and Solomon v. Maynard et uxor.*, decided in the June 1843 term (a time when the chief justice's name was being circulated in high political circles as a possible successor to Sam Houston as president of the Republic), Hemphill was bold enough to scold the losing counsel for rooting their case in the common law.[31] Belittling the English system as one "which . . . can exercise no other authority than that derived from the force of reason," he admonished the lawyers that it was their duty to base their argument "in the former laws of the country," despite the admitted "difficulty arising from the scarcity of books or authorities."[32] Counsel in *Scott v. Maynard* also raised again the issue of the common law pleadings, but Hemphill rebuffed them.

Scott v. Maynard was a gruesomely knotted real estate trial for title, in which the court reporter summarized the nineteenth and final bullet point as this: "The Court say that great assistance is afforded them by the argument of counsel when it is confined to the system of laws by which the rights of the parties are to be governed, the practice of Spanish civil law; but arguments which are based on some other system [in this case upon the common law] serve only to perplex and confound."[33]

A second realm of law that presented Hemphill with an opportunity to preserve the Spanish influence in Texas law was in the rights of married women. Under the common law in effect in most of the United States, wives were virtually the property of their husbands, with very little room to maneuver into meaningful independent lives of their own. In Texas under Spain, wives had enjoyed the benefits of community property: they entered a marriage with property of their own, and if the marriage dissolved they retained their original property and moreover had a right to part of the wealth that they had created as a couple. Even as it adopted the common law as its default standard, the Texas Congress, as it did with pleadings, carved out an exception by embracing the concept of community property.[34] It was inevitable that the two philosophies on the status of women would collide in Texas's Supreme Court, and in *Scott v. Maynard* Hemphill made clear his determination that counsel practicing before the Supreme Court had better acquire a working familiarity with Spanish law, because relationships entered into before Texas independence, whether contracts or marriages, would be governed by the law in force at the time they were entered into.

Hemphill also led the Court in a Latin-influenced approach to the law of debtor and creditor. Whereas in the common law, imprisonment for debt was still common practice, Spanish civil law had taken a milder view toward debt since the days of Ferdinand and Isabella. Countless early settlers came to Texas to escape creditors in their home country.[35] For some, including Royall Wheeler's law partner, Williamson Oldham, their financial miseries descended into embezzlement and flight from justice. Such men did not need Hemphill's command of Spanish law to incorporate some protection for themselves into the Constitution itself, in the twelfth of the Declaration of

Rights: "No person shall be imprisoned for debt in consequence of inability to pay."[36]

In matters that required the Texas Supreme Court to blaze its own path between the civil and common law, Hemphill wrote the most important opinions. Since Hemphill was the one with the Spanish texts and mastery of the civil law, Wheeler and the transient associate judges often felt themselves somewhat dependent upon, not to say captives of, Hemphill's divination. "They were both able jurists," recalled Oran Roberts of Hemphill and Wheeler, "though very different in their habits of thought on legal questions and in their mental organization."[37] The other justices were also more comfortable with the notion of simply Anglicizing Texas's legal affairs, and Hemphill regularly had to exercise his powers of persuasion to get the others on board with his blended approach.

Royall Wheeler, the Vermonter educated in Ohio, in particular did not consider himself a weak brother on the Court by any means, and he occasionally took issue with Hemphill's self-assured, though not universally conceded, preeminence. While the two generally worked well in harness together, their judicial tempers were markedly different. Although Hemphill had amassed an impressive collection of legal texts and seemed to have the mastery of them, Wheeler was struck by Hemphill's apparent laziness when the Court was not in session. After the capital was moved from Austin to Washington-on-the-Brazos in 1842, Hemphill's "custom after a session of the Sup. Court [was] to box up his books & lie about the places appropriated for loafers in Washington in a perfect state of torpor (like a lizard in the winter) until the next Sup. Court." Nor, wrote Wheeler, was Hemphill much admired by the practicing attorneys. "The bar south and west entertain a very moderate respect for Judge Hemphill & are extremely averse to see him retained upon the bench" after statehood was effected. And as for the Hemphill Court's legacy of decisions, "it [is] doubtful how far they will be regarded as settling any thin[g]."[38]

Wheeler was not alone in his misgivings about Hemphill's enchantment with the Spanish system. Anderson Hutchinson, who replaced Hemphill on the Fourth District bench (and thus became an associate judge) when the latter was elevated to chief justice, was if anything more vocal, and employed the rather modern tactic of voicing his grievance in his own written opinions—even when he wrote for the majority. Hemphill spoke Spanish and understood the workings of the civil law; the other judges did not. The case of *Whiting v. Turley* (1842) began as a relatively simple action from Travis County by one Turley to recover the cost of a fence he had contracted to build for Whiting and Slocumb. However, the case got snarled when counsel employed the English mode of pleading, forcing the judges to discuss law versus equity. Hutchinson delivered the unanimous opinion reversing the lower court and ruling in favor of Whiting, but his frustration was clear: "[We are left] to find principles and criteria in a language generally unknown to us . . . [and we must] refer to the doctrines and jurisprudence coming to us from Coahuila. Herein we must obey the legislative will and endure as long as we may the constant perplexities that in consequence annoy and delay us at each step."[39]

In the broader society outside the judiciary, Hemphill, in his sympathy for the certainties of the civil law, was even more in a minority in a Texas that had thrown off the Mexican yoke and was actively seeking to define a new identity free of its Hispanic heritage. Culturally, this took the form of an Anglocentric self-righteousness and repression of the Tejano community that lasted more than a century. And journalistic and lay commentators rooted in that movement took a dubious view of the Texas Court's continued deference to what was seen as Mexican law. Texas in the late 1830s and 1840s saw a flourishing of short-lived newspapers published by ambitious editors who had plied their vocation back in the United States, and they were solidly behind Anglicizing all things Texan.

Even Texas's leading newspaper, the *Telegraph and Texas Register*, which for a time held the contract to publish the official disseminations of the government, complained, "We have now all the evils of both the Civil and the Common Law, but few of the real virtues of either."[40] At the outset of Hemphill's tenure, one contributing correspondent of the newspaper characterized the functioning of the Texas judiciary "as yet almost as confused, irregular, and unharmonious as their first organization." Bitter must have been that writer's disappointment at Hemphill's steering a course away from his call for "a practice at Common Law, in Equity, and of Admiralty, for all the Courts of the Republic."[41]

Word of this tension in the development of Texas jurisprudence also spread to interested observers in the United States. The Texas correspondent of Ohio's *Hesperian* took the view that the common and civil law were utterly incompatible: "The truth is, when the civil or common law are thus brought together, they destroy in many cases the essential principles of each other, like two bodies of opposite natures when united by chemical affinity. The judge in many cases must elect between the two or decide that there is no law at all."[42]

Hemphill, however, seemed to feel he had a clear enough vision of what he was doing. He was conscious of the heterogeneous heritage he was creating in his decisions, which caused Judge Wheeler to carp at one point that

Hemphill was concerned mainly with his legacy: "I suspect that the Ch. J. has at length concocted some learned opinions with which he is pregnant & which he is desirous to promulgate before the expiration of the Republic."[43] Hemphill himself made no apologies. Serving at the Convention of 1845, he made his sympathies clear: "I can not say that I am very much in favor of either chancery or the common-law system. I should much have preferred the civil law to have continued in force for years to come."[44] And he believed that the greatest harm would result if, as some were proposing, cases in chancery (i.e., cases in equity) should be decided by juries, like common law cases. Hemphill had practiced in the chancery courts in South Carolina and knew the dangers of submitting sometimes-complex legal issues to the sympathy of laymen. That proposal, to his relief, was defeated.[45]

Upon reflection, Hemphill's partiality to the civil law was less dramatic then than it seems now, for the state of the common law in the rest of the United States was far less settled in the 1840s than it is today. Modern courts are hedged in by an ever-increasing body of statutes, in addition to 220 years of American precedents to draw on, and are administered by a bench and bar highly trained in accredited law schools. Hemphill's time was vastly different; then, American jurisprudence "had the worst of both worlds: the uncertainty of law that a [civil] code could have provided and an undisciplined, self-serving, often corrupt cadre of poorly trained judges and lawyers responsible for administering a systemless system."[46] In fact, as the American common law continued to accrue cases in its rootless way, a movement gained momentum in the late 1800s to look beyond the boneyard of precedents for guidance toward just results. Legal scholars began "shifting the emphasis of legal thought from the traditional common-law preoccupations" with precedent. This shift is described well by one writer: "Regarding all law, including judicial decisions, to be expressions of social policy, they believed judges should strive to reach decisions that would best further the goals of a free, democratic society. . . . The difference between judges dispassionately declaring what law had always been and judges affirmatively seeking results that would have desirable future effects was a difference of more than mere words: it implied a novel legal system with attributes strikingly different from those of the common-law model."[47]

Thus was born the modern tension between the clichéd characterizations of "strict constructionists" versus "activist judges," but seen from this viewpoint, John Hemphill's approach was a generation or two ahead of his time. Indeed, a later chief justice of the Texas Supreme Court, Reuben Reid Gaines, who himself was called upon to navigate the new emphasis on equity jurisprudence in the late 1800s, noted with approval that Hemphill, "even in deciding questions of common law . . . was prone to make excursions into the domain of the civil law in order to illustrate some principle or to fortify some conclusion."[48]

In the realm of criminal justice, where the English system had long provided the protection of jury trials, while the Spanish had occasionally yielded summary and draconian results, the Texas Congress came down early and emphatically on the side of the common law. In civil matters, they were content to let the Supreme Court guide the course of the law. When the centennial of the Court's first meeting was marked by ceremonies in 1940, Judge Sidney Samuels of Fort Worth acknowledged the early Court's achievement in a Texas that was a blank judicial slate: "How solitary was the first court . . . prescribing its own orbit, rationalizing its own mode of thought. It hewed its decisions out of scant materials . . . and sought to fit its decrees to a virgin frontier."[49]

FOUR

THE FRONTIER COURT

Hemphill's applied vision of Texas as a country that charted its own jurisprudential course, melding the certainty of the civil law with the safeguards of personal liberty found in the common law, excited the most controversy about legal development in the Republic of Texas. However, during its ten-year existence the Court also issued opinions on numerous cases that, while they did not reach such a high level of legal philosophy as the debate over contending legal systems, deeply affected the lives of ordinary Texans, even as they carved out more of the country's unique legal identity. The cases also offer a vivid glimpse of a society at the edge of wilderness, both in geography and in antisocial behavior, and of a society struggling to bring both into some civilized harness.

The Court itself was somewhat sensible of its own rustic beginnings, and adopted the tone that tolerance should be extended to shortcomings in judicial regularity from those early days. When A. P. Nowland of Fort Bend County sued one Jones to recover on a note for $404.90, the Court observed that the document copied in the petition "has no date, and there is no allegation as to its date or place of origin. As is usual in transcripts coming here, the papers in the case are copied without any introductory matter by the clerk showing when they became of record by being filed in the Court. We are even left to suppose [when] the suit was instituted." The justices' recitation of the case proceeds with "we presume . . ." and "there must have been evidence that . . ." Nevertheless, the Court noted that the suit, originating in 1839, "occurred before the legislature had attempted to give us a jurisprudence better understood by the courts, the bar and the people, and at a period when the country itself was in the process of formation; so that manifold allowances are to be indulged."[1]

The high bench's leniency did have its limits, though, and the justices would not reach out to help lawyers who made their appeals with poor preparation. In one case, which "came up . . . unaccompanied with any statement of facts, or Bill of Exceptions," the justices could "discover no error whatsoever in the judgment of the Court below," and so affirmed the result without discussion.[2] In at least one instance, the judges were moved to criticize a petition that reached the Supreme Court as being "so entirely slovenly, so wanting in every essential requisite" that they were at a loss as to what to do with it.[3] Once they did receive proper briefs they discovered a case almost as messy as its record. Wayne Barton, a resident of Travis County, was in the habit of grazing his horse on a tract of land near the Colorado River above the mouth of Onion Creek. The horse took to straying into the proximity of Barton's neighbor, Robert Mitchell, to the latter's annoyance. After the horse disappeared, Mitchell was heard to boast that he had driven the horse to a place where Barton would never find it. Although Barton did not witness the deed, he charged Mitchell with trespass. Mitchell was found liable, and upon his motion he was granted a new trial and found liable again. His appeal to the Supreme Court was grounded in his claim that he could not be found to have committed the trespass without there being any witness to it.

The Court, through Associate Judge William J. Jones, was unsympathetic. Finding that Mitchell's declaration of what he had done should "be taken most strongly against himself," it found further that in a case in which the property could not reasonably be kept under the owner's direct supervision, the proof of the trespass did not have to meet as high a standard as in, say, a personal injury. If the Court held otherwise, wrote Jones, "it will be in the power of the Wrong-doer to commit the most wanton acts of aggression upon the stock of his neighbor, without detection." Texas had had a functioning judiciary long enough that Jones was able to cite one of its own cases as precedent for the holding that when an appeal reached the Supreme Court after multiple trials, it was assumed that the jury had reached a correct result.[4] In the absence of some error, Mitchell's bid for a third trial was turned back, the judgment against him affirmed, and the rule was established that in Texas, litigants could not keep going back to trial until they got the result they wanted.

One area of law in which Texas could not escape the entanglements of Spanish and Mexican law was land. In a republic whose population largely comprised the cash-poor and land-rich, possession of vast land grants, from Spanish and Mexican days as well as later, was avidly sought by heirs, former spouses, children of former spouses, creditors, and sundry relations of the original holders. Moreover, attempts by walleyed individualists to assert that their might made right were not limited to such piddling actions as shooing away a neighbor's horse. During the years of Anglo colonial settlement in Mexican Texas, one of Brazoria County's most prominent landowners,

Warren D. C. Hall, had cast a covetous eye on a thousand-acre tract of his neighbor, James A. E. Phelps. Phelps had received the one-league grant in 1824, and lived on and developed the property. In 1831 Phelps and his wife left for the United States to visit one of their children, leaving their plantation in the care of an overseer and numerous slaves. In their absence, Hall invaded their property, displaced the overseer and slaves, and forcibly occupied the land. When Phelps returned the following spring, Hall compelled him to deed the thousand-acre tract to him in return for the "consideration" of being allowed back onto the remainder of his league. Phelps sued Hall in July of 1838 for damages and to recover his lost land. The jury found for Phelps in all respects, and Hall appealed on several grounds. It was Anderson Hutchinson who delivered the lengthy and occasionally outraged opinion of the Court in 1841.[5]

Alluding to the maxim under the civil law that when one compels a price for abstaining from an act that he was bound by law not to commit anyway, the price should be restored, Hutchinson found this to be simply "sound morals." He also noted that the common law, while not controlling in this case because the land originated as a Mexican grant, embraced the same principle. Of Hall's contention that Phelps had made the conveyance knowingly and for good consideration, Hutchinson found "no shadow of a valid consideration to support it." Moreover, even if Phelps "had acted . . . in a compromise, equity, which is derived from the Civil Law and the fountains of universal justice, would have relieved him."[6] Hall's contention that the suit was not filed in a timely manner—seven years had elapsed between the episode and the filing—was brushed aside with equal brusqueness. "The Court considers . . . the distracted state of Texas from 1832, to 1835, and the revolution that occurred" as abundant reason to allow the suit.[7] Hall's other contention regarding jury instructions also failed, but it was the unsavory aspect of the whole transaction that incensed the Court. Hall, "in the spirit and with the hand of rapacity, . . . in his own audacious words, *reigned sole possessor* of the usurped manor and premises, affecting all the power . . . of a successful marauder of the dark ages."[8] The Court restored Phelps's thousand acres, and in so doing announced with unmistakable clarity to would-be land barons in land-rich Texas that their strong-arm tactics would not prevail against the law.

Bringing ambitious, and audacious, landowners under the control of justice was only one aspect of bringing order to the fringes of settlement. Being a frontier people, Texans expected their courts to vindicate actions that seemed, to them, perfectly in keeping with the nature of their society. During the vivid discourse that accompanied the Texas national election of 1841, Joseph Thompson and two other citizens of Red River County were moved to bet eight hundred dollars on the outcomes with one William Walker.[9] Thompson lost but declined to pay up, and Walker endorsed the note over to Wiley Harrison, who sued and won before a jury of their peers to collect the debt. Betting was an everyday occurrence throughout the Republic, as much a part of daily life as tobacco and whiskey. Thompson appealed to the Texas Supreme Court on the basis that no consideration had ever passed between the parties—an essential element of completing a contract that was needed to render the wager enforceable. The trial judge felt otherwise, and his instruction to the jury was that "betting upon an election was an exercise of judgment, and not so manifestly contrary to public policy" as to void the wager.[10] Of all the associate judges on the Supreme Court, none had more proved himself a man of the people than the Anahuac firebrand Pat Jack. But charged now with the solemnity of setting judicial precedent, Jack spoke for the concurring judges that, quite simply, "contracts of this kind are contrary to good morals, and against public policy."[11]

The following year, however, the high bench reached a different result on similar facts, a wager on a horse race from Matagorda County. The opinion by Associate Judge William Ochiltree in *Cavenah v. Somervill* (1843) criticized "that sort of Judicial Legislation" that led courts to have the arrogance to declare "what is and what is not contrary to public policy," and further announced that the Court would view "with strictest scrutiny" the appeals of those who lost their case in law and appealed in equity.[12] He did not, however, actually reach the moral or public policy question of betting on horse races, finding instead that the holders of the assigned notes, having come to them innocently, were entitled to collect. It was an odd result, but in historical perspective one that was uniquely Texan, for in the earliest days of his colony, Stephen F. Austin had outlawed gambling, but had made an exception for horse racing as an incentive for the acquisition and breeding of improved stock.

The Court resumed its more moral tone in a decision upholding the conviction of Hiram Saddler of Lamar County for public brawling. According to the trial record, Saddler and three others engaged in an "affray": the participants "unlawfully assembled together, in a warlike manner, in a certain . . . public road . . . unlawfully and to the great terror and disturbance of divers good citizens . . . did quarrel and fight and make an affray."[13] Saddler appealed on the ground that his three codefendants had been acquitted, and an "affray" could have occurred only by the consensual participation of all. Judge Ochiltree, for the Court, declined to find that "quarrelling and fighting, *eo nomine* [by that name], are . . . offences known either to the Common Law, or to the Statutes of the Republic of Texas."[14] But that wasn't the point.

The essential element of an "affray" was that it occurred in a public place, the consent of the parties notwithstanding. If they wanted to fight, they should have done it where the public would not have to see them. Saddler's conviction was affirmed, and he would have to endure his punishment, a ten-dollar fine.

Texas also found it necessary to adopt some posture and bearing toward its native Indian tribes, some of whom roamed the frontier in unreduced pride and power, and others of whom dwelt within the pale of settlement and sought accommodation and coexistence. This became a complicated story involving national policy, personal political rivalries, and decisions of the Supreme Court—all of which led Texas in a direction different from that followed by the United States.

President Houston was part of a very small minority in believing that Indians deserved to be treated as equals. He had lived with Cherokees twice for a total of six years, once as a teenager fleeing his oppressive Presbyterian boyhood in Tennessee, and a second time in the Indian Territory as he recovered himself after resigning as governor of Tennessee. President Lamar, on the other hand, hotly criticized Houston's tolerant attitude toward natives. "How long," he demanded, "shall this cruel humanity, this murderous sensibility for the sanguinary savage be practiced? Until other oceans of blood, the blood of our wives and children, shall glut their voracious appetite? . . . The white man and the red man cannot dwell in harmony together. Nature forbids it."[15] Lamar advocated "war to the knife" against all Indians who did not submit to white authority in the most abject way. And Rusk, even as he bore the title of chief justice, took a leading part in Lamar's war to expel Cherokees from East Texas.[16]

The Supreme Court entered the debate in a case that came to them from Bastrop County, where Indians had stolen various horses and mules from P. W. Herbert on the night of May 27, 1842. Bastrop was rather east of the usual Comanche raiding range, but the area had been suffering stock depredations by local tribes such as Wacoes, Keechis, and Tawakonis, whom Sam Houston, in his second term as president, had been currying for peace negotiations. Two days after the theft, Herbert's stock was retaken in a skirmish by a group of men including one Thomas Moore, who lost his own horse in the fracas and replaced it with one of Herbert's mules. Herbert demanded its return; Moore refused. Herbert sued, and Moore defended himself with a novel application of *post limine*, the doctrine of international law providing that personal property lost in war for more than one day and subsequently taken by somebody else became the property of whoever wound up with it. The district court in Austin agreed, allowing Moore to keep the mule, and

Herbert appealed to the Supreme Court. Finding, as it did, that there was no ongoing war with a recognized foreign enemy, and that reliance on *post limine* was therefore unwarranted, would have been sufficient to overturn the case without further exposition. The Court, however, through Associate Judge William J. Jones, examined the ramifications of the case and "the grave and important question . . . before us," and bounded to a vastly more expansive ruling than was strictly needed.[17]

The first issue that he found necessary to settle was to deny Texas tribes the status of independent entities with whom the Republic could treat as equals under international law. The United States regularly concluded treaties with Indian tribes, but Jones chose to note particularly that part of John Marshall's opinion in *Cherokee Nation v. Georgia* (1831) that regarded natives as being in a state of "pupilage": wards of the state "who looked to the government for protection, and relied on its kindness and power."[18] He also noted that both the colonization law of Coahuila y Texas in 1825 and a treaty between the United States and Mexico in 1832 referred to wandering natives as "Indian tribes" and not "Indian nations."[19]

Judge Jones had been Lamar's campaign manager, and he proved himself worthy of his mentor in rhetoric as well.

> No community can be termed a nation, which is not able to enforce its sovereign rights within some fixed territory—which is not independent of all other nations—which cannot lay claim to, nor exercise equal political rights with its neighbors. . . . Shall we apply *post liminy* to Pirates on land, or Indian robbers? Or will it be contended that the Indians rank higher than Pirates? . . . And how do these Indian tribes, the Wacoes and Comanches, live? . . . [T]o avenge their imaginary wrongs, they have uniformly had recourse to rapine and bloodshed. Shall we then dignify them with the proud title of nationality?[20]

Jones's opinion stood in gallant disregard of the fact that Texas natives did have territories, albeit defined in their own terms, and the Comanches at least had managed to defend their range very effectively against white encroachment for many years.

Nevertheless, Jones insisted that their domestic dependency and subjection to Anglo rule "is no more discarded by a revolt against the authorities of the nation, than the rights of the master are weakened or impaired by the disobedience of the slave."[21] Moreover, as a matter of public policy, concluded Jones, sanctioning *post limine* in this case would encourage the unscrupulous of the frontier to trade with Indians for stolen stock, and thus increase mayhem at the fringe of settlement.

At the small cost of requiring Moore to restore Herbert's mule, the Texas Supreme Court was able to demonstrate its truculent bearing toward the native tribes and align themselves with the prevailing sentiment of the people.

Indian considerations extended even into the more mundane realms of developing law, such as bailments—including the obligation to suitably care for another's property that was given in loan. In another case from hard-hit Bastrop County, in early summer of 1844, local resident Donald McDonald borrowed a horse from Lewis Hancock, intending to return the animal the next day. Indians stole the horse during the night, Hancock sued for its three-hundred-dollar value, and the jury awarded him two hundred dollars in damages. McDonald appealed on the strength of an affidavit from one of the jurors that he had not properly understood the judge's instructions.

Judge Milford Norton, writing for the Court, held that "the Law imposed upon the Def[endant] the duty of extraordinary care & diligence in securing a horse gratuitously loaned to him against the extraordinary danger to which it was exposed." Yet, rather than stabling the horse in a barn, tying it near the door, or finding some other means of protecting it, the animal was "left in an open lot at a distance from the house entirely unwatched & unguarded": "This was not such care even as a prudent man would have taken of his own property," let alone a bailment in which McDonald was liable "not mearly for slight but the slightest negligence." The Court was unimpressed by the juror's affidavit, holding that it did not matter whether he understood the instructions as long as the verdict was in accordance with the evidence and the law. Besides, wrote Norton, statements by jurors impeaching their own performance were to be viewed with great caution.[22]

Native Indians, not being citizens, were left to the tender mercy of the Republic, and the several hundred "free persons of color" who lived in Texas found themselves in a similar limbo.

In Harris County, as in the rest of Texas, it was not uncommon for a white person to beat a black person, slave or free, with impunity, because persons of African descent were not permitted to give evidence against Anglos in the courts. However, excessive brutality against black residents was a frequent source of community disapproval, resulting in the ostracism of the offender and the willingness of whites to offer testimony on behalf of the injured.[23] Thus when Jesse Benton, a white resident of Harris County, beat Eli Williams, a free black, and Williams sued Benton, it can be presumed that white witnesses offered their help in obtaining Williams's judgment for damages against Benton. Benton appealed, maintaining that "Eli Williams is of African descent, and not entitled by law to maintain his action, except by his guardian or next friend."[24] (In the common law, "next friend" refers to someone who represents a person unable to bring a suit on his or her own behalf.)

The Texas Supreme Court, bound by a constitution that not only deprived free blacks of citizenship but also declared that "[t]he descendents of Africans shall not be permitted to remain permanently in the Republic without the consent of Congress," saw only a thin path to justice.[25] In an opinion written by Associate Judge Patrick Jack (who complained again of the poor quality of the trial record), the Court found that "we cannot conclude that because they are not entitled to some particular privileges, they are, while actually residing in our country, out of the pale of the protection of the law, and that injuries and aggressions may be wantonly committed on their persons and property, and that when they ask for a redress of such grievances, they are to be told that the Courts of Justice are closed against their complaints." To do other than sustain the judgment for the beaten Eli Williams would be, wrote Jack, "against law, contrary to the spirit of our institutions, and in violation of the dictates of common humanity."[26]

It was at least socially significant, though not a deliberate stroke of irony, that it was Pat Jack who wrote the opinion. Not only was he a card-carrying member of the slavocracy, it was he who, by his machinations to recover slaves who had escaped to Texas from Louisiana, helped precipitate the Anahuac Disturbances, which nearly ignited the Texas Revolution in 1832. Certainly in no other context could he be thought of as a defender of African-American rights in the Republic of Texas.[27]

For a country whose politics had throughout its life been dominated by the rivalry between Sam Houston and Mirabeau Lamar, it was fitting that one of the last cases disposed of by the Republic's Supreme Court was a suit between the two principals. And it was doubly fitting that the suit had made its way through the legal process for years—indeed, throughout most of the nation's existence. *Lamar v. Houston* had its origins in the transfer of the capital from Columbia to Houston in the spring of 1837.[28] The new seat of government, hewn from raw woods on the banks of Buffalo Bayou, was not completed at the time its population began arriving. Indeed, the Congress began meeting under oak boughs lashed to the rafters of the unfinished capitol. President Houston took residence in a two-room dogtrot provided by the town's founder, A. C. Allen; Houston furnished the house at his own expense. At the time of Lamar's succession in December 1838, a new presidential mansion was being completed, and Houston agreed to allow the new chief executive to buy the existing furniture for his own cost, plus freight.[29] It was one of Houston's few magnanimous gestures toward Lamar, and one that he came to bitterly regret, for Lamar changed his mind, and when he returned the furniture, Houston found it, allegedly, damaged beyond usability. Claiming the value of the pieces to have been $2,000, Houston sued Lamar for $1,500, the amount of the claimed damage, in April 1839. Lamar won continuances for a remarkable four years before the case was tried and the jury awarded Houston a judgment of $1,335.86, including interest. Lamar made two payments totaling approximately half the judgment before filing notice of appeal on May 1, 1843. The case was not filed in the Supreme Court for more than a year, after which the Court continued the case to its 1845 term, heard arguments, and gave its decision on December 30, 1845, a day after the U.S. Congress accepted Texas as the twenty-eighth state. Chief Justice Hemphill, noting that payments had already been made to partially satisfy the judgment, found no merit in Lamar's contention that the jury's verdict was contrary to the law and the evidence, and affirmed the result. The associate judges unanimously agreed.

Houston quickly struck Lamar with a writ of execution to collect the remaining debt, but the sheriff returned empty-handed, as there was "no property to be found of Defendant." By 1848, with Houston having had two years' steady income as United States senator, he assigned his interest in the case to his revolutionary comrade Ira Lewis of Matagorda County, if he could collect it.[30] Lamar subsequently remitted two hundred dollars in cash and agreed to convey land for the remainder—a bitter end to a bitter rivalry whose voltage had lit much of Texas politics for the preceding decade.

Taken together, the cases reported by the Supreme Court of the Republic are a clear window on a vivid time. They might never have come to modern notice, however, but for the enterprise of a garrulous young émigré from the North who could indeed have stood as an epitome of those who flooded into Texas during its independence. James Wilmer Dallam was twenty-six when he arrived in Washington-on-the-Brazos in 1844. He was from Baltimore, a banker's son who had taken a degree at Brown University and read for the law under the sponsorship of Reverdy Johnson, later a U.S. attorney general. Dallam left for Texas to make his fortune and settled in Matagorda to practice law, but finding little business on the coast, he moved to the capital. There he was seized with the project of compiling the new country's laws and Supreme Court decisions, a difficult task because of sloppy and incomplete records.[31] He took the manuscript back to the United States, where, with his banker father's help, he was able to get it published. Dallam cleverly included in the title the claim that the digest contained a full accounting of Texas's byzantine land laws.

When he returned to Texas, lawyers and land traders found his book indispensable, and Dallam became financially established. He married the daughter of the late Texas secretary of the navy S. Rhoads Fisher, and found himself a success in Texas society. But if James Dallam was a paragon of the bright young talent that coursed into Texas from the United States, he also exemplified the tragedy that could befall it when least expected. He returned to Matagorda after statehood, but found little happening in the law business. With his literary talents established—in addition to his legal digest he was busily writing romance novels such as *The Lone Star: A Tale of Texas*— he undertook editing a newspaper, the *Colorado Herald*. When invited to relocate to the growing port town of Indianola and start a newspaper there, he accepted, journeying to New Orleans to arrange some affairs. Within days he was dead of yellow fever, age twenty-nine, leaving a young widow and infant daughter.[32]

Dallam's digest of the Republic Supreme Court's cases was not quite complete. When he left for the United States to publish it in the spring of 1845, the Republic and its Court still had another year to live. Those cases were not reported until legal scholar James Paulsen compiled and published them in 1986, too late to have much precedential value, but the stout volume that Dallam did compile was consulted and cited by generations of Texas courts.[33]

FIVE

THE ANTEBELLUM COURT

The annexation of Texas to the United States became effective when accepted by the American Congress on December 29, 1845, but Texas did not surrender its sovereignty until the formal transfer of power on February 19, 1846. In a rustic ceremony at the hewn-log Capitol in Austin, the Republic's last president, Anson Jones, gave a speech, intoning, "The final act in this great drama is now performed. The Republic of Texas is no more." The Lone Star was lowered from the flagpole, and former two-term president Sam Houston stepped forward to take it in his arms. The American flag, now with twenty-eight stars, was raised in its place, and the first legislature of the State of Texas convened immediately: eighteen senators and fifty-five representatives.

The enrolling and engrossing clerk of the Senate, N. C. Raymond, whose job it was to prepare official copies of passed bills for executive signature, observed that body at its task for the next five weeks before writing a friend in some exasperation,

> As yet not a solitary office of the State government except that of Governor has been organized, and as is always the case when so many have a say so in anything . . . mites are made mountains of, and the substance of things are overlooked by many while grappling for the shadows. . . . There has as yet nothing definite been done with regard to taxation, some are for reducing it—a good idea if a fellow wants to make political capital—while others are for increasing.

In the matter of a state judiciary,

> the Districts are yet to [be decided], the probate courts to organize, the justices courts, and a multiplicity of other business which cannot be done untill counties are established. . . . A Bill however has become a law post-

poning the holding of the Courts in the Spring. . . . There will be an entire
reorganization of everything from Justice Courts up to the Supreme bench,
and new laws enacted for the governing of each officer in the discharge of
his several duties. . . . Hemphill as Chief Justice—Lipscomb and Wheeler
as associate justices of the Supreme Court have been confirmed.[1]

Importantly, the new state constitution reduced the number of Supreme
Court justices from the chief and the fluctuating number of district judges to
three permanent figures—a chief justice and two associate justices (no longer
"associate judges")—appointed by the governor for six-year terms with the
concurrence of two-thirds of the Senate.[2] With the uncertainties of a Texas
national currency now behind them, they were to be paid salaries of not less
than two thousand dollars a year. When the legislature finally got around to
the Supreme Court on May 12, it provided that the Court should consider
cases annually at Austin, but subsequent amendments had them meet for
three terms each year: at Austin in November, at Galveston in January, and
at Tyler in April.[3]

As noted, Hemphill and Wheeler were continued from the Supreme
Court of the Republic. The new addition to the high bench of the state was
Abner Lipscomb, fifty-six, a South Carolinian who, like Rusk, had read for
the law in John C. Calhoun's office. He had gone on to serve for twelve years
as chief justice of the Alabama Supreme Court before being elected to the
legislature and then immigrating to Texas in 1839. Almost immediately on
his arrival he was drawn into Lamar's circle, and served that president for a
year as secretary of state. Lipscomb had served with Hemphill in the Constitutional Convention of 1845, where it was Lipscomb who introduced the
resolution approving the annexation terms to join the Union.[4] He lacked the
chief justice's facility in Spanish law, but he otherwise had confident judicial
views of his own.

There had been some support in the 1845 convention for the popular election of judges, which would have followed the national trend toward the
so-called popular sovereignty of the Jacksonian era. There was an extent,
however, to which Texas's legal minds regarded the passion of the masses as
a force to ride and, with luck, control, rather than obstruct and be trampled
by. Many were not, themselves, true believers that the popular will should
always have its way. Thomas Jefferson Rusk, who had been chief justice before Hemphill, was no stranger to electioneering among high-strung yeomen,
having been the popularly elected captain of volunteers from Nacogdoches
during the revolution. But he had also subjected himself to rigorous self-
improvement in letters, the law, and judicial temperament since those days,

and now believed that the popular election of judges was woefully ill suited to fill an office requiring the probity, independence, and courage needed from the bench. "If we have a . . . judiciary . . . which is swayed by popular clamors," he argued at the 1845 convention, "you are on a sea without a compass; your rights of person are not safe; your property is not safe; the reputation of your country is endangered; all is anarchy and confusion." Popular election of judges, he insisted, was a short route to a "weak and vacillating judiciary, destitute of talent and integrity, with no merit beyond that of office seekers, who, if they cannot secure an important office will take a small one."[5]

Hemphill's and Rusk's plea that judges be cut from a finer cloth than elected politicians carried the day at the convention, with the proposal for popular election losing by a vote of 38-19. But the momentum of the times was against them. Texans were still a people susceptible to the notion that frontier egalitarianism could be beneficially extended to the bench. A constitutional amendment providing for the popular election of judges was introduced in the state's First Legislature. It failed, but another that was introduced in the Second Legislature passed and was ratified; in 1851 Texans began going to the polls to elect their judges—including justices of the Supreme Court.[6]

Rusk and Hemphill had no idea, of course, that in taking up the cause to find a better way to select judges than subjecting them to the "popular clamors," they were firing the opening salvo in a debate still unresolved after a century and a half. Still, Texas embarked in 1846 on a fifteen-year journey as a state of the genteel Old South, but it was antebellum life with a difference. Texas was the only southern state to border the western frontier, where the cotton planters kept a lookout for Indian raids, and where the code of gentlemen was rattled by the unlettered expectations of the frontiersmen, whose favor now had to be maintained if a judge wished to continue in office. Therefore, the Supreme Court under the state government, as under the Republic, still found itself having to smooth out some of the more rustic notions of frontier justice and, Solomon-like, split some fine differences. Lipscomb, for instance, writing for the Court in 1854, denied convicted Madison County murderer George Jones's contention that he should have been acquitted because he produced more witnesses than the prosecution. Lipscomb did, however, overturn the conviction on the grounds that for the bailiff to have provided alcohol to the jury during its deliberations constituted reversible error. It was no doubt the first time in Texas legal history that Robert Burns's lines on "bold John Barleycorn" were cited as an authority on the emboldening effects of alcohol. Lipscomb soberly considered the prevalence of the practice, but concluded that since it was impossible to predict for any juror how much liquor would cause his judgment to be impaired, "the only safe rule is to exclude it entirely."[7]

Another frontier issue that the Court had dealt with during the Republic was that of counsel encouraging jurors to impeach their own conduct during a trial, for the purpose of winning a new trial.[8] Hemphill noted with cold disapproval an increasing use of this tactic, and crushed it in *Mason v. Russel's Heirs* (1847) with a comment that affidavits from such jurors should be received by the Court only for the purpose of having grounds to punish them.[9]

Hemphill had played an influential role in framing the Constitution of 1845, and that document embodied his preference that a core of one's personal assets be secure from seizure for debt—a concept that the civil law could trace straight back to a decree of Ferdinand and Isabella, but was unknown in the English common law. It took the form of an exemption from forced sale of family homesteads up to two hundred acres, in value up to two thousand dollars. The same article also enshrined the enhanced legal position of women under Spanish law, decreeing that a husband could not alienate the family homestead "unless by consent of the wife."[10]

From the infancy of statehood, creditors assaulted the homestead exemption in the courts, but Hemphill wrote some of his most forceful opinions in rebuff. In *Sampson and Keene v. Williamson and Wife* (1851), he held a couple's homestead exempt from foreclosure, even though the couple had pledged the place as security for a promissory note.[11] "The homestead," wrote Hemphill, "which is exempted by the Constitution from 'forced sale,' cannot be forced under process from the court; and it matters not what form the contract assumes, nor how willing the head of the family may be, it is an immunity conferred by the Constitution for purposes beyond the mere pleasure of the individual, and cannot be renounced."[12] Lipscomb, an even stronger proponent of debtor protection, concurred separately, but it was too much for Wheeler, who dissented on the grounds that the Williamsons had voluntarily placed the property at risk, and thus it became a voluntary sale when the mortgage was enforced.[13]

Even more stridently in *Shepherd v. Cassiday* (1857), Hemphill held that a homestead was not considered abandoned, and left vulnerable to seizure, merely because the owner relocated.[14] When Margaret Cassiday left her homesteaded house and lot in Bastrop for a sojourn with her children in Austin, she rented the house to a Mr. Teal. After her departure, one James Shepherd obtained a judgment against her, which was satisfied by the forced sale of her house. Cassiday lost at trial, lost on her motion for a new trial, and appealed to the Supreme Court. Evidence conflicted whether she ever intended to return to Bastrop, and Hemphill cited the principle that a homestead was not to be considered abandoned until a new one was acquired. He did concede that such a protected vacancy could not last indefinitely, but "the homestead is not to be regarded as a species of prison bounds, which the owner cannot pass over without pains and penalties." Rather, the principle of the homestead "was intended to secure the peace, repose, independence and subsistence of citizens and families . . . placed beyond the reach of creditors . . . which they could neither enter nor disturb." This principle, declared Hemphill, was "a right so strongly secured, founded upon such high public policy, [that it] can not be lost by the mere absence of the party or family intended to be benefited. . . . His necessities and circumstances may frequently require him to leave his homestead for a greater or less period of time. . . . But let him leave for what purpose he may, or be his intentions what they may, provided they are not those of total relinquishment or abandonment, his right to the exemption cannot be regarded as forfeited."[15]

Having joined with Lipscomb to secure inclusion of the homestead exemption in the state constitution, Hemphill stood on firmer legal ground with his broadside of an opinion than he otherwise would have, but his reliance in part upon "high public policy" was also significant. Courts probing their way to an equitable result have ever pinned their rationale to sound public policy; Hemphill had done so before, and was prepared to do so again. And while Hemphill took the lead, Lipscomb was generally willing to go along, articulating his philosophy in his concurring opinion to *Sampson v. Williamson*: "It was said by Lord Redesdale that, 'the distinction between strict law and equity is never in any country a permanent distinction. Law and equity are in continual progression. . . . A great part of what is now strict law was formerly considered as equity; and the equitable decisions of this age will unavoidably be ranked under the strict law of the next.'"[16]

Wheeler was less amenable to this view, and generally no more likely to be sympathetic to Hemphill's search for equity than he was fond of the chief justice's affinity for the Spanish law. In *Snoddy v. Cage* (1849), the Court gave Texans a measure of relief from debts incurred in "foreign countries" (namely, the United States) at the time Texas was an independent country: Hemphill lengthily reasoned that the Texas Congress had intended "to treat the immigrant debtor with marked favor."[17] Wheeler dissented at equal length in favor of the creditor, quoting an early U.S. justice that "in searching among the fountains rather than the rivulets of the law for its true principles . . . there can be no safer guide than its precedents."[18] Wheeler was also least likely of the trio to remand a case back to a lower court for pleadings to be amended. "Parties are supposed to know their rights," he carped in one dissent, "and to be . . . capable of conducting their causes without requiring the judges . . .

to become their advisers. . . . That would be, to borrow an expression from Chief Justice Marshall, for the court to assume the guardianship of adults as well as infants."[19]

With Hemphill still at the Court's helm under statehood, the status of women before the law continued to be refined, and generally held proof against male challengers who would have prevailed elsewhere in the United States. When Maria de Jesusa Smith of San Antonio was widowed, her path to administer her late husband's estate was blocked by Samuel Smith, his son from a former marriage in the United States, with that wife still living in Missouri, of which the Texas wife had no knowledge. In the case of *Smith v. Smith* (1847), Chief Justice Hemphill ruled that even conceding the legitimacy of the American marriage, "yet we cannot permit . . . such evidence in our courts, in cases where it would operate to the annulling of a marriage, celebrated here according to the laws of the country, and to the destruction of all the rights of the innocent partner and the offspring of the latter marriage."[20] Nor would the dead man's status as a bigamist, if it could be proved, prevent the Texas widow from administering her late husband's estate.

The Texas Court's championing of the rights of women did not, curiously, extend to a more lax view of marriage or make a bad marriage easier to escape. Texas statute provided that a marriage could be dissolved "when either the husband or wife, is guilty of excesses, cruel treatment, or outrages toward the other, if such ill treatment is of such a nature as to render their living together insupportable."[21] In a case that came to the Court from Victoria County, a trial judge had granted a divorce to Mrs. Margaret T. Wright from her husband, John. The evidence was that Mr. Wright had indeed been a bad spouse. When single, Margaret had been a woman of property in De León's colony; after she married, her husband had had her league of land transferred to his own name without her knowledge, and after he removed from Texas, she occupied the land and managed it profitably. In divorcing John, Margaret alleged ill-treatment, but did not enumerate any specific acts of cruelty that brought her to court. Mr. Wright answered in an equally general way that her charges were not true, and when the divorce was granted, he appealed to the Supreme Court.[22]

Hemphill's lengthy exposition dealt mostly with matters of practice, but he did use the occasion to point out an important difference between the common law and the civil law on this point: under the common law, a woman was usually granted alimony while a suit was pending, because as a wife, she had no property or support of her own. In Texas, with its Hispanic heritage, the woman's claim to interim alimony was even stronger precisely because she did have property, which would come back to her after the divorce, and which the husband could be fraudulently using or damaging.

Hemphill wrote for the Court that notwithstanding the statute's silence on the matter of proving specific allegations, the divorce should not have been granted without them, and the decision was reversed. A more conservative ruling could have acknowledged the vagueness of the statute and suggested that the legislature fix it, but the Court's preference for certitude prevented years of frontier "he said, she said."

Hemphill wrote that he joined his two brethren "reluctantly" in the decision—likely because it worked against finding an equitable outcome for Mrs. Wright. In a larger sense, however, Hemphill's views on the status of women before the law could not help being influenced by his own private life. He was a bachelor, but in 1844 he purchased a female slave named Sabina for five hundred dollars. Their first daughter, Theodora, was born in 1849, and a second, Henrietta, followed thereafter. Within the compulsion implied by their respective positions, the relationship seems to have been one of love and respect. Sabina died after several years, leaving Hemphill with the two daughters to raise.

There were no schools for slaves in Texas, so when his daughters were old enough, Hemphill enrolled them in the newly founded Wilberforce University in Xenia, Ohio, whose student body of two hundred was composed substantially of mixed-race children of southern slave owners. Undeterred by the fact that Xenia was a primary stop on the Underground Railroad, which might have put him at physical risk as a slave owner, Hemphill made special arrangements with the school's president, the Reverend Richard Rust, to become his daughters' guardian should anything happen to him. According to Rust, Hemphill had grown estranged from the rest of his family and had confided his worries during visits with his daughters in Ohio. "He was very anxious to make provision for his children," said Rust, "lest his distant relatives for whom he felt no interest might claim and get his property. He said that in case of his death, he intended his property should go to Theodora & Henrietta; and . . . he would make a will and devise it to them."[23] John Hemphill thus found himself in the same predicament as other southern slave owners whose mixed-race children filled Wilberforce College: torn between love of their offspring and duty to the "peculiar institution." But there can be no doubt that it left Hemphill with both a keen understanding the vulnerability of women before the law, and a predisposition to lend a sympathetic ear to persons of color who made their way into court.

Abner Lipscomb won reelection to the high bench in November 1856, but died in Austin just weeks later, leaving a vacancy to fill. Winning the seat and joining his close friend Royall Wheeler on the bench was Oran Milo Roberts, a district judge since statehood and professor of law at the University of San Augustine, which he founded. An Alabama legislator before moving to Texas in 1840, Roberts expressed pro-southern views and ardent admiration of the southern firebrand John C. Calhoun, making Roberts a profound disappointment to his first Texas mentor, Sam Houston, who had appointed him district attorney for San Augustine in 1844.[24]

Indeed, in Texas as elsewhere in the United States during the 1850s, slaves and slavery demanded much consideration from the judiciary, but Texas judges took a distinct legal posture toward the institution, one surprising for the time. When the Texas Supreme Court spoke on the issue, its treatment of the rights of blacks, whether slave or free, was remarkable for its liberality, and for its concentration not on vindicating the institution, but on the law and search for equity in the cases involved.[25] This was certainly in evidence in *Moore v. Minerva* (1856), a case involving a slave woman named Minerva who was emancipated in Ohio and then accompanied her former master to Texas. After his death, Minerva sued his administrator for her freedom; the administrator, relying on a Republic-era law that forbade free blacks from immigrating to Texas, claimed that she was still in bondage.[26] The Texas Court came down squarely for Minerva, declaring, "There is nothing in our law by which she could forfeit her liberty by coming to Texas with her former owner . . . who had emancipated her by deed valid at the time and place it was executed."[27]

In the North, abolition had been a viable movement for two generations, showing a growing vigor by which the South felt increasingly threatened as time passed. Southerners insisted on concessions for the safety of their "peculiar institution," which they received repeatedly: in the Missouri Compromise of 1820, in the Compromise of 1850, in the Kansas-Nebraska Act of 1854, and in the *Dred Scott* decision of the U.S. Supreme Court in 1857. In Texas, those who doubted the rectitude of slavery learned, for their safety's sake, to keep quiet. That there were such doubters, however, was well known.

After the mid-1840s, the Hill Country of west-central Texas was populated by several thousand German settlers who had immigrated under the auspices of the Adelsverein, the association of dukes and princes who sponsored them. Within a very few years, they economically far outstripped the longtime American settlers, and did so without the benefit of slaves, which to the American Texans, who hailed mostly from the South, was unforgivable.[28] Sentiment antipathetic to slavery was also strong in the city of Austin and surrounding counties, and in Texas's northern tier of counties along the Red River. There, many settlers in the Peters Colony were Free-Soilers.[29]

In fact, nearly three-quarters of Texas families owned no slaves, and since a civil war seemed ever more likely, they might still have been persuaded that the Union was worth saving. Texas's former president, Sam Houston, from his seat in the U.S. Senate, underscored his long-standing disapproval of slavery with his opposition to the Kansas-Nebraska Act, which extended slavery north of the old Missouri Compromise line. Proslavery legislators in Texas were so incensed at the aging Houston that they named his replacement to the Senate in 1857, two years before his term expired—an unprecedented insult. That new senator was to be none other than Chief Justice Hemphill, who signaled that he was more than ready to defend the South in the halls of Congress—a high irony for a father supporting two mixed-race daughters.

Nevertheless, in the 1858 election to fill the opening left on the Court when Wheeler took Hemphill's place as chief justice, the seat was won by an ardent Unionist, James Hall Bell. He was a Harvard law graduate with four years' experience as a district judge. Of medium but strong stature, with auburn hair and piercing blue eyes, the thirty-three-year-old Bell was a scion of one of Texas's founding Anglo families.[30] (Attesting to the strength of antisecession sentiment in Texas on the eve of the Civil War, another Unionist of future importance to the Supreme Court, Andrew Jackson Hamilton, was elected to Congress at the same time, and still another, James Throckmorton, entered the legislature.)

Yet it was not merely the presence of Bell on the Court that gave it a liberal bearing on cases involving persons of African descent. The Court's bent in that direction was already confirmed. In the case of *Guess v. Lubbock* (1851), the Court showed itself willing to overlook minor documentary deficiencies in acknowledging a black woman's claim to freedom.[31] Margaret Gess had been the companion and lover of Adam Smith, a white man and business associate of a locally prominent Houston figure, James Morgan (who was himself the employer of the free woman of color Emily West, later famous as the "Yellow Rose of Texas"). Smith came to Texas in 1831, a time when the status of Texas slaves could not have been more confused.[32] Smith acquired Margaret, age about twenty, in a transaction around 1830; they spent ten years together and had a child. Smith used Margaret's money to buy land in his own name, knowing that as a slave in an independent Texas, she would not be permitted to own land herself. At the time they separated in 1840, Smith provided Margaret Gess a document reading, "The bearer, Margaret, a negro woman, about 30 years of age, is free and at liberty to go and do the best she can to make an honest livelihood in the world."[33] It was cosigned by one witness, not the five that the law required if it were to be accepted as a manumission.

When Adam Smith died in 1848, without a will, his nephew and heir, prominent Houston merchant and later Texas governor Francis Richard Lubbock, peremptorily claimed Margaret, her daughter Puss, and her land as his property by inheritance (which meant, one might note, that he was asserting ownership over his own cousin). Margaret brought suit to regain her freedom, although her prospects must have seemed dubious, as the district clerk with whom her lawyer filed the case was none other than her purported master, Lubbock himself. Inexplicably, although Lubbock maintained that Margaret was his slave, he did not challenge her standing to bring the suit, which she could not have done were she in bondage. At trial, the jury, not unpredictably, awarded her and her daughter and her land to Lubbock. Gess obtained the services of former associate judge Benjamin C. Franklin to appeal her cause to the Supreme Court.

Abner Lipscomb wrote the Court's opinion, finding little to compliment in the presentation of either party. He ruled that Margaret's status under either the Republic or the State of Texas was not applicable, since she had been acquired under Mexican sovereignty, thus her status was caught in the web of indecipherable slavery rulings of that era. Otherwise, he noted, because Lubbock had not raised the issue of her standing at trial, her document of manumission had to be accepted as the true state of Adam Smith's mind while he was alive, and "it is doubtful that the relation of master and servant did ever exist."[34] The Court remanded the case for retrial, and Franklin, probably recognizing that the elements of law sent down were too arcane for a jury's understanding, tried the case to the judge. At the second trial, Margaret Gess won her freedom after nearly four years of uncertainty, and Lubbock saw no point in appealing to the Supreme Court again. After this, the free Margaret Gess disappeared from history.[35]

Late in the antebellum era, on the verge of civil war, the case of *Westbrook v. Mitchell* (1859) again demonstrated the Court's punctilious observation of the rights of blacks in the courts, circumscribed though they were.[36] The case arose on the edge of the frontier, in sparsely settled Johnson County, south of what would later be the city of Fort Worth. There, James Westbrook, a miller who owned ten slaves, reached an agreement with a free person of color in his employ, Lewis John Red Rolls. In earlier years, before the family emigrated from Mississippi, Red Rolls had been the slave of Westbrook's father, who had apparently given Red Rolls his freedom. Red Rolls continued in the family's service and accompanied them to Texas. In 1855, Red Rolls needed money and reached an agreement with Westbrook to sell himself back into slavery for a sum of $2,500. This was far above the going rate, but it was possible that Red Rolls knew of the various accounting gimmicks that masters commonly used to avoid paying the full price in such cases—charging them room, board, and other fees; placing funds in escrow, and so forth.[37]

In January of 1858, the legislature enacted a bill prescribing conditions under which free blacks could sell themselves into bondage, with safeguards to prevent its abuse. Later in the year, Red Rolls ran away from the Westbrook place for reasons never entered into the record—perhaps Westbrook had failed to meet the terms of their agreement, or Red Rolls had learned of the new law and realized that his previous deal with Westbrook was no good. He fled, not to freedom in Mexico or the North, but to the nearby Hill County farm of William Mitchell, a former neighbor of the Westbrooks and the owner of a female slave who may have been the mother of Red Rolls's two children. Red Rolls offered to sell himself into slavery to Mitchell, as allowed by the new statute. They agreed on terms and determined to formalize the deal before the local district court, as newly required by law, but did not do so before Westbrook's son arrived at the Mitchell farm to reclaim Red Rolls. Guns were drawn, oaths exchanged, and young Westbrook left with Red Rolls in tow. Mitchell convinced the Hill County authorities to serve the Westbrooks with a kidnapping charge and recover Red Rolls, which they did, but then Westbrook sued Mitchell for the return of his property. At trial, district judge N. W. Battle ruled that Red Rolls was the property of Mitchell on the grounds that free blacks could not sell themselves into slavery before passage of the 1858 statute, which invalidated the agreement between Red Rolls and Westbrook, but then the judge instructed the jury in such a way as to acquit Westbrook of the kidnapping charge.

Westbrook appealed the loss of Red Rolls to the Supreme Court, which heard the case during the Austin term, late in 1859. In rendering the Court's decision upholding Judge Battle's ruling and awarding Red Rolls to Mitchell, Justice James Bell, who was shortly to prove himself only a lukewarm friend of the Confederacy, began at the beginning of slavery's legal thread, citing the *Institutes* of Justinian from the sixth century on how individuals could come to be slaves. Then taking Thomas R. R. Cobb's defense of slavery into account, he ruled that in Texas, before the statute of 1858, the only way one could be a slave was to be born to a slave mother.[38] And in passing the 1858 statute, the legislature was aware of the prospect for abuse, and "evinced the greatest caution in prescribing the manner in which free negroes might enter into the condition of slavery."[39] Bell went on to note the safeguards put in place by the law:

> The act requires all of the proceedings to be of the most public and formal character. The District Courts must have supervision of the matter. The court must be satisfied that there is no fraud; that the proposed master is a person of good repute, and that no good reason exists, why the relation of master and slave should not be formed in the particular case. This caution of the legislature will suggest . . . that there are reasons of public policy why the courts of the State should not [otherwise] recognize the right of free negroes to sell themselves into slavery. The recognition of such a right might lead to its exercise for bad purposes.[40]

Red Rolls, thus, had been free to select a master of his choice, and Westbrook had no relief coming.

These two cases represent only two situations—a former slave seeking confirmation of her freedom, and a free person of color choosing a new master—in which the Texas Supreme Court chose to follow the legal paths most favorable to the black people in question. In *Chandler v. State* (1847), the Court upheld the manslaughter conviction of a master tried for murder in the killing of a slave.[41] David Chandler's attorneys had sought to convince the Court to follow a rule upheld in Virginia and South Carolina, namely, that a slave was in his ancestry a slave by having been captured in war, and the captor held the power of life and death over him, and that relationship passed down through the generations. The opinion written by Royall Wheeler chose to follow the more humane, if legally tenuous, Tennessee rule that slavery was more akin to medieval Norman villeinage, and "it seems especially . . . the intention of our legislation . . . to throw around the *life* of the slave the same protection which is guaranteed to a freeman."[42] Wheeler also wrote the opinion eight years later in *Nix v. State*, which expanded this protection to include assault and battery.[43] In 1857, a similar case involving a white man accused of whipping a black he did not own was, not surprisingly, dismissed on a technicality by the trial court, but the state actually appealed. The Court, in the opinion written by Justice Oran Roberts, rejected the lower court's apparent notion that "a slave is property only, as a horse or any other domestic animal": "We recognize in the slave personal rights," and for a man not his owner to whip him established a prima facie case against the batterer.[44]

Even further beyond what one might have expected from an antebellum state supreme court, the Texas justices announced their intolerance for the shoddy defense of blacks on trial. In the 1847 case of a black man named Nels convicted of murder, Justice Wheeler found it unacceptable that Nels's lawyer had stipulated to (admitted) facts damaging to his defense, intimating that he would never have done so had the defendant been white.[45] Moreover, the Supreme Court later found in *Calvin v. State* (1860) that the state had a duty to provide counsel for blacks who could not afford their own—a progressive notion that would not be enshrined in federal jurisprudence until more than a century later.[46] "The law of the case" in *Calvin*, wrote Justice Bell in reversing a lower-court holding in which defense counsel had agreed to proceed on a flawed indictment, "is precisely the same as if the accused were a free white man, and we cannot strain the law even 'in the estimation of a hair' because the defendant is a slave."[47]

On these and several other points of law, the Texas Supreme Court proved itself the most progressive in the South in standing guard over the rights of blacks, both free and enslaved.[48] If nothing else, these cases illustrate the extent to which some landed Texans had actually convinced themselves that slavery was a benevolent institution. In their view, free persons of color lacked the resources to ever make a good living, and were daily at risk of being kidnapped and sold into bondage; and besides, when a master had invested from four hundred to eight hundred dollars in each slave, he had every incentive to care for them. Such staggering myopia had no basis in fact, of course, and the increasing hysteria with which slavery was championed negated any conviction that the institution was good for the slave as well as the planter. Nor was the Supreme Court's relatively liberal treatment of Texas blacks under the law shared by the press or by ambitious politicians, as secessionist editors and demagogues saw abolitionists behind every bush.

It was probably not an accident that secessionist ardor reached its greatest violence in North Texas, where it was not a majority view and where the pro-Union majority had to be cowed into silence. Only a year after Lewis John Red Rolls was allowed to select the master of his choice—and in Red Rolls's own Johnson County—a Methodist minister from the North, Anthony Bewley, was lynched on suspicion of being an abolitionist. After Bewley was strung up, he was buried long enough to partly decompose, and then dug up, boned, and his skeleton left on the roof of a local shed for children to play with.[49] Such secessionists were beyond reasoning with; they meant to have a war, and with that war came a whole new set of challenges for the Texas Supreme Court.

SIX

THE CIVIL WAR COURT

While history reckons the beginning of the Civil War from the firing on Fort Sumter on April 12, 1861, in Texas the contest over disunion had been raging for years. For a decade, U.S. senator Sam Houston had struggled grimly to steer a middle course through the crisis over slavery, denouncing northern abolitionists in Boston itself, but even more bitterly excoriating the South's extreme secessionists.[1] The latter were determined to establish their own cotton-growing nation, notwithstanding the fact that the North had repeatedly sought to accommodate their demands. Houston was forcibly retired from the senate in 1859 by the Texas Legislature, but among the people, pro-Union sentiment was strong enough to almost immediately elect him governor of the state.[2]

The election of Abraham Lincoln as president in 1860 was the catalyst for the southern breakout. In Texas, proslavery fire-eaters such as Williamson Oldham and Associate Justice Oran Roberts called for a secession convention to withdraw Texas from the United States. The extralegal election of delegates was held on January 8, 1861; the convention met on January 28 and unanimously elected Justice Roberts president; a secession ordinance was quickly passed and slated for a popular referendum on February 23.

Hoping for a judicial opinion that withdrawing Texas from the Union was illegal, Houston turned to the Court but found no help in Wheeler, a secessionist whose reputation for tenaciously held views was equaled by his distaste for arguing about them.[3] Oran Roberts was even less useful; his part in the upcoming rebellion so disgusted Houston that the governor pardoned a murderess from the penitentiary when her lawyer pointed out that it was Roberts who had denied her appeal.[4] Young Bell, however, extended Houston a straw to grasp: although Bell registered the opinion that secession was constitutional, he believed that only the legislature could effect it. That body was not then meeting, and Houston declined to call, and made it known that he would not call, a special session to pull Texas out of the Union. It bought him a little time, but the legislature, many of whose members were also members of the Secession Convention, endorsed the actions of that extralegal body.[5]

When submitted to the people, the referendum passed by a vote of 46,129 to 14,697. That majority was deceptive, however. The ordinance failed in several counties along the Red River, as well as in Austin and most of the surrounding counties. And in fact, the huge majorities piled up for secession in the cotton counties were achieved in part by suspending the practice of secret balloting. When Justice Bell went to cast his vote in Brazoria County, the ballot handed him was a brightly colored piece of pasteboard with the words FOR SECESSION printed on it. As one observer described the scene: "Justice Bell was at that time an expert penman. He raised his right knee and steadied it against the edge of the table at which the election officer sat, placed the ticket on his knee, asked for a pen—which was handed him—with which he thoroughly blotted out the word 'For,' and, in script that was . . . beautifully distinct, he wrote the word 'Against.' The presiding judge . . . [remarked,] 'Judge Bell, I am very sorry to see you cast that vote, and you will regret it.'"[6] It would have taken extraordinary courage for ordinary Texans of Unionist persuasion to face down poll officers in the manner that Bell did. In fact, the vote in Brazoria County was 527 for and 2 against—the other vote coming from Bell's brother.[7] In later years, Chief Justice John William Stayton considered Bell's vote against secession "perhaps the most heroic act of his life, and manifested a self-sacrifice and patriotism which could not be suspected."[8]

When Sam Houston left the U.S. Senate in 1859 and was replaced by Hemphill, Royall T. Wheeler became chief justice. Once the Civil War had begun in earnest, the behavior of Texas's three justices mirrored their differing sentiments about the war. Roberts, who was nearing forty-seven and had authored a dozen opinions since the opening of hostilities, resigned from the bench to organize and lead the Eleventh Texas Infantry.[9] Roberts's chair, after he left, was filled by George Fleming Moore, lately a Confederate army colonel but also, more to the point, the erstwhile court reporter who had prepared the previous three volumes of the Court's cases. Moore's election in 1862 was the beginning of a remarkably long and distinguished, if multiply interrupted, tenure on the Court.[10]

Bell, who at thirty-three was more than a decade younger than Roberts (and of an age when most men in the South were soon to face conscription), rode out most of the war on the Court. He was frank in his opinion that while he sympathized with the Confederate cause, the conflict would prove an unwinnable catastrophe. Oddly, Bell, the only Unionist on the Court, was also the only native Texan, and the diversity he brought to the high bench was also more representative of the population of the state both politically and geographically.[11]

The same ardor for states' rights that had prompted Texas and the other Southern states to leave the Union also frequently made for thorny relations with the Confederate government in Richmond when it tried to assert national powers over its fiercely independent components. The Confederacy's conscription statute predated that of the United States as the first national draft in American history, and the Texas Supreme Court was the first in the country to rule on its legitimacy.[12]

In 1862 a conscript named F. H. Coupland was taken into custody as a deserter by Colonel R. T. P. Allen, on orders of the provost marshal of Travis County. Coupland obtained the services of prominent lawyer George W. Paschal, who obtained a habeas corpus hearing before Chief Justice Wheeler. The writ was issued, ordering the army to show cause why Coupland was being detained, but Confederate authorities arrested and jailed Paschal over remarks deemed subversive in his argument about the Conscription Act— a demonstration of the chill placed on the freedom of speech during the war. He took no further part in the case.[13] Before the habeas corpus writ could be served, Coupland was drafted into the rebel army and released from his original detention; Wheeler then remanded Coupland to the custody of Colonel Allen. Coupland, ordered to rendezvous with his regiment, disappeared and was not present for the full hearing by the Court at the Austin term of 1862.

With Justice Moore writing the opinion, the Court first disposed of questions of practice, such as whether the person seeking relief, Coupland, a presumed deserter because he had not presented himself for muster, had to be present during consideration of the writ.[14] He did not, since once a writ was issued, it could not be undone by the bad acts of either party. But the key to the case, Moore realized, lay with the question whether the Confederate conscription law itself was constitutional. Taking a deep breath, Moore wrote that the members of the Court "address ourselves to the consideration of this question, with a full appreciation of its magnitude and importance, with respect both to public interest and private rights; the liberty of the citizens, and the power of government."[15]

Moore acknowledged "apprehensions of coming danger in the over-zealous advocates of states rights"; had they not felt so strongly about the overreaching powers of a central government, they would not have left the Union. That said, national crises had to be met with strong measures: "But great emergencies like that which now exist will sometimes arise when the

Confederate government is forced to exercise the entire military power that has been granted it. . . . The denial of power to raise such an army . . . is the denial of power to raise a single man." The conscription law was upheld, but only because of the emergency of the moment; "if to-morrow that necessity should cease, its continuance would be as clearly unconstitutional."[16]

Bell dissented hotly. Moore had quoted Story on the Constitution for the proposition that the lessons of the Articles of Confederation had been learned, and central governments had to hold the power to make war, and necessarily therefore had the power to compel their citizens to participate.[17] Bell had studied under Story at Harvard, and he took umbrage at Moore's use of the great scholar to defend the draft. Bell retaliated in kind, brandishing the writings of Calhoun back at the majority, arguing that troops should be raised from militias. The authors of *The Federalist*, according to Calhoun, had fallen "into an error so radical and dangerous, one which has contributed more than all others combined to cast a mist over our system of government, and to confound and lead astray the minds of the community."[18]

"The majority of the court say, the power to raise and support armies is expressly granted," Bell wrote. "This, of course, is not denied; but I beg leave to say, it is not to the purpose. The question is not whether or not the power to raise and support armies is expressly granted; the question is, whether or not the power to raise armies *by conscription* is expressly granted. It will of course be conceded that no such express grant of power [exists]."[19] Bell quoted both Madison and Hamilton, pointing out that although they diverged philosophically and the former became a Jeffersonian Republican while the latter remained a Federalist, they were united in their interpretation that the war power rested on the calling up of state militias. Could it then be possible that such men would give their sanction "to compel every man between the ages of eighteen and forty-five years, to become a regular soldier, subject to the orders of the president? It is not possible."[20]

Furthermore, Bell pointed out, the armies of the United States had proved victorious over the British in the War of 1812 and over the Mexicans in 1846–1848 without resorting to conscription; the Confederate armies had soundly whipped Union forces already without resorting to conscription. Therefore the practice could not be argued as being necessary. "I take leave to say," wrote Bell,

> that nothing, in my judgment, could be a more palpable violation of the constitution and of the rights of citizens. I believe that "the constitution" in the language of Vice President Stephens, "was made for war as well as for peace"; and that there exists no power, in any department of the gov-

ernment of the Confederate states, to transcend it or to suspend it upon any notion of public necessity. I believe that no power exists anywhere in the Confederate government to subject its citizens, not belonging to the army or navy, and not actually serving in the militia, to any military code, or to the will of any military officer, provost marshal or other, or to the jurisdiction of any other tribunal than the ordinary courts of justice established by law.[21]

It was a ringing credo; Bell could not have helped but be aware that at the original application for the habeas corpus writ, Coupland's attorney Paschal had been arrested and jailed by Confederate authorities for the energy of his argument against the conscription statute. In his dissent Bell seemed almost to be daring the provost marshal to arrest him as well.

He was lucky to be left alone, for as the war progressed, dissent became increasingly dangerous. More than forty men were hanged in and around Gainesville for being suspected Unionists; Sam Houston himself complained to friends that Confederate gumshoes kept him under surveillance and questioned his friends about his opinions.[22] Scores were killed or driven out of the German settlements in the Hill Country for their prevalent antislavery attitudes.[23] There was also active resistance to the draft in the heavily German-populated counties southeast of Austin, leading to the declaration of martial law in those counties in January 1863 and the military arrest of large numbers of dissidents.[24]

In September 1863, an unsigned broadside was distributed in Central and Southeast Texas, criticizing the war and protesting the loss of civil liberties. Penned by Houston attorney J. D. Baldwin with his friend Dr. R. R. Peebles of Hempstead, the pamphlet was titled, with dark historical allusion, "Common Sense." They engaged a German immigrant named O. F. Zinke to print the handbill. On October 11, 1863, Baldwin, Peebles, and Zinke were arrested on charges of conspiracy and treason and then spirited to San Antonio by Confederate soldiers acting on orders of Major General John Bankhead "Prince John" Magruder, who had command of the district of Texas, New Mexico, and Arizona. Other arrests followed, and by March of 1864 the struggle between Magruder—who had imposed martial law and suspended habeas corpus without the authority to do so—and the civil government in Texas had reached a boiling point.[25] Peebles's wife had been unable to find an attorney willing to take her husband's case in San Antonio or Houston, but antisecession lawyer John Hancock of Austin sought a writ of habeas corpus from the Supreme Court on March 7, 1864.[26] The Court issued the writ the same day the application was filed.

Justice Moore had written the opinion affirming the right of the Confederacy to draft its cannon fodder, but he proved to be no pushover when it came to matters in which the prerogatives of the Supreme Court were involved. The prisoners were brought to Austin and, pending a ruling, placed in the custody of the Travis County sheriff. In response, Magruder sent a detachment under Major J. H. Sparks, and the prisoners were forcibly removed from civilian custody and returned to military detention.

Moore responded with a writ of attachment and an order to Sparks to show cause why he should not be held in contempt. The major responded with the soldier's defense: he was merely following orders. Under pressure from the judge advocate general, Sparks returned the prisoners to the Court's custody in the sheriff's office before the habeas corpus hearing began on March 28. The Court, while expounding the principle that "neither officers nor soldiers are bound to obey any illegal order of their superior officers," found Major Sparks to be less culpable than his superiors, acknowledging that if he had disobeyed orders out of conviction of conscience, he would have done so at his peril. But Sparks's exculpation only added odium to Magruder's role. Had the prisoners been "doubly guilty beyond all that has been charged against them," it would be far better for them to go free, "unwhipped of justice, than for the civil authorities of the state to be subordinated to military control."[27]

A new writ of attachment was issued, this one to Major General Magruder, summoning him to the Court at its Tyler term on May 16, 1864, to show cause why he should not be held in contempt for ordering Sparks to take the prisoners and for ignoring the writ of habeas corpus. Magruder, through counsel, pointed out that the Confederate Congress had suspended the right of habeas corpus (which it had, after the fact) and that the Texas Court had no jurisdiction; but the justices were having none of that. "It certainly needs neither argument nor authority to show that there is no officer or tribunal, civil or military, known to the law of the land, that could, without a violation of law and a contempt of this court, forcibly take from under its control, and without its consent, said prisoners until final adjudication," wrote Moore. The civil courts, he proclaimed, do not "sit merely for the purpose of registering the edicts of the military authorities."[28]

Magruder, who earned his nickname "Prince John" in the Confederate army because of his high tailoring and lavish entertainments (he had married a rich woman, whom he almost never visited), was an officer of impeccable manners. The Court already had his communication assuring the justices "that he intended no contempt of the court, but entertained for it the most profound respect; that it was his pleasure, at all times, to sustain the civil authorities" and avoid conflicts.[29]

The Court responded coldly that "similar manifestations of exquisite politeness by criminals, while engaged in violating the law, will, perhaps, readily suggest themselves to the readers of fictitious literature, but we doubt if its parallel can be easily found in the dry details of judicial proceedings."[30] Nevertheless, Moore had taken the Court as close to the brink of a constitutional crisis as he dared, so Magruder was fined court costs, and the matter dropped.[31] It was only a symbolic shake of their fists at the Confederate officers when the justices announced their intention to send a copy of the proceedings to the governor so that he might take such action as he thought the good of the state might require. "We have felt called upon to say so much in this case," Moore had concluded, "because, from the position and official responsibility of the principal offender, and the situation of the country, we cannot resort to the ordinary punishment of imprisonment by which such offenses are usually repressed and corrected. Yet the magnitude of the offense . . . forcibly admonish[es] us that the acts of the defendants should not be passed by without the brand of our most decided condemnation."[32]

Unfortunately for the prisoners, when they were released by the civil authorities they were immediately rearrested by the military, who then had the necessary power and authority to do so under the Confederate Suspension Act. Over the next several months, they were shuttled from town to town, in constant danger from angry mobs who had no use for traitors. They were finally taken to Mexico—outside Confederate jurisdiction—and quietly released sometime in late summer of 1864.[33]

Other than conscription cases and other military matters, land title issues and criminal suits occupied the largest blocks on the Court's docket during the war.[34] Regarding other matters, with the coming of the war the Texas Legislature had passed a "stay law," suspending the collection of "debts and liabilities on bonds, promissory notes, bills of exchange, and contracts for the payment of money" until January 1, 1864, or six months after the close of the war if that happened first.[35] The statute did not bring the legal profession to a halt, but as Oran Roberts noted later in his history of Texas, "though the courts were kept open for criminal business relating to military operations, there was little else of a judicial nature transacted during the war period."[36] Attorneys' business was sufficiently affected that when one case reached the Supreme Court that turned on whether a lawyer's office was a public or private place for purposes of playing cards, Justice Bell's tongue was probably only partly in his cheek when he wrote, "A lawyer's office may be a public place during the usual hours of business, and private during the evening and night. A lawyer's office may, also, and in times like the present, many doubtless are very private and quiet and undisturbed places at all hours."[37] (The conviction was affirmed, even though the Court pointed out a defect in the indictment, namely, that while the three defendants were accused of playing cards, it was not specifically alleged that they were playing cards *with each other.*)

Chief Justice Wheeler, once it became clear that the South would be bled to death (and because he was, according to George Paschal, upset at the disdain with which Confederate authorities were treating state courts), committed suicide at his home in Washington County on April 9, 1864, age fifty-four. He had labored on the Court for two decades, fourteen years in Hemphill's large shadow, and the last six as chief justice. Paschal, who became Supreme Court reporter immediately after the war, eulogized him scantly as having "acquired more reputation as a declaimer before juries than as an accurate lawyer."[38] Chroniclers more friendly to the Southern Cause found this somewhat mean and attributed the sentiment to Paschal's Unionism,[39] but even those more kindly disposed had to concede that Wheeler lacked Hemphill's "deep, varied and almost exhaustless learning," as well as Lipscomb's practical sense, yet he "possessed other mental faculties of a high order."[40]

With the last vestige of the "Old Court" of Hemphill, Lipscomb, and Wheeler gone, Oran Roberts left the Confederate army to run for Wheeler's place as chief justice in August 1864. James Bell also threw his hat in the ring for the position, but his past antisecessionist tendencies worked against him, and Roberts beat him by almost a five-to-one margin.[41] Bell's former slot as associate justice was won by yet another popular member of the Confederate military. Although the war had turned badly for the South, early in that year an attempted Northern invasion of Texas via the Red River from Louisiana was soundly, in fact spectacularly, defeated as Union gunboats trapped by low water were pummeled from both banks. One of the heroes of that action was Captain Reuben A. Reeves of Walker's Texas Division. A Kentucky native, Reeves relocated to Palestine in East Texas in 1848, quickly built a successful law practice, and became a prominent landowner with numerous slaves. He had no judicial experience when he was elected to the Supreme Court.[42] By turning out Bell, the populace lost the services of a solid legal mind and seasoned judge, the first casualty of the system of popular election that Rusk and Hemphill had warned against.[43]

With the loss of the war, the conscription cases decided by the Texas Supreme Court were considered historical dross and so were not officially reported. For their historical interest, however, they were collated and printed by one of the Court's reporters soon after the end of the conflict.[44] Scholars have continued to respect the remainder of the Court's work during the war, undoubtedly because the justices had proved their skill and probity in other areas of law for a long period either before the war (Wheeler) or after (Moore, Reeves, Roberts). Of the 310 decisions actually reported from the war years, about a third involved land disputes and required facility with Texas's complicated, multinational land heritage.[45] *Cowan v. Hardeman* (1862), for instance, established the rule that on land deriving from Spanish or Mexican land grants, mineral rights did not convey unless specifically granted; the case was cited as authority a century later.[46] (However, Oran Roberts in one case declined to choose between whether a coastal land grant extended down to mean high tide, as under the common law, or only to the highest high tide, as under Spanish law. In *City of Galveston v. Menard* [1859], he extended the grant down to the water wherever it was, because the clear purpose of the grant was for the construction of a port.)[47] Similarly, an 1863 ruling that for land taken under powers of eminent domain, the owner had to be compensated without discount on the ground that he would benefit from the purpose for which the land was taken, was also cited with approval more than seventy years later.[48]

The decisions of the Civil War Court have been accepted as precedent because they were decisions of a bench convened under the Texas Constitution and interpreting Texas law. For much of the following decade, that would not be the case.[49]

SEVEN

THE RECONSTRUCTION COURTS

As Northern victory became ever more certain, Abraham Lincoln determined upon the course, as articulated in his Second Inaugural Address, that would indulge in "malice toward none, with charity for all." His view of Reconstruction was simple: secession had been illegal; therefore, the Southern states had never really left the Union. As the commander in chief who defeated the rebellion, he would decide the terms of their readmission: the wayward states would have to pledge their renewed allegiance to the Union, revise state constitutions to delete references to slavery, and apply for statehood. The South would be reassimilated into the Union with a minimum of recrimination or constitutional restructuring. Lincoln would have to effect this plan over the hate-filled determination of radicals within his own party, men who wanted to whip and scourge and punish the South not just for the war, but for a generation of intractable pugnacity as well. They argued that the South had indeed left the Union, and now it was Congress's prerogative to dictate the terms of readmission, just as it would do for any other new territory seeking to become part of the country. Lincoln's assassination on April 14, 1865, only five days after Lee's surrender at Appomattox Court House, gave the congressional radicals the momentum they needed to bring their vision to reality.

Lincoln would have had severe difficulties enacting his program over their opposition in any event, and the new president, Andrew Johnson of Tennessee, had nothing like Lincoln's persuasive powers. He was able to at least initiate Lincoln's plans in the phase known as Presidential Reconstruction. Texas's rehabilitation began with the arrival of General Gordon Granger (a minor figure in the war) with eighteen hundred troops to begin the occupation and declare the end of slavery on June 19, 1865 (celebrated afterward as the holiday Juneteenth). He was followed on July 21 by the man Johnson appointed provisional governor, the former Unionist congressman Andrew Jackson Hamilton, who, as war approached, had evaded a secessionist mob in Austin by hiding in the sinkhole at his brother's ranch (later known as Hamilton Pool). He had served as a Union officer during the war, which had prompted another Austin mob to burn his wife and six children out of their home.[1]

Virtually all statewide and even county offices were under Hamilton's appointment. While there were not many who had, like himself, deserted the state to fight for the North, he was fortunate in that there were plenty of moderate Democrats of the Sam Houston mold to choose from, men who had opposed secession but remained quietly at home and supported the troops. Their appointments to fill the long list of jobs were usually acceptable to all. On August 19, Hamilton opened voter registration for an election on January 6, 1866, to send delegates to a convention scheduled to meet in Austin on February 7 to revise the state constitution to omit consideration of slavery. Presidential Reconstruction was proving easier to implement than many had feared, but when the convention set to its task, so far from acting as though the Confederate defeat should soften their long-standing political views, the delegates took full advantage of the moment and northern softness to promulgate a document almost stunning in its restatement of traditional southern mores.[2] Of paramount importance, according to the delegate and former justice Oran Roberts, was to "keep Sambo from the polls" and form "a white man's Govt."[3]

The racial restrictions outlined in the Constitution of 1866 would not operate until given legislative effect, and when the Eleventh Legislature met that autumn, it passed a number of laws that became known collectively as the "Black Codes." Unlike even more unreconstructed southern states, Texas paid some heed to federal oversight by never specifying race in the statutes; they would apply to all citizens, but everyone knew how selectively they would be enforced. As the federal revenue collector for Austin, John L. Haynes, wrote to Unionist former governor Elisha Marshall Pease as the Black Codes passed one by one, the legislature "completed its series of bills to reenslave the negroes."[4] For Congress's benefit, framers like Oran Roberts could point to aspects of the new Texas constitution that improved the station of blacks: they had access to the courts, and they could enter into contracts, own or lease real estate, devise wills and inherit property, and otherwise enjoy the same legal rights as whites. They could not, however, attend public schools, vote, hold office, serve on juries, or testify against white people. Then, among the more odious of the Black Codes, vagrancy laws kept blacks out of the cities and on the plantations, where gun restrictions disarmed them and an apprenticeship statute provided for the virtual indenture of their children from adolescence to adulthood.

The election on June 25, 1866, was to ratify the new constitution and elect a new state government. Pease, who was Hamilton's preferred candidate to succeed him as governor, was defeated by James W. Throckmorton, who had opposed secession, but still served as a Confederate officer.[5] Unlike Pease, Throckmorton stood foursquare against enfranchising even educated freedmen. When the legislature convened, Oran Roberts was chosen U.S. senator, along with a controversial figure from Texas's past, former provisional president of the Republic David G. Burnet.

The new constitution enlarged the Texas Supreme Court from three justices to five, all to be popularly elected. The people retained George Fleming Moore from the previous Court, to be joined by Richard Coke, Stockton P. Donley, George W. Smith, and Asa H. Willie. Charged by the constitution with selecting the chief justice from among themselves, the group gave Moore the nod.

Coke was a gigantic, bearded bear of a man, a Virginian and graduate of William and Mary College with a degree in civil law. He was only twenty-one when he relocated to the frontier village of Waco, which gave him an identity as much western as southern, and he succeeded in legal practice there. His government service opened when Governor Hardin Runnels appointed him in 1859 to a commission established to decide the fate of the Brazos Indian Reservation. At the Secession Convention he had voted with the majority, and then served as an officer in the Fifteenth Texas Infantry throughout the war, and was wounded in Louisiana. Despite this history, Governor A. J. Hamilton found him impressive and appointed him judge of the Nineteenth Judicial District in 1865.[6]

Donley was a Missourian who had studied at Stephen F. Austin's alma mater, Transylvania University in Kentucky. He moved to East Texas in 1846, and shifted his practice from Clarksville to Rusk to Tyler. His specialty was criminal law, at which he gained a formidable reputation as an investigator. He was a private in the Seventh Texas Volunteers, was captured early in the war at Fort Donelson, Tennessee, was exchanged owing to his poor health, and, although remaining in the army, was not returned to the front. He resumed his criminal practice in Tyler until running for the Supreme Court.[7]

George Washington Smith was not the Texas revolutionary figure of the same name, although the two were contemporaries. Born a Kentuckian, and a Texan since 1847, he had developed a lucrative legal practice and railroad interests in Columbus. He was a judge of the Fifth Judicial District from 1859 to 1866, when he was elected to the Supreme Court.[8]

Of the four justices new to the Court, it was Asa Willie who developed the longest association with it. He was named for his uncle, the early Texas figure Asa Hoxey, although he was born in Georgia and taught at a rural school before immigrating to Independence, Texas, at sixteen, to board with his famous relative. His older brother was in law practice at Brenham, where Asa read for the law (the only member of this Supreme Court not to have received formal legal education), joined the bar in 1849, and soon became district attorney for the Third Judicial District.[9] After his brother became attorney general, Willie performed many of the duties of the attorney general's office before opening his own practice in Marshall. He was a staff officer with the Seventh Texas Infantry and, like Donley, was captured at Fort Donelson and spent several months as a prisoner of war before being repatriated. Back in action at Chickamauga, he served with the Army of Tennessee; after the war, he was back in Brenham when elected to the Supreme Court.[10]

Although it functioned under a Reconstruction regime, the Supreme Court of 1866–1867 evaded the scholarly opprobrium later heaped on its successor. It acted under the authority of a state constitution (however disreputable that document may have been), and its few decisions have been respected as precedential by succeeding courts.[11] It began work with a hugely overcrowded docket, owing to the Civil War legislature's suspension of so many of the cases pending at the start of hostilities. Its collective judicial thinking, however, was not always of the highest caliber, as in *Gabel v. City of Houston* (1867), which upheld a ruling against a Houston brewer for selling malt liquor on a Sunday, which was against city ordinance.[12] The appellant's contention was that freedom of religion as protected by the Texas Constitution (of 1845, under which the offense occurred) did not contemplate enforcement of Sundays as a day of worship. The Court disagreed, ruling that Gabel was not forced into religious participation, but he was forced to refrain from hindering others in their religious observances, and bar patrons "may commit riots and breaches of the peace, to the great annoyance of others who may feel it their religious duty to . . . attend worship."[13] The Court based this conclusion on a clause in the Constitution that proclaimed it to be "the duty of the legislature to pass such laws as . . . shall be necessary to protect every religious denomination in the peaceable enjoyment of their own mode of public worship."[14]

Given the tumultuous state of society at the time, there was an amount of rustic justice, often administered by vigilantes, that made its way to the high bench. Justice Donley once had to reverse a conviction for theft because the confession had been made under threat of death.[15]

Inevitably, the Court had some legal detritus from the war years to sweep up, such as whether the purchaser could recover the value of a slave named Jerry who escaped on May 1, 1865. By ruling that Jerry's changed legal status deprived the purchaser of the ability to make good on the debt, the Court found itself under no necessity to calculate the depreciation of the collapsed Confederate currency.[16] Such cerebral opinions were usually the work of Chief Justice Moore. Richard Coke had his own, often more direct, analysis, once denying recovery of the price of a slave to an owner whose runaway was impounded by the sheriff beyond a time, statutorily, when he should have sold him. He recovered nothing, on account of "the utter worthlessness of the slave, arising from his mental insanity."[17] Since he was worthless, there was no value to collect.

Based on the attitudes represented in the Constitution of 1866, Texas probably merited a governmental makeover, but it was larger forces in play that brought about the end of Presidential Reconstruction. On August 20, President Johnson issued a proclamation declaring the rebellion in Texas to be over, and as far as the Throckmorton government was concerned, that closed the book on the Civil War era. As a matter of law, the U.S. Supreme Court later ruled in a case involving prewar Texas bonds that Lincoln's and Johnson's view was correct, that secession had been illegal and the states had never left the Union.[18] Nevertheless, radicals in Congress seized control of the process, impeached (but failed to remove) Johnson, and placed the former rebel states back under military occupation in the phase known as Congressional Reconstruction, which fired generations of southern hatred. While motivated partly by concern over the conditions imposed on southern freedmen, the radicals' hands were not entirely clean either, because seating southern congressional delegations would have weakened their grip on power.[19] The South was divided into military districts, with Texas and Louisiana comprising the Fifth District, under command of Major General Philip Sheridan, in New Orleans, with Major General Charles Griffin to assume command in Texas.[20]

Griffin was a West Point artillerist from Ohio who had switched to the infantry, risen to the post of corps commander, and, with Grant and others, received Lee's surrender. He was a hot-tempered quarreler and meant to endure no backtalk from old-time Texas politicians.[21] He felt especially spurred to severity because the Freedmen's Bureau, established by the federal government to help former slaves assimilate into society and political participation, had been met in Texas with arson, murder, mayhem, and a pointed lack of relief from a judiciary largely stocked with former rebels. Griffin's job was to reduce Texans to acceptance of Congress's terms for readmission: establish yet another state constitution, this one embracing voting rights for freedmen; set up local and state administrations acceptable to the authorities (which, thanks to the disenfranchisement by the so-called Ironclad Oath of those who had engaged in rebellion, largely restricted participation to freedmen and Republicans); and ratify the Fourteenth Amendment, which the Eleventh Legislature had declined to do, not with an act defying the federal government but with a shrug: since it was already law, indulging the formality of a vote would serve no purpose.

Confronted first with the Black Codes and then with the legislature's use of its redistricting powers to gerrymander Unionist judges out of their districts, General Sheridan determined to brook no more "pride in the rebellion" among state officials.[22] The first step was to remove the elected governor, Throckmorton, which Sheridan did on July 30, 1867, and to appoint in his place E. Marshall Pease, whom Throckmorton had lately defeated, but who was on record as not opposing black voting rights. Empowered to sweep away all those regarded as "impediments to Reconstruction," Sheridan then removed the entire Texas Supreme Court. He offered the post of chief justice to Union general Edmund J. Davis, a Florida native but long a resident of Laredo and a leading Republican. Davis declined, and Sheridan turned to Amos Morrill, a Texas lawyer—A. J. Hamilton's partner in Austin—with Massachusetts roots, a good Unionist who had quit the state during the rebellion.[23]

Of the associate justices of what became known as the "Military Court," Albert H. Latimer had acquired undoubted radical cachet, supervising voter registration in North Texas and serving as subassistant commissioner of the Freedmen's Bureau. Also accorded a certain respect as a signer of the Texas Declaration of Independence, Latimer had become a leading Texas Unionist as the debate over secession increased. When war came, his age (his birth date was unknown, but he was surely over sixty) excused him from fighting.[24]

Livingston Lindsay was a Kentucky lawyer and schoolmaster who had come to Texas only in 1860 and gone into legal practice in La Grange. He was appointed to the Military Court in September 1867 and served until the Court was reorganized in 1869. During that period he represented the moderate Republican position as a delegate at the Constitutional Convention of 1868.[25]

A. J. Hamilton himself was named an associate justice, serving on the Court from 1867 until November 1869, when he resigned after losing a close race for governor. In his service at the 1868 convention, Hamilton distinguished himself with an act of statesmanship that also served as his political immolation, in opposing continuation of the Ironclad Oath. E. J. Davis, the Union general who had refused Sheridan's offer to be chief justice, was elected president of the convention. By arguing (along with Lemuel Evans) in favor of broadening the franchise to include those who had been unable to swear to the oath, Hamilton ensured his defeat by Davis when the two opposed each other in the 1869 contest for governor (although even then, it may have been General Reynolds's supervision of the vote counting that handed the election to his favorite by a majority of 809 votes out of nearly 80,000 cast). Hamilton's was an act that Justice Roberts, in his history of Texas, credited to Hamilton's and Lemuel Evans's "devotion to right and their ability to rise above the common prejudice of the day and do justice to their fellow-citizens who had differed with them."[26]

The last of the new associate justices was Colbert Caldwell (spelled "Coldwell" in some sources), a Tennesseean of forty-five whom Hamilton as provisional governor had appointed judge of the Seventh Judicial District. Caldwell did not last the entire term of the Military Court, suffering the fate of a genuine moderate. While giving a speech to a mostly black crowd two months after his appointment—he was campaigning for a seat at the Constitutional Convention—Caldwell survived an assassination attempt at the hands of former rebels who found him too cozy with the occupation. At the convention he performed yeoman service for the freedmen and the Republicans. Unable to escape his history as a former owner of nearly a dozen slaves, however, the army found his zeal for radicalism insufficient, and dismissed him from the Supreme Court late in October 1869.[27]

Two other justices served on the Military Court before it was disbanded in the summer of 1870. Moses B. Walker, a Union officer from Ohio, replaced Albert Latimer on November 27, 1869, after Latimer resigned under military pressure. James Denison, a native of Vermont but a resident of Texas since 1839, replaced the ousted Colbert Caldwell in January 1870.

The decisions of the Military Court have no precedential authority under stare decisis because the Court operated outside the Texas Constitution, their appointments having been made by the military rather than by popular election or gubernatorial appointment.[28] The majority of the cases the Court decided during its thirty-three months of existence were legal holdovers from the war, including monetary disputes stemming from the devalued Confederate currency and the loss of slave property through emancipation, as well as a range of criminal matters. But as one historian has noted, its decisions in such areas as common law marriage, homestead exemptions, contested wills, and warehousemen's negligence are "staples of Texas jurisprudence."[29]

U.S. military authority over Texas officially ended on April 16, 1870, opening the door for civil government to resume under the Constitution of 1869. In addition to bowing to federal requirements, the new constitution reconfigured the Supreme Court by reducing it to three judges (rather than justices), this time appointed by the governor with the concurrence of the Senate, serving in staggered terms of nine years, with one to be appointed every three years. The Tyler and Galveston terms were dispensed with, and until the three meeting places were reinstated by the Constitution of 1874, the Court would meet only in Austin.

The new Court was headed by the newly titled "Presiding Judge" Lemuel Dale Evans, who had stood with A. J. Hamilton in opposing the continuation of the Ironclad Oath at the 1868 Convention.[30] Before the war, Evans had been a Unionist congressman who rented the rooms immediately beneath Senator Houston's at Willard's Hotel. During the Convention of 1845, he had declared an opinion that was more tenable for a politician than a judge, and that he was under some squint to live down: that the judicial system itself was a humbug, "an invention of the darker ages of the world," and that no issue could come to court that could not as well be settled by resort to the Golden Rule. Therefore, there existed "no question of right or wrong which a savage is not as competent to decide . . . as a Storey or a Marshall."[31] Serving with Evans as associate judges were Moses Walker, who had sat on the Military Court, and Wesley Ogden, a lawyer who had practiced in New York and Ohio and whose fifteen years' practice in Port Lavaca, Texas, had come to an end in 1863 when he fled to the North.[32]

At least by sitting under the auspices of the Texas Constitution of 1869, however short-lived it was, this Reconstruction Court escaped the historical ignominy of the appointed Military Court.[33] Or it would have, had it not been for the last disastrous case that it heard. Lemuel Evans, ever the good Unionist, stepped down from the bench when his term expired in September 1873. Wesley Ogden then moved to the presiding chair, and Governor Davis appointed J. D. McAdoo to round out the reconfigured Court. It was an evenhanded appointment, for McAdoo, unlike Ogden, was not a Yankee. Born and raised in Tennessee, he had immigrated to Texas early in its statehood and served Texas in Confederate posts, although not fighting Yankees but guarding the Indian frontier, throughout the Civil War.[34]

The administration of E. J. Davis has been painted in rather darker colors than it deserves by Texas historians unable to shake off the gall of Reconstruction.[35] But Democratic, which at the time inevitably meant ex-Confederate, sentiment against Davis was so inflamed that the Court he appointed was almost universally derided as being composed of minions ready to do his bidding. During the Court's four regular sessions, however, the judges demonstrated considerable independence from the hated "carpetbag" regime— which in fact included relatively few carpetbaggers. It was true that the Court repeatedly upheld Davis's widely resented program of school taxes.[36] But it also took a position contrary to the administration in finding against a prominent German-Texan Unionist, Jacob Kuechler, who had challenged a grant of lands to a railroad that was the project of important Democrats.[37]

Ironically, the Court most notably disappointed Davis in the one clear instance in which the governor, although himself so despised, attempted to rid the state of a genuine example of a delinquent carpetbagger. This was in the (rather appetizing-sounding) case of *Honey v. Graham* (1873).[38] Carpenter George W. Honey of Wisconsin was a Methodist minister, a vocation that carried considerably more voltage in those days, when Methodism was vastly more evangelical and activist than it has since become. During the war Honey had been chaplain of the Fourth Wisconsin Cavalry regiment, and he came to Texas in 1866 on behalf of the American Missionary Association to organize schools for freed slaves.[39] In southern eyes, he was a paradigmatic carpetbagger. In 1869, after serving a stint as Court clerk, he was elected Texas state treasurer on the Radical Republican slate. In April 1872, Honey left the state, indicating that he planned to return in six weeks. When he hadn't returned by May 27, Governor Davis took steps to replace him, charging that he had abandoned his office. (Davis had had quite enough trouble elsewhere trying to keep the administration's hands clean — the adjutant general, James Davidson, who had enraged Texas Democrats with his aggressive use of mostly black state police, had absconded with $30,000 of state money.)[40] Declaring the office of treasurer vacant, Davis appointed Beriah Graham to the post.

Honey sued, claiming that this act was beyond the governor's power, and the Supreme Court eventually agreed.[41] The Court, through Judge (and Colonel) Walker, admitted that Davis had a difficult problem, in that the state treasury was likely being looted by an unbonded caretaker while Honey was absent with no notice of where he had gone or whether he would return. But Davis had no power to declare an elective office vacant, and "it would be better that every dollar in the treasury should be stolen, the vaults and safes thrown into the river and the building reduced to ashes, than that the governor should, in one jot or title [*sic*], violate or impede the due course of the law."[42]

Although vindicated, Honey did not continue in office. After winning his case and, to his thinking, clearing his name (although his claim for damages was dropped), he packed his carpetbag and vacated for the North.

By far the most notorious Supreme Court case heard under the 1869 Constitution, and the case that pinned the appellation "Semicolon Court" on the Davis-appointed Court's entire tenure, arose at a time when the defeated Confederacy had been almost wrung dry by the continued occupation, and when northerners, except for the most wall-eyed of Radical Republicans, were ready to move on to other matters.

For the election of 1873, the Ironclad Oath was lifted, and Texas Democrats were once again allowed into the voting booth. E. J. Davis stood for re-election as the Republican governor, and he was opposed by Richard Coke, the hairy giant and specter of the old days: a member of the Secession Convention, a Confederate captain wounded in battle, and a former associate justice of the Supreme Court who had been removed by General Sheridan in his 1867 purge of "impediments to Reconstruction." After a vivid campaign, Coke unseated Davis by a humiliating margin: 85,549 to 42,663.[43]

Eight years in power was a large investment to walk away from, and Republicans brought suit to challenge the election results in a number of races. The Texas Supreme Court was embroiled in the battle when it received a petition for a writ of habeas corpus from Joseph Rodríguez, then being held in jail in Austin on a warrant from the sheriff in Houston. He was charged with having voted more than once in the election.

Habeas corpus being by its nature a matter of urgency, the justices heard arguments at once. Contending that the Court should not even hear the *Rodríguez* case was Harris County district attorney Frank Spencer, who asserted that it was not a true controversy at all, but a test case concocted to euchre the Court into ruling on the validity of the election. The relevant statute provided that each justice of the peace precinct would be a voting precinct, and that the voting would be held on one day, from eight a.m. to six p.m.[44] At issue was whether this was contrary to the relevant constitutional provision, which specified a four-day voting period.[45] As it became known that Rodríguez's legal fees were being paid by leading Republican politicians, including former Reconstruction governor and Rodríguez's own cocounsel, A. J. Hamilton, this seemed more likely true than not, but Judge McAdoo for the majority ruled that as a matter of law, the Court had no choice but to proceed to a full hearing because Rodríguez's arrest appeared on its face to be legal.[46]

The state's summation was delivered by the brilliant former district judge Alexander W. Terrell, who had balanced for years on the sectional fence: as a Unionist and friend of Sam Houston, he had taken no role in secession, but once war came he fought for the Confederacy.[47] Thus Terrell entered the *Rodríguez* case with something approaching credibility with both sides. Terrell insisted that the Court had no place interjecting itself into a political matter. "If one single case can be found," he intoned, from the earliest dawn of American jurisprudence until now, in which any court has ever held illegal an act under which a legislature was chosen . . . I will admit that I have misunderstood the theory of our government. If the Legislature can hold the general election law constitutional by seating its members, and this court can construe it as unconstitutional in passing upon the election of other officers, the constitution will cease to be a bond of order, and become a bond of anarchy.[48]

Terrell further pleaded the case that Reconstruction had overstayed its welcome.

Three times have the people of Texas since the surrender attempted to establish civil government. Once they were remanded by the federal power to a condition of territorial vassalage; once . . . they were defrauded of their choice by a military commander; and now . . . by the more insidious approaches of judicial construction.[49]

Former governor Hamilton argued the case for Rodríguez. The prominent pro-Union congressman, appointed governor, and Court justice had resumed private practice after losing the governorship to E. J. Davis in 1869. Hamilton played innocently baffled by the charges of perpetrating a fraud upon the Court, and saved his thunderbolts for opposing counsels' own history: "I do not take my lessons in patriotism from gentlemen who, in 1861 . . . gloried in overthrowing the State government and tearing down the United States flag. I never fought against the flag of my country."[50] Rodríguez indeed appeared to be getting lost among the larger and older scores being settled. Hamilton did, however, remember to contend for Rodríguez's writ, claiming that Rodríguez could not be guilty of violating the election law if the election was invalid, and concluding with suitable blandishments to the justices: "I am satisfied that the gentlemen who fill this honorable bench are men—physically, intellectually, morally—who will scorn such unworthy flings and do their duty."[51]

In examining the issue, the Supreme Court took cognizance of the governing clause (article III, section 6) of the state constitution: that elections "shall be held at the county-seats . . . until otherwise provided by law; and the polls shall be opened for four days." And after hearing out both sides, the Court stunned the state by ruling on January 6, 1874, that the 1873 election was invalid. Had the clause mandating a four-day period of election been separated from the rest of the sentence by a mere comma, then it could be argued that that requirement could be changed by the legislature, even as it clearly could change the location of polls from county seats. That was not the case, however. The clause was set off by a semicolon; therefore, it was clear that the constitution required the polls to remain open for four days. Since the polls were open for only one day, the election would have to be replayed. Rodríguez may well have voted more than once, but the fact that he did so in an invalid election meant that he could not be guilty of any punishable offense.

Outrage does not begin to describe the popular reaction to the decision in *Ex parte Rodríguez*. Immediately vilified as the "Semicolon Case," it led the people to mount a coup d'etat to finally force an end to Reconstruction government. Faced with the possibility that Davis would continue in office and delay new elections indefinitely, angry crowds formed militias, armed themselves, and converged on the Capitol. Barricaded in his second-floor office, Governor Davis telegraphed President Ulysses S. Grant for aid in upholding constitutional rule. But Grant, whose generosity to Robert E. Lee and his defeated army helped bring about peace in 1865, now realized that Reconstruction had finally run its vengeful course, and that it was time to let the South resume control of its own affairs. He refused to come to Davis's rescue, and the governor was forced to decamp in disgrace. (Interestingly, in Washington at the time and urging Grant to this conclusion was Texas's ousted Unionist justice, James Hall Bell, who was considered to have thereby at least partially redeemed himself from the positions taken in his earlier opinions.) The new legislature was organized and Richard Coke inaugurated—extralegally—and more than a century would pass before a Republican again held the governorship.

There have been times in the history of American jurisprudence when obstreperous executives have defied court rulings, as when Andrew Jackson famously refused to enforce Cherokee land rights. And state executives routinely dragged their feet in enforcing civil rights decrees in the 1950s and 1960s. But *Ex parte Rodríguez* is perhaps the only state supreme court decision in American history that was reversed by a mob, which was then instrumental in installing a new government. This said something deep and fundamental about the way Texans viewed—and to an extent probably still view—their Supreme Court: that the will of the people is justice, by definition, and the Court's job is to effect it. And when the Court seeks to impose some alternate and alien form of justice, extreme measures can justifiably result.

Writing during World War I, a time when Civil War resentment still lay barely beneath the surface in the South, the usually unflappable and speak-no-evil Harbert Davenport, in the only book-length history of the Texas

Supreme Court, still could not stop himself from whacking the Confederate cane over the head of the Semicolon Court. It had committed, he accused, "the only blot upon the pure, honored, and exalted reputation of the Supreme Court of Texas which has marred the splendor of its history. . . . In the judicial annals of no other country has there been a more lamentable, shameless prostitution of a court of justice to the interest of lawless political conspirators against constitutional government . . . than that disclosed in *Ex parte Rodriguez.*"[52]

The irony was that by the clear grammar of the Constitution, the justices had ruled correctly, although with minimal creativity they could have found the election error to be harmless. The vengeance of the people, however, could not be stemmed. Once installed, Governor Coke revamped the Court with five new members, and the reputation of the whole tenure of the Semicolon Court was banished to the judicial wilderness. It became Texas lore that not one of their opinions was ever cited as precedent, but in reality that canard undermeasured their legacy.[53]

Even the ex-Confederate firebrand Oran M. Roberts, who was particularly sharp in his scorn for the Semicolon Court, during his own later term on the Court refused to reopen cases of railroad subsidies that it had decided. He also cited precedents from the Semicolon Court when he felt its holding was correct, as in *Renn v. Samos* (1871),[54] a question partly involving, appropriately enough, the establishment of insanity.

EIGHT

THE REDEEMER COURT

Richard Coke's highly irregular elevation to the Governor's Mansion in January 1874 gave effect to the popular will, as expressed in his overwhelming election. The downfall of E. J. Davis marked the end of Reconstruction, and Coke's installation marked the coming of the "Redeemers," those who meant to restore as much of antebellum southern ways as they could manage, short of provoking a second war.

Coke's own tenure on the Texas Supreme Court had been cut short by the commanding general of the occupation, but during his brief time there he showed as much regard for the vox populi as it had shown for him. In one of his important decisions, *Stroud v. Springfield* (1866), he upheld a jury verdict even though it had found against the weight of the evidence.[1] Conceding that juries "are the exclusive judges of credibility," Coke as justice would not interfere with their conclusion. As governor, Coke meant in his own Supreme Court appointments to show continued deference to the popular will that had swept him into office. Every one of the men he selected for the high bench had been prominent in the Confederacy.

The coup that propelled him into the governorship did not alter the constitutional process of selecting justices: the amendment of December 2, 1873, took effect, and on January 27, 1874—his twelfth day in office—Coke named his choices to the newly expanded Court.

The new chief justice was an old hand on the high bench: Oran Milo Roberts, associate justice from 1857 to 1862, president of the Secession Convention, and, after being recalled from the field of battle, chief justice after Royall Wheeler killed himself in 1864. After Texas regained statehood at the end of Presidential Reconstruction, Roberts was elected to the U.S. Senate, but with the advent of Congressional Reconstruction, he was never seated. Unfazed, Roberts returned to his home in the East Texas town of Gilmer and opened a private law school, with which he contented himself until Coke tapped his services for Texas once more. Roberts was now just short of sixty years old and (apart from his sentiments about "keeping Sambo away from the polls") had entered a long period of mellowing, a period when his experience and knowledge of law in areas unrelated to the recent war could ballast the Court and generate solid precedents.

The four associate justices were Thomas J. Devine, George F. Moore, Reuben A. Reeves, and William Pitt Ballinger.[2] Thomas Jefferson Devine, fifty-four, was Canadian-born of Irish immigrant parents. He graduated in law from Transylvania University and joined the Kentucky bar before arriving in La Grange in 1844 and finally settling in San Antonio. There he served as district judge for the ten years 1851–1861, and after secession continued as judge for the Western District. When a dispute arose between Mexico and the Confederacy over the cotton trade—an issue of signal importance to the rebel government because cotton was a critical source of income—Devine was sent on a diplomatic mission, which he successfully concluded. He joined many other Texas secessionists in fleeing to Mexico ahead of the occupation, and like most of the others, he returned before long. Devine, however, was arrested for high treason—one of only three Americans to suffer this visitation of Union wrath (the others were Clement Clay and Jefferson Davis). Perhaps motivated partly by pity for the pneumonia that Devine contracted while imprisoned in New Orleans, as well as by calmer thinking, the charges were dropped and Devine was restored to American citizenship in June 1867.[3]

George Fleming Moore's appointment to the Court renewed his association with Oran Roberts, whom Moore had replaced on the Court when Roberts left it to lead his Eleventh Texas Infantry in 1862. (They had also been boyhood friends in Alabama.) A scion of plantation wealth, Moore settled in Crockett, Texas, in 1846 at age twenty-four. In 1858 he and his partner, Richard S. Walker, became court reporters, and they prepared three volumes of *Texas Reports*. Elected to replace Roberts as associate justice in 1862, Moore was elected chief justice by his peers on the Court in 1866, but was removed by the occupation the following year. Back in private practice, he won two cases before the U.S. Supreme Court and became an expert on Texas's labyrinthine land laws.[4] His reappearance on the Court in 1874 was the beginning of a tenure that would eventually include service as chief justice.

Reuben Reeves was the Confederate cavalry captain who had taken moderate Unionist James Hall Bell's open slot in 1864 and served two years on the bench. After taking part in the 1866 Constitutional Convention, Reeves was elected judge of the Ninth District. Of all the members of the Texas judiciary who were stripped of their offices as "impediments to Reconstruction," the charge probably stuck most stubbornly on Reeves, a former slave owner who was said to have denied legal participation to freedmen.[5]

William Pitt Ballinger was a forty-eight-year-old Kentucky native, formerly U.S. district attorney for Texas (1850–1854) before entering successful private practice in Galveston. During the war, he was Confederate receiver (of sequestered enemy property) for Galveston; six weeks after Lee's surrender, Texas governor Pendleton Murrah commissioned Ballinger and Ashbel Smith to travel to New Orleans to seek surrender terms from the commanding general of the occupation there, but the victorious Union saw no need to negotiate.[6]

A couple of Coke's appointments proved to be ephemeral. Ballinger received his commission on February 3, 1874, and he resigned the same day after attending one session of the new Court—the shortest tenure of any member in the Court's history. He had always been ambivalent toward the idea of public office, having declined an associate justiceship in 1871. Ballinger did later serve on the judiciary committee of the 1875 Constitutional Convention, but he refused the nomination for governor in 1878.[7]

To fill the void left by Ballinger, Coke appointed Peter W. Gray, son of William Fairfax Gray, who had chronicled the Convention of 1836, which produced the Texas Declaration of Independence. Sam Houston had appointed younger Gray district attorney for the city of Houston upon the elder's death. After statehood, Gray played an important role in Texas legal history as a member of the First Legislature, authoring the Practice Act of 1846, which continued Texas's Latin heritage of simplified pleadings. Appointed to the Supreme Court on February 11, 1874, Gray accepted the post but was forced to resign in April because of his consumptive health, and he died in Houston the following October at age fifty-five.[8]

Coke's third attempt to plant a justice in this chair finally stuck, and its occupant made a contribution to Texas's growing judicial legacy. Robert Simonton Gould was forty-eight, born in North Carolina to Presbyterian New Englanders. He graduated from the University of Alabama when he was only seventeen. After teaching mathematics he read for the law and entered practice in Mississippi with a former governor before immigrating to Texas in 1850 and settling in Leon County. At the Secession Convention, Gould voted to leave the Union; he later raised a battalion and served as captain, rose to regimental colonel, and was wounded in battle. He had had a taste of the occupation, having been removed from a district judgeship in the 1867 housecleaning of "impediments to Reconstruction."[9]

Justice Devine resigned from the Court in 1875, owing in probably equal measure to concern for his wife's ill health and to the remunerative prospects of successful private practice. His replacement that year, the last of Coke's appointments, might have created something of a judicial legacy had he served longer on the bench, but he was fated for higher office. John Ireland, forty-eight, was a Kentucky lawman (deputy sheriff at twenty, then elected constable for three years) who didn't arrive in Texas until 1853, then was elected mayor of Seguin in 1858. Like his colleagues, he voted for secession at the Convention in 1861, and he rose through the Confederate army from private to lieutenant colonel. Removed from his district judgeship in 1867 as yet another "impediment," Ireland went on to serve in both the state House and Senate, where he gained a reputation as an early foe of railroad interests.[10]

A month after Coke named who would sit on the Court, the legislature fulfilled its constitutional duty and named two more cities where, apart from Austin, the Court would hold terms once each year: they would resume their sessions in Galveston and Tyler.

Texas's line of settlement in 1875 ran north to south roughly from Fort Worth to San Antonio and then southwest to Laredo. East of this line, cities grew and crops flourished, but beyond the pale of civilized government, war with the Comanches and Kiowas raged on the rolling plains, Apaches roamed unchallenged in the Trans-Pecos, frontier towns were beset with factions and saloon fights, and the roads between them were beset with outlaws and highwaymen. One of the Redeemer Court's most celebrated cases, *Horbach v. State* (1875), concerned the "hip-pocket-movement" claim of self-defense. It originated in a saloon fight in Dallas. A local named J. P. Horbach entered the bar to find an argument in progress among the patrons over who owed for a round of drinks. H. K. Thomas, who was well known locally as not just a drunk but a "mean" drunk, demanded of Horbach to know whether he (Thomas) owed for the drinks. When Horbach said he did, Thomas "began to abuse Horbach by heaping upon him curses and epithets of a grossly insulting, outrageous nature."[11] When Horbach tried to make amends, Thomas "stepping back his right foot, threw his right hand behind him, pushing back the skirt of his coat," at which Horbach drew his gun and shot Thomas in the head, killing him.[12]

At trial, the judge disallowed evidence that Thomas was habitually armed and was dangerous when intoxicated, and Horbach lost his claim of self-defense and was convicted for the death. Through Chief Justice Roberts, the Supreme Court declared that the trial judge erred in excluding that evidence and reversed the ruling. The case became infamous, however, as defense attorneys across the state began employing the hip-pocket-movement defense as a strategy to justify almost any shooting—a reliance quite unwarranted by the actual ruling.[13]

With Reconstruction finally dead in its grave, yet another constitutional convention met in 1875 to prepare a state charter that would not bear the taint of occupation. The document that the convention members promulgated reflected their revulsion of the E. J. Davis tenure by emasculating the office of governor to the point that its occupant became little more than a figurehead with interim appointment powers. To place the judiciary back in harness to the popular will, judges were thenceforward to be elected by the people. District courts, which had grown to thirty-five in number, were reduced to twenty-six, with judges elected to four-year terms.[14]

The Supreme Court's declining ability to keep up with its caseload was a major focus of the convention's committee on the judiciary. Over time the Court had fallen some two years behind its docket, which was bad enough for those awaiting an outcome in civil cases, but for those languishing in prison while awaiting an appeal that might free them, it was a travesty. The committee appointed at the convention to draft a new judiciary article comprised the leading legal minds in the state, but with so many strong intellects in one room, each contending for his point of view, agreement proved impossible. "There were nearly as many opinions on the subject," wrote Governor Coke, "as there were members."[15] The committee managed to produce a majority report, but also two minority reports, all undercut by a grab bag of individual opinions.

After the crucible of debate and compromise, the convention produced a new format for the judiciary that, although it passed, was warmly espoused by no one: a Supreme Court of three justices to hear appeals of civil cases arising from the state district courts, with a Court of Appeals to hear all criminal cases as well as civil cases arising from the county courts.[16]

A new election was held in February 1876, and chosen for the new three-member high bench were Chief Justice Roberts, Moore, and Gould. Reeves and Ireland lost their seats and returned to private practice. Ireland, whose modest and somewhat Jeffersonian vision of what Texas should be was out of step with the increasingly self-confident times, was subsequently turned down by the legislature in his bid for a U.S. Senate seat, and then rejected again by the people when he stood for the U.S. House. Texas had not heard the last of him, however, as he eventually made his mark as a two-term governor.

As chief justice, Roberts managed to reinvent himself from Confederate firebrand to an elder statesman of judicial sagacity. This he accomplished through such opinions as that in *Texas Land Company v. Williams* (1878).[17] The case, from Leon County, was a trespass to try title to a contested eleven leagues of land. In setting out the complicated history of this and similar cases, Roberts wrote, "Amidst such a confusion, it is not surprising that the courts of last resort should not be able to retry promptly the cases being tried by twenty-six district judges, and the county judges all over the State, that are brought up by appeals and writs of error." To avoid such procedural messes, the justices "have sought to regulate the mode and order of proceeding in suits under them, so as that the points in controversy . . . should be presented with distinctness and certainty, the want of which, under our present practice produces delay, expense and injustice."[18]

He then turned the opinion into a white paper on the preparation of legal briefs, and expounded upon the Supreme Court's rules of practice. (Perhaps one example of the kind of anomalous, indeed almost absurd, decision that Roberts hoped to avoid in the future, had been rendered in a brief opinion by Justice Devine in 1874. It dismissed an appeal that, for want of the appellant's alleging any points of error, let stand a lower court ruling that a debt paid in Confederate money was sufficient to discharge an obligation.)[19] Roberts had previously been and would be again a law professor, famed for scholarly precision in his speech, even to the point of interrupting himself in midsentence and beginning again with what he thought would be a clearer explanation. He used this voice in *Texas Land Company*, and the case was cited for years as an indispensable primer for the preparation of briefs in accordance with the Court's procedural rules.[20] It was hard to believe that this was the same figure who aimed to "keep Sambo away from the polls."

The new configuration of the Supreme Court pleased virtually no one, but repeated calls for its revamping—by Coke and by his successor, Richard Hubbard—were ignored by the legislature.[21] The Roberts Court, however, continued to make strides to put the Texas judicial house in order. With its rules of practice adequately expounded, the Court then found it necessary to determine what degree of authority to accord decisions of the Civil War- and Reconstruction-era Supreme Courts, with their cakewalk of seating and unseating, appointing and electing, and service under a hodgepodge of constitutions. The opportune case for considering the matter, *Taylor v. Murphy* (1878), came from Harrison County, in an appeal to determine whether a married couple's community property could be levied against to satisfy a judgment against the wife for an obligation undertaken before her marriage.[22] The Military Court appointed by General Sheridan, considering a case with somewhat similar facts in 1867, had concluded that it could.[23] Justice Moore was not inclined to take that decision as controlling, for the reason that the Military Court "did not exercise its functions under and by virtue of the Constitution and laws of the State of Texas, but merely by virtue of military appointment."[24] Moore was willing to accept the 1867 decision as binding on the parties to that case, but he would not accept the precedential value of an essentially foreign tribunal. Moore's ruling, that the husband's separate property was not at risk, was in keeping with Texas's unique development of marital property rights.

In the Court's quest to determine what weight to give the decisions of its predecessor Courts, it was probably inevitable that a case should arise whose issue had been ruled on differently by different Courts.[25] That issue proved to be the constitutionality of the City of San Antonio's sale of railroad bonds. The Military Court had ruled the sale valid; the following Court had reached the opposite conclusion on the grounds that the enabling legislation, whose purpose was not clear from the title of the bill, violated the so-called Caption Clause of the constitution.[26] When a third case in the same matter made it to the Redeemer Court in 1877, Chief Justice Roberts wrote with apparent amusement that from the timing of the suit, it seemed probable that it was "brought to take the opinion again of this court when composed of still another set of justices. . . . [I]t would be unfortunate that it should be thought practicable, on a doubtful question, to easily procure a change of decision with every change in the members who might from time to time compose the Supreme Court."[27]

While he disapproved of relitigating issues among disagreeing Supreme Courts, Roberts ruled that the bond sale was indeed unconstitutional. A fourth case on the same issue, however, then made its way to the U.S Supreme Court, which found the sale constitutional again.[28] When a fifth case on the San Antonio railroad bonds reached the Texas Supreme Court in 1879, the mildly exasperated justices expressed themselves politely, but unmistakably, through Justice Micajah Bonner: the decision of the Military Court in Texas was not binding, "not having been organized under the Constitution and laws of the state, [and] with all due respect to the members who composed that court as individuals, their opinions have not received the same authoritative sanction given to those of the court as regularly constituted."[29] As far as the U.S. Supreme Court ruling was concerned, Texas had not endured a decade of Reconstruction and shaken it off in a people's coup d'etat to be dictated to now by the federal court on a purely state matter: "Although we entertain the very greatest respect for the opinions of that high tribunal, yet we feel it our duty, upon a question which involves the proper construction of a local statute under the Constitution of Texas, to follow the latest decisions of this court."[30]

The terms set out in the 1876 Constitution kept the legislature from meeting during the term of Governor Richard Hubbard (1876), so he should not have borne most of the blame for the growing power of corporations such as railroads and the financial abuses they came to practice, which aroused the hatred of an increasing portion of the population. The state Democratic

Convention of 1878 was thus a contentious one. While former moderate Unionist governor James Throckmorton held one clutch of delegates, the growing power at the convention was held by an ascendant Greenback faction, the forerunners of the Populist movement, which took root to combat the growing corporate influence. The deadlocked delegates discovered one dark horse candidate for governor that they could all support: Chief Justice Roberts. The judicial Cincinnatus was at home in Gilmer, plowing his field and tending his law office, when he learned of his nomination, and he borrowed fifty cents to telegraph his acceptance.[31] He won the Democratic nomination in July 1878 and submitted his resignation as chief justice soon after.

Victorious by a landslide in the election, Roberts was sworn in as the state's seventeenth governor on January 21, 1879. In the same election, George Fleming Moore was elected chief justice, and Micajah Bonner, the judge of the Seventh District, won the associate justice seat vacated by Moore.[32] Born in Alabama, raised in Mississippi, and educated in Kentucky, Bonner had settled in Marshall, Texas, and opened a law practice in 1849. He later relocated to Rusk and went into partnership with Texas's first governor, J. Pinckney Henderson. After Henderson was elected to the U.S. Senate, Bonner took two of his brothers into the firm, then moved to Tyler in 1873 to take over the Seventh District bench.[33]

Texas by the close of the 1870s was undergoing a dramatic transformation. The state had not suffered the devastation visited upon the Deep South, and after the war there was an influx of refugees and paupers from other Confederate states. From a population of 818,579 in the census of 1870, it almost doubled in the next decade, to 1,591,749 in 1880. The Rolling Plains and the Llano Estacado were opened to settlement by the permanent eviction of the Comanches and Kiowas to a reservation in the Indian Territory in 1875, and vast cattle spreads went into operation virtually overnight. There was also rapid growth in the reach and power of business, all of which led people to increasingly resort to the courts.

One of Oran Roberts's first actions as governor was to draw the legislature's attention, once again, to the fact that the Supreme Court was being overwhelmed by new litigation. It was now some nine hundred cases behind its docket, and the Court of Appeals, which handled criminal cases, was two hundred cases behind.[34] The legislature ignored Roberts's call to enlarge the Supreme Court to nine justices, to meet in three sections as they saw need. Roberts insisted on action, however, and called a special session that finally passed an act on July 9, 1879. It created the Commission of Appeals, which was intended to relieve the Supreme Court of a portion of its caseload. A board of three persons "learned in the law," the commission would meet at the same places and times as the Supreme Court. Its members would receive the same salary as the justices, and would dispose of cases that the Court might refer to it.

The commission was a good idea, but its utility was limited by a Supreme Court whose justices were in the habit of doing their own work, and they seldom actually referred cases to it. Indeed, the commissioners complained to Governor Roberts in 1881 that they were not being given enough work to fill their days.[35] Still, when the commission's legality was challenged, the Court through Justice Gould ruled that it was constitutional. It was interpreted to be not a court but a board of arbitration, with no actual jurisdiction, and citizens were not deprived of any rights, because they still had access to the court of last resort.[36] Chief Justice Moore, believing that a court by any other name was still a court, filed a rare dissent. "It matters not whether the commission of appeals is a court or a board of arbitrators," he wrote. The act "not only . . . interferes with the exclusive constitutional jurisdiction of the Supreme Court, but it requires of it the exercise of functions . . . expressly withheld from it by the Constitution, and inconsistent with [its] duty and dignity."[37]

In November 1881, Moore's failing eyesight forced him to take the anguishing step of resigning from the bench, having served twelve years over a span of twenty. Governor Roberts elevated Robert Gould to take his place, and then pulled John William Stayton out of private practice in Victoria to fill the resulting vacancy.

When the old "Colonial" Capitol in Austin caught fire and burned to the ground on November 9, 1881, the Texas Supreme Court's newest member had been on the high bench three days. The appointment of Stayton was shrewder than it seemed from his lack of judicial experience. He was a renowned legal scholar; his personal library, with a heavy salting of Roman and Spanish law, was one of the richest in the state; and he had the reputation of reading forty pages of law every day, save Sundays.

Doubtless this was a holdover from his youth, for few men had fought harder to get an education. A Kentuckian, Stayton was orphaned at fourteen and raised thereafter on the farm of his grandfather, who saw no value in book learning. At seventeen he apprenticed himself to a blacksmith so he could afford to hire a tutor, and then learned more as a teacher's assistant in a county school. He read for the law under the tutelage of an uncle, graduated from the University of Louisville in 1856, and then within a month married and immigrated to Texas. Stayton and his wife Jeannie settled briefly in La Grange before financial straits forced a move to sparsely settled Pleasanton, south of

San Antonio, where he supported himself as a blacksmith and an attorney for the Eighteenth Judicial District. He suspended his legal career to enlist in the Civil War as a private, ending as a captain of cavalry, and settled in Victoria to start a private practice. His appointment was as much a surprise to him as to anyone, but it showed Roberts to be a shrewd judge of character. Met with puzzled exclamations of "Who is he?" Roberts answered that they might not know him then, but in a short time they would know him without need of introduction.[38]

The inadequacies of the Capitol built in 1856 had chafed the state government for some time. The Constitution of 1876 authorized the sale of three million acres of the public domain to finance a new capitol, but left the details to a future legislature, and early in 1881 plans were laid to construct a more suitable building. (The land to be sold, in the far northwest corner of the Panhandle, covered an area larger than Connecticut.) It was purely a coincidence that the existing structure burned in November of that year. A temporary capitol was hastily appropriated just south of the ruins, but for most of the following seven years, the Texas Supreme Court met in rented quarters in the Bruggerhoff Building downtown.

Dedicated in 1888, the new Capitol was a Victorian Romanesque fantasy in rusticated rose-colored granite, stretching two hundred yards east to west and a hundred yards through, its three principal floors each with twenty-two-foot ceilings. It contained 409 rooms, 924 windows, and 404 principal doors; the chambers and corridors were wainscoted with 1,250,000 feet of oak, pine, cedar, walnut, and cherry woodwork. Its dome, at 309 feet, was fourteen feet higher than the dome of the Capitol in Washington, enough to make a symbolic statement about states' rights, which were still not forgotten. In addition to the Senate wing on the east and House wing on the west, vast chambers, each lit with newfangled electric, five-pointed Lone Star chandeliers whose bulbs spelled out TEXAS, the building provided housing for the executive departments, their locations marked by transoms of acid-etched glass imported from England.[39]

The Constitution of 1876 had separated the civil and criminal courts of last resort, and the design for the Capitol took cognizance of the novel arrangement. The newly bifurcated courts were perched on the third floor, overlooking the north portico. The Supreme Court's room and justices' chambers lay on the west side of the north transept, opposite a similar suite on the east for the Court of Appeals. The two were separated by a loggia with a balcony well looking down into the Texas State Library. While decorative, with its lunettes of blue Belgian glass, the feature was actually designed for functional ventilation, allowing hot air to rise into the attic through an inverted cupola of pierced tin—an important feature for a building in which so many legislators would be speaking.

Under the Redeemer Court, those areas of Texas jurisprudence that had developed in unique ways continued to evolve. A wife's stake in community property was strengthened by the holding in *Yancy v. Batte* (1877), in which the deceased wife's heirs were allowed to recover one-half the value of land that the couple had acquired together, but that the husband had sold after being widowed.[40] The person held liable was the innocent purchaser, who had had no notice of claims by any heirs. Texas's traditional zeal for protecting the homestead did have to accommodate one mild limitation. Justice Bonner wrote the opinion in *Ball, Hutchings & Co. v. Lowell* (1882), that while a primary homestead could not be seized for debt, a second homestead could.[41]

Texas was still a largely frontier state, and many of the decisions issuing from its high bench during these years still had to deal with life as real people lived it. Occasionally the Court in its wisdom produced rulings of surprising compassion for the times.

In 1881, the justices struck down a city ordinance from Weatherford that declared "that any prostitute or lewd woman who shall reside in, stay at or inhabit any room, house or place within the limits of this city, or any person who shall knowingly furnish, rent, let or lease any premises or place within the city limits to any prostitute or lewd woman . . . shall be deemed guilty of an offense" punishable by a fine of up to two hundred dollars.[42] The city council had dismissed the mayor, James Milliken, for renting a house to such a woman. The justices held that the city might well outlaw prostitution, but they had no power to create an outlaw class by denying housing to those who were or might be practitioners of the trade. Justice Bonner, speaking for the Court, wrote: "The unfortunate and degraded class against whom the ordinance was mainly intended, however far they may have fallen beneath the true mission of women, . . . are still human beings, entitled to shelter and the protection of the law; and the council did not have the power to so far proscribe them as a class, as to make it a penal offense in any one to rent them a habitation without regard to its use."[43] Such decisions showcased a Texas in transition from a rural identity to an urban one.

Systematizing practice before the Supreme Court, as Justice Roberts did in his famed *Murchison v. Holly* opinion, was only one element of a trend toward greater professionalism and efficiency in legal practice during this period. Another was the establishment of the Texas Bar Association in 1882.

Sixty-five lawyers met in Galveston on July 15 of that year, a suitable choice, since that city was the site of the state's first local bar, founded as early as 1868. When the state association was officially inaugurated that December, Justice Devine became the first president, to help the fledgling organization "advance the science of Jurisprudence, promote the uniformity of legislation and the administration of justice throughout the State, uphold the honor of the profession of the law, and encourage cordial relations among its members."[44] Compulsory membership still lay some decades in the future, so this first formulation of a state bar drew few members, but they were largely drawn from the cream of the crop: judges, expert corporate lawyers, and those with an appellate practice.

Texas found itself in need of this sophisticated pool of legal thought, for the courts increasingly had to take account of the rapidly growing influence, demands, and social considerations brought by big business. The Court's effort to decide land cases, those involving large corporate claims as well as those between individuals, occupied much of its attention during the closing years of the frontier.

Republic Court associate judge Benjamin Cromwell Franklin was the first person to hold a judicial appointment in the Republic of Texas: President David G. Burnet appointed him special district judge in the summer of 1836 to hear an admiralty case six months before Congress assembled to elect judges under the new constitution. Reproduced from the Texas Bar Journal Photo Collection, Archives of the State Bar of Texas.

Republic Court associate judge Robert McAlpin Williamson is credited with holding the first regular session of a district court in the Republic of Texas. Williamson was nicknamed "Three-Legged Willie" because he walked with a wooden crutch strapped beneath his drawn-back right leg. Reproduced from the Texas Bar Journal Photo Collection, Archives of the State Bar of Texas.

Thomas J. Rusk came to Texas chasing men who had embezzled his investments. After serving as revolutionary secretary of war of the Republic, he presided over the first session of the Texas Supreme Court on January 13, 1840, and crafted carefully limited opinions that won the respect of members of the other branches of government. Published with permission of the Tarlton Law Library, Jamail Center for Legal Research, University of Texas School of Law.

Republic Court associate judge R. E. B. Baylor was an ordained Baptist minister whose main contribution to history was his role in founding Baylor University in 1845. Along with Justices Abner Lipscomb and Royall T. Wheeler, he introduced the study of law at Baylor and was on the first faculty when Baylor Law School opened in 1857. Reproduced from the Texas Bar Journal Photo Collection, Archives of the State Bar of Texas.

The three members of the first Supreme Court of the State of Texas, Chief Justice John Hemphill (top) and associate justices Royall T. Wheeler and Abner Lipscomb earned a reputation as "the greatest assemblage of judicial talent in state history" for their erudite, socially progressive opinions. Hemphill, U.S. Senate Historical Office; Wheeler, published with permission of the Tarlton Law Library, Jamail Center for Legal Research, University of Texas School of Law; Lipscomb, Courtesy State Preservation Board, Austin, TX; Accession ID: CHA 1989.451; photographer: Eric Beggs, 7/14/95, Post Conservation.

James Hall Bell, associate justice in the antebellum and Civil War period (1858–1864), was the first native Texan to serve on the Supreme Court, but his antisecessionist stance ran counter to public sentiment, and he failed in his future bids to serve on the Court. Published with permission of the Tarlton Law Library, Jamail Center for Legal Research, University of Texas School of Law.

The three members of the "Semicolon Court," who gained notoriety for their decision in Ex parte Rodríguez *in early 1874, were (seated, left to right) Associate Judge Moses B. Walker, Presiding Judge Wesley Ogden, and Associate Judge J. D. McAdoo. Standing behind them are court reporter E. M. Wheelock (left) and clerk of the court W. F. De Mormandie.* PICA 04708, Austin History Center, Austin Public Library.

The "Redeemer Court" appointed by Governor Richard Coke when he stormed into office in 1874 consisted of (left to right, from top): Chief Justice Oran M. Roberts and Associate Justices Robert S. Gould, George F. Moore, Reuben A. Reeves, and John Ireland. When the Constitution of 1876 reduced the Court to three elected members, Reeves and Ireland lost their bids for election.
Courtesy of the Texas State Library and Archives Commission.

From 1848 until 1881, the Supreme Court was housed in a building on the old Capitol grounds (shown left of the Capitol). When the Capitol burned in 1881, the Supreme Court Building was torn down and the Court offices were moved to temporary quarters while the new Capitol was being built. C00243, Austin History Center, Austin Public Library.

Not long before the Court moved into permanent quarters in the new Capitol in 1888, the justices and their staff posed for photographs in their quarters in the temporary Capitol. Chief Justice John W. Stayton (center) and associate justices Reuben Gaines (seated, left) and A. S. Walker (right) held court in a room adorned only with portraits of the Hemphill Court and an attorney's table with a spittoon placed strategically underneath. Charles S. Morse, clerk of the Court for almost two decades, stands at left. PICA 12941, Austin History Center, Austin Public Library.

Chief Justice Stayton had room to study, write, and even sleep in his private quarters in the temporary Capitol. The scholarly Stayton, who became chief justice in March 1888, was said to have read forty pages of law every day of his adult life, except Sundays. PICA 12936, Austin History Center, Austin Public Library.

The Court library in the temporary Capitol was both a gathering place and a workspace for clerks and other staff. PICA 12945, Austin History Center, Austin Public Library.

*The early twentieth-century Supreme Court composed of (left to right) Associate Justice
Thomas J. Brown, Chief Justice Reuben Gaines, and Associate Justice Frank A. Williams
operated so harmoniously for over a decade that it earned the sobriquet "Consensus Court."*
PICA 12930, Austin History Center, Austin Public Library.

*Deputy clerk H. L. Clamp (center), whose service in the Supreme Court clerk's office is the
longest in history (1902–1954), is shown with clerk F. T. Connerly (right) and deputy clerk J. S.
Myrick in 1914. Clamp wrote a memoir that brings the personalities and characters of several
generations of justices to life.* PICA 12944, Austin History Center, Austin Public Library.

Chief Justice Nelson Phillips, described by one contemporary as "an aristocratic Southern gentleman" whose speech was "sprinkled with Jeffersonian quotations," brought a touch of class to the Supreme Court. Phillips served on the Court from 1912 to 1921, the last six years as chief justice. From the personal family collection of Angela Phillips Pringos Box.

*In 1925 Governor Pat Neff appointed a special Texas Supreme Court to hear the appeal of Johnson v. Darr, a case involving the Woodmen of the World. It was the first all-woman supreme court in the United States. Pictured (*left to right*) are Hattie Henenberg, Hortense Ward (special chief justice), and Ruth Brazzil.* C02798, Austin History Center, Austin Public Library.

Alex Phillips, shown here in 1934, served as the Court's porter for fifty years, spanning the period from Chief Justice John Stayton to Chief Justice Calvin Cureton. "Old Alex" is a recurring presence in the Court lore of that period. PICA 12953, Austin History Center, Austin Public Library.

Chief Justice Calvin M. Cureton (center), Associate Justice John H. Sharp (left), and Associate Justice William Pierson (right) are shown in Cureton's office in the Capitol in 1935, shortly before Pierson was murdered by his son in April. Texas Supreme Court Historical Society, Judge Joe R. Greenhill Collection.

Chief Justice James P. Alexander is congratulated as he takes the bench for the first time in January 1941. Four and a half years later, he would preside over the newly constituted nine-member Supreme Court. Reproduced from the Texas Bar Journal Photo Collection, Archives of the State Bar of Texas.

Chief Justice John A. Hickman (standing, right) shakes hands with Democratic National Committee member Wright Morrow during a testimonial dinner in Houston in 1952. Standing between Hickman and Morrow are business magnates J. W. Evans and Gus Wortham. Also pictured are (seated, left to right) Governor Allan Shivers, Houston mayor Oscar Holcombe, and former governor William P. Hobby. Courtesy of Larry McNeill (private collection).

Associate Justice Meade Griffin (right), who served on the Court from 1949 to 1968, chats with State Representative Jack Hightower during a reception, circa 1954. Hightower later was elected to two terms on the Court, and as a justice he helped found the Texas Supreme Court Historical Society in 1990. Reproduced from the Texas Bar Journal Photo Collection, Archives of the State Bar of Texas.

Justice Ruel C. Walker, acknowledged by his colleagues as one of the brightest legal minds in the history of the Court, takes the oath of office after his reelection in 1965, halfway through his twenty-one-year tenure. Reproduced from the Texas Bar Journal Photo Collection, Archives of the State Bar of Texas.

Justice Don Yarbrough (right), *pictured on the bench with Justices Price Daniel* (center) *and Sears McGee, sat on the Court for six months in 1977 before resigning in the face of impeachment for several criminal indictments.* Reproduced from the Texas Bar Journal Photo Collection, Archives of the State Bar of Texas.

William L. Garwood (left) was appointed to the Court by Governor Bill Clements in 1979, becoming the first Republican justice since Reconstruction. Reproduced from the Texas Bar Journal Photo Collection, Archives of the State Bar of Texas.

District Judge Ruby Kless Sondock became the first woman to serve as a full member of the Court when she was appointed by Governor Bill Clements in 1982. Reproduced from the Texas Bar Journal Photo Collection, Archives of the State Bar of Texas.

*Raul A. Gonzalez was the first Hispanic justice on the Court,
appointed in 1984 by Governor Mark White, then elected in 1986, 1988,
and 1994.* Reproduced from the Texas Bar Journal Photo Collection,
Archives of the State Bar of Texas. Photo by Charles Guerrero.

NINE

THE CAPITOL COURT
AND THE PUBLIC LANDS

In the last decade of the nineteenth century, cases colored by frontier violence or the memory of sectional strife faded into the background, and the Texas Supreme Court mellowed into a new identity. It became known as the "Capitol Court," an ethos absorbed from its sumptuous quarters in the new statehouse.

The Supreme Court room was smaller than the House or Senate chamber, but large enough for the span to be supported by a single fluted column with an exaggerated Corinthian capital. The wide windowsills of red Etowah marble from Georgia topped steam radiators with grilles plated in fourteen-carat gold. The brown- and cream-colored Wilton carpet laid in 1889 featured an elaborate, Jacquard-woven floral pattern, and the twenty-seven-inch-wide strips were hand-stitched together on-site so as to appear seamless. Behind the bench, heavy gold brocatelle draperies framed portraits of justices from the "Old Court": Hemphill, Lipscomb, and Wheeler. The bench itself, a walnut fantasy on a raised dais, was emblazoned with the motto SICUT PA-TRIBUS, SIT DEUS NOBIS, officially translated "As He Was to Our Fathers, May God Be So to Us."[1] H. L. Clamp, who joined the Court as deputy clerk in 1902, offered perhaps a better translation: "As Our Fathers Have Done, May God Do to Us," an admonition that as they judged, so too would they be judged.[2]

A door behind the dais led to the justices' chambers, which were served by a dumbwaiter for shuttling books up from the Texas State Library. The only incongruous distraction from the dignified atmosphere was in the lighting. Believing that electricity was a passing fad, the Capitol's builders fitted the building for gas. The courtroom's initial electric lights, powered by the on-site direct current generator, were attached to their switches with casually strung wires. Proper chandeliers finally followed in 1891, and a two-blade ceiling fan over the bench kept air circulating over the justices.[3]

John William Stayton, the studious lawyer whom Governor Roberts had plucked from private practice to join the Court in 1881, succeeded Asa Willie as chief justice when the latter retired in 1888. (Willie's ascension to chief justice over incumbent Robert Gould in 1882 is described in Chapter 10. In resigning from the Court six years later, Willie cited the insufficient salary as his reason for leaving—neither the first nor the last justice to do so.)[4] Stayton anchored the Capitol Court in that capacity for six years. Two other justices joined the Court in the 1880s, but exited before they could enjoy the splendors of the new Capitol. Charles Shannon West, a South Carolinian, was an Austin attorney and former Texas secretary of state who had been active in the 1875 Constitutional Convention and later helped prepare the *Revised Statutes of Texas*. In 1882, at the age of fifty-three, he was elected to the associate-justice chair that Micajah Bonner had vacated, and he died a few weeks after resigning three years later.[5] His space was filled by Sawnie Robertson, who was only thirty-five and had been one of Oran Roberts's law students at his private school in Gilmer. He resigned after only one year on the high court and went into private practice in Dallas, but died when he was only forty-two.[6]

The jinxed chair next went to Reuben Reid Gaines, fifty, the son of rich Alabama planters. After fighting through the entire war under General Joe Johnston, Gaines gathered up his wife and joined the flood of refugees fleeing the ruined South for Texas. They settled in Clarksville and later Paris; he served four years as district judge, but otherwise spent his time in private practice and Democratic Party politics. His appointment in 1886 opened an unprecedented twenty-five years of service on the Court, eight years as an associate, then succeeding Stayton as chief after his death in 1894, and serving until his retirement in 1911. As an indication of his good breeding and discreet habits, once the Court moved into its Capitol domicile, Gaines could not bring himself to tread in street shoes on the expensive Wilton carpet. Every day when he arrived for work he changed into carpet slippers. After his Court appointment, Gaines abandoned his political activities completely and gained respect for his scrupulous impartiality.[7]

Joining the Court briefly in 1888 was Alexander Stuart Walker of Georgetown, yet another ex-rebel district judge who had been removed from office by military order. He and his law partner, Alexander W. Terrell (another former judge), became the Supreme Court reporters in 1872, the year after Walker helped start the *Democratic Statesman* (one of the precursors of the *Austin American-Statesman*) newspaper. Oran Roberts as governor appointed Walker to the Commission of Appeals when it was created in 1879, and the following year he began a four-year stint as district judge in Austin. Bookish and widely read, Walker left the Supreme Court after serving only ten months (he was defeated in the primary by John Lane Henry), but he continued to serve as its reporter until his death in 1896.[8]

Two other additions to the Capitol Court were more lasting and influential than Walker. Thomas Jefferson (T. J.) Brown, a Georgia native but Texas-raised from the age of ten, graduated from Baylor University with a law degree in 1856. He ended the war as a captain in the Twenty-Second Texas Cavalry and then went into law practice, first in McKinney (where he partnered with future governor James W. Throckmorton) and later in Sherman. In the Texas Legislature in 1888 and 1890, he became a leader in the effort to reform corporate abuses by the railroads and was an early advocate of the movement to form the Texas Railroad Commission.[9] Brown was appointed to the Court in 1893 to fill the vacancy left by John Lane Henry.

Joining the Court the year after Brown, to take Gaines's place when he was elevated to chief, was Leroy Gilbert Denman. One of the rare (up to this time) native Texans, from Guadalupe County, Denman had been a classmate of Woodrow Wilson's at the University of Virginia. He had practiced law privately in New Braunfels and San Antonio before Governor James Hogg appointed him to the high bench, where he served for five years.[10]

When the Texas government reasserted control over its state affairs in 1874, it found itself still in possession of one mighty asset, of which it had not been stripped during war, Reconstruction, and readmission: its vast public domain. Texas was unique among the American states, trading on its ten-year history as an independent nation to retain title to its public domain. After a generation of issuing headrights and military bounty and donation grants, most of the remaining vacant land lay in the western and northwestern portions of the state. During the Civil War, the Comanches and Kiowas had been alert to the withdrawal of federal troops, and in a fury of raiding that all but overwhelmed the Confederate home guard, they threw the line of settlement more than a hundred miles back to the southeast. The return of federal troops to the frontier after the war sparked a sharp series of campaigns that somewhat reduced the Plains Indians' fighting strength, but it was still potent enough that beginning in 1869, the administration of President U. S. Grant instituted the "Peace Policy," which involved feeding them in hopeful substitution of fighting them. Both sides contributed to the scheme's ultimate failure, which led to prosecution of the Red River War in 1874—by chance, the same year of Texas's state resurgence.[11] The final defeat the next year of the Kiowas and Comanches, whose continued reduction was ensured by the establishment of new posts such as Fort Elliott in the Panhandle, suddenly opened nearly incomprehensible vistas to settlement and development.

The year 1876 brought the new state constitution and, with it, a whole new thicket of land issues that ultimately found their way to the docket of the Texas Supreme Court. The conflicts embraced two broad areas, in both of which the Court had to recognize and act in light of the depletion of the public domain and, with that, the end of the frontier.

One set of conflicts—settling ownership disputes between contending parties—bracketed all aspects of the range-war era: open range versus fenced pasture, cowmen versus sheepmen, ranchers versus sodbusters, large operators versus small players, and the fate of the Texas school lands. The second set of conflicts centered on railroads. The 1876 Constitution reversed Texas's earlier hostility toward bartering swaths of the public domain in order to encourage railroads to lay track across the plains. This colossal exchange of land for development engendered complex legal issues that became entangled also in a tide of public sentiment against the railroads over the way they used, and abused, their newfound power.

In tackling issues concerning the public domain, the Court found its job complicated by the rapid change of direction in public policy between succeeding gubernatorial administrations. Oran Roberts, governor from 1879 to 1883, benefited from the state's rapid recovery from Reconstruction, marked by burgeoning population growth. He announced his fiscal policy as a conservative-sounding "pay as you go," and on his watch the state deficit was reduced by a quarter and property taxes were reduced by a substantial 40 percent. While this kept him popular with small landowners, the recovery was financed by the wholesale dispensing of the state's land patrimony, which favored railroads and large-scale land investors.

Roberts's successor in the Governor's Mansion was John Ireland, the former justice whom the voters had not retained on the Court when it was reduced to three members in 1876, and who subsequently failed in his bids for U.S. Senate and House seats. Elected governor in 1882 and reelected in 1884, he served at the height of Texas land conflicts: range wars that pitted cowmen against sheepmen, and the fence-cutting wars after the advent of barbed wire that heralded the end of the open range. His philosophical preference for smaller landholders, and a goal to conserve as much of the public land as Roberts had not given away, probably made him the more genuinely conservative of the two governors. Early in his term, Roberts had advocated the sale of public lands "without limit as to quantity to the purchaser" in order to maximize short-term financial gain. He also used the aridity of the land as a justification, noting that only large-scale operations in West Texas could be economically viable. Ireland, on his accession, began pressing for minimum prices and maximum allowed purchases as a way to favor a more Jeffersonian countryside of small freeholders.[12]

The final aspect that the Court had to consider in its land cases was the nature of the litigants before them. In the freewheeling days of the Republic of Texas, with large league-and-labor Mexican grants at stake, bad actors such as W. D. C. Hall might invade neighbors' properties and actually have the nerve to expect the Supreme Court to vindicate them. (Hall at least was slapped down by the Hemphill Court as a would-be Norman baron.)[13] Now, on the post–Civil War frontier, tracts of land vastly larger were stalked by speculators, squatters, adverse possessors, and others with some color of legality to their claims.

In contests involving the ownership of land, the justices had firm precedents in hand that "actual settlers are favored by the law" over other claimants.[14] What caused much confusion was that many cases came into court in which there was no bad actor. The culprit was legislative and administrative haste to dispense the public land, of which tens of millions of acres had been only nominally explored, let alone surveyed. A homesteader might in good faith settle on his 160 acres, intending to perfect his title with three years' occupancy as the statute required, and be totally unaware that some well-financed entity had purchased a large patent that included his little corner of it. A large "land and cattle company," for its part, might in good faith purchase patent to enough land for a profitable operation, and have no idea that small squatters were already in possession of parts of it. In many cases the closest thing to a bad actor, although more bumbling than bad, was indeed the State of Texas.

Just such an issue came up on appeal in 1878, in the case of *Summers v. Davis*,[15] a complicated trespass action to try title (that is, establish clear title) to a league and labor of land that dated back to Austin's colony. The Court used the case to declare that between competing owners of a tract, the homesteader in actual possession had the right of ownership, restating the earlier rule favoring homesteaders. Indeed, just the occupation of land with the intent to claim it as a headright grant resulted in a presumption of legal ownership and an equitable interest in its title.[16] Just how heavily occupation could weigh in one's favor was demonstrated in an 1884 case originating near Sweetwater, in Nolan County. A poor dirt farmer named Powell settled a 160-acre tract in 1880, intending but neglecting to file a homestead application within the required thirty days. Meanwhile, a speculator named Gammage obtained a headright certificate—a type of land acquisition from the state that did not require actual occupancy—to a much larger tract that included Powell's 160 acres. When the case reached the Supreme Court, even though Gammage held the patent to the land, the Court awarded ownership of the 160 acres to Powell based on his prior occupancy with the intent to homestead.[17]

As throughout the Court's history, virtually every action it took soon enough required an equal but opposite reaction as people tried to take advantage of its rulings. In the case of homesteaders being favored over other claimants, *Powell* and similar cases created the belief in some quarters that briefly squatting on the land, or touching foot on it, or even just intending to settle it, would also prove superior to other claims. These vain hopes the Court had to crush. When a quick thinker named Weaver purchased a "homestead" from an owner who had never in fact lived on the place, the Court recognized instead the patent of one Garrett, who had fulfilled the conditions for receiving it from the state. The 1888 opinion was doubly effective for having been written by Justice Stayton, who had a background in real estate law.[18]

The cases that had the greatest impact on the vast Texas plains were those involving big cattle ranches. An important social context of lawsuits over the grazing range was that they seldom involved cowboys, except, as will be elaborated, as agents of their corporate employers. There had been a time when industrious cowboys, acquiring their own cattle and grazing them on the open range, could become wealthy stockmen. By the middle to late 1870s, however, that era was already well on the wane. With the end of the open range and the advent of barbed wire, a huge capital investment was increasingly required to operate a viable ranch. As funds flowed in from English, Scottish, New York, and Chicago investors, who formed gigantic land and cattle companies, they hired the best lawyers to squeeze the most land out of the state and to squeeze out their competitors, and the cowboy was reduced to a minimum-wage worker with little chance of advancement.[19]

Even that most iconic of Texas cowmen, Charles Goodnight, was himself reduced to the status of glorified foreman. Although he had been among the first to turn cattle onto the range right after the Comanches and Kiowas were driven onto their reservation, the need for cash to compete as a major operator forced him to put up a two-thirds stake in the business for a loan from a British investor named John George Adair, who collected 10 percent interest on it. The initials in the JA Ranch, with which Goodnight's name became forever linked, stood for "John Adair."[20] Goodnight, however, was nothing if not zealous for the expansion of his and his partner's business, and it was Goodnight who came to figure most prominently in cases that reached the Supreme Court.

The 1876 Constitution set aside half of the remaining public domain for the support of a public school system, after which the state moved to derive income by leasing grazing rights to its unoccupied school lands. But key ranchers, who had already fenced in millions of acres, were in no mood to begin paying a fee for what had, traditionally, been free range. Goodnight alone was thought to have enclosed as much as 600,000 acres of land he did not actually own, much of which, in the state's view, was school land. When the Panhandle Stock Association, of which Goodnight was the most important member, saw the legislation inevitably coming, the group moved to make the most of it, lobbying for a law that would offer them twenty-year leases for four cents an acre a year. The state responded in 1883 with a statute that created the State Land Board, composed of five high state officials (governor, treasurer, comptroller, attorney general, and commissioner of the General Land Office), which was empowered to lease land for up to ten years, with tracts put up for competitive bidding, but the grazing lease amount never to be less than four cents an acre. Collusion among the stockmen defeated the plan, since each rancher bid only on the land he had already fenced, for the minimal rent.[21]

Eventually, the attorney general, John D. Templeton, had had enough of the chicanery and brought suit to force Goodnight to remove the fences from state land. Goodnight's lawyers constructed elaborate arguments: the suit should have properly been brought as an action of trespass to try title; the suit could not lie because other ranchers might have an interest in those lands and should have been joined as defendants; and the like. Goodnight prevailed in the trial court, which he generally did, because it would have taken considerable nerve for a Panhandle judge or jury to cross him. The case became known as the "Grass Lease Fight," and when it reached the Supreme Court in 1888 the reversal was thorough. In an opinion written by the scholarly and methodical—and strategically creative—Reuben Reid Gaines, the Court would not be mocked, especially as it was clear that the offending fences were Goodnight's and not anyone else's. Gaines allowed Goodnight's lawyers their points, writing that a suit in trespass to try title might have been an acceptable way for the state to proceed, but nothing required it to do so, and suing Goodnight in a nuisance action to remove his fences, which is what the state did, worked just as well.[22]

The previous year, the Court had reached an opposite result in a bitter case arising in now-defunct Greer County, which was located in far North Texas. There, the Day Land and Cattle Company had sought patent to 144,000 acres of public land, which the state had sold in 1884 pursuant to an 1879 statute mandating sale of one-half of the public domain in the county for payment on the state debt. A new attorney general, James Stephen Hogg, had taken office in 1887, intent on making a name for himself as a populist and reformer. He sued to get the land back, claiming that the statute mandating the sale had appropriated the lands for specific (rather than general) public use, which removed the tract from the jurisdiction of the State Land Board, which therefore had no power to sell it.[23] Hogg won, after which Day Land and Cattle came back to the land board with a bid to lease the same land at six cents an acre. The bid was accepted, and the first year's rent was paid. It was a ruse, however. Day Land and Cattle fenced the land and refused to pay the second year's rent, claiming that if the land board had no authority to sell the acreage, then it had no authority to rent it, either. This time Jim Hogg and the state lost, but for a different reason: the statute authorized the lease of surveyed lands, and the 144,000 acres in question had not been surveyed when the lease was signed. The English common law recognized unsurveyed land as a public commons, and if the state wanted some remedy, it would have to sue under a different theory.[24]

With vast tracts of rich grazing land at stake, it was inevitable that the cattle companies' attorneys would probe every crevice of the legislature's land laws, which were added to in virtually every session and were usually poorly drafted, to find ways to increase their holdings for little or no cost. The 1883 statute that created the State Land Board was tested again in *Smisson v. State* (1888).[25] Soon after the statute was enacted, the board issued an administrative regulation that raised the minimum rate for leasing public lands from four cents to eight cents an acre. A cowman named Smisson leased a tract of public land at the higher rate and also agreed to pay twenty cents an acre for the land that bordered on water. He then turned his cattle out to graze, but tendered only four cents per acre, the amount stated in the original statute. His claim was that any increase in rent would have to be enacted by the legislature, and that the administratively imposed increase was therefore unconstitutional. It was Chief Justice Stayton, the Court's resident authority on land law, who wrote out Smisson's defeat. The legislature, he held, had authorized the land board to lease land; it had not required the board to do so. And if the board leased land, it was authorized to accept competitive bids, which meant that it had the flexibility to negotiate the best possible terms for the state.

In 1883 the legislature, alarmed by the avarice with which the land and cattle companies were creating private empires out of the public domain, had passed a new law forbidding any one purchaser from acquiring more than one section (640 acres) of school land in one county. Also noticing the protracted nature of the resulting lawsuits, which dragged on for years, the lawmakers provided that suits seeking to nullify transactions under this law had to be filed within a year of the sale.[26] Here was a new crevice to exploit. Under this statute, three men in Archer County, F. Lewis, S. J. Moore, and S. T. Jones, and one ranch, the sprawling Wichita Land and Cattle Company, each acquired one section of school land. What the land board did not know was that Lewis, Moore, and Jones were all cowboys employed by Wichita Land and Cattle, and in a short time they conveyed their sections to the company. By the time the scheme was uncovered and a suit filed to undo the transaction, more than a year had passed since the sale. In arguing *State v. Wichita Land and Cattle Company* (1889) the ranch's lawyers righteously cited the statute of limitations. Justice Gaines, just as righteously, cited the doctrine of fraudulent concealment, and the lands went back into the public domain.[27]

One did not have to be a goliath operator like Charles Goodnight or Wichita Land and Cattle to have an eye out for the main chance. If anything, those who had nothing but saw the chance to get something were even more motivated than those who already lived abundantly. In one case, a farmer named Starkweather sold some land to a man named Busk, including acreage that was tenanted by a sharecropper named Lowrie. Sharecropping was about the lowest scale of farming: a farmer like Lowrie, who could not afford a place of his own, tilled the land of another and paid a share of the crop as rent. Once it was realized that Starkweather did not actually own all the land that he had sold, but had merely fenced in part of the public domain, Busk the purchaser and Lowrie the tenant began a race to establish a claim to the still-public land. Busk applied to the state for a patent under a scrap-land statute, repurchased the land from the state, and arranged to have it surveyed. Lowrie, meanwhile, knowing the advantage of possessors, entered the tract and made minimal improvements, including smoothing the area for a homesite and erecting "rock pillars for a house in which he intended to live."[28]

This case, *Busk v. Lowrie*, was decided by the Court in 1893, in a unanimous opinion authored by Justice Thomas Jefferson Brown. The Court reaffirmed its confidence in the general doctrine preferring resident homesteaders, and its willingness to overlook procedural deficiencies such as tardy filings, in order to keep them on the land. It was not, however, prepared to award the land to Lowrie for having jumped onto the land and mortared some rocks together. As expounded by Justice Brown, the law was intended to protect "the actual settler [who] . . . must reside on the land, or occupy preparatory to and with the bona fide intention of residing thereon." Lowrie had not occupied the land until Busk had applied for a patent, which Lowrie knew Busk was going to do. Busk had followed the forms of law and was awarded the parcel.[29]

Busk patented his land under the Scrap Law of 1887, which was passed for the very purpose of divesting the state of such odds and ends as survey errors—evidence enough that the state was aware that it was running out of land, a circumstance that would once have seemed unimaginable. As time passed, in fact, it began to dawn on the Court that the state, like a skilled con artist, had probably sold more of the public domain than it actually possessed. The General Land Office, while it maintained meticulous records of its myriad transactions, had conveniently never devised a method of overall tally. The inevitabilities climaxed in the case of *Hogue v. Baker*, decided in 1898, five years after the U.S. Census Bureau declared the end of the frontier and the same year that historian Frederick Jackson Turner propounded that the frontier had been the primary shaper of the American character.[30]

Would-be landowner R. S. Hogue, after the time-honored custom, settled on 160 acres in West Texas's Scurry County, near the town of Snyder, with the intention of homesteading it. He filed his application and had the land surveyed, but the General Land Office declined to issue him the land, saying that the land in Scurry County available for homesteading was exhausted. Hogue sued for a writ of mandamus to compel the land commissioner, A. J. Baker, to issue the title. After a lengthy consideration of exactly how one-half of unappropriated land should be defined, Chief Justice Gaines was left to conclude that the result hardly mattered: "When the Constitution took effect, the public lands amounted approximately to 75,000,000 of acres, and it is to be presumed that this fact was known to the convention that framed that instrument. One-half of this quantity was more than sufficient to satisfy the outstanding certificates, to encourage the construction of railroads and other internal improvements and to meet every demand made upon them." But the simple truth was that "the half of the public domain not dedicated to the school fund has been exhausted, and . . . it follows that the survey in controversy is not subject to location for the purpose of acquiring a homestead donation."[31] The frontier was finally, legally gone.

The other great stakeholder in the fate of the public lands was the railroads. Overcoming the antipathy expressed toward them in the 1869 Constitution, the Convention of 1876 empowered the legislature, if it chose, to gift the railroads with sixteen sections of land (10,240 acres) for every mile of track they laid. To prevent the concentration of land under any one owner, however, the land would be granted in sections that would alternate, as on a checkerboard, with school lands. And the railroads, furthermore, had to dispose of the grants within five years. (This provision was easily circumvented by one party or another consolidating sections by selling them to an already-large holder for a hundred dollars each.)

The political divisiveness that the railroads caused among the general public divided even Democratic politicians, who were united in other matters. Governor Oran Roberts believed that aiding the railroads would settle the country in the shortest amount of time, and that accomplishing it was worth the hemorrhage of public-domain lands. When John Ireland took over the governorship in 1883, he was little short of horrified by what had taken place, predicting that the people would "turn with deep mutterings from the wicked folly" of casting away their patrimony with both arms.[32] Indeed, Ireland became such a vocal critic of the railroads that they and their allies in the legislature began calling him "Ox-Cart John," after the only mode of transport Texas would have if he had his way. The railroads divided the Texas Supreme Court no less, especially after John Lane Henry joined the Court in January 1889, for in private practice he had been a zealous railroad advocate. Henry was another ex-Confederate, born in Virginia and educated in Tennessee before immigrating to Texas and practicing law in Huntsville and Livingston. Relocating in 1879 to the vicinity of Dallas—whose population had tripled in the preceding decade to more than ten thousand—he served as mayor of East Dallas and as a director of the Dallas and Wichita Railroad in the years preceding his appointment.[33]

During Ireland's second term, he found a powerful ally in the state attorney general, James Stephen Hogg, who was intent on vindicating popular indignation at the most abusive railroad practices. Hogg struck in the case of *Galveston, Harrisburg, and San Antonio Railway Company v. State* (1889).[34] In an instance of excruciatingly bad drafting, the 1876 Constitution defined the public school lands in one place as all the alternate sections of lands surveyed from railroad grants, and in another place as one-half of the public domain of the state. At stake was whether the railroads would get one-half of the lands appropriated to them (sixteen sections per mile of track, less remitting the alternate sections as school land); or whether they would get one-fourth of the lands appropriated (sixteen sections per mile, taken only after one-half the public domain was set aside as school lands). The GH&SA Railway received its land under the first reading, and Hogg sued to get half of it back.

In sum, he should not have lost, but he did. In the view of one commentator, Gaines allowed Henry, the old railroad lawyer, to talk him into a legally doubtful holding because to have done otherwise would have turned public policy on its head and called into question all grants made to the railroads since the policy was begun in 1876. Chief Stayton filed a lengthy and vigorous dissent—a rarity during the amicable days of the Capitol Court. Stayton had been a member of the Convention of 1876 and had spotted this ambiguity in the constitutional language at the time, but the amendment he offered to correct it was defeated.[35]

Being nineteenth-century railroads, of course, they seemed incapable of not eventually overreaching, and the Texas Supreme Court began to find ways to thwart at least some of their ambitions. It was the same GH&SA Railroad that sued the state for its sixteen sections per mile along a line it had begun to construct from San Antonio to El Paso. Because that law had been repealed in 1882, Governor Roberts would not approve the transfer of land. Because the railroad had undertaken construction under the 1876 law granting the lands, it sued. By the time the case reached the Supreme Court in 1896, Gaines had replaced Stayton as chief, and John Lane Henry, the railroad's man, was off the court, replaced by Thomas Jefferson Brown, a former legislator, railroad reformer, and in fact one of those responsible for creating the Texas Railroad Commission.[36]

Gaines for the unanimous Court found a way to deny the railroad the windfall of land without touching the actual issue that the case presented. The GH&SA Railway, he ruled, was a legal successor to the former owner, the bankrupt Buffalo Bayou, Brazos, and Colorado Railroad Company. That charter had empowered the company to build a rail line from Buffalo Bayou, near Houston, to Austin, on the Colorado. Whatever land riches were promised by the legislature in 1876, the GH&SA Railroad could never have assumed more powers than were held by its predecessor, and if it wanted a charter to build a line from San Antonio to El Paso, it should have applied for one.

Even in a case in which a railroad got the legislature to revise its charter so as to allow it to construct an additional line—in this instance, permitting the Houston and Texas Central Railway to lay track from Brenham to Austin— the state sued to get some land back, arguing that the charter had been improperly revised in 1870 in light of the fact that the 1869 Constitution barred land grants to railroads. T. J. Brown, the reform justice, wrote the opinion giving the land back to the state.[37]

A similar logic to that used in the GH&SA Railroad result was applied to another case in 1896. The commissioner of the General Land Office, citing the repeal of the land-for-track legislation, declined to issue land to the Tyler Tap Railroad, which had constructed fifty-four miles of rail line. The tracks had been laid before the repeal, however. When the railroad went broke, its receiver, a man named Thompson, sued the state and lost.[38] This time Gaines found that the legislation repealing the land largesse actually prohibited the commissioner from issuing title to lands earned under the program, and did not merely end the program as of the time the repeal passed.

TEN

THE CAPITOL COURT AND
THE GILDED AGE

The proliferation of railroads changed Texans' lives in fundamental ways. Trains on the plains rendered obsolete the picturesque trail drives of the cowboys, as the development of the cattle car made possible direct shipment to stockyards. For rural and town dweller alike, arrival of the railroad brought life by mail order; all the conveniences of modern times, from windmills to garden seeds to battery-powered invigorating underwear, could be ordered from sales catalogs such as those of Montgomery Ward or Sears, Roebuck. It was true that the railroad companies enriched themselves on lavish land grants, and then pursued predatory business practices, but the economic benefits that they conferred on society were also considerable.

With the railroads insinuating themselves into aspects of Texans' lives that no one expected, it is hardly surprising that Texas courts, and ultimately the Texas Supreme Court, found themselves challenged to apply old doctrines to new situations that called for a willingness to be creative. John Hemphill could only have smiled as the new Court tried in its own way to balance law and equity, to preserve its judicial credibility by staying within its bounds, while still responding—and being seen to respond—to vastly changed times. Sometimes this required an artful selecting of precedents in order to arrive at justice.

At first it appeared that the railroad interests would fare well in the Texas Supreme Court. Chief Justice Gould, appointed early in the Redeemer era and elevated to chief by Governor Oran Roberts in 1881 after George Moore resigned, was not elected to the post in 1882. He was politicked out of it by Asa Willie, the veteran of Presidential Reconstruction who had subsequently been removed by military order. Willie, after serving a term in Congress, had gone into a lucrative private law practice, working often for the railroads. He lobbied the Democratic Convention and hustled the nomination away from Gould. Gould believed that part of the reason for his defeat was that he shared the same last name with the infamous railroad robber baron Jay Gould.[1] Here was highlighted an unexpected aspect of the elective system of choosing judges: before they could be elected, they had to be nominated, and it seemed that the party pols who did the nominating proved as susceptible to misperception and insistent buttonholing as the people at large could prove susceptible to passionate times and pithy campaign slogans. (Gould, forced off the bench, yet made himself useful. He and former governor Roberts became the first law faculty at the new University of Texas, at which Gould excelled for the next twenty years. He resigned shortly before his death in 1904.)[2]

Statutory regulation of large corporate businesses still lay largely in the future. The United States had entered what the writer Mark Twain called the "Gilded Age," an era of virtually laissez-faire capitalism, in which exploitation of labor and invulnerability from the repercussions of predatory conduct accrued to the profit of a small but grotesquely wealthy class of "robber barons." The courts, when involved with this class at all, were not deciding conflicts between business practices and government regulation. Rather, they used the existing realms of the common law, such as torts, to measure what responsibility, if any, these huge combines had to the broader community.[3] The Texas Supreme Court justices were keenly aware of the social upheaval that the growing power of business was causing, quoting in an 1893 case from scholarly commentary that "the formation of gigantic combinations . . . in late years has created alarm and excited the liveliest interest in the public mind. The amount of discussion which it has invoked . . . is probably without parallel."[4]

The early 1880s marked a turning point in the Court's willingness to interject itself in the matters of business law, finding liability and upholding large damage awards that it had previously found too bold. John William Stayton, who had joined the Court only one year before Willie, proved especially willing to reach into equity, when necessary, to see that justice was done. The years 1882 and 1883 were pivotal. In *P. J. Willis Bros. v. McNeil* (1882), Justice Micajah Bonner in his opinion admitted that "[e]xemplary damages are said to rest in the sound discretion of the jury. This discretion is often abused, but the courts, from the very necessity of the case, are frequently embarrassed in deciding where the line of proper discretion ends, and where that of arbitrary abuse commences."[5] In this case of actual damages of $1,084.50, Bonner held that an exemplary damage award of $12,000 was excessive. He also, not insignificantly, invited legislative attention to the propriety of fixing such amounts by statute in order to relieve the courts of the burden of uncertainty and the accusation of overreaching.

Stayton dissented in *McNeil,* and the following year he began to take a leading role in extending remedies to victims of railroad negligence.[6] State law required railroads to maintain cattle guards along their lines in such repair as to prevent damage to other property from stock crossing their lines. This the Texas and St. Louis Railroad failed to do, and stray cattle trampled the growing crops of farmer Josephus Young. Young sued, but the railroad pleaded the doctrine that individuals have a duty to protect themselves from the wrongdoing of others if they can do so at modest trouble and expense. The trial judge agreed and gave a summary judgment for the Texas and St. Louis.

When the case came to the Supreme Court, Stayton reversed the judgment.[7] The danger to the railroad interests lay in his reasoning that "[c]onsidering the dangerous character of the business of maintaining and operating railways, the high degree of care necessary therein, and the importance of such companies having the exclusive control of their roadways and their construction, it would seem that they should not be relieved from liability."[8] It simply asked too much of farmer Young to know how to construct, and pay for constructing, the cattle guards needed to keep stock out of his field. The statute gave Young the right to construct his own cattle guards, but did not impose the duty to do so.

Railroad companies also began losing personal-injury verdicts with greater regularity; one key case involved A. L. De Milley, who was a passenger on a Texas and Pacific train when his car struck a broken rail and careened down a thirty-foot embankment, injuring him seriously and permanently. A jury found in his favor, awarding him four thousand dollars, and the railroad appealed, claiming that the defect in the specific broken rail had not been discoverable upon inspection, and that the trial court had erred in allowing witness testimony about the poor condition of sections of track that were not the direct cause of the accident. "While a single defect might escape the observation of even a careful man," wrote Stayton, "the general dangerous condition of a railway is a fact to which a jury may look for the purpose not only of ascertaining the degree of care used by the owner, but also for the purpose of showing the indifference of the owner to the safety of those whom it undertakes to transport."[9]

In each of these cases, it would have been easy for the Court to back the trial judges when they circumvented juries by granting summary judgments, issuing directed verdicts, or even wording their jury instructions in such a way as to obtain a desired result. However, the Supreme Court evinced a decided preference to let juries decide issues for themselves, and no one needed to remind the corporate entities that the majority of the people in Texas were solidly populist in their leanings, and juries more likely than not would seize an opportunity to punish them. The railroads, of course, wriggled ever more creatively in their arguments to escape liability. In *Ormond v. Hayes, Receiver* (1883), Mary Ormond of Jacksonville sued the International & Great Northern Railroad and its receiver for thirty thousand dollars in the death of her husband.[10] They were passengers on a train and also had a large shipment of household furnishings in the baggage car. The railroad had agreed to stop at a section house a quarter mile from the Jacksonville station to allow them to disembark and unload, but the train did not do so. When they stopped in Jacksonville and the Ormonds got off, the husband proceeded to the baggage car to supervise the unloading of his goods. While he was doing so, the train started forward, striking and killing him. The railroad's contention was that when Ormond set foot on the ground he ceased being a passenger under the railroad's care, and moreover when he helped in removing his goods from the baggage car, he became for those moments a servant of the railroad equal to the paid employees, to whom the line did not owe the same care as to a paying passenger, and furthermore he was killed as a result of his own carelessness and mischance.

This time it was Justice Charles Shannon West who lowered the boom on the railroad: "[W]e think [Ormond] had a right to go to the baggage car for the purpose of identifying and claiming his property and receiving it from the employees of the defendants, and if he did no more than simply aid and assist defendant's employees in . . . removing his own baggage from the car to the platform . . . that the relation of carrier and passenger had not entirely ceased."[11]

Whether it was because people began to understand that they could actually recover judgments from the mighty railroads, or because of the explosion in Texas business, cases involving the transportation and communication industries proliferated through the 1880s. In the tally of one commentator, this class of suits accounted for only 10–13 percent of the Supreme Court's cases in 1882 and 1883, increasing to 20 percent in 1884 and 25 percent by 1895.[12]

While the Court certainly did not leap aboard any populist bandwagon, the justices undeniably bent the common law where they could to provide relief for the injured and take the railroads down a peg when their conduct merited it. One prime example grew out of a tragic accident involving a child. The Denison, Texas, rail yard of the Houston and Texas Central Railroad included a roundhouse, where locomotives and rolling stock were repaired, and a turntable, a huge, rotating apparatus on which locomotives were turned and headed back out in the opposite direction. The rail yard lay next to a field with a pond where local boys, including one S. P. Simpson, age ten, were accustomed to fish and play. One day the boys entered the rail yard, which was not fenced, and began playing on the turntable. Simpson's right leg became caught in the mechanism and was crushed; his family sued, and the jury awarded them $3,500 in damages. The railroad appealed, claiming that they should not be held liable when the injuries occurred as the result of a trespass.[13]

Stayton's opinion in the 1883 case noted that the turntable was never secured in such a way that it could not be used, and that it was obscured from oversight by intervening yards and coal bins. "The entry upon such a place was not a trespass," ruled Stayton, when committed by a child, "for it is the duty of every person to use due care to prevent injury to such persons, even from dangerous machinery upon the premises of the owner, if its character be such as to attract children to it for amusement."[14] Extending far beyond young Simpson's mangled leg, the case was the beginning of the state's adoption of the doctrine of attractive nuisance, and in the view of one commentator, the "beginning of modern tort law in Texas."[15]

When the injured parties seeking recovery from the railroads were adults, it almost seemed as if the Court were willing to consider, in individual cases, just how vile the company's behavior was in assessing what kind of justice to render. Indeed, the Court all but admitted this in *Texas and Pacific Railway Company v. Gay* (1895).[16] A railway employee named John M. Gay was killed in Parker County when the coupling pin between the engine and tender worked itself free and he was crushed between them. The legal hurdles for Mrs. Gay, who brought suit on behalf of herself and their young daughter, were formidable. There is no wrongful-death action under the common law; it has a statutory basis. And the Texas wrongful-death statute allowed actions only against principals; the Texas and Pacific had placed itself in receivership under a federal court in Louisiana, so it appeared that there could be no recovery. The receivership was "ostensibly upon the ground that it was largely indebted to the Missouri Pacific Railway Company, which debt it was unable to pay, and that its roadbed was in bad condition . . . when in truth and in fact no such real indebtedness existed." The railroad continued to operate in receivership "free from the annoyance of its local creditors," and with the federal court blissfully ignorant of the scheme to avoid liability.[17]

John Gay's heirs were awarded a judgment in April 1894, when the Court held the railroad nonetheless to be a defendant, in view of the collusion of the receiver. A year later, however, the parties were back in the Supreme Court. The Texas wrongful-death statute had been amended to allow action against receivers, but by the time that was done, the statute of limitations had taken hold, allowing the Texas and Pacific to argue that the case be dismissed on that ground—especially since John Brown, the receiver, had died anyway. The justices were not sympathetic; whatever action might be lost to Mrs. Gay, the statute of limitations would not even begin to run on the minor daughter until she came of age.

In his opinion, Justice Leroy Gilbert Denman took one especially bold step, allowing the testimony of the railroad's own employees to the effect that coupling pins normally had a slot-and-key mechanism at their lower end to prevent them from working free, and the one that killed John Gay did not, but now they were used in all cases. Such testimony would have been inadmissible to support an inference of negligence in most jurisdictions, and later became inadmissible in Texas.[18]

Simultaneously with the railroad rulings, the Supreme Court also decided a series of cases involving telegraph companies, which ranked not far below railroads in public disfavor. Here too the Court used the cases to extend the reach of Texas tort law. This trend began quite early with the important case of *So Relle v. Western Union Telegraph Company* (1881).[19] On January 16, 1874, Austin businessman C. O. So Relle's mother died near Giddings. A near relative wrote out a message informing So Relle of that fact and requesting him to come on the night train. He delivered the message to the Western Union station, paid the fee, and was told the telegram would be promptly sent. In fact, it was not sent for several days, causing So Relle to miss his mother's funeral. He sued Western Union for fifty thousand dollars for his anguish, but he lost at trial when the telegraph company pointed out that while the occurrence was unfortunate, it did not give rise to a cause of action. Mental anguish might be an element to consider in actual damages, but it did not constitute damages in and of itself in the absence of physical injury. The trial court agreed and dismissed the suit.

When the case landed at the Commission of Appeals, however, the commissioners were able to find two earlier Texas cases (both of them concerning railroads) that fell the other way. They also cited a recent scholarly text registering the opinion that "[i]n case of delay or total failure of delivery of messages relating to matters not connected with business, such as personal or domestic matters, we do not think that the company in fault ought to escape with mere nominal damages." The text went on to mention that such a delay in announcing a death could produce an injury to the feelings that could not be easily estimated in money, "but for which a jury should be at liberty to award fair damages."[20] Buttressing its decision further, the commission pointed out that "telegraph companies enjoy special franchises and privileges under the law," and that telegrams, by their very nature, were sent only on matters of importance to the parties. It took some sophistry, but seven years after the death of So Relle's mother, the Commission of Appeals declared for the first time that mental anguish without accompanying physical injury could be regarded as harm for which actual damages could be recovered, and not merely as an element of punitive or exemplary damages.

The rule laid down in *So Relle* was applied but muddied in a case based on similar facts in 1883. There, the Gulf, Central, and Santa Fe Railway was also the telegraph operator, which failed to timely deliver a telegram from J. T. Levy, a farmer near Cleburne. Distraught that his wife had died in childbirth (the infant also died), Levy had telegraphed his father, a hundred miles distant, to appeal for emotional support and financial help with the burial. In the wake of *So Relle*, both Levys, father and son, separately sued the railroad. Both cases, on appeal, were decided by the Supreme Court on the same day. Stayton's opinions were carefully modulated. That the jury could consider the son's pain and suffering was unquestioned, since he had sustained a financial loss as well. However, Stayton ruled that the jury should not have been told of young Levy's financial distress, which was preexisting, not caused by the failure to send the wire, and served only to inflame the jury. He also held that the telegraph operator had a duty only to its paying customers, which the father was not, and he was excluded from recovery.[21]

In 1889 the Texas Legislature finally heeded the growing clamor to rein in growing business power with a state antitrust statute, a year before the passage of the Sherman Anti-Trust Act by Congress. The statute was challenged in 1895, but the case had an ironic twist.[22] The Anheuser-Busch Brewing Association, one of the largest in the United States, had licensed two local jobbers in El Paso named Houck and Dieter as their exclusive distributors for that area. When the Texas antitrust law was passed, Busch canceled the exclusive agreement, claiming that to maintain it would violate the Texas law. This opened the door to competing distributors, which prompted Houck and Dieter to refuse to pay for their last shipment of beer. Busch sued the two for the price of the beer, thus putting the local distributors in the position of having to claim that the antitrust law was unconstitutional. There was more to the case than that, however. Evidence developed at trial that Houck and Dieter had leased all the beer-cooling capacity in El Paso and probably meant to corner the beer market in that city. Reuben Gaines had recently become chief justice when the case came up. Rather than presume that the nefarious design was in the larger company, Gaines focused on the statute, which was held to be constitutional. The case was remanded, with good sense: if the jury found that Anheuser-Busch had made the agreement with Houck and Dieter in furtherance of a scheme to restrict trade, then Busch could not recover. If the jury found, however, that Busch genuinely renounced the contract after learning of its antitrust implications, and was innocent of any design to restrict trade, then it could recover the price of the beer.

As had so often happened through its history, the Court balanced a stroke on the right with a stroke on the left. The conservative stroke had come two years earlier, when Gaines was still an associate justice. Texas's growing commerce and population had led to unprecedented growth in the insurance industry, and Gaines had to split some legal hairs to limit the scope of the new antitrust law to the transportation (read: railroad) and communication (read: telegraph) industries. It took nine typeset pages in *Texas Reports* to do it. Gaines noted that the case, *Queen Insurance Company v. State* (1893),[23] did not arise out of an action in which someone claimed harm; it was brought by the state attorney general to nullify an agreement among an association of fire insurance companies, which had met to standardize rates and commissions statewide. The state won at trial and in the civil appeals court before the insurance group took it to the Supreme Court. In his opinion, Gaines agreed that the deal was "possibly unenforceable among its members." Still, though perhaps somewhat suspect, the agreement to standardize rates "was not enjoinable by the public, nor a ground for forfeiting its members' franchises, since the business is not one in which the public has an interest as in that of a common carrier." The companies that the antitrust statute intended to regulate, wrote Gaines, either had power of eminent domain, or were dealers in commodities that were necessities of life, or engaged in a professional service to which the public was entitled. This combination of fire insurance companies might actually be detrimental to the public, and sound public policy might require its suppression, yet "the court cannot extend the rule merely by reason of their opinion as to what the law ought to be."[24] That was a political question, and the Court would interpret such statutes in the narrowest way; if the legislature meant to include the insurance industry in antitrust regulation, it would have to do so specifically.

In 1891, two years after passing the antitrust law, the legislature, under prodding from Governor Hogg, who had vigorously campaigned on this issue, and in response to a new amendment to the Constitution, created the Texas Railroad Commission. The railroads' well-documented rapacity in the land-grant game, and such practices as the charging of preferential rates to certain customers, merited scrutiny on their own, but during the 1880s the complexion of the industry had changed dramatically with the consolidation of the many state lines into the ownership of a handful of very powerful interests. Jay Gould came to control the Texas and Pacific, Katy, and International and Great Northern. Two other major players were the Southern Pacific and the Atchison, Topeka, and Santa Fe.

The railroads of course were quick to challenge any notion of state regulation. While the powers of the Texas Railroad Commission were limited in some cases, the overall legitimacy of the agency was upheld in 1894 in *Gulf, Colorado, and Santa Fe Railway Co. v. Eddins*.[25] There, the railroad had contended that for the state to presume to regulate railroads infringed on the interstate commerce powers of the federal government. A civil appeals court ruled otherwise, that "although state legislation may indirectly, incidentally, and remotely affect interstate commerce, it will not burden, regulate, and impede it."[26]

Three years later, Justice T. J. Brown reinforced that decision from the high court. In *Railroad Commission of Texas v. Houston and Central Texas Railway Co.*, it was apparent from the railroads' pleadings that they meant to gut the commission utterly, seeking a judgment affirming that its "rules and regulations are unreasonable, unfair, unjust, and unlawful, and that the same be canceled and held for naught . . . that the commission was and is without jurisdiction, power, or authority, under the constitution of this state, and the statute creating said commission . . . [be] set aside and annulled."[27] The Houston and Central actually won its case at trial, but when it reached the Third Court of Civil Appeals, that tribunal certified its questions and handed them up to the Supreme Court. Justice Brown was calm in his assurance that in individual cases of this nature, "courts will determine the question of the reasonableness and justice of any matter by the same rules as if it were an issue in other classes of suits."[28] Beyond that, the law creating the Texas Railroad Commission had provided for judicial review of its decisions; therefore, creating the commission could not be seen as the taking of private property without due process.

In finding ways to give effect to the populist sentiment of the people, the Texas Supreme Court stood in contrast to more conservative eastern state supreme courts, and to the federal Supreme Court, which buttressed the free-enterprise claims of the business community. One commentator noted a speech by Justice David Josiah Brewer of the U.S. Supreme Court in which he admonished the New York Bar Association to beware "the greedy hand of the many from filching from the few that which they have honestly acquired."[29] The Texas Court, rather, mirrored the stance of the state executive and legislature. It was part of the political cunning of Governor Jim Hogg, when confronted by the growing throng of populist support, to advocate enough reforms to attract more voters to the Democratic Party and thereby hamstring the Populist Party, but to steer clear of such radical reforms as would genuinely damage Texas business.

The Texas Supreme Court was able to find in the common law enough flexibility to provide relief for ordinary citizens who got trampled by big business, but was equally able to balance that endorsement of equity with self-restraint, deferring to the legislature to carry out the bulk of business regulation. No less than in the earliest days of the Supreme Court under T. J. Rusk, their discretion during those years of social upheaval preserved their judicial credibility.

ELEVEN

THE CONSENSUS COURT

J. G. Denman resigned from the Court on May 1, 1899, after serving five years and authoring 146 opinions. From private practice he came and to private practice he returned, still only forty-four years old, later to chair the board of the San Antonio National Bank. Replacing Denman was the highly experienced Frank Alvin Williams, the product of an antebellum Mississippi plantation.[1] Nine years old when the Civil War began, orphaned by sixteen and his way of life gone, Williams immigrated to Texas at twenty to live with his sister in Crockett. He read for the law with his brother-in-law, practiced for twelve years, and served as judge of the Third Judicial District for eight years, followed by seven years on the new civil appeals court in Galveston before Governor Joe Sayers tapped him for the Supreme Court.

Partly because the justices had preferred to do their own work and had not made use of the Commission of Appeals as they could have, and partly because a Texas emerging into the twentieth century generated an unprecedented mass of litigation, the Supreme Court had again fallen behind in its business. (As Justice Gaines once remarked to the deputy clerk, "There will be lots of cases pending before the Court when I am dead and gone, so why worry?")[2] In 1891 a constitutional amendment was ratified, to take effect the following year, overhauling the judicial system to provide the justices some relief whether they wanted it or not. To clarify the function of the Court of Appeals, it was renamed the Court of Criminal Appeals, and it maintained its appellate jurisdiction over all criminal cases. More importantly, the Commission of Appeals was abolished and replaced with an intermediate level of courts of civil appeals, which became the obligatory first avenues of recourse for those losing in district court. The intent was to save the Supreme Court's time by having it primarily decide conflicts among the civil appeals courts' rulings. Meeting in a special session in 1892, the legislature designated Fort

Worth, Austin, and Galveston as the cities to host the civil appeals courts, each with three justices. Dallas and San Antonio were added the following year, and Texarkana in 1907.[3] Gaines, however, was a hands-on justice, and as loath to relinquish oversight of the law to lower-level courts of appeal as he had been to refer questions to the Commission of Appeals. In the 1898 case of *Choate v. San Antonio and Aransas Pass Railway Co.*, the Court expanded its jurisdiction in ruling that while the weight to be given to evidence was a question of fact for the jury, whether there *was* any evidence was a question of law that the Supreme Court could review from the courts of appeals.[4]

Three justices on each appellate bench was felt to be the optimal number.[5] To seat more would increase the cost of maintaining the court, and differing points of view would become redundant when three were just as likely to provide, or at least understand, the possible points of view in a case. Collegiality was also a consideration, and with the Supreme Court as a functioning example, three would have been a hard number on which to improve. Indeed, especially after Denman resigned and was replaced by Williams, the Court composed of Gaines, T. J. Brown, and Williams entered a period of stability, with no personnel changes for almost twelve years. And their amicable working relationship was such that the "Capitol Court" gained a new sobriquet: the "Consensus Court." In that whole span of time, stretching across a dozen volumes of *Texas Reports*, there were filed a grand total of only six dissents: one by Gaines, two by Williams, and three by Brown.[6] And this was at a time when the increasing complexity of the law and the increasing sophistry of argument gave every opportunity for the three to disagree.

When one of them did dissent, it was almost with regret. Such was the tone of T. J. Brown's disagreement with the ruling in the "Smallpox Case" arising in Greenville in 1903.[7] The Katy Railroad maintained a hospital there for its employees. A surgeon at the hospital employed a nurse who, in caring for an employee with smallpox, went out in public without disinfecting himself. Local resident W. A. Freeman caught the disease and died. His widow, Annie Freeman, sued the Katy for negligence and won at trial. Although by now the railroads might have felt that going to the Supreme Court was a fool's errand, Gaines found that a statute in question had eliminated the doctrine of *respondeat superior* (by which an employer could be held responsible for the bad acts of an employee) from the case, and with Williams's agreement, reversed the decision.

"A careful study of the opinion of the majority," wrote Brown in his dissent, "has not brought my mind to a concurrence with the forcible reasoning of my associates." The five-and-a-half typeset pages of his exposition, however, make clear the depth of his consternation at the majority holding, opining that it "applies to a remedial statute the most rigid rule of construction, thereby limiting the liability instead of promoting the remedy."[8]

No doubt much of the collegial tone of the Court was set by Chief Justice Gaines. His open-mindedness was evinced when Frank Williams, the relative newcomer, filed in 1908 the era's only recorded concurring opinion (that is, agreeing in the end result of the case, but not necessarily in its scope or logic).[9] A Cooke County farmer named John Reasor lived on a homestead of ninety acres, and over time purchased tracts of twenty-nine, ten, and two acres, all within a mile of his own farm. He leased the tracts out to sharecroppers, using his share of the produce to support his family. When Reasor died broke, the smaller tracts were sold to pay his debts, but when his minor children came of age, they sued to recover them on the claim that the homestead extended to all. Gaines and Brown were convinced; Williams was not. The other justices agreed to a rehearing, and were subsequently converted to Williams's point of view.[10] A rehearing was a rarity for Gaines.[11] With a strong dislike for dictation, he wrote out his own opinions in legible longhand, limiting each one to six pages, which required him to refine his thinking before ever touching pen to paper. He seldom changed his mind, and to do so for Williams showed great deference.

The format of their conferences was simple: in considering a writ of error, Gaines would read the opinion from the court of appeals, although he did so in a fast, scholarly mumble. Brown was hard of hearing, and deputy clerk H. L. Clamp would repeat the text for him into an Acousticon hearing aid. Williams would read the application for the writ, and in the minority of cases in which an error was found in the court below, they would agree to hear arguments.[12]

Gaines and Williams became warm friends; both were outdoorsmen and frequently went on hunting and fishing trips, often with court clerk Fred Connerly, deputy clerk Clamp, and never without Old Alex, the Court porter who became the camp cook. Gaines sometimes forgot to pack his gun, but never failed to remember the case of beer. T. J. Brown was more straitlaced, a Sunday-school teacher with a large following in the Christian Church. Only occasionally would he go roughing it with Gaines and Williams; on one occasion they set out in pleasant weather, but were overtaken by a storm and got a frigid soaking without benefit of a tent. Seeing Brown sitting miserably on a flat rock to avoid sitting on the wet ground, Connerly offered him a tin cup of whiskey. Brown, who was a prohibitionist, refused at first, but relented after he started shaking. "Circumstances," he declared, "alters cases." According to Clamp, Brown seemed to enjoy his experiment with alcohol and became quite jolly and talkative.[13]

Justice Gaines was a man of regular habits off the bench as well as on, summoning the porter to bring him his street shoes every afternoon at five (he always wore carpet slippers while working), and telephoning Weed's Stable (the number was 223) to send his horse and buggy to the front of the Capitol at 5:15 for his daily drive. Often he was accompanied by Clamp, whom he regaled with law stories as they took in the fresh air. Gaines was an odd duck of a chief justice, a whittler and a storyteller who would lounge about the clerks' office in a great rocking chair, convulsing them with tales but never laughing at his own jokes. After work and his drive, he would repair to the Austin Club, watching keenly the rivalries between the clerks over the billiard tables, but never playing. Late at night he would retire to his rooms in the McDonald Building, where he lived with his wife Louisa. No shrinking violet herself, she sometimes resented being left alone. Once she locked him out, and when he knocked she cracked the door and whispered, "Is that you, John?" After exploding, "Who in the hell is John?" he took her point and later enjoyed telling that story on himself.

He could meet great adversity with equanimity, but if a gust of wind blew his hat off, he could erupt into a fierce torrent. He hated being surprised. One story became a legend at Austin's Driskill Hotel. Gaines sometimes reserved the hotel's large dining room to host dignitaries for dinner, and on this occasion had ordered a turkey. He rose to carve it, a task that he always appropriated to himself, as he considered no one could do better than he. While Gaines stood, the waiter pulled his chair back to give him more room, but neglected to replace it. The carving done, Gaines seated himself grandly in the nonexistent chair and crashed to the floor, grabbing the tablecloth on his way down and upsetting the entire feast. Seizing the carving knife, he chased the waiter out of the room, down the stairs, and, by one account, down the street. Back in the dining room, he took his seat and resumed gracious conversation as though nothing had happened.[14]

In the Court's conference room such outbursts sometimes took the form of throwing books or inkwells, at which Brown and Williams would flee to their own chambers. After Gaines calmed down, the porter would say, "Jedge, if you is through with your tantrum, I will pick up things and call the other Jedges."[15]

At home in Clarksville, in northeast Texas, Gaines had been a mainstay of Democratic politics, elected twice as district judge, but when he became a justice he abandoned political pursuits entirely. T. J. Brown could not have been more different in that regard. As a two-term legislator who was in the vanguard of the reform movement, he relished politics and remained well connected, and he kept the clerks busy as he dictated long letters to such political operatives as Colonel E. M. House, who engineered the election of two Texas governors before turning his attention to Woodrow Wilson. Gaines, for all his joie de vivre, was quiet and unassuming; Brown was a fiery stump speaker. Gaines enjoyed the creature comforts; Brown was a spartan, a believer in a cold bath and vigorous walk before breakfast. Gaines had his daily constitutional in his buggy; Brown would walk with his long staff from his house at Fourteenth Street and San Antonio as far as the Insane Asylum west of Hyde Park, where he would sometimes stop to chat with the patients.[16]

There were important points of sympathy among the three justices. Gaines and Brown were former Confederate rebels; Williams was from a Mississippi planter family but had been too young to fight in the war. Gaines had Louisa and one daughter; Williams and his wife Laura had five children. Brown, laid low by the death of his wife Louise (with whom he had seven children), prevailed on deputy clerk Clamp and his wife to move into his spacious house with him and his daughter. Williams probably had the best legal recall of the three; sometimes during their conferences he would reach for a volume of reported cases and turn to the page he wanted without needing a citation to find it. (Not surprisingly, Williams was a master of puzzles. He bought a newspaper each day from Joe, the vendor, and gave only a cursory glance at the news before attacking and quickly defeating the crossword puzzle).[17] Like Gaines, he wrote out his opinions rather than dictating them, but became temperamental when quizzed about his illegible hand, leaving Clamp to decipher his scrawl as best he could.[18]

The Consensus Court was an eccentric trio to preserve the unique judicial legacy that Texas had nurtured for the previous sixty years, especially as discontented women started pressing for more rights. Texas women had long enjoyed a more elevated status before the law than that of women in states without a civil law heritage. Two generations of blending the civil law's regard for women with the common law view of marriage, however, had confused that stature. There was a degree to which Texas women had come to suffer the "disabilities of coverture," which meant that single women were better off before the law than married women. To an extent, Texas wives' identities were merged with those of their husbands; although a wife might leave a marriage with her own property and a share of the community property, the husband possessed the lion's share of power during the marriage.[19]

During the years of the Gaines Court, plaintiffs sought new and ingenious ways of getting to the assets of married women, and Texas courts were sometimes compelled to exercise some creativity in order to protect them. Some efforts reached only as high as the courts of appeals, and the Supreme Court, its main job now defined as refereeing inconsistencies among the proliferating courts of civil appeals, let those opinions speak for it. In *Anderson v. Neighbors* (1901), the judiciary turned back an effort to declare that married women, because their identities under the common law merged with their husbands', could not be "persons" for the purpose of buying school land. In this case, not surprisingly, someone was trying to take an unfair advantage. Mrs. J. H. Anderson had bought land in Pecos County from the state five years before, and had made valuable improvements. The suit was brought by one E. B. Neighbors, a potential lessee, who, if Mrs. Anderson had been ruled ineligible to make the purchase, stood to gain the use of the improvements. The decision confirmed that Texas wives had rights "as absolute as those of their husbands" to acquire and hold property.[20]

However, when another plaintiff relied on a wife's legal independence in an attempt to seize her assets to satisfy a debt she had contracted on behalf of her husband, another appeals court dipped into the common law just enough to protect her. Mrs. Elmira Ewalt contracted the services of Mrs. Chidgey, a nurse, to care for her dying husband, who ran up a bill of $160 before he expired on the first day of the twentieth century. Mrs. Chidgey also briefly nursed Mrs. Ewalt in her last illness, thereby increasing the latter's indebtedness a further $15 before she too died. Seeking to recoup her just due, Mrs. Chidgey sued the Ewalts' executor, J. B. Flannery, for $175 from Elmira Ewalt's estate.[21] It had long been established that a Texas wife possessed a narrowly construed right to make contracts necessary to look after her own welfare and that of her children, but in *Flannery* the Court declined to extend that right to contract care for her husband. One commentator found the ruling positive insofar as it shielded Mrs. Ewalt from the debt she undertook, but noted the corollary disincentive for businesses to cooperate with a wife trying to provide care for her spouse.[22] Ultimately, justice was served when Mrs. Chidgey was allowed to recover $160 from the Ewalts' community property under the theory of an implied contract.

Thus, as a general proposition, the Texas wife was compensated, after a fashion, for giving up the legal advantages of spinsterhood by being doubly protected: if she were party to a note or contract without her husband's knowledge, the deal was not enforceable against her, the same as though she were a minor or a mental incompetent; and if she did so with his permission, she was held to be his agent, and her personal property was not at risk in a judgment. In fact, the cases in which that principle was clarified illustrated just how completely a man could be left holding the bag. In one, decided in 1907, Mrs. M. J. Richburg signed two notes, of $272.65 and $272.70, to set her two sons up in business. She made one $75 payment before defaulting. Her lender, one Sherwood, expected her sons to pay him from the proceeds of their businesses, but according to Justice Brown, Sherwood knew of Mrs. Richburg's status when he lent her the money, and so was out of luck.[23] In the other case, Mary Edwards, acting for herself and as agent for her husband H. L. Edwards, and as attorney in fact for one Helen Cooper, hired an architect named Annan to design a two-story building for the improvement of their lot in El Paso. When Mrs. Edwards was able to pay only $15 toward the fee, Cooper claimed that she knew nothing of the deal, and Mrs. Edwards pleaded her coverture, and so her husband was stuck with the tab, as a court of appeals ruled in 1910.[24]

Not all such cases worked to the benefit of wily women who could play the angles. Inevitably there were unscrupulous husbands who sought to take advantage of their wives' lack of legal competency. This was a matter on which the Gaines Court spoke in 1903 when one particular cad of a husband named Dority gave himself a comfortable living from his wife's property while making no provision for her upkeep. Helen Dority was in ill health, but supported herself with a poultry business and dairy cows, which were her separate property. Her husband B. P. Dority was hale, a wheelwright, but lazy and venal. Not only had he contributed nothing to his wife's support for the two years before the trial, but he had also leased out and lived on the income from her ranch, since, as the husband, he had the governance of her separate property while in the marriage. After twenty-six years of marriage, Mrs. Dority sued for divorce, which was granted by the district court but reversed by the civil appeals court, which ruled that there were no grounds for divorce.

In *Dority v. Dority* (1903), the Supreme Court's ruling, so far from merging her person in his, fell like a blade to cut him off from her property, and affirmed her right to manage her own affairs. Reluctantly, Justice Williams hinted that he had to create some law to reach his result, that the cases he cited "may not wholly apply to a case like this," but they do "affirm the principle that his right of management is dependent upon the discharge of duties which go hand in hand with that right."[25]

Another cad of a husband was the cause of an exception being carved out of the rule of spousal privilege, the doctrine that communications between a husband and wife could not be used as evidence. After the couple divorced, the husband alleged that he had contracted a venereal disease from his wife, and she sued him for slander. She had actually caught the malady from him, but the trial court disallowed her testimony on the grounds of spousal privilege. His confessing to having an infection, if he had done so, was communicated during the marriage and was not admissible. It took a court of appeals in 1901 to set the matter straight: in the case of a husband's injury to a wife, spousal privilege would not apply.[26]

A similar disability of the marriage coverture doctrine stated, as a general proposition, that a wife could not bring a lawsuit without her husband's joining in it. In 1893 the legislature passed a statute allowing a wife whose husband was a drunk to serve formal notice to vendors not to sell liquor to him, on pain of having their bond revoked.[27] When Mrs. Kate Tipton failed to get a saloon dealer, R. F. Wright, to stop selling alcohol to her husband after she gave the statutory notice, she filed an action to revoke the vendor's bond. In defense, the vendor maintained that Mrs. Tipton, being a mere wife, could not bring the action without her husband—the drunkard—joining in it. On these facts, the Court in 1898 had no difficulty extending legal competency to Mrs. Tipton as a necessary extension of the law. To hold otherwise would render the statute "a farce, and unworthy of any legislative body."[28]

In cases in which someone other than the husband falsely disparaged a woman's virtue, the Consensus Court was chivalrous enough to finally make them actionable, which up to that time the Court had not been. Once again it was a little bit of a reach. T. J. Brown wrote in *Hatcher v. Range* (1904) that previous decisions of the Court "were reluctant to follow precedents so unreasonable and unjust," but conceded that "we are equally bound by those precedents, unless there be present in this case a sound reason why they should be disregarded." This reason he found in an 1879 statute that placed slander on the same legal footing as libel, a law that had been previously overlooked, and that provided the basis for a new rule. "We therefore conclude that under the law as it now exists in this State, words spoken or written which 'falsely and maliciously' . . . impute to a female want of chastity are actionable, without showing special damages therefrom."[29]

At the turn of the nineteenth century into the twentieth the rights of Texas married women before the law were in active ferment in the legislature as well. A variety of bills had been introduced in 1897 that aimed to lessen the "disability of coverture," but they failed to pass.[30] Opposition gradually eroded, and in 1911 the legislature passed a statute allowing a wife to be declared single for the purpose of going into business.[31] Also in that year, some of Texas's small rank of professional women undertook a campaign to gain control of their assets during marriage. They were led by Hortense Sparks Ward, who in 1910 had become the first woman to pass the state bar exam. In a trumpet blast of a pamphlet, she complained that for women to reacquire their property after a marriage ended (and she was a divorcée) was not good enough. A husband, she wrote, "may even mortgage or sell every piece of furniture in the home, and she is helpless to prevent [it], even if her earnings have paid for every piece. He has a right to sell her dresses if he sees fit."[32] In 1913 the legislature succumbed to her relentless bulldogging and passed the Married Woman's Property Rights Law, finally giving Texas wives exclusive control of their separate property during marriage.[33]

In addition to empowering a wife to preserve the integrity of her home, the Court not surprisingly also strengthened the rights of a mother in the raising of her children. The dispute arose in the case of Alice Dillard, an impoverished widow who was reduced to moving in with an uncle, who agreed to keep her, but required her to find another home for her son, Austin. Pressed by circumstances, she gave the boy into the care of foster parents Daniel Deaton and his wife, who could better provide for him, on the promise that she would not change her mind and require his return. Within a few years she remarried and now as Alice Wood found her station in life much improved. With her husband, she sued to have Austin returned to her, but lost both at trial and in the civil appeals court. The couple then brought a habeas corpus action to the Supreme Court.[34] Through T. J. Brown, the justices in 1900 conceded that the Deatons had grown attached to the boy, and that his "interest would be as well, if not better, subserved by remaining" in their possession. However, concluded Brown, "God, in His wisdom, has placed upon the father and mother the obligation to nurture, educate, protect and guide their offspring, and has qualified them . . . by writing in their hearts sentiments of affection and establishing between them and their children ties which cannot exist between the children and any other persons."[35] To leave Austin in the care of the Deatons would require establishing greater unfitness on the part of Alice Wood than had been shown.

The Consensus Court and its immediate predecessor (the Gaines-Brown-Denman Court) also worked to vindicate that other great feature of Texans' domestic security, the homestead exemption. Texas had shielded homesteads from seizure for debt for two generations, but still came plaintiffs with new theories and new arguments attempting to chip away at it. The justices in the main continued to protect this icon of Texas's unique jurisprudence, and on those rare occasions when they let themselves be led astray, they proved capable of repentance.

This exemption had never, of course, extended to protection from the government. Homesteads could still be seized for tax delinquency, so it was probably inevitable that local authorities would push to extend the definition of "taxes" in order to broaden the circumstances in which a homestead could be taken. As far back as *Higgins v. Bordages* (1895), the Court had found it necessary to revisit the matter da capo, from the beginning, in order to overrule one of its own mistakes.[36] The City of Beaumont required certain residents either to construct sidewalks on their properties, or be assessed a fee for the city to do it. Henry and Mary Higgins paid little mind to the directive, and the city laid the sidewalk along their lot and billed them the twenty-dollar fee, which they declined to pay. The city seized their lot, which was their homestead and was worth some six hundred dollars, and sold it to one Bordages for thirty-five dollars.

It was T. J. Brown who authored the lecture this time: "The Constitution of this State . . . has in such plain and unmistakable language defined and limited the liability of homesteads to forced sale that no department of the State government can disregard it. From the inception of homestead exemptions in this State, the changes have been in the direction of larger exemptions and more perfect protection."[37] The Court's expansive interpretation, Brown noted, had been endorsed by the succession of constitutional conventions: "Whether it is good or bad policy is not a question for the courts. The Constitution is paramount, and must be observed and enforced."[38]

In the present case, the property was seized for delinquency of "assessments for local improvements." The city had not argued that the "assessment" was a tax either general or special, but contended that its forced collection was as appropriate as if it had been an actual tax. Brown disagreed: "Our courts have held that such assessments are not included" in any definition of a general tax, and lacked the specific purpose needed to regard it as a special tax. The remarkable aspect of *Higgins* was that in it, Brown forcefully overruled the Court's previous decision in *Lufkin v. City of Galveston* (1885), which the Court now found to be "directly antagonistic to the express provisions of the Constitution of this State . . . in antagonism to a long line of decisions of our own courts upon kindred questions."[39]

A Supreme Court cannot do much more to apologize for a previous lapse in judgment, but having done so, the Court almost immediately refined the holding in *Higgins* to mitigate the damage that its judicial waffling had caused. In *Storrie v. Cortes* (1896), the Court ruled that a contractor who had relied on *Lufkin* before it was overturned could seek a civil judgment against a property owner who balked at paying his share of the cost of improvements; he simply could not seize his homestead.[40]

While the Consensus Court generally acted in continuity with the long Texas heritage in the realms of women's rights and the sanctity of the homestead, there was one area in which it broke with tradition. One of the earliest ways, dating back to 1731, that Texas had straightened the road to justice was in its use of simplified pleadings. By long practice, defendants who claimed that third parties were liable to them in a proceeding were allowed to bring them into a suit as a way of avoiding multiple actions. In *United States Fidelity & Guaranty Co. v. Fossati* (1904), the Court disallowed the practice, a stance that generated historical criticism.[41] Charles T. McCormick, who was later dean of the University of Texas Law School (1940–1949), went so far as to write that this new direction "showed a tendency to narrow and restrict rather than to develop and extend these liberal Texas procedural institutions," and worked against the tradition that "exalts the purpose above the letter, the substance above the form."[42] The hindrances thrown down by *Fossati* and similar cases were smoothed out by statute in 1919.

In 1900 the Court found itself taking on a case concerning the freedom of religion.[43] This was a realm of conflict usually litigated in the federal courts, but as it involved a contest over property ownership, it wound up on the state docket. The late nineteenth and early twentieth centuries were a time of active religious ferment in Texas. The Methodist Church, which in former years had been evangelical and vociferous, settled more onto a back bench, surrendering the active chase of souls to the Baptists. Other denominations, such as the Church of Christ, were even more vocal in their claim to be the only narrow road to salvation, and whole new denominations such as the Nazarenes and Seventh-day Adventists were founded in or centered in Texas, and all competed gamely for converts. The Baptists, whose traditional theology allowed individuals freedom of conscience, had been dividing and subdividing for decades over doctrinal disagreements.

When the Baptist Church of Paris, Texas, was founded in April 1861, subscribed with contributions from a number of citizens in the community, it aligned itself with the New Hampshire Articles of Faith. Over time, however, the religious sentiment of the majority modified, and when they publicly professed a competing confession, the minority who held to the New Hampshire Confession sued for ownership of the church building, claiming to be the true Paris Baptist Church.

The Court, through Justice Brown, was reluctant to get involved: "Courts cannot decide between conflicting opinions upon theological questions."[44] To do so in this instance would require the Court to divine the intentions of those who had supported the founding of the institution. If the plaintiffs prevailed, the church would "be deprived of the power to change or modify that declaration . . . and to change it would not only forfeit their rights in the property, but would deprive them absolutely of their membership in good standing in the church, which, to a Christian, was of greater value than houses or land."[45] In awarding the church property to the majority who had changed their confession, Brown noted the "common knowledge that in this country houses of religious worship are usually built by subscription" from across the spectrum of the community, and it would become an "absurdity" to suppose that the Methodist or Jew who contributed to erecting the church had any preference for the specific confession of the members.[46]

By 1911 the justices of the Consensus Court had worked together hard and amiably for more than a decade. Reuben Gaines was seventy-five and, for all his clocklike regularity, tiring. Brown was the same age, hearing cases through his Acousticon and supporting himself on his great staff when he walked. Williams was only sixty, but increasingly vociferous in his dissatisfaction over their pay. Importantly presaged by Stayton, the Gaines Court had escorted Texas from the frontier into the industrial age with wisdom, discretion, and impeccable judicial temperament. How fast it would fall apart.

TWELVE

THE WRENCH IN THE GEARS

The Consensus Court's decade of amicable productivity spent some of its last capital upholding the constitutionality of the Texas Railroad Commission and its rulings. Whereas a few years earlier, the Court had let stand the *Eddins* case, holding that the commission violated no federal prerogatives, now it held the agency equally good against a claim that it violated the state constitution's mandate that a bill's purpose be stated in its name.[1] In 1905, in *International and Great Northern Railroad Company v. Railroad Commission of Texas*, the Court conceded that the commission's right "to correct abuses" was not specified in the title of the bill, and that the language in question was capable of two constructions, one constitutional and one not—in which case the rule was to read it in the permissible way.[2] However, in looking at the power granted to the commission to remedy extortion and discrimination and to set rates, the Court concluded that the purpose of the law creating the Railroad Commission was reasonably clear from its title and therefore constitutionally sound.

With a similar touch of creativity, the Court ruled in 1907 that a state tax on the railroads did not take their property without due process of law.[3] This was achieved by holding that the tax, while *equal* to 1 percent of their gross receipts, was not actually a tax *on* their receipts, but rather an excise tax for the privilege of doing business. The rail line pressed its point, as zealously as railroads typically had, that a state excise tax could not be levied on interstate commerce. The Court held, however, that the 1 percent tax on gross receipts was only a measure to determine the amount of excise tax to be levied for doing business within the state. The railroads were still a long way from being out of arguments—claiming, for instance, that a law requiring a state tax board to assess a valuation of intangible assets violated the constitution because that document mandated that railroad assets be valued by each county tax assessor. The Court calmly pointed out, again in 1907, that intangible assets, obviously, were not located in any one county, but that did not immunize them from taxation.[4]

Occasionally the railroads won a round, as when the Texas and Pacific Railway Company escaped paying a Texas franchise tax by virtue of its charter's having been issued by the Congress of the United States.[5] The Court also decided in favor of a line whose intangible assets were taxed at a rate higher than that imposed on other businesses in the county.[6] But in the main, the Consensus Court closed out its era by maintaining its strict but not unreasonable holdings on the right of the state to tax and regulate the large railroad companies, whose behavior, if given their will, would have reverted to the excesses of the most predatory days of the Gilded Age.

The Texas Court also began to make itself felt in a completely new field of law, one that would only grow in importance in the decades to come. The Industrial Age had since its beginning been powered by coal. Until the middle of the nineteenth century, lamps were fueled largely by whale oil, and then by kerosene, a derivative obtained by refining crude petroleum. The presence of oil in East Texas had been known ever since Spanish ships put in and caulked their seams with tar from coastal seeps. In Corsicana in 1894, drillers trying to reach an aquifer to augment the municipal water supply kept striking oil instead, and had to cap the wells—only to see petroleum leaking out of the ground around the pipes. Commercial interest in Texas oil led to production of about 66,000 barrels in 1897.[7] This glut nearly wrecked the fledgling business, however, since there was not yet a way to process the crude in state. Construction of the first Texas refinery, which turned out profitable amounts of gasoline and kerosene, pointed to a future of vast wealth.

In southeast Texas, at Spindletop Hill near Beaumont, an eccentric brickmaker and girls' Sunday-school teacher named Pattillo Higgins had suffered years of derision for nursing his pet theory that oil would pool beneath geologic features known as salt domes, of which Spindletop was one. He was vindicated on the tenth day of the new century, January 10, 1901: the ground shook, pipe began shooting out of the bore hole, and a geyser of crude oil blew the crosspiece from the top of the derrick.[8] Texas tea had arrived, American industry would never be the same, and Texas wildcatters, investors, landowners, refiners, pipeline operators, and everyone else involved in the new bonanza would begin suing each other like mad. Oil and gas as a legal discipline came on the scene, and the oil patch fell heir to all the sophistry perfected by railroad lawyers over the preceding thirty years to obtain advantageous business positions.

As acknowledged by oil and gas law authority A. W. Walker, Jr., petroleum was "a species of property that had hitherto seldom been the subject of judicial notice," which led to judicial improvisation: "In the absence of controlling precedent . . . the courts at first attempted by analogy to pigeon-hole oil and gas under the category of some other type of property which, in the court's mind, it seemed most to resemble."[9] Was oil a static mineral, for instance, like iron ore or gold, or, being liquid, did it flow underground in streams? Actually a field of oil is static until punctured by a well, when it then begins flowing toward that well, perhaps away from the property of a neighbor who wanted the oil under his ground for himself. One of the first solutions enunciated, with disastrous implications for any goal of conservation, was that a landowner losing oil from beneath his own ground and up a neighbor's well should seek relief by drilling his own well and getting the oil first! In 1921, one Texas court was reduced to speculating whether petroleum deposits did not have a "fugitive nature, since they are supposed to percolate restlessly about under the surface of the earth, even as the birds fly from field to field."[10]

"A better understanding of the nature of oil and gas," wrote Walker, "soon revealed that in many respects oil and gas was a species of property unique unto itself, and that rules of law that worked very well when applied to other species of property were wholly inadequate and unjust in their operation when applied to oil and gas."[11] All the Court needed to do was to import a resident expert in the field to guide the justices through the strange new cases.

The Consensus Court began to unravel with the resignation of the picturesque Reuben Gaines on January 5, 1911. He was seventy-four and in declining health, and after suffering a slight stroke he retired to his wife Louisa, in whose company he survived another three years before succumbing to a larger stroke. One of the most significant of Texas justices, Gaines left a legacy of hundreds of opinions from his twenty-four years on the Court, which, as a group, ushered Texas from the frontier into the twentieth century. It was a career carried out with courtly demeanor—setting aside the incident of chasing that Driskill waiter with the carving knife—and he prided himself on his lack of party fervor. In fact, during his years on the bench it was said that he never gave a political speech, in his own behalf or that of another.[12] It therefore seems ironic that the timing of his retirement should have excited any comment. But his resignation came just weeks before Governor Tom Campbell would be replaced by governor-elect Oscar Colquitt, thus allowing Campbell to name the next justice. Campbell was a prohibitionist; Colquitt was ardently opposed. By 1911, no corner of social discourse in Texas remained unsinged by the firestorm over whether to outlaw alcohol.[13]

Justice Gaines was said to never forget to take a case of beer on his hunting trips, but he was too much a judge to have expressed his views publicly on a subject that might come before the Court in controversy. The public debate over prohibition, however, was pervasive. The movement had its roots in the whiskey-soaked history of the West, including Texas.[14] On the frontier, most towns had multiple saloons before they had a church; at U.S. Army posts, unfitness for duty owing to alcohol might number half the soldiers on any given day. There was a reason that Texas had passed the statute allowing wives to give notice to barkeepers not to serve their husbands. It was beyond question that families had suffered, wives been beaten, and children been neglected. The fact that Texas was rapidly industrializing tended to concentrate the evils of alcohol in, if anything, a more urban and visible environment.

The effort to dry out the populace began quite early in Texas history, with proselytizing by the Women's Christian Temperance Union, which distributed the pledge to "taste not, touch not, and handle not" the demonic spirits.[15] Political efforts, however, met with resounding defeats. A referendum for statewide compulsory prohibition, which got on the ballot in 1887, was beaten by ninety thousand votes. The "dry" forces then turned to intensive local organizing, winning passage of an amendment in 1891 that allowed the local option within subdivisions of counties, which meant that voters in a precinct could decide whether the town would be wet or dry. Squeezed between hotly competing wet and dry lobbies, the legislature ignored petitions sent it from 1908 to 1910 to place a statewide prohibition amendment on the ballot. In 1910, Colquitt, an avowed wet (the drys alleged that his middle initial, B, stood for Budweiser), won the governorship with a plurality, but not a majority of votes. By the year that Justice Gaines retired, 1911, Texas was sharply divided between dry counties in the fundamentalist Protestant north and east, wet counties in the Hispanic south and German west, and the south-central and urban areas fighting out a crazy quilt of wet and dry precincts within each county.[16] A statewide prohibition amendment finally appeared on the ballot that year; it saw the largest turnout of voters ever in Texas up to that time, 468,000, and the measure was defeated by about 6,000, with signs of voting manipulation across the board. Political tempers in Texas at the time Justice Gaines retired approached the boiling point.

Gaines had just suffered a stroke, and it seems likely that he did not give the political ramifications of a Court vacancy any thought. But his leaving set off a chain of events that saw his beloved Court become highly politicized, and saw nine different men come and go from the high bench in the following decade. The venerable T. J. Brown, Diogenes with his lamplit shepherd's crook, was elevated to replace Gaines as chief, and Governor Campbell appointed William F. Ramsey as associate justice to bring the Court back up to strength. It was a lateral move from the Court of Criminal Appeals, which gave Ramsey's résumé a unique aspect, for no one else had ever occupied a seat on both benches. He was fifty-six, a longtime lawyer and banker from Johnson County, raised in Alvarado and maintaining a prominent law practice in Cleburne. He had had no judicial experience when appointed to the Court of Criminal Appeals, but he had spent a year as board chairman of the Prison Commission. His main qualification for the Supreme Court was his long association with Campbell, with whom he shared the prohibitionist passion.[17]

Once the façade of the Consensus Court cracked, it fell quickly. Frank Williams was next to leave, resigning only two and a half months after Gaines retired. Williams had sent signals to the legislature that four thousand dollars a year was not enough compensation for justices of the Supreme Court. He, at least, could not live on that, and suggested six thousand as more appropriate. The legislature failed to heed his warning, and Williams made good on his threat to leave.[18] The newly installed Governor Oscar B. Colquitt replaced him with Joseph B. Dibrell of Seguin, a onetime schoolteacher who had served his district for eight years in the Texas Senate and risen to president pro tempore. In Austin, Dibrell was also known for his socially prominent wife, Ella. His first wife and the mother of their four children had died in 1898; Ella bore him three more, and was an early leader in Austin's arts scene. She was a founder of the Texas Fine Arts Association, and when the great German-American sculptor Elisabet Ney died in 1908, Ella purchased Formosa, Ney's home and studio in Hyde Park, as a memorial and museum.[19] Deputy clerk H. L. Clamp found Dibrell kind and affable: "He possessed a clean mind and I never heard him speak an unkind word against any one, nor tell an obscene joke."[20]

Whether it was because the times were felt to be changing too fast, or because of the new chemistry among justices distracted by the brawl over prohibition, traditional areas of Texas jurisprudence did not enjoy the nurturing that they had had under previous tenures. The new Court proved less willing to craft reasonable justice for wives when a strict observance of their legal disabilities could lead to an absurd conclusion. In 1913 it let stand a civil appeals court ruling that a murdered wife's heirs could not bring a wrongful death action against her husband. A wife could divorce her husband for cruelty, but spouses could not sue each other for torts, including assault. Had she survived, she could have divorced him, but could not have recovered for the assault; therefore, her heirs were not given any greater standing than she would have had.[21]

Fortunately for their advancement, however, women had come to enjoy increasing statutory protection, thanks to the constant pressure of suffragists such as Hortense Sparks Ward. In 1911 they had won the right to go to court and have their disabilities of coverture removed so that they could go into business; in 1913 they were granted a share in the management of their community property. In 1915 a new statute declared a wife's legal recovery for injuries to be her separate property, and in 1917 income from her separate property was declared to be separate property.[22] Since the legislature met only every two years, women's progress was very steady indeed. It was not altogether surprising, however, since the movement for the advancement of women, who were so often the victims of drunken husbands, had planted itself firmly within the prohibition camp, which was ascendant in the legislature. Dry lawmakers needed every ally they could muster, even women for whose cause they might otherwise not have been overly sympathetic.

Ramsey had soon found himself to be more committed as a prohibitionist than as a member of the Supreme Court. Thinking that he would be more effective as a dry governor than a dry justice, he resigned in March 1912 after only fourteen months on the Court, determined to topple Budweiser Colquitt. "We here in the office," recalled deputy clerk Clamp, "and many others elsewhere, tried to persuade him not to make the race, but to no avail."[23] Ramsey ran hard against Colquitt and alcohol in the Democratic primary, but failed badly, after which he moved to Dallas and entered private practice with his son. With the dry Ramsey off the bench, this time Colquitt put a wet in the chair more partisan than Dibrell. The new vacancy he filled with Nelson Phillips of Hillsboro; he had some judicial experience (two years as judge of the Eighteenth Judicial District) and had served as chairman of the 1910 state Democratic convention. Phillips had shared a speaking podium with Colquitt at wet rallies in years past and had appeared as counsel at the side of dry leaders when vindictive wets in the legislature held Inquisition-like hearings on the failure of the 1911 prohibition amendment.[24] Phillips also represented a changing of the guard on the Supreme Court. He was a native Texan, which was still unusual on that bench, and he was born in 1873, too young to remember the Civil War or even Reconstruction. He was studious; people in Hillsboro remembered that in his youth he would use the lamps in the county courthouse to study late into the nights.[25] Though not yet forty, he had transcended those Texas roots in a number of ways: his clothes were tailored in London, he was an equestrian who preferred the English riding saddle, and he raised Great Danes.[26] He told good stories, loved a fine cigar, and respected his new office deeply. One change Phillips brought to the Court was that he had deputy clerk Clamp organize a tennis club. Clamp had two courts laid out on a nearby vacant lot, and about fifteen men in the Court's circle used them hard. Phillips was probably the best player, but he was given competition by first assistant attorney general G. B. Smedley and prominent Austin lawyer Charlie Black.[27]

William Ramsey's seat was up for reelection at the time he resigned to run for governor in 1912, so Phillips, as a wet and a Colquitt ally, had to instantly defend his chair from an onslaught of prohibitionists, including civil appeals judges Ocie Speer and R. A. Pleasants, and the righteous Baptist dean of the University of Texas Law School, John C. Townes.[28] Dividing their forces worked against the drys; Phillips retained his seat even though he received only 30 percent of the fractured vote.[29] Over the next decade, he crafted a respected niche for himself in real estate law and the statute of frauds, but especially in mineral law, where he interpreted the constitution to allow the state to reserve mineral rights on land that it sold, a decision that ultimately resulted in vast state revenue.[30]

The drys were not done yet, however, for Dibrell's chair was also up for contest. (In fact, by an accident of the calendar and the recent resignations, all three seats on the Supreme Court were in play that year, but no one dared challenge the legendary chief T. J. Brown.) Although he had served a long stint in the state Senate, Dibrell was of the old school, and thought it undignified for a justice to get out and electioneer for his job. Indeed, under the 1876 Constitution, by which justices were elected by the people, no one had ever had the effrontery to oppose a sitting justice for his seat in a primary contest.

The bitter and growing social schism over alcohol, however, shattered that decorum. In the 1912 primary, Dibrell found himself opposed by a prohibitionist zealot who relished campaigning, William E. Hawkins. Fifty years old, a Louisiana native and a minister's son, Hawkins had attended the forerunner of Tulane University before graduating from Southwestern University in Georgetown, Texas. He read for the law in the office of University of Texas regent Seth Shepard, an old Texas hand who had played a leading role in Texas's redemption from Reconstruction (and who ironically was a vocal opponent of prohibition). After nearly twenty years in practice, Hawkins was appointed first assistant attorney general for Dallas and then, briefly, commissioner of insurance and banking.[31] It was the dry governor Tom Campbell who had appointed Hawkins to that position, but the latter's truculent self-righteousness later led Campbell to demand his resignation. The deliberative and presumably impartial office of Supreme Court justice was perhaps not the most appropriate one for a candidate so strongly identified with the single hottest political issue of the day—the more so for a candidate with no judicial experience. Once he announced which seat he would run for, Hawkins issued press releases that had the effect of urging other drys to stay out of his race.[32] That, plus his vigor on the campaign trail and his magnificently judicial profile—a majestic nose and prominent square chin, a luxuriant moustache—whipped the dry vote into a frenzy and they overwhelmed the diffident Dibrell, who, after his defeat, returned to private practice in Seguin.

Newspapers noticed the change in tone in the judicial contests. An opinion editorial in the *Dallas Morning News* had foreseen it in 1911, warning that "the pushing man may secure undue prominence over the abler but more modest candidate and an unseemly political scramble for a high judicial office may take place. . . . [T]hen a candidate's real qualifications are not so much considered as the extent of his partisan adhesion."[33] The piece went on to assert that neither a wet nor a dry who sought the Supreme Court for that issue alone deserved it. Rusk and Hemphill had warned two generations earlier that this day would come.

A case came to the Supreme Court the following year (1913) that put Hawkins the prohibitionist on the spot: largely rural Clay County, east of Wichita Falls, had a solidly entrenched dry regime, which imposed a tax for doing business in the county on the Texas Brewing Company of Fort Worth. That business activity consisted of mailing circulars promoting its products to residents of Clay County. The contention was ludicrous on its face, and the county was bound to lose. Hawkins, as the prohibitionist flag bearer, could not be seen to vote against Clay County's tax, so he escaped the predicament by dissenting without comment.[34] It began to dawn on Hawkins that life as a Supreme Court justice would be less a crusade than he thought it would be.

For all the energy he had expended in winning election to the Supreme Court, once Hawkins took his seat he proved himself habitually lax in articulating his views in written opinions. A few times at first, but then dozens and ultimately scores of times, he circulated notes such as, "I dissent and will file my views later." He would then let the matter pass, thus holding up the disposition of case after case. Eventually he left behind more than a hundred dissents, concurrences, and "statements."[35]

He often voiced passionate views on them, to the extent that if he had spent the time in writing opinions that he did in lecturing his fellow justices, the Court might not have sunk so deep into its backlog. In one instance, as recalled by deputy clerk Clamp, Hawkins hectored and shook his finger at Chief Justice Brown in support of a contested law until, finally given a chance to respond, Brown snapped, "That statute ain't worth a damn." Brown was said to always regret this rare lapse in judicial temperament, but his frustration only grew as the Court's output slowed to a crawl.[36] From ninety-six opinions produced by the Court in 1911, and seventy-five in 1912, the number plunged to forty-six in 1913 as the backlog on its docket ballooned. Chief Justice Brown clung to the time-honored three-man configuration of the Court and opposed expanding it as a remedy to speed things along. Enamored of the glory days of the Consensus Court, he protested to the Texas Bar Association's Special Committee on Judicial Reform that when the justices consider a case, "we do not divide them out, and give so many to each judge, but each man does all the work he can, and before any opinion is written we all get together, and go over every question in the case again, and pass upon it, and agree upon it."[37] That comity had produced whole years in which not a single dissent was filed; he had never met an obstacle like Hawkins, but he was not ready to give up on him yet.

Brown was keenly aware that they had a problem; he estimated that the Court was three years behind on its docket, and "it is useless to read these statements in the newspapers saying that we are nearly [caught] up . . . for simply the men who write it do not know what they are writing about."[38] The chief justice, elderly and infirm as he was, was carrying more than his share of the load. In 1913, Hawkins's first full year on the Court, Brown wrote twenty-four majority opinions, Phillips seventeen, and Hawkins four. The next year, the vigorous Phillips took more of the load, authoring forty-three opinions, Brown twenty-seven, and Hawkins two.[39] Hawkins, however, was far outdistancing Brown and Phillips in concurrences and dissents, most of which he never got around to writing, but when he did, he had trouble keeping to the point. One of his rare majority opinions filled twenty-one typeset pages in *Texas Reports*. In their joint concurring opinion, Brown and Phillips wrote tiredly, "We prefer to confine this decision to what we regard as the sole question presented . . . without reference to the other questions discussed in the opinion of Mr. Justice Hawkins."[40]

"It is not necessary to write a dissertation on the law in every case," chided Brown in a later statement to the state bar association; "make it brief so as to enable us to dispatch more business."[41] Not every opinion, he said, needed to be written with a view to posterity. Because of Hawkins's lack of legal training, he felt compelled to research his opinions in the laws of as many states as he could get his hands on, material that Brown and Phillips would regard as secondary at best, but then he would completely overlook an essential element that set the case at hand apart from all the others. Brown was patient and courteous without fail, seldom going beyond what he wrote in *Dallas County v. Lively* (1914), in response to Hawkins's dissent, with its near-biblical exegesis on the word "extra": "Justice Hawkins has made a laborious and extensive search into the authorities; but we believe he has found no case that reaches the distinguishing feature of this [one.]"[42]

When Hawkins did manage to get dissents written and filed, Court historian Harbert Davenport described them as of a high standard, but that says more about Davenport's baseline level of platitudes that he wrote about all justices.[43] Two cases that Davenport mentioned were actually interesting, however. One was Hawkins's disapproval of the result in *St. Louis and Southwestern Railway v. Griffin* (1914), in which he would have upheld the state "blacklisting" statute, which the majority declared unconstitutional.[44] The law gave a discharged employee the right to obtain from his former employer a written statement of why he was fired. Thomas Griffin obtained such a letter, stating that he had been discharged for inexperience and incompetence, upon which he sued, alleging that the statement was a lie. The Court ruled that the right of free speech implies a right to silence, and employers could not be compelled to give such a statement.

The other interesting example was Hawkins's dissent in *Ex parte Mitchell* (1915), in which he would have declared unconstitutional Texas's "local option pool-hall" statute—not surprising for a prohibitionist ramrod.[45] The statute in question had placed the legality of pool halls under local option, rather after the manner of allowing the local adoption of prohibition. The opinion by Phillips held that the statute was an illegal delegation of legislative powers and allowed a general law of the state to be overruled by a county, both of which rendered it unconstitutional. In his (unusual for him) brief dissent, Hawkins pointed out that the early Texas decision that the Court relied on had actually been decided merely on its defective pleading, not for any constitutional import.[46]

Chief Justice Brown's eyesight continued to weaken as he advanced through his seventies. He still enjoyed his evening walks around the Capitol grounds, illuminated now with a lantern hung from a crooked staff. Not keeping to the sidewalk, his habit was to stroll down the middle of the street; he still taught a Wednesday-night Bible class, so deputy clerk Clamp took it upon himself to accompany Brown on his walks to and from church to make sure he did not get run down by an automobile.[47] Stomach cancer finally claimed T. J. Brown in May 1915.

A new governor who had just taken over from Colquitt, James E. Ferguson (also an avowed wet), appointed Phillips chief justice in June. He then appointed James E. Yantis, a former state senator from Waco and more recently assistant attorney general, as associate justice. Yantis was almost sixty, and he served on the Court only three years before his declining health forced him to resign in 1918. After Ferguson was impeached and had resigned from office—the only Texas governor to suffer that fate—the new chief executive, William P. Hobby, replaced Yantis with Thomas B. Greenwood, a lawyer in private practice in Palestine. At forty-five, he was only a year older than

Nelson Phillips and had no experience on the bench. However, his successful practice of twenty-five years had led to a seat on the University of Texas Board of Regents. In his sixteen years on the Supreme Court, Greenwood distinguished himself in real estate law, negligence, and the growing field of oil and gas.[48]

Still, Hawkins's foot-dragging crippled the Court's productivity. One analysis undertaken many years later showed that in 1907, the 61 cases that the Consensus Court heard were disposed of, on average, in six and a half months. By 1913, the caseload had increased only to 106, but parties could generally not expect a final disposition for five years.[49] Both the state bar association and the legislature recognized that the Court was in crisis. Task forces were formed, meetings held, and plans put forward. In 1915 a proposed constitutional amendment to expand the Court to five justices was beaten badly at the polls. One idea that gained traction and actually was put into effect came from former justice Frank Alvin Williams, who had quit the Court over the shabby pay.[50] The legislature passed a statute enabling the chief justice—now Phillips—to appoint a "Committee of Judges" from the courts of appeals to take over the duty of reviewing applications for writs of error. When that act was attacked as an unconstitutional delegation of power, the Court upheld it, with Hawkins dissenting.[51]

Ultimately, though, the solution was found in re-creating the old Commission of Appeals. Soon after taking over gubernatorial responsibilities in 1917, William Hobby began calling special sessions of the legislature, which was then out of its biennial session, to consider an agenda of pressing issues: ratifying national prohibition, which was finally to have its day; granting women the right to vote in primaries; and creating an appeals commission to help the Supreme Court.

The first iteration of the Commission of Appeals had been subverted by the Capitol Court's reluctance to use it, and it was discarded with the creation of courts of civil appeals in 1891. Times were different now, however. The statute was enacted and signed. Hobby appointed six commissioners, whose jurisdiction extended to cases given them by the Supreme Court and (importantly) cases whose parties agreed to their review. In its first two years, the commission disposed of more than 250 cases and finally set the Supreme Court back on a path toward a credible calendar.[52]

William Hawkins left the Court in 1921, to the relief of most followers of Texas jurisprudence, and with prohibition the law of the land, his zeal was no longer needed in public service. He entered private practice with his son in the little town of Breckenridge and later Abilene.

Hawkins's career on the bench did leave one legacy that he would not have anticipated. Besides the new Commission of Appeals, which began to clean up the mess he left behind, the sentiment for more fundamental judicial reform received a shot of energy. Assessing the now-contested primaries and the degree to which lowbrow politicking had been injected into them, the Texas Bar Association's Committee on Jurisprudence and Law Reform suggested that candidates for judge thenceforward "be selected by a nominating convention and thus as far as possible . . . the judiciary be kept out of politics and relieved . . . from the disastrous consequences to the judiciary of the primary election system."[53] It was a sentiment endorsed by civil appeals Judge R. A. Pleasants, who had lost to Nelson Phillips in 1912: "[T]he greatest need in this state today is to divorce the selection of our judges from politics, and not have the judiciary elected at political primaries."[54]

THIRTEEN

THE CURETON COURT

Just at the end of Hawkins's tenure, the Supreme Court added a new man to the staff, second deputy clerk Carl Lyda, who would work for the Court for the next forty-five years. Hawkins's reputation as the deadweight that sank the Court's efficiency might have taken a toll on him, as he struck Lyda as "a man who continually 'carried a chip on his shoulder,' especially in his relationship with the other justices and personnel of the Court."[1]

Not surprisingly, Hawkins was unable to hold on to his seat on the Court, losing the 1920 Democratic primary to Judge William Pierson of the Eighth Judicial District. Pierson was another in the growing set of native Texans who replaced aging Confederates born in the Deep South. He was fifty, a native of Gilmer, well rounded, with a degree in literature from Baylor followed by one in law from the University of Texas, having trailed newly elected governor Pat M. Neff through both institutions by a couple of years. Pierson entered the state legislature in 1901 (two years after Neff), where he sponsored a bill establishing the colleges that later became Texas Woman's University and Texas State University. He then returned to his private legal practice in Greenville, where he and his wife had three children, and was elected district judge in 1912. The Eighth Judicial District had become a front line in the crusade to impose prohibition, and Pierson's decisions in seven cases involving breweries gave him statewide visibility among the prohibitionist factions of the Democratic Party. Quiet and scholarly, he served as a trustee of Burleson College in Greenville, and was a member of the Texas State Historical Association.[2] Pierson also struck the clerks as a kind Christian gentleman, but they perceived that he was saddened by his own somewhat frail health, and more by a siege of family problems, not the least of which was his six-year-old younger son, Howard. Shortly before Pierson's swearing-in, he lifted young Howard into his chair on the distinguished bench to show him the view of the courtroom, and Carl Lyda described the boy's reaction as "resentful." The boy was clearly, in country parlance, not right.[3] Nevertheless, Pierson took well to the Supreme Court, and his long tenure, along with that of Greenwood, helped stop the revolving door that had been spinning since Gaines left in 1911.

That stability was ensured with the appointment of a new chief justice. Cigar-savoring, deity-invoking, tennis-playing Nelson Phillips resigned in November 1921 after a decade on the Court, six of them as chief. He was not yet fifty, and his new job as general counsel to Southwestern Bell Telephone in Dallas carried less dignity but a lot more money.[4] He later went into practice with his son, Nelson Phillips, Jr., until he died of heart disease, at sixty-six, in 1939. (To the astonishment of the Court's clerks, Phillips remembered which small personal items of his they had ever expressed admiration for. After his death, Nelson Junior delivered to the Court a gold-headed cane for deputy clerk Clamp, a silver-topped tobacco humidor for second deputy clerk Lyda, and two rare books for deputy clerk Joe Byrne.)[5]

To replace Phillips, Governor Neff turned to the Texas attorney general, Calvin Maples Cureton, forty-seven, a curious mixture of friendly humility that stemmed from his origins on a ranch in Bosque County, and the conceit that came from having taught himself most of what he knew about the law. He had attended four years at Central "College" in Walnut Springs until he was fifteen, then worked on the family ranch, and he enjoyed regaling the Court's clerks with stories of studying on horseback. His real experience in higher education, at the University of Virginia, was cut short after only one year by the financial panic of 1893. Back in Texas, he read for the law and was admitted to the bar the year before he volunteered for the Spanish-American War. After that he represented Bosque County in the legislature for two terms before being hired as first assistant attorney general in 1913 and elected attorney general in 1918.[6] When Neff approached him about the vacancy on the Supreme Court, Cureton—cheekily for a man with no judicial experience—indicated that he would accept the post as chief justice, but not associate.[7]

The triumvirate of Cureton, Greenwood, and Pierson reigned for fourteen amicable years, the only drama in conferences stemming from the fact that while Cureton and Pierson were always quiet and courtly, Thomas Greenwood did not think that his views were being assimilated unless he raised his voice. "At times," wrote Clamp, "you could hear him clear across the building."[8]

Interestingly, the case for which the Cureton Court is most remembered is not one that broke significant legal ground. It was, however, a landmark of Texas social history, for after Cureton, Greenwood, and Pierson all were required by law to recuse themselves on ethical grounds, the case was heard by a special Texas Supreme Court composed entirely of women.[9]

It concerned the Woodmen of the World, a fraternal organization that provided life insurance and other financial services to its members. That group was founded in Omaha, Nebraska, in 1890, and within a decade grew to write nearly a quarter of a billion dollars in life insurance.[10] The growing influence was seen in the proliferation of their distinctive tree-stump headstones in cemeteries around the nation. The Woodmen also played a role in disaster relief, beginning with the Galveston hurricane of 1900, at which time the organization's treasurer was Texan Morris Sheppard, who later became the state's longest-serving U.S. senator.[11] By 1920, most of Texas's leading lawyers and politicians were members. In June of 1922, one W. T. Johnson sued J. M. Darr of El Paso and won a judgment to collect long-overdue debts. Darr was the owner of various tracts of land in the city, which Johnson moved to seize to satisfy the judgment. However, Darr held the tracts as trustee for the local chapter, called a "camp," of the Woodmen of the World. The deeds showing Darr as owner had been duly filed; those revealing him to be the trustee of the equitable owner, the Woodmen, had not been filed. The Woodmen trustees sued Johnson to void his creditor lien on properties of which they were the equitable owners.

The trial court held for the Woodmen on a lot that was occupied by a tenant, but found for Johnson in the matter of the unoccupied lots. The Woodmen took the matter to the El Paso Court of Civil Appeals, which vindicated the group on December 6, 1923, in reversing the trial court, and Johnson appealed to the Texas Supreme Court.[12]

In the 1920s, secret societies and mysterious lodges were in high fashion, and the business connections made in them were very much the way for a man to get ahead. Former justice William Ramsey, by way of example, not only was a member of the Woodmen of the World, but also was a Mason, an Elk, a Knight of Pythias, and a Red Man of the Improved Order.[13] (His good standing as a Presbyterian was somewhat less exotic.) As ubiquitous as membership in the Woodmen of the World was in Texas legal circles, the group had been involved in Texas lawsuits before, three of which had reached the Supreme Court.[14] The insurance premiums that members paid were tied to the group's expenditures the year before, giving members who were judges a financial stake in the outcome of a legal action and thus requiring their disqualification from hearing the case. In each of the three instances, the members of the Supreme Court had certified their recusal to Neff, causing him to appoint special justices. In each instance he had appointed non-Woodmen male members of bench and bar to perform the duty.

On March 8, 1924, Cureton certified to Neff the Court's inability to hear *Johnson v. Darr*, and the governor was required by the constitution to act "immediately" to appoint the special court. Neff, however, sat on the issue for nearly ten months, and at some point made a discreet inquiry that made its way to the Supreme Court's deputy clerk, H. L. Clamp, namely, whether it would be legal to appoint women to the special court. His response was that as long as the minimal constitutional requirements were satisfied — seven years' practice of law and thirty years of age — it would be legal.[15] On January 1, 1925, only a week before the Court's scheduled hearing, Neff announced his appointments: all were female.

The need for a special court coincided with active changes in the legal status of Texas women. A Texas statute enacted in March 1918 granted them the right to vote in primary elections, and then a year later Texas became the first southern state to ratify the Nineteenth Amendment to the U.S. Constitution, which extended the voting franchise to women across the country. *Johnson v. Darr* came to the Supreme Court at the beginning of Chief Justice Cureton's tenure, but it was the very end of Pat Neff's gubernatorial term. He was shortly to be succeeded by Miriam A. ("Ma") Ferguson, the first woman elected governor in the United States (although by a few days she would become the second to be inaugurated).

While Neff had not endorsed Ferguson's campaign — she was running virtually as a surrogate and as vindication for her husband, James E. Ferguson, the former governor who had been impeached in 1917 — Neff had warmly espoused female suffrage, selected a woman as his private secretary, and consistently appointed women to Texas boards and commissions.[16] Undoubtedly, Neff had also observed challenges to these progressive changes as they made their way to the high bench, for the political empowerment of females did not take place by unanimous consent. The statute allowing women to vote in state primaries was hauled to the Supreme Court in 1920 for a ruling on its constitutionality, a muster that it passed in *Koy v. Schneider*.[17] The Court's rationale was that a party primary was not an "election" for purposes of constitutional qualification, even though it was common knowledge that victory in the Democratic primary was tantamount to election. That was too fine a distinction for Chief Justice Phillips, who dissented that the Court had acted against the clear language of the constitution, which provided only for male suffrage.

Women suffered a setback in the Court of Criminal Appeals, though, which ruled in 1921 that merely allowing women to vote did not entitle them to sit on grand juries.[18] Reaching this result required the exercise of some rather attenuated logic: the constitutional provision for juries referred to men serving on them. To allow women on a jury meant that a jury composed entirely of women could conceivably be impaneled, and that would violate the constitution. The fact that the Criminal Appeals Court decided an actual case based on a highly imaginative hypothetical one was not allowed to stand in the way of the needed decision. The Cureton Court also threw a punch at women's rights, declaring the 1917 law giving wives the proceeds of their separate property as separate income to be unconstitutional. Their logic was that "the legislature might alter powers of management and rules of liability," but the 1917 law sought to change property definitions in a way that was a step too far.[19]

Ma Ferguson's own campaign for governor had been legally challenged all the way to the Texas Supreme Court on the justification that the state constitution used the words "he" and "his" in setting out gubernatorial qualifications. The Court held that use of the masculine pronouns was the accepted common practice for denoting both sexes, and that "the truths of current history" were that the right to cast ballots had rendered women eligible for office.[20]

Thus, while the conventional story for many years was that Neff appointed the so-called All-Woman Supreme Court because he was unable to find male judges or attorneys who were not disqualified by membership in the Woodmen of the World, Neff's record of previously appointing men to hear Woodmen cases makes it more likely that his intent was to strike a blow for the political advancement of women as he departed office.[21]

One of Neff's choices was Hortense Sparks Ward, whose intense lobbying had resulted in passage of the Married Woman's Property Rights Law in 1913. Since then she had become the first Texas woman certified to practice before the U.S. Supreme Court, and she drafted the bill that allowed women to vote in the primaries, in consequence of which she was honored as the first woman to register to vote in Harris County. She was now nearly fifty and married to a judge, whom she had met while employed as a court reporter.[22] The other two appointees were Edith E. Wilmans, who had represented a Dallas district in the Thirty-Eighth Legislature, and Nellie Robertson, a county attorney from Granbury. Neff's action rocked the Texas judiciary and its followers to the core.

Newspapers trumpeted the story, but word quickly came back to Neff that Wilmans and Richardson lacked the seven years' practice requirement—by two months and three months, respectively. They removed themselves from consideration, and Neff appointed in their stead Hattie Leah Henenberg, thirty-one, who ran the Dallas Bar Association's program of legal aid for the poor, and Ruth Virginia Brazzil, thirty-six, who as a life insurance company lawyer in Galveston would likely have insight into the Woodmen of the World trust issues. (In her private and domestic way she was, however, opposed to female suffrage, a position in which she was not entirely alone among members of her sex.) Fortunately for Neff's purposes, this second round of appointments stuck, for beyond this five, there were only about two dozen more female lawyers in Texas to choose from.[23]

The *Dallas Morning News* accurately captured the significance of the occasion: "All records were shattered. . . . It was a healthy New Year gift of recognition to the woman barrister of today. This is the first instance a woman has been appointed to sit on the supreme bench; it is the first time a higher court is to be composed entirely of women."[24] And it was inevitable that someone would state the obvious, as John William Stayton wrote in *Holland's* magazine, that the new justices "were a good deal better looking than the Supreme Court which regularly deliberates on the third floor of the capitol."[25]

The All-Woman Supreme Court, the first in the United States, convened on January 8, 1925, with Hortense Ward as special chief justice, to consider whether to grant the writ of error and hear the case. Chief Justice Cureton administered their oaths, which caused some amusement when they came to the passage affirming that they had never participated in a duel.

At the hearing on January 8, the All-Woman Court issued the writ of error, and oral arguments were heard on January 30. At their last meeting on May 23, they gave their decision upholding the El Paso Court of Appeals, agreeing that even secret trusts did not have to be recorded. In subsequent decades, *Johnson v. Darr* has provided the deciding precedent some thirty times, in only one of which was the gender of the court even mentioned.[26]

The All-Woman Court's decision was the most celebrated of Calvin Cureton's tenure, but perhaps the most incendiary, even if not the most important, was one that purported to settle issues of Texas water law. Cureton, for all his studious application to the law, was at root largely an autodidact. Like many self-taught scholars, he had a tendency to show off his learning with exposition that went beyond the needs of the case at hand. Deputy clerk Clamp considered him the antithesis of Reuben Gaines, who limited his opinions to six hand-drafted pages, while Cureton's were unnecessarily verbose. And like many autodidacts he was occasionally not just wrong, but wrong with a majestic certitude, which could have ill effect when he assigned himself the task of writing the opinions on what he felt were the most important cases.[27]

Motl v. Boyd (1926)[28] was a Gordian knot of a water dispute from largely arid Tom Green County, concerning the right to pump irrigation water from a small private reservoir on Spring Creek, a tributary—and in the drought of the 1920s, a dribbly tributary—of the South Concho River. The contending landowners' tracts were located in different surveys, although both tracts bordered the stream. The previous owner of the upstream tract had thirty-five years earlier allowed the previous owner of the downstream tract to construct a dam, which impounded a lake of some 105 acres, and an irrigation ditch. The present downstream owners now sued to prevent the upstream owners from drawing water from the stream for irrigation. It was a case that embodied a quagmire of conflicts between the English common law of riparian water rights, in which a right to use a flowing stream normally came with the land, and Spanish civil law, in which an owner had no right to the water that flowed by or through his land unless that right was specifically conveyed when the land was purchased. It was a legal schism in which Texas, with its bicultural history, had always had one foot on the dock and one on the boat. And in West Texas, where nonirrigated land sold for only a small fraction of the price paid for land that could be watered, it was a case of monetary importance. The issues, noted Cureton, were "insisted on with so much force and so earnestly that we have concluded to investigate the whole subject."[29] Those who were familiar with Cureton's method of tabulating the minutiae of a case could only settle back for a long read.

During an exhaustive exploration of Texas history, Cureton took notice that when Stephen F. Austin meted the boundaries of land grants to his colonists, he elongated the tracts so that each would have frontage on a stream for irrigation. Therefore, the English doctrine of riparian rights must have been what was at work. Cureton then factored in later statutory elements, such as the definition of a navigable stream as one having banks thirty feet apart—a definition that Spring Creek minimally met, although not many on the scene would have described a subtributary of the South Concho River as navigable. He therefore opted for the common law model and concluded that the upstream landowners had rights to the stream—or would have had, had the previous owner not conveyed those rights to the previous downstream owner, an act that limited the present upstream owner's right to irrigation to storm waters above the stream's usual flow. Cureton's opinion was meticulously scholarly and, in the context of Texas's heritage, dead wrong, but it would be nearly forty years before *Motl v. Boyd* and the cases that later cited it as controlling authority would be given a thorough ordering.[30]

As Cureton tried his autodidactic best in such areas as water law, Thomas Greenwood carved out a specialty for himself in cases involving oil and gas. Within a year of the discovery of oil at Spindletop in 1901, more than five hundred oil companies were chartered in Texas, including those that later became Gulf, Sun, Texaco, Mobil, and Exxon. In those freewheeling glory days of the "wildcatters," investors, drillers, and landowners alike were out to make the best of it, and with sharp dealing and subterfuge left, right, and center, there was a reason that the first discovery became known as "Swindletop." In one sensational episode the Waters-Pierce Oil Company, a clandestine subsidiary of John D. Rockefeller's Standard Oil monopoly, fraudulently obtained a state charter to participate in the Texas free-for-all. It was ultimately fined $1,808,483.33 (including interest) under the state's antitrust laws, a ruling upheld by the U.S. Supreme Court. In response to the State of Texas's demand that the full amount be paid in cash, several old-fashioned carriages were loaded with small bills and gold coins and paraded up Congress Avenue to the Capitol.[31]

Subsequent fields that "blew in" during the following five years were now referred to as part of the "First Boom." They only presaged what would follow. The second boom, which followed in 1911 at Electra and Iowa Park near Wichita Falls, was dwarfed by the fields in Ranger, Breckenridge, and Desdemona in 1917 and 1918. Texas Supreme Court decisions before Greenwood joined the bench in 1918 had sometimes been inconsistent, as when the justices settled that the surface owner generally owned the oil beneath him in *Texas v. Daugherty* (1915).[32] Apparently not wanting to call attention to the Court's own lack of expertise, however, the justices made the holding without expressly overruling a previous case to the contrary.[33] Greenwood's long series of opinions began to systematize the field. One of his first opinions, issued in 1919, set out the duties of lessee and lessor in pursuit of the underground wealth.[34] *Stephens County v. Mid-Kansas Oil and Gas Company* (1923) is considered his keystone work, since it "defined the nature of the estate created by the ordinary oil and gas lease, [and] stabilized the legal status of a lease and the estate created by it."[35] In 1929, his opinion in *W. T. Waggoner Estate v. Sigler Oil Co.* outlined the preferred nature of redress as damages, although in extraordinary circumstances the Court would employ equity and require a forfeiture of the lease.[36] In *Sheffield v. Hogg* (1934), Greenwood went on to define the parties' interest in royalties.[37] Probably not since the Court's reliance on John Hemphill for guidance in Spanish law had it looked so much to the expertise of one justice in a given area of law.

The Cureton Court had reigned for fourteen years when Thomas Greenwood decided not to seek reelection in 1934. The solid reputation that he took with him into private practice in Austin did not suffer when he partnered with Dan Moody, the Texas attorney general who had upended the Ferguson machine and served two terms as governor. Winning election to Greenwood's seat (not appointed, something of a rarity) was John Henry Sharp, a judge with five years' experience on the Commission of Appeals. He was the same age as Cureton, now sixty, a fellow Central Texan with a BA from Southwestern University in Georgetown, and like Cureton had "read for the law" privately, without the benefit of a formal legal education. Sharp had established his practice in Ennis, south of Dallas, where he served eight years as president of the school board and four years as mayor. Once ensconced in the Supreme Court, he stayed for eighteen dutiful years.[38]

A much more wrenching change of tenure came the following year. On the night of Wednesday, April 24, 1935, Austin police received a call from Seton Hospital. Howard Pierson, the twenty-one-year-old son of Justice William Pierson, was being treated for a gunshot wound in the arm. He stated that he and his parents had been car riding on Bull Creek Road about four miles west of the city, on their way to a pecan experiment station on the Colorado River, when they were stopped by two men who brandished pistols. As reported in the *Dallas Morning News*, Howard told police that as the robbers took their money and watches, his father said, "I'll see that you're punished for this." According to his story a struggle ensued, the pair began shooting, and Howard fled into bushes to hide. His father and mother, he said, were killed: "I tried to drag them and get them to the car but I couldn't make it." Instead, he drove back into town and reported the incident at the hospital. His wound dressed, Howard accompanied officers back out to Bull Creek Road to locate the bodies. Word of the tragedy spread through Austin like lightning. The legislature adjourned a night session to await word of the Piersons' fate. Chief Justice Cureton was informed, and he joined police in a search of the site.[39]

The *Dallas Morning News*, however, went to print with the wrong story. Inconsistencies in Howard's account led police to suspect that he was the killer. After a nine-hour interrogation, he confessed, admitting that he had shot himself in the arm to cover the crime, and led police to the spot where he had hidden the gun, spent shells, and his parents' effects. Asked why he had done it, Howard replied obliquely, "[A] reason"; when the whole story was told, he said, the world would know that he had had to do it. Justice Pierson's grief over his son's mental disturbance had been common knowledge for years, but now Howard spilled out a torrent of recrimination, that his parents had always favored their other two children and had thwarted his ambition to become a great scientist. He claimed he was really adopted, and he recalled in detail many slights and disappointments dating back to his early childhood.[40] Howard had recently lost a job as an oil field worker. Pierson, knowing of his mental problems, had declined to finance his return to college to study science. Found in one of Howard's pockets were two bloodstained letters that his father had written several days before, soliciting employment for Howard. A jury eventually found him insane.

The Piersons' bodies reposed in the Supreme Court for a day before the funeral. It was undoubtedly intended to honor Pierson's history with the Court, but clerk Lyda found it deplorable: "[It was] the most ill conceived and obnoxious experience during the time I was with the court—and probably of my whole life.... [D]uring that day and far into the night thousands of total strangers filed by to view their remains. Most of these people had never heard of the Piersons before the news of their tragic deaths . . . and were impelled strictly by morbid curiosity and not by sympathy or any decent concern."[41] The ordeal ended with services at the First Baptist Church and burial in the Texas State Cemetery.

To replace Pierson, Texas's New Deal governor, Jimmy Allred, turned to Richard Critz, who had served on the Commission of Appeals since 1927. He was yet another Central Texan who had attended Southwestern University and, like Cureton and Sharp, had read for the law without the benefit of formal training. Eight years as Williamson County judge, starting in 1910, were followed by a decade of private practice in Taylor. In that practice he assisted Georgetown's daring young district attorney Dan Moody (who was also from Taylor) in the prosecution of local Ku Klux Klan members. It was Moody, as governor, who appointed Critz to the Commission of Appeals.[42] On that bench Critz proved himself highly competent, but developed a frosty judicial temperament that led to the most dramatic Supreme Court election of the following decade.

FOURTEEN

THE WARTIME COURT

Chief Justice Cureton had suffered for many years from chronic heart disease, and a heart attack ended his life on April 8, 1940. He was sixty-five, and had bested the tenure of the legendary John Hemphill with nineteen years' service as chief justice. His death heralded the beginning of an era of rapid changes on the Court, in personnel, in mode of operation, and in the sophistication required to survive as a justice in an increasingly politicized arena.

With less than a year until the next election, Governor W. Lee O'Daniel appointed seventy-one-year-old William Folsom Moore to replace Cureton as chief justice. A native and lifelong resident of Paris, where he had served as Democratic Party chairman, Moore had served two terms in the Texas House and had recently been taken on as first assistant attorney general. It was a thin résumé for a chief justice, and he declined to seek reelection in his own right, but he served as a placeholder until those more qualified could compete for the office.[1] (Moore's appointment was a warm-up exercise for O'Daniel, who repeated the technique for his own advancement. When U.S. senator Morris Sheppard died suddenly on April 9, 1941, O'Daniel appointed the frail, eighty-six-year-old surviving son of Sam Houston to the post, knowing he could not possibly retain it, and then ran for and won the Senate seat himself.)[2]

Elected chief justice in 1940 to succeed Moore was the remarkable James Patterson Alexander. Fifty-eight, raised on a farm near Waco, Alexander believed that one's obligation to the civic good extended beyond those hours when the courthouse was open. Elected county judge in 1916 as a newlywed, he paired his judgment of first-time juvenile delinquents with personal mentoring, inviting wayward youths into his home. In 1920, after serving two terms as county judge, he was elected judge of the Nineteenth District Court in Waco. The same year, he was invited to join Baylor University's new law faculty, where he taught for the following two decades. In the ten years preceding his election to the Supreme Court, he served on the bench of the Tenth District Appeals Court. Alexander's advocacy of judicial reform and his strong work ethic led his colleagues to urge him to run for the open chief justice seat in 1940. He was the first to be elected to that office by popular vote who had not previously served on the Supreme Court.[3] He devoted much of what spare time he had to farming, in which he kept an avid interest, and he was a skilled beekeeper. During the Great Depression, believing that foreclosure and dispossession ripped to the heart of the American social fabric, he sold several tracts of land on easy terms to those who needed it.

As chief justice for the next seven years, Alexander combated judicial inefficiency by leading the effort to revise the Texas Rules of Civil Procedure. The court system around the state, however, entered a decline and experienced growing backlogs, owing largely to neglect on the part of the state executive: O'Daniel's departure for the U.S. Senate elevated Coke Stevenson to the Governor's Mansion in August 1941. Corrupt and cornpone as the O'Daniel administration had been, his popular tax cuts had put Texas into serious debt. Stevenson, a flinty archconservative who made his own breakfast and drove himself to the Capitol every morning, was taciturn (his motto parodied a beatitude: "Blessed is he who sayeth nothing, for he shall not be misquoted") and earned him the sobriquet "Calculatin' Coke."[4] During the preceding decades, the legislature had sought to deal with Texas's growing judicial burden by providing the state with the most complex and top-heavy appeals system in the United States: forty-seven appellate judges scattered among eleven courts of civil appeals, the Court of Criminal Appeals, the Civil Commission of Appeals, and the Supreme Court. This was eleven judges more than were found in the second-most appeals-heavy state, California, and fourteen more than in New York, whose population was more than double that of Texas. Keenly aware of the bloated state judiciary, Stevenson decided, as an austerity measure, not to replace deceased or retiring judges. This of course made the judicial tangle even worse.

The justices and entire staff of the Supreme Court gathered in the conference room to listen to Roosevelt's "Day of Infamy" speech on December 8, 1941, and his request for a declaration of war against Japan. The three briefing attorneys, J. V. Hammett, Clarence Guittard, and future chief justice Joe Greenhill, all declared on the spot their intention to enlist, which left Justices Alexander, Sharp, and Critz in a bind. The three briefing attorneys were more than just crack legal researchers; after briefing the cases they were assigned to conduct mock oral arguments in order to sharpen the justices' grasp of the issues.[5] With the drain of manpower to the war effort both at home and abroad, the Supreme Court made a nimble adjustment to womanpower instead, with the hiring of female briefing attorneys. The pay for men had been two hundred dollars a month, an amount that Chief Justice Alexander felt somewhat embarrassed about when he hired Greenhill in the summer of 1941, writing, "If you are making more than $200.00 per month there, you might prefer to remain there and not move here and begin drawing your salary" until the time he was needed. (Alexander needn't have worried, as Greenhill was not getting paid regularly where he worked.)[6]

The Court did not lower the salary in contemplation of hiring women, although the justices made it absolutely clear that their employment was for the duration of the war only, after which the former clerks would be offered their jobs back. In all likelihood, providing equal pay for equal work was less on their minds than protecting their budget from the parsimonious Stevenson.[7] Hiring women worked out well from another standpoint: although there were not a great many female attorneys in Texas, a selection of them was available because most law firms would not hire women.[8] Additionally, some of the women who did go to law school responded to the pressure of finding themselves interlopers in this male bastion by excelling.

While enrolled at the University of Texas Law School, one of the brightest, Ione Steele, married one of her professors, the criminal-law authority George Stumberg, who was widowed with two daughters. She was accomplished in her own right, graduating in 1937 as editor in chief of the *Texas Law Review*, second in her class, and a member of the Order of the Coif. Upon graduation, she did not seek legal employment, but assumed the role of rearing Stumberg's two daughters and the one they had together. It was Chief Justice Alexander who recruited this fallow talent, and after obtaining the blessing of her husband, who was serving in North Africa, Stumberg accepted the job.

Texas attorney general Gerald C. Mann supplied the second briefing attorney, surrendering his editor of the attorney general opinions, Virginia Grubbs, who was in her last semester at the University of Texas Law School. She was, however, engaged to another member of Mann's staff, and soon took a leave of absence from the Court to marry. She was quickly hired away by the Houston law firm later known as Baker Botts.

The third female briefing attorney approached the Court of her own volition — Mary Kate Parker, who was secretary to the chairman of the state insurance board. She was no less a legal whiz than her colleagues, graduating from the University of Texas at nineteen and summa cum laude from the University of Texas Law School in 1934. Deeper into the war era, Beth O'Neil worked as briefing attorney from the fall of 1944 until the end of the war in Europe.

In Texas, the flight from rural areas into the cities that had begun during the Great Depression in the quest for jobs only accelerated with the opening of countless factories to supply the war effort beginning in 1942. In fact, the sudden shortage of skilled workers, the advent of rationing, and other war-related exigencies stressed Texas society in unprecedented ways. Despite this, litigation fell off during the war, and the Court made progress in whittling down its long-infamous backlog.

One of the cases decided during the war was intimately connected with Governor Stevenson and the influence of Texas Democrats on the national scene. Franklin D. Roosevelt had taken over the presidency just as the Depression-gripped country reached rock bottom. The Democratic power structure in Texas was deeply conservative and suspicious of the so-cial spending that was the centerpiece of FDR's New Deal. Party leaders went along with it at first because Roosevelt's vice president was John Nance Garner, the former U.S. House Speaker, a Texan from Uvalde and heir ap-parent to the White House after FDR's traditional two terms. When Roose-velt threw over custom and ran for a third term, after having tried to replace anti–New Deal Texas congressmen such as Martin Dies and Richard Kleberg, and then jettisoning Garner for a new vice president, he made mortal ene-mies in the Texas Democratic Party. Texas voters in 1940 rebuked their party leaders and gave FDR his third term with more than 80 percent of the state vote, but the 1944 Texas Democratic Convention selected anti-Roosevelt rep-resentatives to the Electoral College. Once cooler heads prevailed, a second convention named electors who could be counted on to vote for Roosevelt. In the case of *Seay v. Latham* (1944), the Court found no constitutional reason why the party could not replace the rebellious electors.[9] As one commen-tator has noted, the case showed the potential effect of a state-party feud on a national election, a precursor to the 2000 U.S. Supreme Court decision in *Bush v. Gore*.[10]

Hostile as the Texas political powers were to the Roosevelt policies, they were, if anything, even more hostile to the labor movement, and the legisla-ture required anyone attempting to unionize workers to register. Labor orga-nizer R. J. Thomas deliberately broke the law in order to set up a test case; the Court in *Ex parte Thomas* (1943) had no trouble holding that the police power of the state embraced the compulsory registration of labor organizers; the U.S. Supreme Court disagreed and reversed the decision.[11]

As the successful outcome of the war became more certain, servicemen began returning, and Ione Stumberg resigned her position when her husband resumed his teaching at the University of Texas. Alexander replaced her with newly minted UT Law graduate Mel Ruth Ramsey, whom he blended only gradually into the Court's routine, first having her review opinions from the civil appeals courts before allowing her to brief cases. She worked only eight months, from March to November 1945, when Joe Greenhill returned, having been told that his old job would be waiting for him.[12]

While Coke Stevenson watched federal war spending in Texas lift the economy, working citizens rationed their commodities, labored in war production, and agonized over the safety of the nearly three-quarter of a million Texans in uniform. Anti-Axis feeling was high. Patriotism can be undiscerning, however, a fact that left one associate justice in grave vulnerability at the polls.

Richard Critz (pronounced with a long *i*) had been appointed to the high bench after the murder of Justice Pierson in 1935. Although a father of four with a reputation as an old softie where his family was concerned, his imperious demeanor on the bench earned him powerful enemies. He had not enjoyed law practice, but found his identity on the Supreme Court, where, according to his son-in-law, later congressman, J. J. "Jake" Pickle, he could "read and study, read and study, and write."[13] Over the years this scholarship manifested itself in the Court's development of the "substantial evidence" rule, and in the method by which the Court considered oil regulation cases.[14] Critz was, however, a last holdout of judges who disdained politics, and his hauteur was legendary. He seldom deigned to even speak to the Court's briefing attorneys, including his own, the recently hired Joe Greenhill, who recalled that Critz came by his office no more than ten times.[15] During oral argument, if an attorney staked out a position with which he disagreed, he would make a disparaging comment (one was, "I believe that's the silliest thing I've ever heard") and turn his chair around for the remainder of the argument.

One lawyer who lost cases before the Supreme Court both as advocate and as litigant was Angus Wynne, a former president of the state bar. Livid at losing one particular case before the high court in 1942, in which Critz had written the opinion reversing the trial court and the court of appeals, Wynne was in Hillsboro and encountered a local attorney, Robert W. Calvert, a former Texas House Speaker and future Supreme Court justice.[16] To Calvert, Wynne vowed to run a candidate against Critz in the next election and unseat him.

Angus Wynne went to his task with a vengeance, finding a ready candidate in Gordon Simpson, a native of Gilmer, a graduate of Baylor and then UT Law, his study for the latter degree having been interrupted by service in World War I. Like Wynne, Simpson was a former president of the state bar and a former state representative, and best of all, Simpson was out of the country, serving with the judge advocate general's office in Italy, which left Wynne free to run a campaign of absolutely squalid dishonesty.

Critz saw the storm coming and raised money, which he spent on dignified advertising. Despite Critz's reputation of being cold and impatient, his judicial record was exemplary, and he ran with the endorsement of the huge majority of newspapers and local bar associations. Wynne, however, knew more about modern campaigning. He lay low and let Critz finish first in the primary, knowing he would have to face Simpson in the runoff. Then his propaganda issued without stopping. Advertisements warned the Texas voter, in the most alarming terms, that the state Supreme Court actually chose the cases it wanted to hear, that the people did not have any right to be heard there. The clear message was that the writ of error system, which in fact was constitutionally mandated and imposed on the Supreme Court to limit its jurisdiction and reduce its docket, was undemocratic, with the implication that somehow it was Critz's fault. Worse, Wynne's campaign for Simpson deliberately mispronounced Critz's name to rhyme with Fritz, which was American slang for a German soldier, vaguely associating him with Nazi Germany. Simpson's service in uniform was boldly touted, and the allegation was made with no proof offered that Critz (rhymes with Fritz) had uttered awful calumnies against this American hero in uniform, "behind his back, and while he can't say one word in his own defense."[17] It was grotesque, but Critz never answered in kind, running only high-toned endorsements of his experience and good character.

As two historians who researched the election noted, attention the day of the voting was focused on the liberation of Paris, and Texas residents anyway were loath to use their rationed gasoline and rubber to drive to polling stations for a mere judicial runoff.[18] The result was that Critz was decisively defeated. Simpson himself had never left Italy and probably had no idea what had been done in his name until he returned—although one might argue he should have resigned the instant he became certain of Wynne's dishonesty.

Those connected with the Court were all too aware of how Simpson had won his seat, but perhaps because they now had to work with him, they made no issue of it. Longtime deputy clerk Clamp found him a hard worker and "the personification of a Southern Gentleman."[19] Greenhill later recalled the dirty tricks of Wynne's campaign for Simpson, but also noted how unpopular Critz had made himself with some segments of the bar, suggesting an acceptance that Critz's immolation was to some degree self-lit.[20] Once he took his seat, Simpson proved to be a good judge, and progressive enough in his attitudes to hire a female clerk even though the war was nearing its conclusion and male attorneys were coming back on the market. However, he lacked Critz's adoration of study and reflection and writing, and of being a justice. He resigned from the Court halfway through his term (during several months of which he was on leave of absence in Germany to review the convictions of Nazi war criminals) to become the General American Oil Company's vice president and general counsel. Angus Wynne's mission of vengeance essentially robbed Texas of an outstanding jurist and replaced him with a bright but less than fully dedicated journeyman.

Whether because of the travesty of the Critz-Simpson contest or because the pressure for judicial reform had never really gone away, in 1946 the Texas Civil Judicial Council put forth a constitutional amendment that would have mandated merit selection of all Texas judges.[21] The legislature, most of whose members had at least a working familiarity with electoral shenanigans, passed the amendment on to the voters, where it failed. This had not been the case in the previous legislative session, when lawmakers responded to calls for an expanded Supreme Court with a proposed amendment increasing the Court from three to nine members. While there had been incremental growth of the appellate courts through statutes, efforts to reform the state judiciary at the constitutional level had previously proved fruitless. Texans had twice defeated proposed amendments to increase the size of the Supreme Court, so the Judiciary Article of the Texas Constitution had remained unchanged since the creation of the Court of Criminal Appeals and the courts of civil appeals in 1891. During 1945, however, the tide changed quickly. A constitutional amendment passed out of the legislature in March, was ratified by voters in a special election in August, and went into effect in September. The amendment provided that the enlarged Court would consist of the three justices in office and the six sitting judges of the Commission of Appeals, who would be elevated to associate justices. They would serve six-year terms, with three members standing for election every two years.[22]

Extensive consideration had gone into the method of selecting justices for the newly enlarged Court. The dean of the University of Texas School of Law, Charles T. McCormick, authored a thought-provoking article in 1943 in which he admitted that "[n]o constitutional mechanism can be devised which will make certain the choice of the best qualified men as judges." Texas, he pointed out, had during its history tried the election of judges by the legislative branch and appointment by the executive branch, and finally election by the people, a method that gained momentum during the rabble sovereignty of the Jacksonian era. McCormick argued against the popular election of Supreme Court justices, first because the institution of the direct primary gave a candidate's showmanship before the voters as much weight as his qualifications and judicial temperament, which could be more carefully weighed at a party convention, and second because of Texas's rampant urbanization. "The voter in the big city does not know . . . the candidate for a judgeship as the country voter may," he wrote, and furthermore, a large-city judge who manages to make a name for himself through grandstanding "is not likely to be the kind of jurist that lawyers admire."[23] McCormick had to conclude, however, that Texans' preference for holding judges, however ill qualified, to short leashes by direct election to short terms was probably immutable. McCormick's article was one of the most articulate early volleys in an open-ended cannonade of argument to find a more rational method of selecting judges who were qualified, impartial, and not beholden to a particular constituency—which he held to be a near impossibility in a partisan election.

When it came to the selection of six judges to round out the augmented Court, Dean McCormick almost got his way. In his article he had argued for the appointment of new judges by the chief justice, or by a consortium of impartial sitting judges, which he hoped would thwart a governor's temptation to appoint political cronies. In support of this contention, he offered the example of the six judges on the Commission of Appeals: "Every lawyer in Texas will testify to the excellent results attained by vesting in the Supreme Court the choice of the judges of the Commission of Appeals."[24]

Commentary that the commissioners were as qualified as the justices proved to be no idle boast, as the new members of the Court included some formidable legal minds.[25] Graham B. Smedley was the senior commissioner to be elevated to the Court, having been appointed by Miriam Ferguson in 1933. He was an authority on oil and gas law; in the early years of the century, while the Supreme Court was trying to get a bearing on how the law should treat those unique resources, Smedley was assistant attorney general in that field for six years beginning in 1913, as well as in the areas of school lands and water law. He later switched sides to become counsel for the Continental Oil Company, and authored a digest of Texas oil and gas law. Twelve years on the commission gave him his judicial voice, although it was a shrill one, and his colleagues often felt the sting of his independent-minded disdain. Elected and reelected to the Supreme Court, he gained the sobriquet the "Great Dissenter" after Oliver Wendell Holmes, who had equal difficulty persuading others to his point of view. Smedley died in office on June 16, 1954, after nearly nine years on the Court.[26]

Few Brewster had spent more than two decades rising through the legal hierarchy in Bell County, from county attorney to district attorney to district judge. He was notably religious, attended Baylor University and Howard Payne College (both Baptist schools), and had written articles on the salutary effect of clergy on society. He was also the author of a book, *Search and Seizure* (1931), outlining how far the state could go in ferreting out violators of prohibition. He had just served a year as president of the state bar when he was named to the Commission of Appeals late in 1941. In his twelve years on the Supreme Court, Brewster was noted both for his scholarship and for defusing tense discussions with well-timed humor.[27] Probably not just because he had to work with Smedley, Brewster authored a scholarly but occasionally lighthearted history of dissent on the Texas Court.[28]

In many ways the most remarkable of the new crop of justices was John Edward Hickman, sixty-two, one of the last Texas justices to boast frontier bona fides. Born in the Williamson County community of Liberty Hill in 1883, he was set to work at a young age by the untimely death of his father. Still he managed to graduate from the Liberty Hill Normal and Business College in 1902 and took a job teaching in a one-room school at Hog Mountain, not far from Killeen. After further studies at Southwestern University in Georgetown and the University of Texas, Hickman took a job as baseball coach and principal at the high school in Lampasas. After graduating at the top of his class from the University of Texas Law School in 1910, and then serving as quizmaster for the Class of 1911, his rise through the legal profession was slow and deliberate. He opened an oil and gas practice in Dublin, Texas, and then, following the new discoveries, in Breckenridge. He won a seat on the Eleventh Court of Civil Appeals in Eastland in 1927. The reform governor Dan Moody appointed him chief justice of that court a year later, and he served seven years before the Supreme Court named him to the Commission of Appeals in 1935.[29]

Hickman was also considered little short of a force of nature in the area of religion. He was born into the Cumberland Presbyterian Church, on which he soured after he was blocked from becoming a deacon while still a teenager. He turned to the Methodist Church, of which he became a passionate exponent. After moving to Austin, he assumed teaching duties of a Bible class at University Methodist Church, which gained such fame that members of other churches — even a synagogue — attended. One of his students was Joe R. Greenhill, who recalled that Hickman's Sunday school class "got so big that it had to meet in a theater across the street," adding, "I was an Episcopalian, but I went to Hickman's Bible class."[30] Several other members of the Court also attended University Methodist, and indeed it was boasted around the church (if not by Hickman) that on any given Sunday morning, a quorum of the Court could be found listening to him expound on the Bible.

While the expansion of the Court to nine justices occurred with procedural smoothness, it was marred by a politically sensitive case that immediately pitted the original three members against the newcomers.[31] The case in question was one of those labyrinths involving early land laws of Mexico and Texas as modified by subsequent treaties, constitutions, statutes, and court decisions; modern land speculators whose actual interest in the case was largely not part of the record; and the political strengths and vulnerabilities of the lawyers and judges involved.

The suit, *Texas v. Balli*, began in 1940 when Texas's popular attorney general, the former football hero Gerald Mann, filed a trespass to try title against the heirs of Padre Nicolas Balli, longtime claimants to ownership of Padre Island, a hundred-mile-long barrier island off the shore of South Texas.[32] Original documents that would have clearly established the Ballis' ownership had long since been lost, although their probable ownership was reconstructed from subsequent documents relating to surveys of the land. Off the record was the interest of Gilbert Kerlin, a New York lawyer who had purchased the Ballis' interest in Padre Island and financed their end of the litigation. By the time the case reached trial, hundreds of defendants (possible landowners) had been joined, and oil companies with an eye on potential oil leases provided more legal muscle for the Balli heirs.

After a string of continuances, the suit went to trial in January 1942 in Nueces County, the state's choice of venue in order to avoid the internecine political-judicial relationships permeating the counties farther south. Most particularly, the state wanted to neutralize any influence that might be wielded by one of the defendants' lead attorneys, former state House Speaker Francis Seabury, who was deeply involved in South Texas politics. Last-minute agreements among the parties provided for the case to be heard by a judge, which was sensible because its complexity would have bamboozled any jury of laymen; and it further stipulated that the judge need not decide who actually owned the island—that was a circus that the now-united defendants could battle out for themselves once the State of Texas was vanquished. The only matter that needed to be decided at the moment was the validity of the state's ownership claim.

Both the trial court and the Fourth Court of Appeals in San Antonio found for the defendants in all respects. Associate Justice James R. Norvell of the latter court, who was later to serve on the Supreme Court, wrote the opinion. He was from the Rio Grande Valley and had extensive experience with Spanish and Mexican land issues. In June 1943, he affirmed the district court's ruling, finding conveniently that although the Balli family could not legally have been granted more than twelve leagues of land (53,136 acres), the additional eighteen leagues (79,704 acres) of land on Padre Island had accreted there naturally during the intervening century or so—which might have been geophysically impossible, but allowed him to pass the case up to the Supreme Court.

The state had several sound grounds for appeal, including doubt that the original Ballis had ever perfected their title, improbability that Padre Island had actually more than doubled its size by natural accretion, and the failure of subsequent Balli heirs to observe constitutional surveying requirements. In what was probably not their wisest move, the justices referred the case to one of the three-member panels of the Commission of Appeals, perhaps thinking to sidestep the political dilemma of opposing either the popular attorney general or the politically powerful collection of attorneys for the Balli heirs.[33] That panel, consisting of Slatton, Smedley, and Taylor, affirmed the lower courts' decisions. The Court adopted the commissioners' decision in December 1944.

Not until later did Alexander and Sharp (by then joined by the newly elected Simpson) realize that they had given their endorsement to a likely bad decision. Curiously, although the standard motion for rehearing would have been filed in January 1945, and normally would have been acted on reasonably soon afterward, voting on the motion did not occur until November 1945, after the commissioners had become full-fledged justices. As a result, although all three members of the original Court issued dissenting opinions, the majority of the new nine-member Court voted to uphold the original opinion. Ownership of Padre Island therefore remained in private hands, outside the jurisdiction and protection of the state.

The result of the *Balli* case soured Chief Justice Alexander in a way that could not be repaired. He had limited his dissent to matters of law, noting that since the Ballis, under Mexican law of the time, could not have purchased more than twelve leagues of land, and since both the field notes of the survey and the payment made were for 11.15 leagues of land, he could not find how they could be awarded all thirty leagues, 133,000 acres, of Padre Island. On a personal level, Alexander may have carried his concerns about the case a step further, even purportedly suggesting that the Balli family had helped finance the successful constitutional amendment that expanded the Court to include the commissioners, and thereby gain a majority.[34]

In point of fact, tensions had been building between the commission and the Court for several years. It became obvious that a philosophical sea change was brewing, from the number of cases that found all six commissioners on the side of a case opposed by two or even all three justices. In the commission's work, its members sat en banc with the Court in hearing cases and issuing opinions, but they could not vote. Joe Greenhill noted the number of "2–7 majority opinions": "Two justices would vote one way, and the other justice and all six commissioners the other. The two justices' votes would prevail."[35]

Whatever the circumstances, Chief Justice Alexander emerged from *Balli* a bitter man. He still had more than two years left to serve, often in dissent. One of the most important cases to issue from the Court in that period was *Trapp v. Shell Oil Co.* (1946), which confirmed the authority of the Texas Railroad Commission to limit oil production for purposes of conservation as long as its action was backed by substantial evidence.[36] Alexander dissented sharply, having previously written the majority opinion in *Railroad Commission v. Shell Oil Company* (1942), which specifically restricted the use of the substantial-evidence rule in agency hearings.[37] In his dissent, he also contended that the delegation of judicial powers to an agency of the executive branch violated the constitution's separation of powers.[38] His opinion was not shared by Justice Slatton and others, however, and at least for the time being, the substantial-evidence rule was accepted as the standard in administrative hearings. Even more significant over the long run, as one commentator has noted, *Trapp* marked the beginning of a trend toward ever-greater regulatory oversight of business interests by executive agencies.[39]

Deputy clerk Clamp had long thought that Alexander took his job too seriously, and indeed from his early days as McLennan County judge, his career had been marked by a relentless work ethic.[40] He lacked the recreational outlets the preceding chiefs had found so useful—Gaines's and Williams's fishing trips, Phillips's tennis—and this may have taken its toll. Alexander died of heart disease in Austin on New Year's Day 1948, the seventh anniversary of his accession.

FIFTEEN

THE FIFTIES COURT

When Alexander died, Governor Beauford Jester appointed the popular, Bible-teaching John Hickman as chief justice and filled the vacancy on the Court with prominent Houston attorney Wilmer St. John Garwood. Garwood was the scion of an important political family in Bastrop—his father had served in both the state House and Senate—and was representative of a new breed of Texas justice. Impeccably educated at Georgetown University, the University of Texas, and Harvard, Garwood and his generation of more urbane and scholarly jurists began to shift the perception of the Texas Supreme Court away from its uniquely colorful heritage. Chief Justice Hickman's health was not robust, and Garwood sometimes stood in as acting chief during his decade on the Court.[1]

Local color was not dead yet, however, as following Garwood onto the Court in 1949 was Meade F. Griffin from the Texas Panhandle. Born in Cottonwood (Callahan County), he was formerly county attorney and then mayor of Tulia (Swisher County), and served as county judge in Plainview (Hale County) before spending seven years as district attorney of the Sixty-Fourth Judicial District. He was a past president of the state bar, and had served as prosecution subsection chief during the war crimes trials in Germany. Griffin's subsequent two decades on the Court place him in a very select company of judicial longevity, and after his retirement in December 1968 he was appointed a special judge of the Court of Criminal Appeals, making him one of a very few to serve on both benches.[2]

The fifties opened with a number of other personnel changes on the Supreme Court. Since being run as Angus Wynne's weapon to unseat Richard Critz, Gordon Simpson had served three and a half creditable years on the Court, but resigned to enter private practice in Dallas. Appointed to that vacancy was Ralph Hicks Harvey, a native of northeast Texas who had taught history and Latin before entering a judicial career that had taken him as high as the Sixth Court of Appeals. He died in September 1950 after only a year and a half on the high bench, two months before the general election.[3] Interestingly, despite having a terminal illness, Harvey had run for his seat on the Court in the July 1950 Democratic primary. He lost to Robert W. Calvert, who, before being elected in November, was appointed by Governor Jester to complete Harvey's term. (Harvey's term expired on December 31, and Calvert's service would have begun on January 3 had he not been appointed to the seat.)[4]

Calvert, forty-five, was a man who had already demonstrated immense determination to succeed. He was the son of a Tennessee sharecropper, so poor that when his father died, his mother was compelled to place Robert and his sister in the Corsicana State Orphans' Home. Surviving ten Dickensian years there, nearly dying in the influenza epidemic in 1918 (his sister did perish), he embarked on a course of legal study at the University of Texas. It took eight years to complete his education, allowing for times he could not afford to continue. He graduated in 1931, settled in Hillsboro to practice, entered politics, and in six years was Speaker of the Texas House. He returned to Hillsboro's local politics after being defeated in a run for attorney general in 1938.[5] In his run for associate justice in 1950, he had the advantage of voter confusion over his name, which was similar to that of Texas state comptroller Robert S. Calvert, and also a timely advertising campaign by Calvert Whiskey. "I couldn't have bought that for a million dollars," he recalled near the end of his life.[6] His luck was Texas's gain, however, for his own twenty-two years on the Court were highly distinguished.

With the Court expanded to nine members, an increasing number of justices came and went, but a few stayed long enough to leave their mark. After Beauford Jester became the only Texas governor to die in office, his successor, Allan Shivers, appointed Clyde Earl Smith, judge of the Seventy-Fifth Judicial District, to fill a vacancy on the Court in 1950. His was a Texas Horatio Alger story, with a Shivers family connection. Born into grinding poverty in the hardscrabble Hill Country of Central Texas in 1897, Smith's tenant-farmer father died when Clyde was only four, and he spent several years at a Catholic orphanage in San Antonio while his widowed mother struggled to make ends meet. He eventually returned to his family, but they remained poor, even after his mother remarried. As a teenager in the East Texas logging community of Woodville, Clyde subsisted on a variety of menial jobs—bicycle messenger, peanut vendor, delivery boy, night telephone operator. He was noticed by a local judge, Robert Shivers, who allowed him to study law in his office. Woodville was the seat of Tyler County, and once admitted to the bar, Smith embarked on several years as county and district attorney. His career faltered when he was defeated in Depression-era races for attorney general, Congress, and the Railroad Commission. He had served for seven years as Seventy-Fifth District Judge when Judge Shivers's son, now governor, elevated him to the Supreme Court. He went on to spend two decades there, a judicial progressive who supported the concept of nonpartisan elections for judges.[7]

Elected to the Court in 1950 was Will R. Wilson, Sr., a Dallas native who graduated first in his class from Southern Methodist University Law School and served two terms as Dallas district attorney. Interestingly, one of Wilson's most enduring contributions during his Supreme Court years—in addition to his well-known work on the federal *Tidelands* case—was a paper he delivered at a water-law conference sponsored by the University of Texas Law School. Titled "A Reappraisal of *Motl v. Boyd*," the paper (published in 1955) suggested that the 1926 case authored by Chief Justice Cureton was based on an incorrect interpretation of Spanish law. As will be seen, that suggestion was the beginning of the end of *Motl v. Boyd*.[8]

Wilson served as associate justice from January 1951 until June 1956, when he resigned to run a successful campaign for state attorney general. He later served as assistant U.S. attorney general in the Nixon administration.[9]

Following Wilson onto the Court in 1953 was Frank Pugh Culver, an Alabama native who came to Texas when his father, a Methodist minister, accepted the presidency of the school that later became Texas Wesleyan University in Fort Worth. A law graduate of the University of Texas following undergraduate study at Vanderbilt, Culver had taught Latin (like Justice Harvey) and English in the high school at Winnsboro before settling in Fort Worth, where he served as assistant district attorney and then as judge of the Seventeenth District Court for twenty-two years, with time out for extensive military service in both world wars. He had been on the Second Court of Civil Appeals for only a year when he ran for and won a seat on the Supreme Court, where he served two full six-year terms.[10]

Another two-decade member of the Court was Ruel Carlile Walker, appointed associate justice by Governor Shivers upon the death of Graham Smedley in 1954. A native of Cleburne, Walker exited the University of Texas Law School in 1934 as editor in chief of the *Texas Law Review*, and with highest honors. He worked as an investigator for the Attorney General's Office before returning to Cleburne for private practice and heavy involvement in local and then state Democratic Party affairs. In twenty-one years on the Court, Walker became a leader not just for his scholarship, but for his efforts as a consensus builder, allowing the Court to speak with a more united voice than it otherwise might have.[11] It was a stewardship that came at a particularly opportune moment, since Smedley had been the senior associate justice. That station carried with it a role as elder statesman that transcended Court politics and personalities and fostered the smooth operation of the Court and cooperative relationships among the justices. Smedley had taken the job uncommonly seriously, and Walker's particular gifts carried forward the operation of a Court that was increasingly composed of newcomers.[12]

Indeed, the whole ethos of the Hickman Court was one of not rocking the boat, of deferring to the legislature whenever the justices sensed the temptation to remedy an outrageous situation with a judicial solution. The Court had a sterling opportunity to do so—to emulate the Stayton Court's *So Relle* boldness—when it reviewed *Harned v. E-Z Finance Co.* (1953), in which the plaintiffs sued a moneylender not just for usury but for the intentional infliction of emotional distress.[13] There was no question of the defendants' egregious conduct, and the Court admitted that there were good reasons of public policy why there should be a "new tort" of intentional emotional distress, but it was not going to take that step. That was a job for the legislature.

The Hickman Court's position on the limited role of the judiciary was not the default result of inaction; it was an implementation of philosophy. One example was an inheritance case that required the Court to decide whether to apply in Texas the ancient Rule in Shelley's Case, a hoary medievalism originally intended to protect the rental interest of the feudal baron in his castle. Over time it had become a common law doctrine in England that effectively denied property owners the right to bequeath property by inheritance to a specific person and that person's heirs. Most jurisdictions, including England in 1925, had jettisoned it. The Court's opinion polled the status of the rule in various states: "The Legislatures in a majority of states have abolished the rule in whole or in part, and it appears that in one state, Vermont, it was abolished by judicial decree."[14] Texas, however, was manifestly not Vermont, and citing Texas's very first statute—that the common law would be made the authority of decision in the state—the justices upheld application of the Rule, but with a specific recommendation to the legislature that it be repealed by statute.

There was, of course, a swamp of pettifoggery into which even the Hickman Court would not follow. In a case from Dallas in which a trial court had declared two minor children to be dependent and neglected, the appeals court reversed. Following the Supreme Court's example of punctilious obedience to the applicable statutes, the appeals court pointed out that the district court was meeting in a physical location that had been annexed to the city of Dallas in 1947, whereas an arcane statute provided that the district court was required to hold its session in an area of Dallas that was within the city limits at the time it became the county seat 107 years before. The Supreme

Court's opinion was one of the more impatient that it ever issued: "What difference can it make?"[15]

Then, too, some cases did not lend themselves to a legislative remedy because of the present and ongoing hardship or cost to one of the parties. In such a case, the Hickman Court could prove as formidably adroit with its reasoning as any of its predecessors. In an administrative ruling in 1953, the Texas Railroad Commission, which had long since succeeded to oversight of the oil and gas industry, ordered all production shut down in the huge Spraberry Field in West Texas. Some 1,800 wells in the field were flaring off casing-head gas in gargantuan quantities. Charged by statute with preventing waste of an irreplaceable natural resource, the Railroad Commission halted the flow from those wells until some means could be found to harness and market the gas. However, some 468 wells in the field were not flaring gas, and had they been allowed to continue pumping, they would have had an unfair impact on the "correlative rights" of the restrained producers of the same field. So the Railroad Commission just shut down all the wells. The amount of money being lost was colossal, and the affected companies took the matter to court.[16]

In its ruling, the Court lauded the Railroad Commission for its dedication to duty. It had "made a courageous effort to prevent the waste of gas." Further, the Court acknowledged that in the future, "it may be through the use of administrative devices not available to the courts" that additional means could be found to prevent waste and protect correlative rights.[17] For the present hour, however, the justices found a bright white hair to split: the commission had the statutory power to shut down a field to prevent waste, and it also had the statutory power to *limit* production to protect correlative rights, but the statute did not specifically convey the power to *stop* production in order to protect correlative rights. Therefore, the Court held that the administrative order to shut down the nonwasteful wells was void, and the Railroad Commission was instructed to stop enforcing the order at Spraberry Field. The more obvious construction would have been that the right to limit production implied the right to stringently limit production, but the day was saved for hundreds of drillers, at perhaps not too great a cost to the Court's otherwise staunch principles. (In the same year, the Court also rendered its mite to the history of spousal rights, holding that oil produced from a well on a spouse's separate property, and the royalty paid for it, remained separate property.)[18]

Fortunes were made or lost depending on the Court's rulings in oil and gas cases, but there was another precious underground resource that demanded increasing consideration, without which life itself could not be sustained. During the middle 1950s, Texas suffered under a crushing drought, and it was inevitable both that water rights cases should make their way to the Court and that the mischief wrought by the late chief justice Cureton's analysis of the ownership of groundwater would have more damage to do. Because Cureton had adopted the common law doctrine that a property owner owned from the center of the earth to the dome of the sky, those who owned wells could pump with abandon, drying up their neighbors' land to dust. Two cases now reached the Texas Supreme Court pleading that the state adopt the "American" system of correlative rights, even as had been done in the oil patch.

The first involved a private landowner named Williams, in Pecos County, whose lavish mechanized pumping had dried up Comanche Springs, which had formed part of the municipal water supply of Fort Stockton for many years.[19] The second involved a municipality, the City of Corpus Christi, which owned wells in Atascosa County, from which the city pumped as much as ten million gallons a day into the Nueces River to feed its down-stream reservoir.[20] Some 70 percent of the water never reached its destination because of seepage and evaporation, and the City of Pleasanton, in Atascosa County, was left high and dry. The opinion was written by Justice Calvert, who at fifty, after five years on the Court, was not only becoming a workhorse but also asserting the kind of natural leadership that had made great justices in the past, such as Hemphill and Gaines. He was smart, affable (he drank Falstaff), and strict in his interpretation of the law.[21] Part of that strict inter-pretation, however, was his dedication to stare decisis and the firewall that he erected between his own sentiments (including a clear vision of where justice lay in a case) and the decision mandated by the law and the precedents.

Citing Texas cases going back to the Gaines Court of 1904, including Cure-ton's determined ignoring of the clear and appropriate equity available under Spanish law, Calvert and the Court held for the pumpers in both cases.[22] Calvert did have some additional cover, in that Texas's hyper-amended Con-stitution, in article XVI, section 59, gave the legislature the power, if it chose to exercise it, to prohibit wasteful water pumping, but so far the lawmakers had not done so. "The legislature is now in session," he wrote serenely. "It will have this opinion before adjournment. It will recognize the problem. If it wishes to declare that the transportation of water in conduits which permit the escape of a large percentage is wasteful and unlawful it will have ample time in which to do it."[23]

In 1954, the Court heard a case that ostensibly involved "harmless error" in improper argument to a jury, but that raised racial implications heralding much of the unrest in the decade to come. Only the year before, the justices had ruled that for a counsel's improper jury argument to cause a reversal in a case, it had to be shown that the argument was intended to mislead the jury and probably did mislead the jury.[24] But then they heard arguments in *Texas Employers Insurance Association v. Haywood*, in which an African American man sued for and won total permanent disability status under the state's workmen's compensation law.[25] At trial, the insurance company put two other African American men on the witness stand to testify that the plaintiff's injuries were not that serious. During his closing argument to the jury, the plaintiff's lawyer attacked the two defense witnesses as not being "somebody that you could believe," and stated that the defense should have put (presumably more credible) white witnesses on the stand. The insurance company, which stood to have to pay the claim, appealed that the plaintiff's lawyer's argument to the jury was improper.

The Supreme Court did not hesitate to say that it found "not one whit of evidence" that the two witnesses "either found pleasure in or stood to gain by giving testimony that ran counter to the best interest of the member of their own race. Certainly, their race alone was not a badge of perjury." The Court held that the plaintiff's argument was improper—nothing more than an "appeal to racial prejudice"—and the judgment was reversed.[26]

The timing of *Haywood* was fortuitously in step with larger, national trends, because in May 1954 the U.S. Supreme Court dropped a bombshell on the American public with its ruling in *Brown v. Board of Education*, holding that public schools statutorily segregated by race were inherently unequal and therefore unconstitutional.[27] The decision was a tardy cannonball into the façade of the antebellum South, for a map of school segregation at the time of the suit revealed that the states in the country that required African American children to be taught in separate schools duplicated the membership of the Confederacy, plus the border states of Missouri, Kentucky, West Virginia, Maryland, and Delaware.

Reaction throughout the South was one of outrage and defiance. Texas had already suffered one body blow (after four years of dodging and weaving) in its fight against integration, having lost the monumental *Sweatt v. Painter* case in 1950, which forced the desegregation of the University of Texas School of Law.[28] After *Brown*, the state's intransigence was met with further lawsuits in federal courts, one of which was filed by the Texas NAACP to desegregate the public school district in Mansfield. The keystone of the hostility in Texas was the state executive: Allan Shivers sent Texas Rangers to Mansfield to maintain the status quo, discourage agitation, and see to it that black students continued to be bused to classes in Fort Worth. The Texas Supreme Court, whatever the justices' private sentiments, followed the federal order faithfully. The matter came to the Court in the case of *McKinney v. Blankenship*

(1955).[29] The dispute placed at risk the hard-won Gilmer-Aikin laws of 1949, which standardized state educational requirements, consolidated school districts, revamped the state's oversight framework, and allocated state funding to each district according to its student population, counted separately by race.[30] The suit, brought by a coalition of citizens' groups, sought declaratory relief via a ruling that no state funds could be spent on public education in a way that was contrary to the Texas Constitution—which required the racial segregation of schools. The opinion was a judicial high-wire act, preserving as much of the Gilmer-Aikin system as did not conflict with the federal decision, thus preserving school financing for the coming biennium, but clearly declaring unconstitutional those parts of the law, and indeed those parts of the state constitution, that conflicted with *Brown*.

In this politically and racially charged atmosphere, between 1957 and 1958 the Supreme Court gained and almost lost one of the brightest lights in its history. During the decade, the Democratic Party in Texas had all but rent itself into two warring factions: a liberal wing, rooted in the New Deal and now anchored by U.S. senator Ralph Yarborough, and a frostily conservative, anti–New Deal, mostly segregationist establishment that passed from Allan Shivers to a somewhat more moderate Price Daniel, who became governor in January 1957. The state's most important political figure, U.S. Senate majority leader Lyndon B. Johnson, walked a tightrope between them, almost magically playing both ends against the middle.

Against this backdrop, a dying Few Brewster resigned from the Court in September 1957. In his dozen years as a justice, he earned the reputation as a courteous scholar, and his publication in 1954 of an article favoring desegregation of the state bar probably identified him as more liberal in his sentiments than most of his colleagues.[31] To fill the vacancy, Governor Daniel turned to Joe R. Greenhill, the former briefing attorney for the Court who had risen to first assistant attorney general before entering private practice. In the capacity of first assistant attorney general in 1948 (under Daniel as attorney general), Greenhill had argued the state's position against integrating the University of Texas Law School in *Sweatt v. Painter*. He was ethically bound by the canons to represent the state zealously, and could not otherwise be called a racist. Also in that position, Greenhill settled a case challenging Anglo-Latino school segregation in South Texas by integrating the schools.[32] He later became a friend—although perhaps a wary friend—of his opposing counsel in *Sweatt*, Thurgood Marshall.[33] Nonetheless, his conservative credentials were established, and when Greenhill had to run to hold his seat on the Court the year after he was appointed, the liberal side of the party decided to fight for it.

Opposing Greenhill in the primary was state district judge Sarah T.

Hughes of Dallas, eighteen years his senior and the first woman to run for a seat on the high bench. She had first been appointed to the Fourteenth District Court by Governor Jimmy Allred during the height of the New Deal in 1935 after five years in the legislature, and had been solidly reelected ever since. In an era in which female politicians were still a novelty, the ultimate compliment was, "She thinks like a man." (It is unlikely, though, that one of Judge Hughes's campaign events would have featured the same draw as one of Greenhill's speeches. In a campaign appearance before the Houston Junior Bar, Greenhill was followed onstage by the famous stripper Candy Barr.)[34] With a few exceptions, Greenhill ran with business and bar support; Hughes ran with labor and ethnic support, and came within an eyelash of upsetting him. The vote was 580,994 (50.6 percent) to 566,807 (49.4 percent). As Hughes later admitted, Texas justice would have suffered without Greenhill's twenty-five years on the Supreme Court.[35]

Anxious to make a good impression, Greenhill in his first major opinion provided an encyclopedic accounting of relevant decisions from other jurisdictions.[36] The 1959 case was from the City of Lubbock, which had utilized its power under the Texas Urban Renewal Statute to acquire property by condemnation, which was then sold at arguably fair market value, but for less than the cost of its acquisition and clearing. This action was challenged as not being a taking for "public use" within the meaning of the statute, and also as amounting to a granting of public money to individuals, which was unconstitutional. Greenhill's withering scholarship carried the day with a unanimous opinion upholding the constitutionality of the city's actions, but great was his deflation when, in conference, the highly respected Calvert admitted that he had not read the footnotes past number twenty. "He disliked any footnotes," wrote Greenhill in his journal notes.[37]

By tradition, the justices divided matters of Court administration among themselves, and the one responsible for the Court's physical accommodation, "bricks and sticks" duty, as they called it, was Justice Garwood. Probably more impatient than the others with their antiquated quarters in the Capitol, with its antique bench, which had been sawn apart and extended to accommodate nine justices, the far-flung offices, and the dumbwaiter that fetched books from an inadequate library, Garwood set the machinery in motion to move to Court to its own building.

Funding such a project would be an issue. There was one ready pool of money, the Confederate Pension Fund, but dipping into it ignited the slow fuse of an incendiary device that took decades to explode. Especially in the wake of school integration and the beginnings of a push for civil rights by African Americans, conservative Texans seeking to push back against the tide of history gave greater public honor to their Confederate heritage. And public sentiment, like a bump in the carpet, when denied one expression will find another. Texas had always made some modest financial provision for its Confederate veterans and their widows. Those men had now passed from the scene, the final encampment of the United Confederate Veterans having struck their tents in Norfolk, Virginia, in May 1951. But owing to the number of young girls who, early in the century, had married aging rebels with at least one eye on that financial security, the Confederate Pension Fund was still a functioning entity. As those ladies died off, the fund was obligated to ever-fewer disbursements, so when the legislature finally bowed to the need for the Texas Supreme Court to have its own building, it seized on the suggestion to pay for it with the Confederate Pension Fund and to dedicate it to those who fought for the Southern Cause. It seemed like a good idea at the time; the chagrin and reckoning would come a few decades later.

Construction began on a plot immediately northwest of the Capitol, over-looked by the windows of the old Supreme Court chamber. Chief Justice Hickman presided over the laying of the cornerstone on December 2, 1957. Built of the same pink granite as the Capitol, but of starkly modern architec-ture, the building was finished in twenty months, in August 1959, and dedi-cated in December of that year.[38]

"For the first time in the history of our state," bragged Texas State Bar president (and former justice) A. J. Folley of Amarillo during the dedication ceremonies, "we now have a building, a courtroom and a justices' cham-bers commensurate with the dignity and importance of this great court."[39] The Court had indeed come far since hearing its first cases in Asa Brigham's cabin at Second Street and Congress in 1840, but the modernization was not welcomed by all. The Capitol courtroom held more than seven decades of memories. Second deputy clerk Carl Lyda often came in to work at night, as indeed did all the clerks. Once when he came in unannounced, he found "Old Alex, our ancient Negro porter, sitting alone in the darkness": "When I asked what he was doing, he . . . answered, 'I was jes settin here visitin with Jedge Gaines, Jedge Brown and Jedge Yantis. They lef when you opened the door.'"[40]

They would especially miss the bench. The venerable walnut "SICUT PA-TRIBUS SIT DEUS NOBIS" bench in the Capitol's third-floor Supreme Court room, expanded to accommodate nine justices but still sternly overseen by portraits of Hemphill, Wheeler, and Lipscomb, would not make the transi-tion with them. One of the justices, who declined to go on the record for attribution, described the new marble bench as looking like a soda fountain. "I've threatened," he said, "none too seriously of course, to take up public donations and tear out the new one and replace it with the bench we have now." Another justice, also unwilling to be named, said, "Had the architects tried, it is difficult to see how they could have designed a building more ill-suited to our needs." A third registered a more moderate opinion: "It is true that it is poorly arranged in some respects. But it is so much better than what we have now that I'm not complaining."[41]

One aspect that came in for special criticism was that the clerk's office had been relegated to the basement. For as long as anyone could remember, the clerk's office was not just the storeroom for the oft-consulted case histories, but the social locus of the old Court, where a weary justice could take a rocking chair and tell some stories, mentor clerks, and cultivate the tribe. The new facility was sterile. When the Court convened in its new pink granite strongbox, the justices (for the first time in Texas history, curiously) appeared in judicial robes. A self-conscious Chief Justice Hickman declared that the new garb was "not to satisfy our own vanity, but in recognition of the fact that we are beginning a new era in the court's history."[42] Actually, according to Justice Greenhill, it was the occasionally stifling conditions in the Capitol courtroom that had led to their not wearing robes up to that time. The new Court, unlike the Capitol, had air conditioning.

SIXTEEN

THE CALVERT COURT

Late in Hickman's tenure, two more important justices joined the Court. James Rankin Norvell, fifty-four, had the distinction of being the first nonnative to come east to Texas instead of west from the Old South. Born and raised in Colorado, he obtained his law degree from the University of Colorado before settling in the Rio Grande Valley in 1926. There the lack of legal work led him into detours, one with a title company and one with a railroad, before starting his own law firm in 1930. He had no judicial experience when Governor "Pappy" O'Daniel placed him on the Fourth Court of Civil Appeals in San Antonio a decade later. On that bench, though, he not only distinguished himself but also taught at St. Mary's School of Law for his entire sixteen-year tenure. Norvell ran for and won an open seat on the Court in 1956.[1] (Abner McCall, who had been appointed associate justice by Governor Shivers when Will Wilson resigned in June to run for attorney general, declined to run to hold the seat.)[2]

In 1959 the distinguished Justice Garwood retired from the Court, soon after moving the institution into the new building that he had advocated for. He was only sixty-four, and had plenty of good service left in him: eight years heading the Texas Civil Judicial Council while teaching at the University of Texas and Southern Methodist University and engaging in private practice. No wonder he supported a mandatory retirement age of seventy-five for Texas judges; he wouldn't have had time to do everything else.

Winning the vacant seat was Robert William Hamilton, only three years younger than the retiring Garwood but destined for twelve productive years on the high bench. A native of the verdant Tyler area, he worked his way through law school by dividing his time: teaching and coaching in the Panhandle town of Plainview during the school year, then removing to Austin for summer classes at the University of Texas. It took eight years, but Hamilton's ability to hew to a method and see jobs through was his bedrock. He settled in Stanton in 1929, serving as county and then district attorney before moving to nearby Midland for sixteen years in private practice. That region's booming oil industry gave Hamilton a background in mineral law that served him well in later years. Two years as judge of the Seventieth Judicial District preceded his appointment as chief justice of the Eighth Court of Civil Appeals in El Paso. There he proved himself a workhorse, authoring more than 350 opinions in five years.[3]

Chief Justice Hickman was around long enough to get the Supreme Court moved into its new temple, but at seventy-seven he declined to run for another term in 1960. He stepped down in January 1961, after an appellate career of thirty-three years, sixteen of them on the Supreme Court and thirteen of those as chief. He had written more than four hundred opinions, received numerous awards and honorary degrees, and was the first Texan to chair the National Conference of State Chief Justices. He lived a year more in retirement, and died in April 1962, shortly after turning seventy-nine.[4]

In private consultations, Hickman had indicated his preference that either Griffin or Calvert should run for his seat.[5] Griffin declined, although he remained on the Court until 1968. Calvert's eleven years on the Court had earned him an enormous reservoir of respect that swept him to victory in the election by a margin of almost two to one. Governor Daniel filled Calvert's empty associate's chair with his secretary of state, Zollie Coffer Steakley, Jr. He was fifty-three, wiry, bantamweight but perhaps the best athlete in the Court's history: while various justices had been coaches, Steakley had once been offered a professional baseball contract after graduating from Baptist-affiliated Simmons University in Abilene in 1929. He went to law school instead, then went into private practice in Sweetwater while helping his father at his auto dealership. After returning to Austin, his tenure as assistant attorney general was interrupted by a stint in naval intelligence during the war, followed by a decade in private practice. Interestingly, the religious instruction that had been lost with Hickman's retirement was regained with Steakley. Whereas Hickman's Bible classes had to be held in the Tower Theater to accommodate the crowds, Steakley, in addition to everything else, taught a radio Bible class that had a large following in Central and East Texas.[6]

Thus composed, the Calvert Court was remarkably stable, given that three of the justices faced election every other year. It was a formidable assembly of talent, which was fortunate because not long after Calvert took charge, the Supreme Court was presented with a challenging case, unlike any it had ever faced. It was a class action by landowners whose property bordered the Rio Grande, seeking to be confirmed in their riparian rights to draw irrigation water from the river. The trial court, relying on the oft-cited *Motl v. Boyd* from the 1926 Cureton Court, which established riparian rights throughout Texas, agreed that they did. The Fourth Court of Civil Appeals in San Antonio, stunningly, reversed. In a lengthy, punctiliously scholarly history lesson that began in thirteenth-century Spain, the San Antonio court momentously placed Texas water law on the same footing as Texas land law, establishing that the law of the sovereign at the time the land was originally patented controlled whether Spanish or English rights came with it. The farms adjacent to the Rio Grande originated in Spanish land grants, so the controlling law was that of Spain and Mexico, which at no time had a system of riparian rights. Any right to use the water in a bordering stream had to be specifically conveyed by the sovereign. The current landowners therefore had no appurtenant (that is, legally accompanying) riparian right to irrigate.[7]

It was an act of breathtaking presumption for a civil appeals court, but the genius of *State v. Valmont Plantations* (1961) was that it threw over Cureton's mistakes in *Motl* without actually overruling the case, which, of course, a lower court could not do. In the appeals court's words: "*Motl v. Boyd* is *stare decisis* on many matters which were in issue. On those matters we are bound. We do not presume to overrule the case. . . . We are not, however, bound by dicta, commentary, or advisory remarks. . . . We assert that no Texas Court has heretofore been called upon to decide whether Spanish and Mexican land grants have appurtenant irrigation rights similar to the common-law riparian right."[8] By holding that those elements of *Motl* that had come most into play were, in fact, mere dicta (expressions of opinion) not central to the ruling, *Valmont* gave Texas a fresh start on the issue of water law, with a minimum of disrespect to stare decisis. The author of this audacious opinion was Andrew Jackson ("Jack") Pope, who had sat on the San Antonio Civil Appeals Court since 1950, building brick by brick a reputation as one of Texas's most honest, hardworking, capable, and scholarly judges.

Not all of Pope's colleagues on the San Antonio bench agreed with his approach, however, and there was a vigorous dissent to *Valmont* from Chief Justice W. O. Murray. *Motl v. Boyd*, he insisted, had been cited as controlling authority in scores of cases since, and stare decisis required that it be respected as settled law, notwithstanding alternative approaches that could be suggested by a more exacting reading of Spanish and Mexican history. "There can be no doubt that Chief Justice Cureton seriously intended to lay down the law governing the rights of all landowners to use waters from navigable streams and rivers in Texas," he wrote, "whether or not such lands were originally within Spanish or Mexican grants. . . . And, further, there can be no doubt that the bench and bar of this State accepted such law as settled, and followed it up to the present time. . . . Certainly, *Motl v. Boyd* is one of the most celebrated cases rendered by our Supreme Court and should not lightly be disregarded." In addition, any dicta in *Motl* were judicial in nature and should be followed, and not dismissed as mere obiter dicta.[9]

Chief Justice Murray was not unreasonable in his analysis. If Pope really believed that *Valmont* represented an issue of first impression not bound by stare decisis, there would have been no reason for him to expend nearly thirty pages of ammunition shooting holes through Cureton's *Motl* decision. No Texas judge ever showed more deference to the jots and tittles of precedent than Robert Calvert, and here he seemed to have a rebellion on his hands in the Fourth Court of Appeals. After carefully reading Pope's hefty opinion, and considering all that was at stake, the Supreme Court took a step that it never had previously. It adopted Pope's opinion, verbatim, as its own.[10]

No other vacancy opened on the Supreme Court until 1964, when Frank Culver retired after two full terms. Elected to the open seat was none other than Jack Pope. Now fifty, he was a native of Abilene, a graduate of Abilene Christian College, and a staunch member of the Church of Christ. Not much bigger than Zollie Steakley, Pope had, like Steakley, been a navy man during the war, but in college had played tennis instead of baseball. He was law review editor at the University of Texas, and after graduating in 1937, he relocated to Corpus Christi to join his uncle, former state representative Walter E. Pope, in practicing law and running the family business concerns. Pope had the distinction of having been appointed to the bench by three different governors: by Coke Stevenson to the Ninety-Fourth District Court in 1946, by Beauford Jester to the same bench in 1947, and by Allan Shivers to the Fourth Civil Appeals Court in 1950. Unlike justices who pined for reform in how judges were selected, Pope acquired a zest for campaigning and was good at it, winning three terms on the appellate bench before being elected to the Supreme Court.[11]

In Austin, however, Pope was the junior justice, and he discovered that Calvert ran a tight ship. Prerogatives among the justices were accorded by seniority, right down to access to the men's room. It was a busy calendar, and Pope had to adjust to keep up. "Monday was 'application day,'" he wrote in a later tribute to Calvert, "Tuesday was 'opinion day,' and Wednesday was 'argument day.'"[12] The first thing that Calvert insisted upon was punctuality, for the Court could not function without it. Toward the end of Calvert's term, former governor Price Daniel was appointed associate justice when Clyde Smith stepped down. Daniel and his entourage were late for the swearing-in ceremony, but Calvert opened the program anyway, even though the front row of seats was vacant. Ex-governor of Texas he may have been, but on the Supreme Court, Daniel had better be on time, and now he had lowest priority for the Court's men's room as well.

Calvert also insisted that all discussions of cases be done when the justices were all together in conference; private lobbying for a point of view was forbidden. Concomitant with that, Calvert's rule was that whatever was said in conference, stayed in conference. Disagreements, particular arguments advanced by a justice, and disgruntled feelings were strictly to be left in the room, and not to poison their collegiality beyond there. In the conferences, Calvert moderated and habitually spoke last. And outside the regularly scheduled conferences, justices, even as in the old days, were summoned to hear special causes such as writs of mandamus or habeas corpus. Jack Pope, who treasured his time to read and research and think, found it a grueling schedule.

Little escaped Calvert's eagle eye. He was always respectful to counsel, but in oral argument would reduce unprepared attorneys to tears. By tradition, incoming cases were assigned to the nine justices in strict rotation; it was Calvert who noticed that some of the more experienced briefing attorneys knew whose turn it was, and would seed the calendar with cases they thought deserved to succeed or fail by routing them to particular justices. Calvert found it advisable to "upset that little applecart."[13]

The justices were a disparate group, ranging from the strict conservatism of Meade Griffin and Graham Smedley to the old-style populism of Clyde Smith.[14] Politically, Calvert believed himself somewhat to the left of most of them, but judicially he was a firm adherent of the limited role of the courts. Calvert was at times only grudgingly tolerant of the philosophical distance between those he called his "law men" and his "equity boys."[15] The "law men" were the strictest constructionists, determined to give litigants not a thimble's measure more relief than the constitution required, whereas the "equity boys" were more sensitive to cases in which a wrong had gone unrighted, and might be willing to bend an interpretation to see justice done. Whereas a future conservative generation would chastise the latter as "activist judges," Calvert understood that the courts are at times the last chance for someone hoping to obtain justice, and he understood the obstacles to obtaining justice from a sometimes backward, malleable, and corruptible legislature. But neither argument got him past what he understood as the constitutional limitations on the judiciary. He was a "law man." It was a philosophy molded before Calvert ever joined the Supreme Court; he understood politics and corruption, having chaired the executive committee of the Texas Democratic Party in the 1948 U.S. Senate election in which Lyndon Johnson defeated Coke Stevenson with the aid of delayed returns—the election that led to Johnson being given the sobriquet "Landslide Lyndon." With clear evidence of fraud before them and bearing the duty of canvassing the election results, Calvert had consulted the case of *Ferguson v. Huggins* (1932) and felt constrained to conclude that the executive committee had not the power to do anything about it; their function was purely ministerial.[16]

He followed that philosophy even when it cost him emotionally, in cases for which he felt keen sympathy.[17] Joe Greenhill, who could not often be charged with liberal sentiments, later recalled that "Calvert did not hesitate to follow an established rule even if it appeared to reach an unpopular or undesirable result in a particular case. Since he disciplined himself rigidly to follow the law, he was impatient with judges who would want to depart from the rule to reach an equitable or just result. . . . I must confess that on some occasions I fell into Calvert's classification of 'equity boys.' In some respects, I was almost as firm in my views as he was, and I could feel Calvert's displeasure."[18]

But by his own rule, Calvert left those rancors in the conference room, and otherwise was the most human of justices, with a ready laugh and a penchant for jokes.[19] He could be wounded by accusations that his justice was untempered by mercy, especially when they came from justices who sat on the Court long after he was gone. Many years after Calvert retired, he answered back to a carp from later justice C. L. Ray, who claimed, "When Calvert was here, an oil company, an insurance company, a utility company, or a bank could not lose a case." Calvert was quick to point out decisions of his era that disproved such a blanket assertion.[20]

One opinion that he was particularly proud of was *Landers v. East Texas Salt Water Disposal Co.* (1952), which overruled previous cases to allow joint tortfeasors (those accused of committing a civil wrong) to be sued in the same action. In the past, Calvert wrote, "our courts seem to have embraced the philosophy . . . that it is better that the injured party lose all of his damages than that any of several wrongdoers should pay more of the damages than he individually and separately caused. If such has been the law from the standpoint of justice, it should not have been."[21]

Such lapses into sympathy, rare as they were, raised alarms for someone as conservative as Smedley. "Calvert," he declared as they left the conference room one day after a particularly pointed session, "I am going to make a conservative out of you yet." Calvert responded, "Judge, you just keep working at it. You just keep working at it."[22]

Jack Pope also noted that there were those certain times when Calvert "took the next step in novel cases or those that moved beyond the periphery of the existing case law."[23] But Calvert had a strict test before he would take that step: "My own philosophy is that a prior decision should not be overruled unless it becomes clear from its use and influence over a reasonable period of time that it is more harmful than beneficial to society as a whole or to a substantial segment thereof."[24]

One such case in point signaled a foreseeable end to the doctrine of charitable immunity. In frontier days, before the omnipresence of insurance companies, Texas adopted as public policy the law that churches and other charitable institutions could not be held liable for certain torts that others might be sued for. That doctrine had become manifestly antiquated, and when a case arrived on the docket in 1966 involving an individual who had been injured in a collision with a church bus, the immunity was upheld but the Court, in a concurring opinion by Joe Greenhill, warned that the sun was setting on that day and that charitable institutions should obtain insurance coverage. Calvert's dissenting opinion went even further: "I would abolish [the doctrine of charitable immunity] outright . . . and would agree to abolish it prospectively so that liability would attach only in cases arising hereafter."[25] Two years later the doctrine was indeed scrapped.

On some issues, the legislature took pressure off the Supreme Court. Apart from a short streak of laws passed in the Progressive Era, it was the Supreme Court that for generations had taken the point on the status of Texas women before the law. Passage of the Matrimonial Property Act of 1967, however, enfolded into the Texas Family Code two years later, brought Texas statutes into harmony with long tradition, as well as with laws in the rest of the country.[26]

In the area of real estate law, the Calvert Court provided mostly stability. It did, however, venture new protection for home buyers in *Humber v. Morton* (1968), which imposed an implied warranty of minimum quality on the seller, rather than relying on the shopworn doctrine of caveat emptor on the part of the buyer.[27] In this case, a widow named Humber purchased a house in Morton's development; unknown to her, the chimney had a hole that opened into the attic. She lit the fireplace, burned the house down, and sued the builder. The case, tragic as it was, was well outside the sympathy of the "law men," but Justice Norvell pressed hard to hear it and wrote the opinion, which in Calvert's view hung on one lone decision from "a very obscure lower court somewhere."

The defense argued that the fireplace was the work of an independent contractor for which Morton was not responsible, and that builders in Texas had never been held to such a standard as a warranty of habitability. Norvell's opinion, from which only Meade Griffin dissented, was packed tight with cases and commentary on the long, slow demise of caveat emptor as a meaningful doctrine, going back as far as Justice Joseph Story's commentary on sales from 1856. "The purchase of a home is not an everyday transaction for the average family," wrote Norvell, "and in many instances is the most important transaction of a lifetime. To apply the rule of caveat emptor to an inexperienced buyer, and in favor of a builder who is daily engaged in the business of building and selling houses, is manifestly a denial of justice." While Norvell's historical summary made the Court's implementation of an implied warranty seem only a small step in a long progression, he then resorted also to public policy: caveat emptor "does a disservice not only to the ordinary prudent purchaser, but to the industry itself by lending encouragement to the unscrupulous, fly-by-night operator and purveyor of shoddy work." [28]

This was a day that the "equity boys" carried, but Calvert thereafter needled Norvell with the claim made by the builder's attorney on his motion to rehear, namely, that Norvell reminded him "of the fellow who saw the lone Indian in the woods and from that concluded that all Indians march in single file." [29] The "Widow Humber Case" would prove to be an important one in future years, if only as a measure of the political swings through which the Supreme Court was about to go.

This was not the last fun Calvert and Norvell had together, despite their differences. One December, Norvell drew a habeas corpus petition from a woman, named Joy, in jail for failure to produce a child in a custody dispute. Finding in her favor, Norvell drafted the order to read, "'Tis the Christmas season. Let Joy be unrestrained and unconfined." Calvert was sold. "I tried my best to get him to leave it in there," he recalled, telling Norvell, "We're too staid up here anyhow." But Norvell would not write such an unconventional order. [30]

After eight years with Calvert as chief, attrition began to take its toll on his court. Norvell retired in 1968, and Governor John Connally appointed Thomas Morrow Reavley of the 167th District Court in Austin to succeed him. Reavley was forty-seven, a native of Quitman, another navy veteran from World War II, but he was a Harvard JD among all the University of Texas alumni. Four years on the 167th District bench was his only judicial experience, although he had had brief stints as county attorney in Nacogdoches and Texas secretary of state. Still, Reavley developed a close friendship with the vastly more experienced Calvert in a short time. [31]

Meade Griffin also retired in 1968, and William Sears McGee was elected to the seat that he occupied for the next eighteen years. He was fifty-one when he donned his robe, a Houston native, University of Texas Law graduate, and yet another navy man. His legal experience had come in numerous fits and starts: private practice in oil and gas briefly before the war, then six years as a Harris County court at law judge, during two of which he also taught at the University of Houston College of Law. Governor Shivers appointed him to the 151st District Court bench in 1954, but he resigned a year later to resume private practice before finally settling down for ten years as Fifty-Fifth District Court judge.[32]

When Clyde Smith retired in December 1970, Price Daniel was appointed to replace him, and he served for the next eight years. A native of Dayton and resident of nearby Liberty in deep southeast Texas, Daniel was unique on the Court in various ways: as a former attorney general, U.S. senator, and governor, he had more political experience than any of the other justices, and he was the only one to have begun professional life as a journalist (for the *Fort Worth Star-Telegram* and the *Waco News-Tribune*). He was an army man on a Court packed with navy veterans, and a graduate of Baylor for both undergraduate and law degrees.[33]

Rounding out the new generation of justices was James Gray Denton, who was fifty-three when he joined the Court in 1971 to fill the seat vacated by Bob Hamilton. He was cut from the predominant cloth: native of Bonham, University of Texas law degree just before the war started, navy service, returned to Lubbock where he had obtained his undergraduate degree at Texas Tech. There he served seven years on the Ninety-Ninth District Court bench before moving to Amarillo as chief justice of the Seventh Court of Civil Appeals.[34]

As Calvert passed sixty-five, he began to think of retirement. He was still vigorous, and it was said that Governor Connally had sounded him out about succeeding him as governor, but Calvert declined. A dying Graham Smedley had counseled him some years before that Calvert's best service to the state was in the judiciary.[35] Even as a politician before his Court service, Calvert had aided the courts, getting a bill passed to give the Supreme Court rule-making power in civil cases, and in helping draft the Texas Rules of Civil Procedure that were adopted in 1941.[36] No doubt his service as he left the Court would serve the same cause.

Calvert's congratulatory address in 1971 to the Houston Bar Association on its hundredth anniversary inadvertently served also as his valedictory to the tumultuous 1960s. A remarkable speech, it showed a thoughtful, more mellowed Calvert, sensitive to the doubts that the younger generation displayed about the integrity of the judicial system. He applauded the local bar for a recent public relations effort at improving its image, but reminded members that "if public opinion of lawyers generally is to be enhanced, the judiciary must first earn and hold public respect." He quoted with approval a new female attorney who exhorted her newly sworn colleagues to become "the dissatisfied bar . . . dissatisfied with a local legal system that overlooks a social problem until someone actually files a lawsuit complaining—dissatisfied with a local legal system that by and large leaves it to the federal government to make legal processes available for the indigent . . . that talks much but does little about" current social ills.[37]

If he could, Calvert declared, he would "write rules of practice and procedure which in the trial of cases would minimize the technical skills of lawyers and maximize the legal rights of the litigants." He surrendered none of his conservatism, however. Those intimate with the Court knew of Calvert's anguish at those occasions when, as a matter of law, he felt compelled to rule against a litigant who had fairness firmly on his side. "I would not be misunderstood," he declared. Once his ideal rules were in place, they would be applied equally, to all, "and not according to what at the moment may be our views of the 'justice of the case.'"

"A changing society," he concluded, "is demanding something better than we have had, and we had better start listening with an attentive ear." One improvement that Calvert endorsed was the removal of politics from judicial selection, but he complained that the constitutional amendment for merit selection of appellate judges was languishing in a legislature more concerned with liquor by the drink.

Calvert retired in 1972, after twenty-two years on the Court, half of them as chief justice, near the end serving also as chairman of the National Council of Chief Justices. He authored 378 opinions, considered no-nonsense and to the point. In his last year as chief, Calvert formed a task force to propose revisions to the state constitution's judicial article to reform the way state judges are selected, away from partisan elections. After holding eight conferences around the state to gather input, the task force prepared a plan recommending that the legislature put before the voters an amendment for merit selection, and if that were rejected, to submit to the voters a proposal at least for nonpartisan judicial elections. The legislature eventually rejected the proposal.[38]

However, soon after Calvert left the Court, voters did approve creation of a constitutional revision commission to formulate a complete overhaul of the state's fundamental document. The Constitution of 1876 was still the one in effect, although it was now all but indecipherable for being overgrown with amendments. The legislature became a killing field for reform proposals as no fewer than fifteen met their end there over the next four sessions.[39] More than a decade after he left the bench, Calvert was still advocating for merit selection of judges.[40] Still vigorous as he approached eighty, he served as a member of the Texas State Ethics Advisory Commission in 1984 and 1985. By the time he died a decade later, few jurists in Texas had enjoyed such universal respect for having navigated commitments both to justice and to the circumscribed role of the judiciary under the constitution.

SEVENTEEN

THE COURT IN FLUX

Calvert was followed as chief justice in 1972 by Joe Robert Greenhill, whose association with the Supreme Court dated back to his days as a briefing attorney on the eve of World War II. As a jurist he was regarded as slightly to the left of Calvert and just a touch more willing to invoke equity to see justice done in a case. He was devoted to the institution and keenly interested in recording its history.[1]

One area in which the Greenhill Court had its work set out for it was in administrative law. Two U.S. Supreme Court decisions in 1970 and 1972 announced a formula for modern due process to be followed by states in administrative hearings.[2] Expediency in this area of law was of particular interest to Greenhill; even before joining the Court, he had taken the highly unconventional step of filing a brief in a Texas case as an amicus curiae, even though as special assistant attorney general he was already counsel for one of the parties.[3] After the Texas Legislature passed the Administrative Procedure and Texas Register Act in 1975, the Court had the pieces in place to craft a coherent, efficient process for the hearing and appeal of administrative matters.[4] Commentary on its effort was generally favorable.[5]

In the absence of such clear guidelines, however, the Greenhill Court moved cautiously when entering new legal territory. One example was in the real estate decision handed down in *Friendswood Development Company v. Smith-Southwest Industries, Inc.* (1978).[6] Here the Court for the first time imposed liability on the pumper for damage to neighbors resulting from excessive removal of groundwater. Recognizing that it was taking a new step, the Court provided that the principle was to be applied prospectively, from that time on, and was not to be applied to the case at hand, or retroactively. And even then, Greenhill was relieved when the legislature stepped in with an appropriate new statute, which rendered the Court's decision less activist.[7]

He did not just wait and hope, however. In addition to his Court duties, Greenhill was also a prolific writer, and sometimes published articles on topics of judicial moment, which could then be disseminated among legislators to call their attention to tatters in the legal fabric that needed to be mended.[8] The success of such a method, importantly, hung upon the profound respect that the legislature accorded him. That comity was about to be placed in danger by the increasingly political nature of Supreme Court elections.

Texas's partisan election of justices suffered its most public embarrassment with the election of Don B. Yarbrough to the Supreme Court in 1976. In down-ballot elections, apathetic Texas voters had long elected to office persons with the advantage of well-known names—the long-time state treasurer, Jesse James, was replaced by Warren G. Harding, for example, and it will be recalled that in 1950, Robert W. Calvert unseated an incumbent with a boost from a timely campaign by Calvert Whiskey and the presence on the ballot of state comptroller Robert S. Calvert.

In 1976, Yarbrough drew on the name identification of Donald H. Yarborough, a three-time candidate for governor, and Texas's former U. S. senator, Ralph Yarborough. Don B. Yarbrough was a virtual unknown, only thirty-four and a onetime staff attorney for an evangelical religious organization, Campus Crusade for Christ. The principal contestant for the Supreme Court seat was the chief justice of the Fourth Court of Civil Appeals, Charles W. Barrow, whom the members of the state bar favored in their traditional straw poll by a vote of 10,186 to 1,741, almost six to one.[9] There was no Republican candidate for the seat, so getting the Democratic nomination was tantamount to winning the general election. While Barrow waged a typically dignified campaign, emphasizing his experience and qualifications, Yarbrough ran on his youth and religiosity, and against the influence of the state's powerful law firms, which, he alleged, dictated results from the benches. He also rode the wave of the post-Watergate era, pitting fresh blood against the "good-ole boys," including Barrow. "I think someone smoking stodgy old cigars for fifteen years in some San Antonio appellate court," he said, "should be retired and not elevated to a higher position."[10] Yarbrough also cited the Bible— Chronicles, chapter 19—to promise that he would decide cases based on the laws of God, not man. Religion-loving Texans bought it all, along with the famous name, and when the primary smoke cleared, Yarbrough had nearly eight hundred thousand votes to Barrow's five hundred thousand.

Yarbrough was not entirely devoid of legal experience. He was a Dallas native, had graduated from the University of Texas Law School in 1964, and had gained expertise in the area of water law, practicing as attorney for the Texas Water Rights Commission and serving as secretary of the state bar's Committee on Water Law. Then he joined Campus Crusade for Christ, became a missionary, and moved to California to act as that organization's general counsel. When he returned to Texas in 1970, he entered into a long string of dubious business transactions that began to unravel during the months between the spring primary and the November general election. Yarbrough won the primary on May 1; two days later, he admitted in a press conference (after having deflected questions during the primary campaign) that there were "six or seven" lawsuits pending against him for defaulted bank loans. When press reports on May 4 increased the number of lawsuits to eleven, Texas Republicans investigated the chance of running someone against him in November. Under the Election Code, however, a candidate would have had to file more than three months earlier in order to appear on the November ballot, and the idea for a write-in effort was dropped as impractical.[11]

In June, Yarbrough lost a $100,000 judgment in a civil trial whose jury found his conduct fraudulent and grossly negligent in his legal practice, and once the spotlight centered on him, it became more widely known that his business dealings had been under scrutiny by the Houston Police Department, the Harris County district attorney, the Texas State Securities Commission, and the Federal Bureau of Investigation. The investigations depicted him as selling stolen IBM stock for a Houston dentist; kiting loans; buying a bank with the very money he had borrowed from it; squeezing a power of attorney from a woman dying of cancer and undertaking legal actions in her name without her knowledge; and more. In response, the state bar began taking steps to disbar him, but then it was pointed out, first, that most of the investigations had not yet matured into indictments, let alone convictions, and second, disbarment might not keep him off the Supreme Court. While the constitution requires that justices be lawyers, it does not specify that they be *practicing* lawyers.[12] The legal community then mounted a write-in campaign supported by both political parties, cleverly choosing as their candidate a district judge named Sam Houston. Despite their efforts, and those of a second write-in candidate, Yarbrough won the general election by a huge margin.[13] The prominent Houston attorney and Watergate prosecutor Leon Jaworski, speaking to the Texas Trial Lawyers Association in early December, said that the state's lawyers had "made every effort" to inform the voters what they were getting into, to no avail. He asserted also that Yarbrough should not be allowed to serve on the Supreme Court, a stance that the state bar's membership debated hotly in the coming months. The voters had, after all, made their choice, and there was no legal justification at that point for not honoring that choice.[14]

Yarbrough touted his election to the Supreme Court as evidence of God's will, and he took his seat on the high bench on January 2, 1977—less than a month after soliciting a former partner to murder a witness against him (a fact still unknown to the public).[15] Yarbrough took his oath in a robe borrowed from Chief Justice Greenhill, who swore him in. As the extent of his legal difficulties became known—the number of lawsuits pending against him had reached sixteen, state and federal—he became socially isolated on the Court, and Greenhill circumscribed his duties to the extent that he could.[16]

In June 1977, Yarbrough was indicted for allegedly forging a car title and then lying in court. Finally facing legislative proceedings to remove him from office, he resigned from the Court in July. The next March, he was sentenced to two to five years in prison, but while out on bond awaiting appeal, he removed to the Caribbean island of Grenada, which had no extradition treaty with the United States. There he attended medical school, and in 1983, while auditing a medical course on the nearby island of St. Vincent, which did have an extradition agreement, he was nabbed by federal marshals. He was returned to Texas to serve a five-year sentence for perjury, and in 1986 was convicted on federal bribery charges and received six years more.[17]

After Yarbrough's resignation in July 1977, Governor Dolph Briscoe appointed to the vacancy the man whom Yarbrough had defeated in the primary, Charles Barrow of the Fourth Court of Civil Appeals. He had served on that bench for fifteen years, having been appointed to it on the death in an automobile accident of its previous holder, his father. Barrow quickly settled in to become a workhorse of the Court and a prolific author of opinions.

While it could be argued that Yarbrough's election was a fluke (although given the electorate's penchant to pull the lever for famous names living or dead, it probably was not), it did herald a period of changes on the Court, of almost revolving-door rapidity.

Dolph Briscoe had been elected governor in 1972, and he had presided over a constitutional change that lengthened the gubernatorial term of office from two years to four. Succumbing to the temptation to be the first Texas chief executive to serve ten years, he announced for a third term in 1978. Texans traditionally frown on third terms, and Briscoe was beaten in the Democratic primary by the state attorney general, John L. Hill. In the general election, Hill faced an electoral novice, Dallas oilman William P. Clements, who had won the Republican primary with the help of large infusions of cash from his own fortune. In former days it would have been a walkover for Hill. However, Briscoe had also presided over an unprecedented change in demographics: the Texas population had increased by three million during the seventies, half of them out-of-state immigrants who felt no loyalty to Texas's tradition of Democratic rule. The victory was a squeaker decided by one-half of 1 percent, but at the end, Texas had its first Republican governor since E. J. Davis was run out of the Capitol in 1874.

Texas Democrats went into collective mourning, but Chief Justice Greenhill sensed an opportunity to exert some leadership in improving the lot of Texas courts at every level. Thinking not just of his own Court, he called attention in his 1979 State of the Judiciary message to the legislature (the first communiqué of its kind) to the declining health of the Court's sister supreme tribunal, the Court of Criminal Appeals. Greenhill used his position as chief to lobby for a constitutional amendment to give the intermediate courts of appeal criminal jurisdiction as well in order to ease the crushing backlog of cases in that court. Greenhill appealed to his old college friend, Governor Clements, for support, and the two pressed the case at a joint press conference.[18] The legislature heeded his call and put forward the amendment, and it was ratified by popular vote in November 1980.[19]

Greenhill issued a second appeal in his 1981 message, noting that despite the jurisdictional change, the system for criminal appeals was still drowning in its backlog, which had ballooned from about thirty-two hundred cases in 1979 to more than four thousand in 1980. Justice delayed, he reminded the legislature, was justice denied, and it took nearly three years for a convict even to get his appeal to oral argument.[20] He urged legislators to appropriate the added resources needed to handle the influx of criminal cases in the intermediate courts of appeal.

Continuing on the issue of funding, Greenhill emphasized the necessity of the state courts retaining the confidence of the people, noting that "the quality of the judiciary can rise no higher than the quality of persons you can attract to, and retain in, the system."[21] The judiciary, he reminded them, was the third coequal branch of the government, yet its legislative appropriation was less than one-third of 1 percent of the state budget.

Another important subject drew Greenhill's notice in the 1981 message. On the partisan election of judges, he said, "Many of us have been trying for years to get the Judiciary out of partisan politics. . . . There is a place for party politics in the election of the executive and legislative persons. You, and they, *and the parties*, have a platform. There *are no* meaningful party platforms for the Judiciary. The judge cannot favor a person, or his lawyer, because of his party. The judge must administer justice equally without regard to the persons before the bench. . . . Election of judges by 'the big lever' is, in my opinion, a poor method." Greenhill conceded that his personal preference for merit selection was politically impossible at that time to achieve, but he urged the legislature to seriously consider at least the nonpartisan election of judges, "just as we now elect our mayors and school boards."[22]

While Greenhill believed in reforming the Court toward merit-based selection, he also lived in a real and very political world, and Texas politics had entered a period of tumultuous change. The new generation of justices that began to take seats on the Supreme Court was increasingly disinclined to accept Greenhill's vision of justice as inherited from Calvert. Franklin Spears was elected to the Court in 1978, and had the distinction of having served as state representative, state senator, and then ten years as judge of the Fifty-Seventh District Court in San Antonio. He became an intellectual anchor of the Court's new progressive wing.[23] In November 1980 he was joined by Cread L. Ray, Jr., of Marshall, who was also a multiterm legislator and appellate judge.[24] Ray, as a measure of the Court's leftward shift, squeaked to victory over incumbent William Lockhart Garwood, forty-nine, a Republican and Clements's first Court appointment. Garwood had been appointed in November 1979 to replace an elected Democrat, six-year associate justice Samuel D. Johnson, Jr., who resigned when President Jimmy Carter appointed him to the U.S. Fifth Circuit Court of Appeals. Garwood was the son of the distinguished Justice Wilmer St. John Garwood, giving him the distinction of being the first second-generation Court member as well as the first Republican on the Court since Reconstruction. He had been on the Court for only a year when Ray reclaimed the seat for the Democrats.[25]

Greenhill had moved toward a strict, conservative approach to the law, and he was increasingly disturbed by the Court's leftward drift, its willingness to uphold large plaintiff verdicts and reach into the realm of equity for decisions that a pure observance of precedent could not sustain. And while Greenhill could occasionally see his way clear to such a result in tort cases, his consternation grew when the Court began applying this method in matters relating to contracts, an area where, in his view, courts should be more reluctant to interfere. "Particularly in contract law," he told an interviewer, "people embark on a course of conduct or a business venture . . . either upon their own knowledge of the law or upon legal advice from counsel, preferably the latter. When people pay for legal advice and take it, the Court should be very slow to say that we're going to change the law."[26]

An unapologetic progressive who believed that a court's function is to provide justice as well as to interpret the law, William Wayne Kilgarlin of Houston was defeated in the 1982 Democratic primary for a seat on the Court by the more judicially conservative incumbent, James G. Denton. When Denton died of a heart attack that summer, party officials placed Kilgarlin on the ballot, and he was elected, unopposed, in November. (In the interim, Governor Clements had appointed Judge Ruby Kless Sondock of the 234th District Court in Houston to Denton's seat, making her the first woman to serve on the Court since the Woodmen of the World special court six decades before. She did not want the job permanently and declined to seek election.)[27]

Kilgarlin was another with a mixed background of law and politics: he had entered the state House of Representatives at the age of only twenty-five, before he went to law school, and at the time he was elected to the Court was judge of the 215th District Court in Houston.[28] His election was the last straw for Greenhill. Faced with the prospect of serving the last two years of his term as part of a conservative minority, he struck back. In early October 1982, before the general election, Greenhill resigned in order to give the choice of appointment to Governor Clements, who could be relied on to name another conservative to the post. Clements did not name a replacement before the election, which he lost to moderate Democrat Mark White, the state's attorney general. When he continued his search for a replacement after the election, Democrats in the state Senate went apoplectic. The word in the cloakroom was that being still the majority party, they would humiliate the outgoing governor by derailing any judicial appointment he might make, no matter who it was. A group of fourteen Democratic senators sent a letter vowing to oppose any appointment that Clements might make, on the principle that the prerogative rightly belonged to the incoming governor.

Clements's response, and it was brilliant, was to appoint the hugely re-spected Jack Pope—a Democrat who had already announced his retirement from the Court—to be chief justice. He was sworn in on November 29, 1982, six days after his appointment had been announced to the public. But Senate opposition to Clements's lame-duck appointments continued, and the position of chief justice was one that the so-called Group of Fourteen strongly believed should be reserved for White. Despite the fact that Pope was a Democrat, they mounted a campaign to block his confirmation when the legislature convened in January 1983.

Governor White, under pressure to use his prerogative to recall the late nominations of his predecessor, conveyed to the Senate a list of appointments that he wanted withdrawn, but Pope's name was not on it. As senatorial opposition began to erode, one senator attempted to save face by crafting a deal with Pope allowing him to have the honor of being chief justice—if he would promptly resign and let White make a new appointment. Pope, who was as close to incorruptible as any jurist in Texas history, bristled at the suggestion. "Shoot me down in flames," he said, "but I will not make a deal." A public letter from retired chief justice Calvert called Senate attempts to sideline him "insulting to a person of Justice Pope's integrity" and pointed out that making a deal to obtain confirmation of his appointment would have violated the oath of office that he had already taken.[29] When White finally stated publicly that he wanted Pope to be confirmed, Senate opposition crumbled, and the appointment was confirmed by a vote of 29–2 on February 3.[30]

Greenhill's strategic move, then, had had its desired effect. At least in the short run, the Court would be in the hands of a dependable leader. Greenhill had stepped down after a decade as chief justice and twenty-five years altogether on the high bench—a longevity that outlasted every prior justice. It was the beginning of a long and honored retirement in which Greenhill not only practiced law, but made himself useful as head of the Texas Bar Foundation, a cofounder of the Texas Supreme Court Historical Society, and counsel for Baker Botts LLP, where he led efforts to give disadvantaged citizens better access to the legal system by encouraging arbitration. His vigorous golden years extended almost three decades after he retired from the Court; he passed away in Austin in February 2011, at the age of ninety-six.

Naming a replacement for such a titan would have been difficult in any circumstance, but in Jack Pope the Court found a dynamo more than equal to the challenge. Exhausting as he had originally found the Court's schedule, he had disciplined himself to maintain an active publishing and speaking profile, with his wife Allene often reading cases and memos to him as he drove to deliver a speech.[31] In his previous years on the Court, Pope had led initiatives to streamline Court procedures and tighten the ethical canons by which all attorneys were bound. Even before his appointment as chief justice was confirmed, he stepped forward to give the State of the Judiciary Address, focusing his remarks on reforms needed to improve the legal system. He reminded the legislature that every law it passed had repercussions in the courts:

> Every legislative session generates new causes of actions, remedies, and crimes. A stack of worthy bills is neither self-enacting nor self-enforcing. Some judge must eyeball every person who violates the new law.
>
> Legislation impacts the need for more courtrooms, judges, bailiffs, court reporters, and appellate judges. Legislative impact costs money and when costs are created we do no service to the public by failing to tell you of our increased needs. You do yourselves no service by refusing to support the implementation of what you have created.[32]

For just one example, Pope cited the Deceptive Trade Practices Act (1973), which, he said, "cut across existing contract, fraud, insurance, and warranty law," and whose newly created remedies had deluged the judiciary with new cases. Few doubted his word when he said he could give scores of other examples. Reiterating a theme introduced by Greenhill, Pope pointed out that the judicial branch is not expensive to run. "If every budget request sought by the judiciary were granted," he told legislators, "it would be less than the utility and maintenance bill of the University of Texas at Austin." His plea had its effect: that year the legislature responded with an $8 million per fiscal year increase in appropriations to the judiciary.[33]

Even as the courts became better funded, however, the Supreme Court was thrown into greater intellectual turmoil as the old conservative consensus continued to erode. The Court lost one of its ablest workers when Charles Barrow resigned in November 1984 to become dean of the Baylor Law School. Between stints on the Fourth Court of Appeals and the Supreme Court, he had authored more than six hundred opinions. With Mark White now in the Governor's Mansion, he filled the vacancy with a historic appointment: the first Latino to take a seat on the Supreme Court, Raul A. Gonzalez. Not merely Latino in surname, Gonzalez's life embodied the struggle of Mexican Americans. Born in 1940 in the Rio Grande Valley's produce-shipping center of Weslaco, he had grown up in the fields, picking tomatoes, onions, and cabbages with his migrant-worker parents, even as his mother imbued him with the necessity of getting an education if he were ever to break out of poverty. He entered the University of Texas in 1959, immersing himself in the campaigns for civil rights while working toward a government degree. He followed his BA with a JD from the University of Houston and embarked on a career that served his community: first the Houston Legal Foundation, then to Brownsville as assistant U.S. attorney, then two years as attorney for the Catholic Diocese of Brownsville. It was a Democrat, Briscoe, who first appointed Gonzalez to a district court bench, the Republican Clements who elevated him to the Thirteenth Court of Appeals, and White who placed him on the Supreme Court, where he spent fourteen productive years.[34]

Losing Barrow was only a prelude to a greater loss for the Court: Jack Pope, a year older than Greenhill, declined to run for reelection in 1984 and retired the following January, almost seventy-two years old. He had sat as a judge—district, appellate, and Supreme Court—for thirty-eight continuous years, longer than any other in Texas history, and he had authored more than eleven hundred opinions, also a record.[35]

Elected chief justice to succeed him was John Hill, whom William Clements had so narrowly defeated for governor in 1978. A native of Breckenridge, and an honor graduate of the University of Texas Law School, Hill had had a successful career as a trial lawyer in Houston before serving as secretary of state and then six years as attorney general.[36] In the latter role he had represented the state five times before the U.S. Supreme Court and had made dozens of arguments before the state's courts, including the Supreme Court, a hands-on approach that served him well in his campaign for chief justice and subsequent service on the Court.[37]

While Hill represented a voice for the judicial mainstream, the Court's leftward direction gained momentum with the addition in 1986 of state senator Oscar Mauzy of Dallas, who had gained a reputation as one of the most liberal members of that body. The son of a labor organizer who died when Oscar was only three, Mauzy was raised as one of eight children in the poverty of Houston's Fifth Ward during the Great Depression. He joined the navy as soon as he came of age and served as a radar man on the USS *Washington*, the ship that bombarded Saipan and Okinawa.

Afterward employed in an oil refinery, Mauzy left for the University of Texas under the benefits of the GI Bill. During his second year of law school, he organized a student strike against changes in the course catalog, students whom he then represented in negotiating a settlement with the school's dean, the formidable Page Keeton.[38]

After graduating, Mauzy relocated to Dallas and practiced labor law until he was elected to the state Senate in 1966. Thirteen years later, his rebellious spirit reared again as he defied the lieutenant governor (and presiding officer of the Senate, the redoubtable William P. Hobby, Jr.) over a bill that would have mandated that the Texas presidential primary be held on a separate day from the primaries for state offices—a move that would have advanced the presidential ambitions of former governor John Connally and blunted progressive influence in the state. Unable to muster votes to defeat the bill, Mauzy led eleven other senators into hiding, denying the Senate a quorum. Dubbed the "Killer Bees," the senators evaded a vigorous manhunt by the Texas Rangers until the bill was withdrawn.[39]

The episode made for grand political theater, and Mauzy rose to become president pro tempore of the state Senate, but it did not bode well for his judicial temperament on the Supreme Court. Indeed the Court, as it closed out its first century and a half, launched itself in a progressive direction that no one even a decade before would have predicted. The liberal justices imposed their weight in such areas as insurance law, warranty protections for home buyers, and a variety of tort cases whose philosophical thread had begun in more conservative times.

Insurance companies had traditionally relied on finding some misrepresentation (or error) by a policyholder in his or her application as a way to avoid payment when a claim was made. Beginning with *Mayes v. Massachu-*

setts Mutual Life Insurance Co. (1980), the Texas Court required that an insurer prove the consumer's "intent to deceive" before it could invalidate the policy.[40] The misrepresentation also had to be shown to be material to the claim.[41]

What the Court recognized in *Mayes* was that consumers did not have anything close to the bargaining power that the insurance companies had in the issuance of policies, where meaningful negotiation was rarely if ever part of the process. Placing a heavier burden of proof on the insurer served both to curb the power of the insurance company and to bring some balance to the relationship between seller and buyer.[42]

In a similar vein, a thread of cases arose on the issue of protecting home buyers from unscrupulous builders of shoddy or even dangerous houses. As Texas emerged from the frontier era the general rule was, predictably, caveat emptor: let the buyer beware. A builder had no particular duty to build a safe and habitable house, because the buyer was putatively able to inspect the dwelling and decide whether to purchase it. Since those days, however, Texas had entered the era of large-scale developers of whole subdivisions, and of builders' associations that generated preprinted sales contracts, with buyers left to take it or leave it. The Court took an unexpected step in the direction of consumer protection as early as 1968 in *Humber v. Morton* (discussed in the previous chapter), in which Justice Robert Norvell ruled that "the old rule of *caveat emptor* does not satisfy the demands of justice in such cases."[43]

Humber might not have made the Court a nanny to the unwary citizen, but it may well have taken the Court too far out of its comfort zone. In 1982, even after the addition of more justices sympathetic to the plaintiff's bar, the Court revisited the issue and retreated in *G-W-L, Inc. v. Robichaux*.[44] "The parties to a contract," intoned Clements appointee Ruby Sondock in the old style, "have an obligation to protect themselves by reading what they sign." In this case, a builder sought to insulate himself from *Humber* by inserting into the contract a specific waiver of any implied warranties, including for the sagging roof over which Robichaux sued. And this, to the Court, barring "some basis for finding fraud," was sufficient. While scholarly commentary that *Robichaux* reinstituted caveat emptor may have overreacted, the case did erode consumer protection in this field.[45] Three justices vigorously dissented from the result, and as the plaintiff-friendly complexion of the Court continued to strengthen, they revisited the issue yet again in 1987 in *Melody Homes Manufacturing Co. v. Barnes*.[46] Here the Court not only overruled *Robichaux* but also buttressed *Humber* with the ruling that implied warranties of habitability and good workmanship could not be waived.

Although *Melody Homes* was perfectly defensible on its own merits, the increasingly political tension on the Court was apparent when Raul Gonzalez, who was uncomfortable with the result, asked what could justify repudiating such a recently decided precedent, and Oscar Mauzy offered "the voters of this state" as authority for taking the Court in a new direction.[47] It was a stance that would have horrified previous generations of justices respectful of stare decisis.

Thus, in an important way, the Texas Supreme Court ended its first century and a half much as it had begun: searching for an identity. The challenges that faced the Court at that point were no less momentous than any in its past: it would soon be called upon to decide matters of huge social importance, such as dismantling the state's system of financing public schools. And even as one chief justice after another called for reforming the process of selecting justices, the Court would soon be rocked by a humiliating scandal and given a total ideological makeover by the voters.[48] But also in its immediate future lay great social progress, such as the election of an African American chief justice and more female and Latino justices, allowing it to reflect the state's diversity.[49]

For most of its first 150 years, the Texas Supreme Court reflected the values and aspirations of the state's people. But how to do that in modern Texas, with thirty million people who belong to competing constituencies and are more diverse and more strident than ever before, will surely challenge the Court in ways undreamed of by past justices. One can only hope that the current justices will return to the question asked by the early Court: what serves us best?

James Collinsworth, 1836–1838

John Birdsall, 1838

Thomas J. Rusk, 1838–1840

John Hemphill, 1840–1858

Royall T. Wheeler, 1858–1864

Oran M. Roberts, 1864–1865; 1874–1878

George F. Moore, 1866–1867; 1878–1881

Amos Morrill, 1867–1870

Lemuel D. Evans, 1870–1873   *Wesley B. Ogden, 1873–1874*

Robert S. Gould, 1881–1882   *Asa H. Willie, 1882–1888*

John W. Stayton, 1888–1894

Reuben R. Gaines, 1894–1911

Thomas J. Brown, 1911–1915

Nelson Phillips, 1915–1921

Calvin M. Cureton, 1921–1940

William F. Moore, 1940–1941

James P. Alexander, 1941–1948

John E. Hickman, 1948–1961

Robert W. Calvert, 1961–1972   *Joe R. Greenhill, 1972–1982*

Andrew Jackson "Jack" Pope, 1982–1985

John L. Hill, 1985–1988

Thomas R. Phillips, 1988–2004

Wallace B. Jefferson, 2004–present

MILESTONES IN THE ORGANIZATION AND OPERATION OF THE TEXAS SUPREME COURT

1836

Mar. 17   Constitution of the new Republic of Texas calls for creation of a Supreme Court led by a chief justice, and three to eight district courts whose judges serve ex officio as associate judges of the Supreme Court.

Dec. 15   Republic Congress passes the first of a series of acts organizing the judiciary.

Dec. 16   Congress elects James Collinsworth as chief justice.

Dec. 22   Congress elects four district judges, who will also serve as associate judges of the Supreme Court: Shelby Corzine, Benjamin C. Franklin, Robert McAlpin Williamson, and James W. Robinson.

1837

Dec. 4   First scheduled Supreme Court session is canceled due to lack of quorum.

Dec. 14   Congress passes a law to fine absent associate judges $1,000.

1838

May 24   Congress adds a fifth district court and elects E. T. Branch as judge.

July 11   Chief Justice James Collinsworth drowns in Galveston Bay, possibly a suicide.

Aug. 10   President Sam Houston appoints John Birdsall as chief justice, pending approval of Congress.

Dec. 12   Congress elects Thomas J. Rusk as chief justice; he is on a military campaign against the Indians and is unaware of his election.

1839

Jan. 7   The 1839 Court term is canceled because of the absence of the chief justice, whose presence is required by the Constitution.

Jan. 21   Rusk learns of his election as chief justice.

1840

Jan. 13   Supreme Court convenes for the first time, with Chief Justice Rusk presiding.

Jan. 20   Associate Judge/District Judge James Robinson resigns under threat of impeachment.

          John Hemphill is elected judge of the Fourth District Court to replace Robinson and takes his seat on the Supreme Court.

          Congress adopts the English common law as the basis for Texas jurisprudence.

Jan. 24   First Supreme Court session ends, having disposed of forty-nine cases and issued eighteen opinions.

Mar. 19   Judge Hemphill, in San Antonio to hold court, kills a Comanche with a dagger in self-defense during the Council House Fight.

June 30   Chief Justice Rusk's resignation is accepted by President Lamar.

Dec. 5   Congress elects Judge Hemphill chief justice to replace Rusk.

1841

Jan. 11   Chief Justice Hemphill convenes his first Supreme Court session.

1845

Feb. 3   Congress provides that the next Court session will begin on the third Monday in December.

Summer   James Dallam publishes the opinions of the Republic Court, 1840–1844.

Oct.   Anticipating annexation, Texas adopts a new constitution, which establishes a full-time three-member Supreme Court, appointed by the governor for six-year terms.

Dec. 15   Final session of the Republic Supreme Court convenes in Austin.

Dec. 29   Constitution of the State of Texas is ratified by the United States, resulting in the annexation of Texas as the twenty-eighth state in the Union.

1846

Jan. 5   Final session of the Republic Supreme Court adjourns; thirty cases were decided, but will not be reported until 1986.

Jan. 22   Judicial terms expire.

Feb. 19   Power is officially transferred from the Republic to the State of Texas.

Mar. 2   The Texas Senate confirms the governor's appointments of Chief Justice John Hemphill and Associate Justices Royall Wheeler and Abner Lipscomb to the Supreme Court of the State of Texas.

1850

           By constitutional amendment, justices are to be elected by the people rather than appointed by the governor; effective 1851.

1851

           Court sessions are held in Galveston in winter, Tyler in summer, Austin in fall.

Aug. 4   John Hemphill is elected chief justice by the voters.

1856

Dec. 8   Abner Lipscomb dies in office.

1857

Feb. 2   Oran Roberts is elected to take Lipscomb's place as associate justice.

1858

Oct.   John Hemphill resigns from the Court when he is elected to the U.S. Senate, replacing Sam Houston. Royall Tyler takes Hemphill's place as chief justice, having been elected by the voters on Aug. 2.

1861

Feb. 23   Texas voters ratify secession from the Union, effective March 2.

Apr. 1   Article 4 of the new constitution vests judicial power in the Supreme Court, district courts, and inferior courts as established by the legislature. Supreme Court justices in office prior to secession remain in office.

1864

Apr. 9   Chief Justice Wheeler commits suicide at his home.

Aug. 1   Oran Roberts is elected chief justice and takes office in November.

1866

June 25   First Reconstruction constitution is ratified, enlarging the Court from three to five justices, popularly elected for ten-year terms. The chief justice is to be selected by the five justices from their own number. The general election is held the same day.

Aug.   George Fleming Moore is selected chief justice by his fellow justices.
              George W. Paschal publishes his *Digest of the Laws of Texas*.

1867

Sept. 10   All Supreme Court members are removed by the U.S. military as "impediments to Reconstruction" and replaced with Union sympathizers.

1869

Nov. 30   Constitution of 1869, the so-called Radical Reconstruction Constitution, is adopted by the voters. It calls for a Supreme Court of three judges, appointed by the governor with the consent of the Senate for nine-year staggered terms; the judge whose term ends first serves as presiding judge. Court is to meet annually in Austin; the Constitution abolishes the Galveston and Tyler sessions.

1870

Mar. 30   Texas is readmitted to the Union; military government ends in April.

1873

Dec. 2   Voters approve a constitutional amendment that expands the Supreme Court from three to five members, headed by a chief justice.

1874

Jan. 6   Semicolon Court, in *Ex parte Rodríguez*, declares state general election of December 1873 unconstitutional; newly elected government under Gov. Richard Coke refuses to accept decision.

Jan. 29   Gov. Coke appoints five new members of the Court; Oran Roberts becomes chief justice.

Feb. 27   Legislature implements the new constitutional amendment that calls for the Court to again hold terms in Austin, Galveston, and Tyler.

1876

Feb. 15   Constitution of 1876 establishes Supreme Court of three justices, elected by the people for six-year terms; a chief justice is the presiding officer. Court of Appeals is established with final jurisdiction in criminal cases and some civil cases. Court meets from October through June in Austin and up to two other locations in the state.
              Oran Roberts is elected chief justice; George F. Moore and Robert S. Gould are associate justices.

Apr.   The reconfigured Court convenes.

1878

Oct. 1   Chief Justice Roberts resigns to run for governor.

Nov. 5   Roberts is elected governor. George F. Moore is elected chief justice.

1879

Feb. 21   Legislature passes the Texas Revised Civil Statutes.

July 9   Legislature creates Commission of Appeals to hear cases pending in the Supreme Court and Court of Appeals.

Sept. 1   Texas Revised Civil Statutes take effect.

1881

Nov. 1   Chief Justice Moore resigns.

Nov. 2   Robert S. Gould is appointed chief justice by Gov. Oran Roberts.

Nov. 9   Capitol is destroyed by fire.

1882

May 3   Legislature sets new rules for the publication of the Court's decisions and specifies that subsequent volumes of *Texas Reports* must be copyrighted by the State of Texas.

Nov. 7   Asa Willie is elected chief justice, having won the Democratic primary over incumbent Gould.

Dec. 12   Texas Bar Association is officially inaugurated.

1888

Mar. 3   Chief Justice Willie resigns.

John W. Stayton is appointed chief justice by Gov. Sul Ross; elected to the post in November.

Apr. 21   New Capitol opens to the public; the Court moves into its new quarters on the north wing of the third and fourth floors, where it will remain for seven decades.

H. P. N. Gammel's ten-volume *Laws of Texas, 1822–1897* is published.

1892

Constitutional amendment passed in 1891 eliminates Commission of Appeals, changes Court of Appeals to Court of Criminal Appeals, with final jurisdiction in all criminal cases, and designates Supreme Court as court of final jurisdiction in all civil cases except those appealed from county trial courts. All sessions of the Supreme Court are to be held in Austin; no longer a circuit court.

1894

July 5   Chief Justice Stayton dies in office.

Reuben R. Gaines is appointed chief justice by Gov. Jim Hogg; elected in November.

1899

The Court composed of Chief Justice Gaines and Associate Justices T. J. Brown and F. A. Williams begins a decade of high productivity and amicability.

1911

Jan. 1   Reuben Gaines resigns as chief justice.

Jan. 5   Thomas J. Brown is appointed chief justice by Gov. Campbell; elected in 1912.

1913

Jan.   William E. Hawkins begins an eight-year stint as associate justice, bringing the Court's productivity to a virtual standstill.

1915

May 26   Chief Justice Brown dies in office.

May 27   Nelson Phillips is appointed chief justice by Gov. Colquitt; elected in 1916.

1917

Harbert Davenport's *History of the Supreme Court of the State of Texas* is published.

1918

Legislature reestablishes Commission of Appeals to assist the Supreme Court in keeping up with its docket. The commission has two sections of three members each, appointed by the governor for six-year terms.

1919

Legislature creates the Board of Law Examiners as an arm of the Supreme Court to administer law examinations for the Texas bar.

1921

Nov. 16   Chief Justice Phillips resigns.

Nov. 17   C. M. Cureton is appointed chief justice by Gov. Neff; elected in 1922.

1925

Jan.   Gov. Pat Neff appoints the first all-woman supreme court in the nation, a temporary court to hear *Johnson v. Darr*, a case involving the Woodmen of the World; the Cureton Court is recused.

1929

Legislature establishes Texas Civil Judicial Council to make a continual study of the state's civil courts; chief justice is a member.

1930

Legislature authorizes the Supreme Court to appoint members of the Commission of Appeals.

1939

Apr. 12   State Bar Act creating the integrated bar is enacted into law; implementation is left to the Supreme Court.
              Court Rules Act confers on the Supreme Court full rule-making power in civil judicial proceedings.

1940

Jan. 13   Supreme Court marks the one-hundredth anniversary of the first session of the State of Texas Court with ceremonies in the courtroom, Chief Justice Calvin Cureton presiding.

Feb. 22   Supreme Court promulgates the first set of rules under the Texas Rules of Civil Procedure.

Apr. 8   Chief Justice Cureton dies in office.
              William Folsom Moore is appointed chief justice by Gov. O'Daniel; does not seek election in November.

Nov. 5 James P. Alexander is elected chief justice, the first to be elected to that position without having served previously on the Court by appointment or as associate justice.

1941

 Briefing attorney position is created to assist Supreme Court justices; future chief justice Joe R. Greenhill is one of three appointed.

1945

Aug. 25 Constitutional amendment increases the membership of the Supreme Court from three to nine members. Commission of Appeals is abolished, and its six members become associate justices of the Supreme Court. James P. Alexander continues as chief justice.

Sept. 21 Nine-member Court convenes for the first time.

1948

Jan. 1 Chief Justice Alexander dies in office.

Jan. 7 John E. Hickman is appointed chief justice by Gov. Beauford Jester.

1957

Dec. 2 Cornerstone is laid for the new Texas Supreme Court Building, which will house the courtrooms and chambers of the Supreme Court and Court of Criminal Appeals, and a judicial administration building, which will house their support offices; the complex is just west of the Capitol.

1958

July 26 In the state Democratic primary, incumbent justice Joe R. Greenhill narrowly defeats state district judge Sarah Hughes in a race for the Supreme Court; Hughes is the first woman to run for election to the Court.

1959

Dec. 3 Court moves from the old courtroom in the Capitol to the courtroom in the new Supreme Court Building, where it holds its first session and dedication ceremonies.

1960

Nov. 8 Robert W. Calvert is elected chief justice to replace the retiring chief justice, John Hickman.

1966

Nov. 8 Constitutional amendment increases the size of the Court of Criminal Appeals from three to five elected members.

1971

Sept. 1 Supreme Court Library is abolished by statute and replaced with the Texas State Law Library.

1972

Oct. 4 Chief Justice Calvert retires.

 Joe R. Greenhill is appointed chief justice by Gov. Preston Smith.

1973

Mar. As authorized by a constitutional amendment passed in November 1972, a constitutional commission meets to draft recommendations for a new constitution to replace the Constitution of 1876. Former chief justice Robert W. Calvert is chair.

1974

Jan. 8   Sixty-Third Legislature convenes as a constitutional convention to draft a new constitution based on the Calvert Commission's recommendations; the convention fails to produce a document to submit to the voters.

July 16   Supreme Court establishes the Texas Board of Legal Specialization to certify attorneys in legal specialty areas for the first time.

July 25   Supreme Court adopts a new Code of Judicial Conduct by a rule of court; effective September 1.

1975

Sept. 1   The Texas Judicial Civil Council is renamed the Texas Judicial Council.

1976

Don Yarbrough wins Democratic primary, then election to the Court, despite pending criminal indictments.

1977

Jan.–July   Justice Yarbrough serves six months on the Court, then resigns in July before he is impeached.

Sept. 1   Legislature creates the Office of Court Administration to assist judges and justices in their administrative duties and examine court dockets, practices, and procedures.

Nov. 6   Constitutional amendment expands the Court of Criminal Appeals to nine members, effective January 1, 1978.

1979

Jan. 31   Chief Justice Greenhill delivers the first State of the Judiciary address to the legislature.

Sept. 1   The legislature amends the State Bar Act to reestablish the state bar as a public corporation and an administrative agency of the judicial branch under the Supreme Court.

Nov.   William L. Garwood is appointed associate justice by Gov. Bill Clements, the first Republican to serve on the Court since Reconstruction; he fails to be elected in 1980.

1980

Nov. 4   Voters pass an amendment to the judicial article of the constitution that extends intermediate criminal appellate jurisdiction to the courts of civil appeals and renames them courts of appeals. The constitutional amendment also changes the titles of the nonpresiding members of the Supreme Court from "associate justice" to "justice."

1982

June 25   State district judge Ruby Kless Sondock is appointed to the Court by Gov. Clements, the first woman to serve as a regular (as opposed to special) justice; completes the remaining months of James Denton's term but does not run for election in November.

Oct. 25   Chief Justice Joe Greenhill resigns.

Nov. 25   Justice Jack Pope is appointed chief justice by Gov. Clements; takes office on November 29.

1984

Oct. 8   Judge Raul A. Gonzalez of the Thirteenth Court of Appeals is appointed to the Court by Gov. Mark White, the first Hispanic justice; elected in 1986.

Nov. 6   John L. Hill, Jr., is elected chief justice to replace the retiring Jack Pope, whose resignation is effective in January 1985.

1987

Aug. 26   Chief Justice Hill announces his resignation, effective January 1988.

Nov.   State district judge Thomas R. Phillips is appointed chief justice by Gov. Clements, the first Republican to hold that post; elected in 1988.

Dec. 6   CBS's *60 Minutes* airs an episode called "Is Justice for Sale?" focusing negative public attention on the Texas judiciary.

1990

Jan. 13   Court celebrates the sesquicentennial of the first session, with Chief Justice Phillips presiding.

           The Texas Supreme Court Historical Society is established when former chief justices Robert W. Calvert, Joe R. Greenhill, and Jack Pope file the articles of incorporation; Justice Jack Hightower is its first president.

1992

Nov. 3   State district judge Rose Spector becomes the first woman to be elected to the Supreme Court.

1993

June 11   The remodeled judicial administration building adjacent to the Supreme Court Building is named for U.S. Supreme Court justice Tom C. Clark, the only Texan to sit on the nation's highest court.

1996

June 7   A third building in the judicial complex is dedicated in honor of Price Daniel, Jr., former Texas Supreme Court justice and former governor and attorney general of Texas.

2001

Apr. 18   Wallace B. Jefferson is appointed justice by Gov. George W. Bush, the first African American on the Court; elected in 2002.

2004

Sept. 14   Justice Jefferson is appointed chief justice by Gov. Rick Perry, the first African American to hold that post; elected in 2006.

JUSTICES OF THE TEXAS SUPREME COURT, 1836–2012, WITH APPOINTMENT/ELECTION DATES

JUSTICES OF THE REPUBLIC OF TEXAS
(DECEMBER 1836–JANUARY 1846)

The Republic Supreme Court consisted of a chief justice and from three to eight associate judges, elected by Congress. The associate judges were the judges of the district courts.

Chief Justices

James T. Collinsworth (December 1836–July 1838)
John Birdsall (August 1838–December 1838)
Thomas Jefferson Rusk (December 1838–June 1840)
John Hemphill (December 1840–January 1846)

Associate Judges

Shelby Corzine, 1836–1839
Benjamin Cromwell Franklin, 1836–1839
Robert McAlpin Williamson, 1836–1839
James W. Robinson, 1836–1840
Henry Whiting Fontaine, 1838–1839
Edward Thomas Branch, 1838–1840
Ezekiel Wimberly Cullen, 1839
John Scott, 1839
John T. Mills, 1839–1845
John Hemphill, 1840
Thomas Johnson, 1840
Anthony B. Shelby, 1840–1841
Richardson A. Scurry, 1840–1841
George Whitfield Terrell, 1840–1842
John M. Hansford, 1840–1842
William Jefferson Jones, 1840–1845

Anderson Hutchinson, 1841–1843
Patrick Churchill Jack, 1841–1844
Richard Morris, 1841–1844
Robert Emmett Bledsoe Baylor, 1841–1846
William Beck Ochiltree, 1842–1845
William Early Jones, 1843–1846
Royall Tyler Wheeler, 1844–1845
John Baker Jones, 1845–1846
Milford Phillips Norton, 1845–1846

JUSTICES OF THE STATE OF TEXAS (1846–1861)
AND OF TEXAS UNDER THE CONFEDERACY (1861–1865)

Justices were appointed by the governor from 1846 to 1851; they were elected by the people beginning in 1851. The Texas Constitution under the Confederacy did not change the Court.

Chief Justices

John Hemphill (March 1846–October 1858)
1846: appointed by Gov. Henderson
1851: elected (unopposed)
1856: elected (unopposed)
1858: resigned to become U.S. senator

Royall T. Wheeler (October 1858–April 1864)
Aug. 1858: elected chief justice (unopposed); assumed position in October
1864: died in office (suicide)

Oran M. Roberts (November 1864–1865)
1864: elected versus James H. Bell (to take Wheeler's place)
1865: resigned/removed from office at end of Civil War

Associate Justices

Royall T. Wheeler (March 1846–August 1858)
1846: appointed by Gov. Henderson
1851: elected (unopposed)
1856: elected (unopposed)
1858: elected chief justice (unopposed); assumed position in October

Abner S. Lipscomb (March 1846–November 1856)
1846: appointed by Gov. Henderson
1851: elected (unopposed)
1856: elected (unopposed)
1856: died in office

Oran M. Roberts (1857–October 1862)
1857: elected versus Peter W. Gray, Thomas J. Jennings, John Taylor, and Benjamin C. Franklin (taking Lipscomb's place)
1862: resigned to fight in the Civil War

James H. Bell (August 1858–August 1864)
1858: elected (as Independent) versus C. W. Buckley (Democrat); assumed position in October
1864: term expired; defeated in bid to be chief justice

George F. Moore (October 1862–June 1866)
1862: elected versus Reuben A. Reeves, Medacus A. Long, Thomas J. Jennings, and William W. Wallace

Reuben A. Reeves (August 1864–1865, 1876)
1864: elected versus C. W. Buckley (Democrat) and John Sayles
1865: resigned/removed from office at end of Civil War

JUSTICES DURING PRESIDENTIAL
RECONSTRUCTION (1866–1867)

Under the Constitution of 1866, the Supreme Court was increased from three justices to five, popularly elected for ten-year terms. The chief justice was selected by elected justices. All members of this Court were removed by U.S. military authorities in September 1867 as "impediments to Reconstruction."

Chief Justice

George F. Moore (August 1866–September 1867)

Associate Justices

Richard Coke (August 1866–September 1867)
Stockton P. Donley (August 1866–September 1867)
George W. Smith (August 1866–September 1867)
Asa H. Willie (August 1866–September 1867)

JUSTICES APPOINTED BY THE
U.S. MILITARY (1867–1870)

Chief Justice

Amos Morrill (September 1867–July 1870)

Associate Justices

Livingston Lindsay (September 1867–July 1870)
Albert H. Latimer (September 1867–November 1869)
Colbert Coldwell (September 1867–October 1869)
Andrew J. Hamilton (November 1867–October 1869)
Moses B. Walker (December 1869–July 1870)
James Denison (January 1870–July 1870)
C. B. Sabin (March 1870, no record of service)

JUDGES IN CONGRESSIONAL RECONSTRUCTION
(1870–JANUARY 1874)

Under the Constitution of 1869, the Supreme Court consisted of three judges, appointed by the governor and headed by a presiding judge.

Presiding Judge

Lemuel D. Evans (July 1870–August 1873)
Wesley Ogden (August 1873–January 1874)

Associate Judges

Wesley Odgen (July 1870–August 1873)
Moses B. Walker (July 1870–January 1874)
J. D. McAdoo (August 1873–January 1874)

JUSTICES IN THE POST-RECONSTRUCTION
"REDEEMER" ERA (JANUARY 1874–APRIL 1876)

Under an amendment to the Constitution of 1869, the Supreme Court expanded to five members, headed by a chief justice. Governor Richard Coke made the appointments in January 1874 after the Reconstruction judges' terms expired.

Chief Justice

Oran M. Roberts (January 1874–April 1876)

Associate Justices

Reuben A. Reeves (January 1874–April 1976)
Thomas J. Devine (January 1874–September 1875)
John Ireland (September 1875–April 1876)
George F. Moore (February 1874–April 1876)
William P. Ballinger (February 3, 1874, resigned same day)
Peter W. Gray (February 1874–April 1876)
Robert S. Gould (May 1874–April 1876)

JUSTICES UNDER THE CONSTITUTION OF 1876
(APRIL 1876–SEPTEMBER 1945)

Under the Constitution of 1876, the number of justices returned to three, elected by the people for six-year terms.

Chief Justices

Oran M. Roberts (April 1876–October 1878)
1876: elected (unopposed)
1878: resigned to become governor

George F. Moore (November 1878–November 1881)
1878: appointed by Gov. Hubbard to fill Roberts's place
1878: elected versus James H. Bell (Republican)
1881: resigned

Robert S. Gould (November 1881–December 1882)
1881: appointed by Gov. Roberts to fill Moore's place
1882: defeated in bid for Democratic nomination

Asa H. Willie (December 1882–March 1888)
1882: elected (unopposed) on Democratic Party ticket with Stayton and West
1888: resigned

John W. Stayton (March 1888–July 1894)
Mar. 1888: appointed by Gov. Ross to fill Willie's place

Nov. 1888: elected (unopposed) on Democratic Party ticket with Henry and Gaines
July 1894: died in office

Reuben R. Gaines (July 1894–January 1911)
July 1894: appointed by Gov. Hogg to fill Stayton's place
Nov. 1894: elected versus Thomas J. Russell (People's Party), J. M. McCormick (Republican)
1900: elected versus J. M. McCormick (Republican)
1906: elected versus Frank B. Stanley (Republican), William D. Simpson (Socialist)
1911: resigned

Thomas J. Brown (January 1911–May 1915)
1911: appointed by Gov. Campbell to fill Gaines's place
1912: elected versus Eugene Marshall (Republican), E. O. Meitzen (Socialist)
1915: died in office

Nelson Phillips (June 1915–November 1921)
1915: appointed by Gov. Colquitt to fill Brown's place
1916: elected (unopposed)
1918: elected versus G. N. Harrison (Republican)
1921: resigned

Calvin M. Cureton (December 1921–April 1940)
1921: appointed by Gov. Neff to fill Phillips's place
1922: elected versus W. H. Wilson (Republican)
1924: elected versus C. O. Harris (Republican)
1930: elected versus C. K. McDowell (Republican), D. W. King (Socialist)
1936: elected versus C. W. Johnson, Jr. (Republican), George C. Edwards (Socialist)
1940: died in office

William F. Moore (April 1940–January 1941)
1940: appointed by Gov. O'Daniel to fill Cureton's place; did not seek election

James P. Alexander (January 1941–September 1945)
1940: elected versus L. J. Benckenstein (Republican)
1945: retained position in reconfigured, nine-member Court

Associate Justices

George F. Moore (April 1876–October 1878)
1876: elected (unopposed)
1878: appointed chief justice by Gov. Hubbard

Robert S. Gould (April 1876–November 1881)
1876: elected (unopposed)
1881: appointed chief justice by Gov. Roberts to fill Moore's place

Micajah H. Bonner (November 1878–December 1882)
1878: appointed by Gov. Hubbard to fill Moore's place
1878: elected versus Leroy W. Cooper (Republican)
1882: retired

John W. Stayton (November 1881–March 1888)
1881: appointed by Gov. Roberts to fill Gould's place
1882: elected (unopposed) on Democratic Party ticket with Willie and West
1888: appointed by Gov. Ross to replace Chief Justice Willie

Charles S. West (December 1882–September 1885)
1882: appointed by Gov. Roberts to fill Walker's place
1882: elected (unopposed) on Democratic Party ticket with Willie and Stayton
1885: resigned

Sawnie Robertson (October 1885–September 1886)
1885: appointed by Gov. Ireland to fill West's place
1886: resigned

Reuben R. Gaines (September 1886–July 1894)
1886: appointed by Gov. Ireland to fill Robertson's place
1888: elected (unopposed) on Democratic Party ticket with Henry and Stayton
1894: appointed chief justice by Gov. Hogg to fill Stayton's place

A. S. Walker (April 1888–January 1889)
1888: appointed by Gov. Ross to fill Stayton's place; did not seek election

J. L. Henry (January 1889–May 1893)
1888: elected (unopposed) on Democratic Party ticket with Stayton and Gaines
1893: resigned

Thomas J. Brown (May 1893–January 1911)
1893: appointed by Gov. Hogg to fill Henry's place
1894: elected on Democratic ticket, versus C. H. Maris and C. O. Harris (Republicans)
1911: appointed by Gov. Campbell to fill Gaines's place

Leroy G. Denman (July 1894–May 1899)
1894: appointed by Gov. Hogg to fill Gaines's place
1894: elected on Democratic ticket, versus C. H. Maris and C. O. Harris (Republicans)
1899: resigned

Frank A. Williams (May 1899–April 1911)
1899: appointed by Gov. Sayers to fill Denman's place
1900: elected versus George D. Green (People's Party), Frank B. Stanley (Republican)
1902: elected (unopposed)
1908: elected versus C. W. Starling (Republican)
1911: resigned

William F. Ramsey (January 1911–April 1912)
1911: appointed by Gov. Colquitt to fill Brown's place
1912: resigned to run for governor (defeated)

J. B. Dibrell (April 1911–January 1913)
1911: appointed by Gov. Colquitt to fill Williams's place
1912: defeated in Democratic primary by William E. Hawkins

Nelson Phillips (April 1912–June 1915)
1912: appointed by Gov. Colquitt to fill Ramsey's place
Nov. 1912: elected versus U.S. Goen (Progressive), J. Walter Cocke (Republican)
1915: appointed by Gov. Ferguson to replace Brown as chief justice

William E. Hawkins (January 1913–January 1921)
1913: elected versus J. M. McCormick (Progressive), T. M. Kennedy (Republican)
1914: elected (unopposed)
1920: lost Democratic primary bid for reelection (to William Pierson)

James E. Yantis (June 1915–March 1918)
1915: appointed by Gov. Ferguson to fill Phillips's place
1916: elected (unopposed)
1918: resigned

Thomas B. Greenwood (April 1918–December 1934)
1918: appointed by Gov. Hobby to fill Yantis's place
1918: elected versus C. O. Harris (Republican)
1922: elected versus J. H. McBroon (Republican)
1928: elected versus M. A. Smith (Socialist)
1934: resigned

John H. Sharp (December 1934–1945)
1934: elected versus Irl F. Kennerly (Republican), Guy L. Smith (Socialist)
1940: elected versus Joe Ingraham (Republican)
1945: maintained position after constitutional amendment

William Pierson (January 1921–April 1935)
1920: elected versus C. O. Harris (Republican), H. B. Short (American), Henry Faulk (Socialist)
1926: elected versus G. N. Harrison (Republican), G. W. M. Taylor (Socialist)
1932: elected (unopposed)
1935: died in office

Richard Critz (May 1935–January 1945)
1935: appointed by Gov. Allred to fill Pierson's place
1936: elected versus Joe Ingraham (Republican), J. R. Barrett (Socialist)
1945: defeated in bid for reelection

Gordon Simpson (January 1945–September 1945)
1944: elected versus Carl C. Stearns (Republican)
1945: maintained position after constitutional amendment

JUSTICES SINCE 1945 (UNDER THE CONSTITUTION OF 1876)

In September 1945, when a constitutional amendment increased the Supreme Court from three justices to nine, the six commissioners of the Supreme Court Commission of Appeals became associate justices. With the advent of staggered terms, the justices began running for election under a place system; the chief justice holds place 1, and the justices hold places 2–9.

Chief Justice, Place 1

James P. Alexander (September 21, 1945–January 1, 1948)
1945: maintained position under constitutional amendment
1946: elected versus G. C. Mann (Republican)
1948: died in office

John E. Hickman (January 7, 1948–January 3, 1961)
1948: appointed by Gov. Jester to replace Chief Justice Alexander
1948: elected (unopposed)
1954: elected (unopposed)
1961: retired

Robert W. Calvert (January 3, 1961–October 4, 1972)
1960: elected (unopposed)
1966: elected (unopposed)
1972: retired

Joe R. Greenhill (October 4, 1972–October 25, 1982)
1972: appointed by Gov. Smith to fill Calvert's place
1972: elected (unopposed)
1978: elected (unopposed)
1982: retired

Andrew Jackson "Jack" Pope (November 29, 1982–January 4, 1985)
1982: appointed by Gov. Clements to fill Greenhill's place
1985: retired

John L. Hill, Jr. (January 5, 1985–January 4, 1988)
1984: elected versus John L. Bates (Republican)
1988: resigned

Thomas R. Phillips (January 4, 1988–September 3, 2004)
1987: appointed by Gov. Clements to fill Hill's place
1988: elected versus Ted Robertson (Democrat)
1990: elected versus Oscar Mauzy (Democrat)
1996: elected versus Andrew Jackson Kupper (Democrat), David Parker (Libertarian)
2002: elected versus R. G. Baker (Democrat), E. J. Flynn (Libertarian)
2004: retired

Wallace B. Jefferson (September 20, 2004–; term ends in 2014)
2004: appointed by Gov. Perry to fill Phillips's place
2006: elected versus Tom Oxford (Libertarian)
2008: elected versus Jim Jordan (Democrat), Tom Oxford (Libertarian)

Justices, Place 2

John H. Sharp (September 21, 1945–December 31, 1952)
1945: maintained position
1946: elected versus Howell Ward (Republican)
1953: retired

Frank P. Culver, Jr. (January 1, 1953–January 1, 1965)
1952: elected (unopposed)
1958: elected (unopposed)
1965: retired

Andrew Jackson "Jack" Pope (January 4, 1965–November 29, 1982)
1964: elected versus T. E. Kennerly (Republican)
1970: elected (unopposed)
1976: elected (unopposed)
1982: appointed chief justice by Gov. Clements

Ted Z. Robertson (December 2, 1982–December 31, 1988)
1982: appointed by Gov. Clements to fill Pope's place
1982: elected versus John L. Bates (Republican)
1988: defeated in bid for chief justice position

Lloyd Doggett (January 1, 1989–December 31, 1994)
1988: elected versus Paul Murphy (Republican)
1994: did not seek reelection

Priscilla R. Owen (January 1, 1995–June 6, 2005)
1994: elected versus Jimmy Carroll (Democrat)
2000: elected versus Joe Alfred Izen, Jr. (Libertarian)
2005: resigned

Don R. Willett (August 24, 2005–; term ends in 2012)
2005: appointed by Gov. Perry to replace Owen
2006: elected versus William E. Moody (Democrat), Wade Wilson (Libertarian)

Justices, Place 3

Gordon Simpson (September 21, 1945–March 1, 1949)
1945: maintained position when Court expanded
1949: resigned

R. H. Harvey (March 1, 1949–September 8, 1950)
1949: appointed by Gov. Jester to fill Simpson's place
1950: died in office

Robert W. Calvert (September 18, 1950–January 3, 1961)
1950: appointed by Gov. Jester to fill Harvey's place, then elected in November
1956: elected versus John R. Anthony (Constitution Party)
1960: elected chief justice

Zollie Steakley (January 3, 1961–December 31, 1980)
1961: appointed by Gov. Daniel to fill Calvert's place
1962: elected (unopposed)
1968: elected (unopposed)

1974: elected (unopposed)
1981: retired

James P. Wallace (January 1, 1981–September 1, 1988)
1980: elected versus Jim Brady (Republican)
1986: elected versus Wiley H. Rawlins (Republican)
1988: resigned

Eugene A. Cook (September 1, 1988–December 31, 1992)
1988: appointed by Gov. Clements to fill Wallace's place
1988: elected versus Karl Bayer (Democrat)
1992: defeated in reelection bid

Rose Spector (January 1, 1993–December 31, 1998)
1992: elected versus Eugene Cook (Republican)
1998: defeated in reelection bid

Harriet O'Neill (January 1, 1999–June 20, 2010)
1998: elected versus Rose Spector (Democrat)
2004: elected (unopposed)
2010: retired

Debra Lehrmann (June 21, 2010–; term ends in 2016)
2010: appointed by Gov. Perry to replace O'Neill
2010: elected versus Jim Sharp (Democrat), William Bryan Strange III (Libertarian)

Justices, Place 4

Graham B. Smedley (September 21, 1945–June 16, 1954)
1945: automatically promoted under constitutional amendment
1946: elected versus S. D. Bennett (Republican)
1952: elected (unopposed)
1954: died in office

Ruel C. Walker (October 19, 1954–September 30, 1975)
1954: appointed by Gov. Shivers to replace Smedley
1954: elected (unopposed)
1958: elected (unopposed)
1964: elected (unopposed)
1970: elected (unopposed)
1975: retired

Ross E. Doughty (October 1, 1975–December 31, 1976)
1975: appointed by Gov. Briscoe to replace Walker
1976: resigned

Donald B. Yarbrough (January 1, 1977–July 1977)
1976: elected versus Sam Houston (write-in) and Tom Lorance (write-in)
1977: resigned

Charles W. Barrow (July 25, 1977–September 30, 1984)
1977: appointed by Gov. Briscoe to replace Yarbrough
1978: elected (unopposed)
1982: elected (unopposed)
1984: retired

Raul A. Gonzalez (October 8, 1984–December 31, 1998)
1984: appointed by Gov. White to take Barrow's place
1986: elected versus John L. Bates (Republican)
1988: elected versus Charles Ben Howell (Republican), Calvin W. Scholz (Libertarian)
1994: elected versus John B. Hawley (Libertarian)
1999: retired

Alberto R. Gonzales (November 12, 1998–December 22, 2000)
1998: appointed by Gov. Bush to complete Gonzalez's term
2000: elected versus Lance Smith (Libertarian)
2000: resigned to become White House counsel to President George W. Bush

Wallace B. Jefferson (April 18, 2001–September 20, 2004)
2001: appointed by Gov. Perry to take Gonzales's place
2002: elected versus William E. Moody (Democrat)
2004: appointed chief justice by Gov. Perry to take Phillips's place

David M. Medina (November 10, 2004–; term ends in 2012)
2004: appointed by Gov. Perry to take Jefferson's place
2006: elected versus Jerry Adkins (Libertarian)

Justices, Place 5

William M. Taylor (September 21, 1945–December 31, 1950)
1945: automatically promoted under constitutional amendment
1951: retired

Will Wilson (January 2, 1951–June 1, 1956)
1950: elected (unopposed)
1956: resigned to run for state attorney general

Abner V. McCall (June 15, 1956–December 31, 1956)
1956: appointed by Gov. Shivers to fill Wilson's place; resigned at end of term

James R. Norvell (January 1, 1957–October 10, 1968)
1956: elected (unopposed)
1962: elected (unopposed)
1968: retired

Thomas M. Reavley (October 10, 1968–October 1, 1977)
1968: appointed by Gov. Connally to take Norvell's place
1968: elected (unopposed)
1974: elected (unopposed)
1977: retired

T. C. Chadick (October 5, 1977–December 31, 1978)
1977: appointed by Gov. Briscoe to fill Reavley's place
1978: defeated in bid for Democratic nomination

Robert M. Campbell (December 1, 1978–February 1, 1988)
1978: elected (unopposed)
1980: elected (unopposed)
1986: elected versus Nathan E. White, Jr. (Republican)
1988: resigned

Barbara Culver (February 1, 1988–December 7, 1988)
1988: appointed by Gov. Clements to fill Campbell's place
1988: defeated in bid for election

Jack Hightower (December 7, 1988–January 1, 1996)
1988: elected versus Barbara Culver (Republican)
1992: elected versus John D. Montgomery (Republican)
1996: retired

Greg Abbott (January 2, 1996–June 6, 2001)
1996: appointed by Gov. Bush to fill Hightower's place
1996: elected versus John B. Hawley (Libertarian)
1998: elected versus David Van Os (Democrat)
2001: resigned to run for state attorney general

Xavier Rodriguez (September 7, 2001–November 6, 2002)
2001: appointed by Gov. Perry to fill Abbott's place
2002: defeated in primary bid for election

Steven Wayne Smith (November 20, 2002–December 31, 2004)
2002: elected versus Margaret Mirabel (Democrat)
2004: defeated in primary bid for reelection

Paul W. Green (January 1, 2005–; term ends in 2016)
2004: elected (unopposed)
2010: elected versus William E. Moody (Democrat), Tom Oxford (Libertarian)

Justices, Place 6

John E. Hickman (September 21, 1945–January 5, 1948)
1945: automatically promoted under constitutional amendment
1946: elected versus Andrew Longake (Republican)
1948: appointed chief justice by Gov. Jester to replace Alexander

Wilmer St. John Garwood (January 14, 1948–December 31, 1958)
1948: elected (unopposed)
1952: elected (unopposed)
1959: retired

Robert W. Hamilton (January 1, 1959–December 31, 1970)
1958: elected versus John Q. Adams (Republican)
1964: elected (unopposed)
1971: retired

James G. Denton (January 1, 1971–June 10, 1982)
1970: elected (unopposed)
1976: elected (unopposed)
1982: died in office

Ruby Kless Sondock (June 25, 1982–December 31, 1982)
1982: appointed by Gov. Clements to fill Denton's place
1982: did not seek election

William W. Kilgarlin (January 1, 1983–December 31, 1988)
1982: elected (unopposed)
1988: defeated in bid for reelection

Nathan L. Hecht (January 1, 1989–; term ends in 2012)
1988: elected versus William Kilgarlin (Democrat)
1994: elected versus Alice Oliver Parrott (Democrat)
2000: elected versus Mike Jacobellis (Libertarian), Ben G. Levy (Green)
2006: elected versus Todd Phillippi (Libertarian)

Justices, Place 7

C. S. Slatton (September 21, 1945–October 1, 1947)
1945: automatically promoted under constitutional amendment
1947: resigned

James P. Hart (October 1, 1947–November 15, 1950)
1947: appointed by Gov. Jester to fill Slatton's place
1948: elected (unopposed)
1950: resigned

Clyde E. Smith (November 15, 1950–December 31, 1970)
1950: appointed by Gov. Shivers to fill Hart's place
1952: elected (unopposed)
1960: elected (unopposed)
1966: elected (unopposed)
19971: retired

M. Price Daniel (January 1, 1971–December 31, 1978)
1971: appointed by Gov. Preston Smith to fill Smith's place
1972: elected (unopposed)
1979: retired

Franklin S. Spears (January 1, 1979–December 31, 1990)
1978: elected (unopposed)
1984: elected (unopposed)
1991: retired

John Cornyn (January 2, 1991–October 18, 1997)
1990: elected versus Gene Kelly (Democrat)
1996: elected versus Patricia Barron (Democrat), Thomas Stults (Libertarian)
1997: resigned to run for state attorney general

Deborah Hankinson (October 28, 1997–December 31, 2002)
1997: appointed by Gov. Bush to Cornyn's place
1998: elected versus Jerry Scarborough (Democrat)
2002: did not seek reelection

Dale Wainwright (January 1, 2003–; term ends in 2014)
2002: elected versus J. Parsons (Democrat), Brad Rockwell (Green)
2008: elected versus S. Houston (Democrat), D. G. Smith (Libertarian)

Justices, Place 8

Few Brewster (September 21, 1945–September 20, 1957)
1945: automatically promoted under constitutional amendment
1948: elected (unopposed)
1954: elected (unopposed)
1957: retired

Joe R. Greenhill (October 1, 1957–October 4, 1972)
1957: appointed by Gov. Daniel to fill Brewster's place
1958: elected (unopposed)
1960: elected (unopposed)
1966: elected (unopposed)
1972: appointed chief justice by Gov. Smith to fill Calvert's place

Hawthorne Phillips (October 4, 1972–December 31, 1972)
1972: appointed by Gov. Smith to fill Greenhill's place
1972: term ended

Sam Johnson (January 1, 1973–October 16, 1979)
1972: elected (unopposed)
1978: elected (unopposed)
1979: resigned to accept appointment on U.S. Court of Appeals, Fifth Circuit

William L. Garwood (November 15, 1979–December 31, 1980)
1979: appointed by Gov. Clements to fill Johnson's place
1980: defeated in bid for election

C. L. Ray, Jr. (November 25, 1980–December 31, 1990)
1980: elected versus William L. Garwood (Republican)
1984: elected (unopposed)
1991: retired

Robert Gammage (January 1, 1991–August 31, 1995)
1990: elected versus Charles Ben Howell (Republican)
1995: retired

James A. Baker (September 1, 1995–August 31, 2002)
1995: appointed by Gov. Bush to fill Gammage's place

1996: elected versus Gene Kelly (Democrat), Ellen Flume (Libertarian)
2002: retired

Michael H. Schneider (September 6, 2002–September 20, 2004)
2002: appointed by Gov. Perry to take Baker's place
2002: elected versus Linda Reyna Yanez (Democrat), Quanah Parker (Libertarian)
2004: resigned to accept appointment to U.S. District Court

Phil Johnson (April 11, 2005–; term ends in 2014)
2006: appointed by Gov. Perry to fill Schneider's place
2006: elected versus Jay Cookingham (Libertarian)
2008: elected versus Linda Reyna Yanez (Democrat), Drew Shirley (Libertarian)

Justices, Place 9

A. J. Folley (September 21, 1945–April 1, 1949)
1945: automatically promoted under constitutional amendment
1949: resigned

Meade F. Griffin (April 1, 1949–December 31, 1968)
1949: appointed by Gov. Jester to fill Folley's place
1950: elected (unopposed)
1956: elected (unopposed)
1962: elected (unopposed)
1969: retired

W. Sears McGee (January 1, 1969–December 31, 1986)
1968: elected (unopposed)
1974: elected (unopposed)
1980: elected (unopposed)
1987: retired

Oscar H. Mauzy (January 3, 1987–December 31, 1993)
1986: elected versus Charles Ben Howell (Republican)
1990: ran for chief justice (defeated by Phillips)
1992: defeated in reelection bid

Craig T. Enoch (January 1, 1993–October 1, 2003)
1992: elected versus Oscar Mauzy (Democrat), Alfred Adask (Libertarian)
1998: elected versus Mike Westergren (Democrat)
2003: retired

Scott A. Brister (November 21, 2003–September 7, 2009)
2003: appointed by Gov. Perry to fill Enoch's place
2004: elected versus David Van Os (Democrat)
2009: resigned

Eva Guzman (October 8, 2009–; term ends in 2016)
2009: appointed by Gov. Perry to fill Brister's place
2010: elected versus Blake Bailey (Democrat)

Sources: Supreme Court of Texas, "Court History," and "Texas Supreme Court Election History, 1851–2010," online at http://www.supreme.courts.state.tx.us/court/history.asp; Thomas R. Phillips, "Popular Elections for the Texas Supreme Court," draft manuscript, October 26, 2010; University of Texas at Austin, Tarlton Law Library, "Justices of Texas, 1836–1986," http://tarlton.law.utexas.edu/justices/.

NOTES

PROLOGUE

1. "Court Structure of Texas," Texas Courts Online, accessed February 4, 2011, http://www.courts.state.tx.us/.

2. Quoted in Paulsen, "Community Property and Women's Rights," 643n6.

3. Ibid., 660–667.

4. See generally W. D. Phillips and C. R. Phillips, *Worlds of Christopher Columbus*, and Cohen, *Christopher Columbus*.

5. It is virtually impossible to find unanimity regarding the interpretation of this protean monarch and complex woman. Two different views of her, one vintage and one modern, can be gained from Walsh, *Isabella of Spain*, and Rubin, *Isabella of Castile*.

6. The latest translation of Cabeza de Vaca's *Relación*, Krieger's *We Came Naked and Barefoot*, is well annotated and has largely supplanted Bandelier, *The Journey of Cabeza de Vaca*, long the standard.

7. For the Karankawas, see generally La Vere, *Texas Indians*; Newcomb, *Indians of Texas*; Ricklis, *Karankawa Indians of Texas*; and, in more detail, Gatschet, *Karankawa Indians*; for the quotation, see Krieger, *We Came Naked and Barefoot*, 26.

CHAPTER 1

1. For two good histories of the Spanish period, see Vigness, *Spanish Texas, 1519–1810*, and Chipman, *Spanish Texas, 1519–1821*. Of the subsequent entradas, see Day, *Coronado's Quest*, and the October 1941 issue of *Southwestern Historical Quarterly* (vol. 45, no. 2), which is devoted to the Moscoso expedition.

2. See Weddle, *French Thorn*.

3. Casis, "Carta de Don Damian Manzanet," 308. Following publication of this article in 1899, Herbert Bolton discovered documents clearly showing the correct spelling to be "Massanet," which has become standard (Bolton, "Notes and Fragments," 101).

4. Casis, "Carta de Don Damian Manzanet," 308.

5. Barrios's administration is usually considered the shadiest of the era (McKnight, "Hispanic Legal Antecedents," 2–4). See generally Bolton, *Texas in the Middle Eighteenth Century*, and also Weddle, *San Saba Mission*, for an account of his being outsmarted by the Apaches.

6. Early San Antonio history is ably chronicled in Teja, *San Antonio de Béxar*. For a standard treatment of Aguayo's resettlement of Texas, see Buckley, "The Aguayo Expedition."

7. See Austin, "Municipal Government of San Fernando de Bexar," for a treatment of the Canary Islanders' resettlement in Texas.

8. McKnight, "Hispanic Legal Antecedents," 7–8.

9. Ibid., 5–6.

10. According to Jack Jackson, others in the settlement could also write legibly (*Los Mesteños*, 69, 71).

11. McKnight, "Hispanic Legal Antecedents," 10–11.

12. Ibid., 6–7. An expansive account of the Menchaca and Hernández families' ranching operations is in Jackson, *Los Mesteños*, 57 ff.

13. Jackson, *Los Mesteños*, 70.

14. McKnight, "Hispanic Legal Antecedents," 7.

15. Ibid., 9.

16. Ibid., 8–9.

17. For accounts of two of the more important filibusters, see Jacobs, *Tarnished Warrior*, and Wilson and Jackson, *Philip Nolan and Texas*.

18. One filibustering casualty, James Long, had captured the town of Goliad before he was defeated; he then spent months being hauled from jail to jail during the tumult of the Mexican Revolution. He was finally shot while in the custody of Felix Trespalacios, who became the first governor of Texas under the administration of an independent Mexico. Long was probably killed because he knew too much about Trespalacios's counterrevolutionary machinations. For the larger context, see Bradley, "Fighting for Texas."

19. For a biography of Moses Austin, see Gracy, *Moses Austin*.

20. The 1783 Census, certified by Governor Domingo Cabello (Bob Bullock Texas State History Museum).

21. For Martínez's discreet handling of the revolutionary tumult, see Almaráz, "Governor Antonio Martínez."

22. Austin to the Colonists, 5 June 1824, quoted in E. Barker, *Life of Stephen F. Austin*, 44.

23. Austin to [probably] Edward Lovelace, 22 November 1822, in Moses and Stephen F. Austin Papers (hereafter cited as Austin Papers), 1:555.

24. McKnight, "Stephen Austin's Legalistic Concerns," 255.

25. Ibid. This appellate scheme was later mirrored in important aspects by the Supreme Court of the Republic.

26. Cantrell, *Stephen F. Austin*, 128–129.

27. Townes, "Development of the Judicial System of Texas," 32.

28. *Laws and Decrees of Coahuila and Texas*, 4.

29. Constitution of Coahuila y Tejas, title III, art. 172.

30. Davenport, *Supreme Court of Texas*, 2–3.

31. Austin's headaches in administering his colony are well summarized in Cantrell, *Stephen F. Austin*, which largely but not entirely supplanted E. Barker, *Life of Stephen F. Austin*.

32. "Manuel Mier y Terán's Letter to President Guadalupe Victoria, 30 June 1828," and "The Law of April 6, 1830," in Wallace, Vigness, and Ward, *Documents of Texas History*, 65–67.

33. Contrasting interpretations of the so-called Anahuac Disturbances can be found in Rowe, "The Disturbances at Anahuac in 1832" (1903), a traditional account, and in Henson, *Juan Davis Bradburn* (1982), a highly revisionist one.

34. Quoted in Davenport, *Supreme Court of Texas*, 3–4.

35. Constitution of Coahuila y Tejas, title III, art. 192.

36. *Laws and Decrees of Coahuila and Texas*, no. 136, p. 151; also in Gammel, *Laws of Texas*, 1:261.

37. An informal and highly readable summary of Texas legal history in the Mexican and early Anglo periods of Texas is Wharton, "Early Judicial History of Texas."

38. Davenport, *Supreme Court of Texas*, 3–4.

39. A modern interpretation of Chambers is lacking. There is one biography— Chambers, *Life of General T. J. Chambers*—and he was the subject of the master's thesis by the Texas historian Llerena Friend in 1928. See Margaret Swett Henson, "Chambers, Thomas Jefferson," *Handbook of Texas Online*, http://www.tshaonline.org/handbook/online/articles/fch08.

40. Davenport characterizes Chambers's rise as having occurred by the exercise of his "persuasive manners" (*Supreme Court of Texas*, 4–5).

41. *Laws and Decrees of Coahuila and Texas*, no. 277, pp. 254–270; also in Gammel, *Laws of Texas*, 1:364–380.

42. The limitations of the Chambers Jury Law demonstrate "the very great influence exerted by the Mexican element in the legislature, and the small headway that the common law was making" (Markham, "Reception of the Common Law in Texas," 905–906).

43. Yoakum, *History of Texas*, 1:323–324.

44. See generally Chambers, *Life of General T. J. Chambers*.

CHAPTER 2

1. The antipathy between Burnet and Houston was of long standing, Houston having in June 1832 undertaken to represent the colonial ambitions of a Tennessee consortium, the Galveston Bay and Texas Land Company, of which Burnet was a principal, and which never paid Houston his retainer ("Agreement Between Houston and Prentiss," June 1, 1832, in Williams and Barker, *Writings of Sam Houston*, 1:229–230; Friend, *Sam Houston: Great Designer*, 42; J. L. Haley, *Sam Houston*, 87).

2. Herbert Gambrell, "Jones, Anson," *Handbook of Texas Online,* http://www.tsha online.org/handbook/online/articles/fjo42.

3. See generally Kemp, "Capitol at Columbia." For a more colorful memoir of the town and its environs, see Lubbock, *Six Decades in Texas,* 36.

4. Constitution of the Republic of Texas, art. IV (1836).

5. These false starts to the beginning of the Supreme Court are summarized in Chapter 3 of this book, but they are fleshed out much more completely in Paulsen, "Short History of the Supreme Court," 248–253.

6. See Hightower, "Freemasonry and the Law of Texas," 7–8.

7. Collinsworth's name was also spelled "Collingsworth" in a number of nineteenth-century sources, and Texas's Collingsworth County was named in his honor. In 1936, the Supreme Court of Texas officially adopted the spelling of his name without the *g* ("In Memoriam," 126 Tex. xxxi). This book follows that convention, notwithstanding that Collinsworth himself occasionally added the *g* to his name (Paulsen, "Judges of the Supreme Court," 311n28).

8. Joe E. Ericson, "Collinsworth, James," *Handbook of Texas Online,* http://www.tsha online.org/handbook/online/articles/fco97.

9. Siegel, *Political History of the Texas Republic,* 98.

10. Paulsen, "Short History of the Supreme Court," 251–252.

11. Looscan, "Life and Service of John Birdsall," 46.

12. Commanding Nacogdoches volunteers during the siege of Béxar, Rusk approached the walls with cavalry: "They fired their cannon but done us no damage all we want is . . . reinforcements and some thing like organization" (Rusk to Houston, November 14, 1835, quoted in J. L. Haley, *Sam Houston,* 116).

13. In May 1838, the Congress had moved the meeting date for the Supreme Court from December to January. According to Paulsen, Rusk did not learn of his election until January 21, 1839, after the January session should have been held ("Short History of the Supreme Court," 252). Therefore, no session was held until January 1840.

14. Lynch, *Bench and Bar of Texas,* 67, quoted in Paulsen, "Judges of the Supreme Court," 316.

15. Lynch, *Bench and Bar of Texas,* 69–73; Davenport, *Supreme Court of Texas,* 14–16; Paulsen, "Judges of the Supreme Court," 317–321; Thomas W. Cutrer, "Hemphill, John," *Handbook of Texas Online,* http://www.tshaonline.org/handbook/online/articles/fhe13.

16. Paulsen, "Judges of the Supreme Court," 321n97.

17. The various omnibus biographies of the Texas judiciary are uniformly uncritical, especially those contained in Lynch, *Bench and Bar of Texas,* and Davenport, *Supreme Court of Texas.* A more modern compilation on the website of the University of Texas School of Law—Tarlton Law Library's "Justices of Texas, 1836–1986"—continues this respectful but less-than-critical treatment: http://tarlton.law.utexas.edu/justices/. By far the best summation of the early judges is Paulsen, "Judges of the Supreme Court," 306 ff. The following brief capsules of the associate judges are drawn from these sources, as well as from entries in *The New Handbook of Texas* and *The Handbook of Texas Online,* http://www.tshaonline.org/handbook/online.

18. Paulsen, "Judges of the Supreme Court," 326.

19. *Telegraph and Texas Register*, May 12, 1841, quoted in Paulsen, "Judges of the Supreme Court," 294.

20. A later Congress and President Houston supported Johnson's claim for pay, while the Supreme Court ruled in *Shelby v. Johnson*, Dallam 597 (Tex. 1844) for Shelby (Paulsen, "Short History of the Supreme Court," 293–295).

21. *Duggan v. Cole* (Tex. 1845), 65 Tex. L. Rev. 412 (Paulsen rep. 1986). James Paulsen was appointed by the Texas Supreme Court as "Reporter of Decisions for the 1845 Term," and the 1986 issue of the *Texas Law Review* became the official publication of those decisions, which were not included in *Dallam's Digest* and were not reported by the state in the *Texas Reports*. This cite conforms to the format specified in Paulsen's "Missing Cases of the Republic" (375).

22. Louis W. Kemp, "Franklin, Benjamin C.," *Handbook of Texas Online*, http://www.tshaonline.org/handbook/online/articles/ffr02.

23. See Neu, "The Case of the Brig *Pocket*," 276–295. Before the post went to Franklin, it was offered to Collinsworth on April 12, who declined it. Interestingly, the same frontier chaos that kept the Supreme Court from meeting for the first two years of its existence also prevented Franklin from hearing the *Pocket* case until midsummer (282–283).

24. Kemp, "Franklin, Benjamin Cromwell." Dixon and Kemp identify Franklin as judge of the Third Judicial District (*Heroes of San Jacinto*, 278); it was correctly cited as the Second District in the *Handbook of Texas* article.

25. Tarlton Law Library, "Justices of Texas, 1836–1986." If this and the sources cited therein are accurate, Fontaine fathered one child a year from the age of sixteen (or a bit older if twins were produced), which would have shown remarkable vigor even by frontier standards.

26. Because the Republic Constitution failed to provide a process for filling vacancies on the bench between congressional sessions, the interim appointments by presidents were not technically legal. Such appointments were occasionally contested.

27. *Haynie v. Republic* (Tex. 1845), 65 Tex. L. Rev. 379 (Paulsen rep. 1986). In addition to legal practice, Jones in later years was a planter, rancher, and railroad developer, and after the Civil War, he subdivided some of his land for sale to freedmen on easy terms.

28. See Wallace, Vigness, and Ward, *Documents of Texas History*, and John V. Haggard, "Neutral Ground," *Handbook of Texas Online*, http://www.tshaonline.org/handbook/online/articles/nbn02.

29. Variants of the incident are legion, but see Wynn, "History of the Civil Courts in Texas," 3–4; and Paulsen, "Short History of the Supreme Court," 246.

30. Travis L. Summerlin, "Baylor, Robert Emmett Bledsoe," *Handbook of Texas Online*, http://www.tshaonline.org/handbook/online/articles/fbaav.

31. Lynch, *Bench and Bar of Texas*, 77.

32. Paulsen, "Judges of the Supreme Court," 325.

33. Paulsen, "Short History of the Supreme Court," 280n269. Louis Kemp's capsule biography of Robinson in the *Handbook of Texas Online* (http://www.tshaonline.org/handbook/online/articles/fro37) discreetly omits this controversial episode.

34. Jodye Lynn Dickson Schilz, "Council House Fight," *Handbook of Texas Online*, http://www.tshaonline.org/handbook/online/articles/btc01; Paulsen, "Short History of the Supreme Court," 255.

35. Lynch, *Bench and Bar of Texas*, 74–75.

36. See generally Hart, *Alphonse in Austin*. DuBois's numbered dispatches, translated by Nancy Barker in *The French Legation in Texas*, have a few missing items, presumably the ones eaten by Bullock's pigs. DuBois got his revenge: his brother-in-law was the French finance minister who denied Texas a five-million-dollar loan that was sorely needed.

37. Santa Anna's two 1842 invasions of Texas can also be seen as reactions to the aggressive expansionism of the Lamar administration; see Campbell, *Gone to Texas*, 173–175.

38. Paulson, "Judges of the Supreme Court," 334–335.

39. Ibid., 340.

40. Terrell to Houston, July 25, 1841, Sam Houston Papers.

41. Paulsen, "Judges of the Supreme Court," 359.

42. Paulsen, "Short History of the Supreme Court," 263. In later years, Ochiltree was most noted for the ardor of his support for the Confederacy, being elected to the Secession Convention and then to the Congress in Richmond (Robert Bruce Blake, "Ochiltree, William Beck," *Handbook of Texas Online*, http://www.tshaonline.org/handbook/online/articles/foc02).

43. Davenport, *Supreme Court of Texas*, 25.

CHAPTER 3

1. Lynch, *Bench and Bar of Texas*, 275.

2. Hogan, *Texas Republic*, 247.

3. Paulsen, "Short History of the Supreme Court," 265–266.

4. J. L. Haley, *Sam Houston*, 245–253.

5. Paulsen, "Short History of the Supreme Court," 267.

6. Hogan, *Texas Republic*, 248.

7. Quoted in Muir, *Texas in 1837*, 92.

8. Constitution of the Republic of Texas, art. IV, sec. 13.

9. Paulsen, "Short History of the Supreme Court," 240–242, 283–301.

10. Act of December 15, 1836, Gammel, *Laws of Texas* (1898), 1:1139.

11. Act of December 22, 1836, in ibid., 1:1258.

12. Wharton, "Early Judicial History of Texas," 311.

13. Act of December 14, 1837, Gammel, *Laws of Texas*, 1:1400.

14. Paulsen, "Short History of the Supreme Court," 252–253. Paulsen cites a letter from Memucan Hunt to President Lamar dated December 25, 1839 (253n90).

15. Philquist, "Supreme Court of Texas," 7.

16. Paulsen, "Short History of the Supreme Court," 253.

17. McGown, "Supreme Court of the Republic of Texas," 16.

18. *Dangerfield v. Secretary of State*, Dallam 358, 359 (1840).

19. *Harvey v. Patterson*, Dallam 369, 370 (1840).

20. Ibid., at 370.

21. *Board of Land Commissioners of Milam County v. Bell*, Dallam 366 (1840).

22. Ibid., at 368.

23. McGown, "Supreme Court of the Republic of Texas," 18–19.

24. An Act to Adopt the Common Law of England, to Repeal Certain Mexican Laws, and to Regulate the Marital Rights of Parties, Gammel, *Laws of Texas*, 2:177.

25. Partially excepted from this were states that had served time under jurisdictions observant of the civil law—the French in Louisiana and the Spanish in Florida.

26. *Grassmeyer v. Beeson*, 13 Tex. 524, 531 (1855). The adoption, or not, of the common law is treated at length in Markham, "Reception of the Common Law in Texas," 910 ff., and F. W. Hall, "Adoption of the Common Law by Texas."

27. *Fowler v. Poor*, Dallam 403 (1841).

28. Ibid., cited in Townes, "Development of the Judicial System," 52.

29. *Hamilton v. Blank*, Dallam 587 (1844).

30. Townes, "Development of the Judicial System," 52.

31. *Scott and Solomon v. Maynard et uxor.*, Dallam 548 (1843). For Hemphill as a possible president of the Republic, see Siegel, *Political History of the Texas Republic*, 235.

32. *Scott and Solomon*, Dallam at 553.

33. Ibid., at 548.

34. Gammel, *Laws of Texas*, 2:177–180.

35. Ashford, "Jacksonian Liberalism and Spanish Law," 8 ff.

36. Constitution of the Republic of Texas, Declaration of Rights, no. 12 (1836).

37. "Remarks of Oran Roberts," quoted in Gaines, "John Hemphill," 23–24.

38. Wheeler to O. M. Roberts, November 21, 1845, quoted in Hogan, *Texas Republic*, 254. James Paulsen notes that Wheeler later recanted this negative judgment of Hemphill (correspondence with author, June 2011). In a letter to Roberts dated May 29, 1847, Wheeler said he was "happy to have found abundant reason to change that opinion," and viewed Hemphill as "a very strong man and exceedingly safe judge." Paulsen explains that Wheeler's 1845 criticism arose from his unhappiness with Hemphill's decision to hold a December session of the Supreme Court, which interfered with Wheeler's plan to take his ailing wife out of state to recuperate.

39. *Whiting v. Turley*, Dallam 453, 455 (1842), analyzed in McGown, "Supreme Court of the Republic of Texas," 6.

40. *Telegraph and Texas Register*, July 31, 1839. Notably, this article appeared before Congress passed the 1840 act favoring the English common law.

41. *Telegraph and Texas Register*, December 30, 1840.

42. Quoted in Muir, *Texas in 1837*, 92.

43. Wheeler to O. M. Roberts, November 21, 1845. Again, Paulsen observes that this early criticism stemmed from Wheeler's unhappiness over the December session.

44. Quoted in Gaines, "John Hemphill," 11.

45. Weeks, *Journals of the Convention*, 191, 198. Equity jurisprudence developed in England as an adjunct to the common law (and statutory law) in response to cases that either

did not have common law precedents or required remedies not provided by the common law. For example, the common law remedy for breach of contract was generally payment of monetary damages, whereas the remedy in an equity case might be to compel specific performance—that is, exact performance of the contract as promised—if damages would be inadequate recompense. Equity cases were heard in courts of chancery, so called because equity was developed as a prerogative of the lord chancellor of England.

46. Woodard, "Common Law and Common-Law Legal Systems," 512.

47. Ibid., 513.

48. Gaines, "John Hemphill," 22.

49. Address by the Honorable Sidney L. Samuels, in Texas Supreme Court, *Report of Ceremony Commemorating the 100 Years of Existence of the Supreme Court of Texas*, 19, quoted in McKnight, "Tracings of Texas Legal History," 271.

CHAPTER 4

1. *Jones v. Nowland*, Dallam 452 (1842).

2. *Doss v. Cradock*, Dallam 592 (1842).

3. *Mitchell v. Barton*, Dallam 632 (1842).

4. *Fulton v. Craddock*, Dallam 458 (1842).

5. *Hall v. Phelps*, Dallam 435 (1841).

6. Ibid., at 440.

7. Ibid., at 441.

8. Ibid., at 438 (emphasis in the original).

9. The presidential contest that year between Sam Houston and David Burnet, mirrored down ballot by their partisans, reached a level of ferocity scarcely equaled at any other time in Texas politics; see J. L. Haley, *Sam Houston*, 224–226.

10. Quoted in the Supreme Court's decision in the case, *Thompson v. Harrison*, Dallam, 466 (1842).

11. Ibid.

12. *Cavenah v. Somervill*, Dallam 532, 534 (1843).

13. *Saddler v. The Republic*, Dallam 610, 611 (1843).

14. Ibid., at 611.

15. Mirabeau Lamar, Inaugural Address, December 13, 1838, quoted in J. L. Haley, *Texas: From the Frontier to Spindletop*, 91.

16. Rusk acted in his capacity as general of militia, an office to which the Congress elected him over President Houston's veto; see generally Everett, *Texas Cherokees*.

17. *P. W. Herbert v. Thomas A. Moore*, Dallam 592 (1842).

18. *Cherokee Nation v. Georgia*, 30 U.S. 1 (1831). Jones was highly artful in selecting Marshall's characterization of the Cherokee in this ruling as being in a state of pupilage. Marshall's decision was explicit that "from time immemorial the Cherokee Nation have composed a sovereign and independent state, and in this character have been repeatedly recognized, and still stand recognized by the United States."

19. *Herbert*, Dallam at 594.

20. Ibid., at 596.

21. Ibid., at 595.

22. *Donald McDonald v. Lewis Hancock*, 65 Tex. L. Rev. 388 (Paulsen rep. 1986). This was one of the "missing cases" of the Republic that was reported by James Paulsen in 1986. It was argued during the Court's final term on December 18, 1845, and was decided on January 2, 1846, two days after annexation.

23. Sam Houston, by way of example, was known to buy slaves out from under cruel "drivers" and to attempt to reunite black families who had been separated on the auction block; see generally Hamilton, *My Master*. In later years, when Hamilton was cheated of several months' wages by a derisive employer, Hamilton solicited the help of a local judge, who forced the employer to pay up, under threat of a horsewhipping.

24. *Benton v. Williams*, Dallam 496 (1843).

25. Ibid., at 497.

26. Ibid., at 496–497.

27. See Henson, "Anahuac Disturbances," *Handbook of Texas Online*.

28. *Lamar v. Houston* (Tex. 1845); Tex. L. Rev. 65, (Paulsen rep. 1986), 382.

29. "Statement of Stephen Z. Hoyle" (October 1838), Sam Houston Papers. For more on this story, see Paulsen, "Houston v. Lamar," 16.

30. *Lamar v. Houston* (Tex. 1845); Tex. L. Rev. 65, (Paulsen rep. 1986), 385. Houston probably assigned his interest to Lewis in satisfaction of a debt to him, for Lewis had lent Houston money before.

31. According to Paulsen, the Republic Congress finally passed legislation in 1840 calling for the appointment of a reporter for the Supreme Court, but it specified that decisions were not to be published until a volume of at least four hundred pages could be produced ("Short History of the Supreme Court," 274–276). This minimum was not met before the Republic was dissolved. Dallam's *Digest* was therefore the only compendium of cases, and although it is not technically "official," it has been cited continually by the state's courts.

32. Lynch, *Bench and Bar of Texas*, 251–253; Kate Dallam Gregory, "Dallam, James Wilmer," *Handbook of Texas Online*, http://www.tshaonline.org/handbook/online/articles/fda05.

33. Paulsen, "Missing Cases of the Republic," 372.

CHAPTER 5

1. N. C. Raymond to John E. King, 23 March 1846, in D. C. Hall, "Raymond's Report on the Legislature," 82–83.

2. Texas Constitution of 1845, art. IV, sec. 2, 5.

3. Davenport, *Supreme Court of Texas*, 29. The exact days they were to meet were changed by the Fourth and Fifth Legislatures (Gammel, *Laws of Texas*, vol. 3: *Laws of the Fourth Legislature*, 896; *Laws of the Fifth Legislature*, 1543).

4. Mary J. Highsmith, "Lipscomb, Abner Smith," *Handbook of Texas Online*, http://www.tshaonline.org/handbook/online/articles/fli14.

5. Weeks, *Debates of the Texas Convention*, 288–289. Quoted in Klemme, "Jacksonian Justice," 437–438.

6. In fact, the popular election of judges gained such traction that no new state entered the Union with an appointed judiciary for more than a century (Klemme, "Jacksonian Justice," 438).

7. *Jones v. State*, 13 Tex. 168 (1854). Jones on appeal also contended that a witness for the state should have been excluded on account of her want of chastity. Lipscomb ruled that her deficient morals, while regrettable, did not render her legally infamous, and the truth of her testimony was for the jury to assess (ibid., at 176).

8. See, for example, *Herbert v. Moore*, Dallam 592 (1842).

9. *Mason v. Russel's Heirs*, 1 Tex. 720 (1847).

10. Texas Constitution of 1845, art. VII, sec. 22.

11. *Sampson and Keene v. Williamson and Wife*, 6 Tex. 102 (1851).

12. Ibid. Not surprisingly for Hemphill, he went on to suggest "the readoption of the Spanish or a more simple form of mortgage. The form in use is deceptive and fictitious" (ibid., at 115).

13. As a member of the Constitutional Convention of 1845, Lipscomb introduced the resolution that the legislature be authorized to pass laws protecting property from forced sale (Weeks, *Journals of the Convention*, 83). Online at http://tarlton.law.utexas.edu/constitutions/pdf/images/index1845.html (accessed February 21, 2011).

14. *Shepherd v. Cassiday*, 20 Tex. 24 (1857).

15. Ibid., at 29–30.

16. *Sampson v. Williamson*, 6 Tex. at 120–121.

17. *Snoddy v. Cage*, 5 Tex. 106 (1849).

18. Ibid., at 126. Wheeler cited a concurring opinion by Justice Henry Baldwin in *Holmes v. Jennison*, 39 U.S. 540 (1840).

19. *Coles v. Kelsey*, 2 Tex. 541, 559 (1847). One thing that may have drawn such a pithy response from Wheeler was that Lipscomb's extraordinarily verbose majority opinion seemed to echo Hemphill in extolling the virtues of a hybridized system of pleading.

20. *Smith v. Smith*, 1 Tex. 621, 624 (1847).

21. Rev. Tex. Civ. Stat., art. 2977.

22. *Wright v. Wright*, 3 Tex. 168 (1848), cited by Gaines in "John Hemphill," 20.

23. Deposition of Richard Rust, July 1, 1871, and cause no. 3074, *Theodora Hemphill v. James Hemphill et al.*, Travis County, June Term, 1871 (Vertical File "John Hemphill," Austin History Center). Perhaps it was the potential scandal that caused Hemphill to postpone making the will he intended. He died in 1862, and his estate had not been settled by 1870, when Theodora (Henrietta had died) sued Hemphill's white relatives for a share of the estate. They settled with her for $1,700. Legal scholar James Paulsen (see works cited herein) has done a great deal of research on Hemphill and his Court, the publication of which is much to be hoped for.

24. Ford Dixon, "Roberts, Oran Milo," *Handbook of Texas Online*, http://www.tsha

online.org/handbook/online/articles/fro18. Dixon wrote more expansively about Roberts in an article in Nunn, *Ten More Texans in Gray*. Houston's disgust with Roberts reached its apogee over the 1861 Secession Convention.

25. Nash outlines six considerations on which the Texas Supreme Court could have circumscribed the legal protections extended to slaves and free blacks, but instead held open the courthouse door to them ("Trial Rights of Blacks").

26. Act of February 5, 1840, in Gammel, *Laws of Texas*, 2:325–326.

27. *Moore v. Minerva*, 17 Tex. 20 (1856).

28. In Gillespie County, the focus of the German colony in west-central Texas, only five families owned even a single slave on the eve of the Civil War. East of there, in New Braunfels and in German settlements more embedded in the majority cotton culture, Germans learned to accept slavery as a fact of life, or else keep quiet; see J. L. Haley, *Passionate Nation*, 299–300.

29. For a map of the results of the Secession Referendum, see Richardson, *Lone Star State*, 199; for a general discussion, see Connor, *Peters Colony of Texas*.

30. Lynch, *Bench and Bar of Texas*, 293–294; Davenport, *Supreme Court of Texas*, 55–58. When Stephen F. Austin first entered Texas, in July 1821, he found Bell's father, Josiah Bell of Missouri, an old friend, illegally squatting on land near Nacogdoches. He brought Bell into his own colonial enterprise and left Bell in charge of his settlers when he departed for Mexico to arrange his affairs (Cantrell, *Stephen F. Austin*, 91, 110; E. Barker, *Life of Stephen F. Austin*, 35, 41).

31. *Guess v. Lubbock*, 5 Tex. 535 (1851). Notwithstanding the style of the case, the most common spelling of her name in contemporary records is "Gess" (Davidson, "One Woman's Fight for Freedom," in Campbell, *Laws of Slavery in Texas*, 87–93).

32. The question is considered as lucidly as it can be in Davidson, "One Woman's Fight for Freedom."

33. Ibid., 89.

34. *Guess*, 5 Tex. 551.

35. Davidson, "One Woman's Fight for Freedom," 92.

36. *Westbrook v. Mitchell*, 24 Tex. 560 (1859).

37. Pugsley, "The Runaway Slave Who Was Free." Pugsley's research and reporting on this remarkable series of events are groundbreaking. The information in the following narrative is derived from his paper.

38. Cobb, *Law of Negro Slavery*. Cobb, a Georgia legal scholar, was a vigorous advocate of slavery.

39. *Westbrook*, 24 Tex. 562.

40. Ibid.

41. *Chandler v. State*, 2 Tex. 305 (1847). The importance of this case is discussed in Nash, "Trial Rights of Blacks," 625–627.

42. *Chandler*, 2 Tex. 310.

43. *Nix v. State*, 13 Tex. 575 (1855).

44. *State v. Stephenson*, 20 Tex. 151 (1857).

45. *Nels v. State*, 2 Tex. 280 (1847).

46. *Calvin v. State*, 25 Tex. 789 (1860).

47. Ibid., at 796.

48. The most detailed study of this phenomenon is Nash, "Trial Rights of Blacks," 622–625.

49. Bewley had been implicated, without good evidence, in the "Texas Troubles," a series of downtown fires across North Texas. According to a rumor propagated in the absence of evidence by secessionist newspapers, the arson was a Northern conspiracy intended to start a slave insurrection. See Donald E. Reynolds, "Bewley, Anthony," *Handbook of Texas Online*, http://www.tshaonline.org/handbook/online/articles/fbe71, and works there cited; also W. White, "Texas Slave Insurrection."

CHAPTER 6

1. See Houston, "Extracts from a Speech on Slavery, Tremont Temple, Boston," February 22, 1855, in Williams and Barker, *Writings of Sam Houston*, 6:167–177.

2. During the campaign for governor, Houston gave only one speech ("Speech at Nacogdoches," July 7, 1859, in Williams and Barker, *Writings of Sam Houston*, 7:343–367), remembering that his vociferous defense of the Union had resulted in his defeat in running for the same office two years before. His enmity for secession, however, was a vivid part of the public record.

3. Lynch, *Bench and Bar of Texas*, 95.

4. Kittrell, *Governors Who Have Been*, quoted in Welch, *Texas Governor*, 36; Houston, Pardon of Mary Monroe, February 11, 1860 [1861], Sam Houston Executive Record Book, Texas State Archives.

5. Friend, *Sam Houston: Great Designer*, 331; Maher, "Sam Houston and Secession," 453.

6. McCormick, *Scotch-Irish in Ireland and America*, 130–131, quoted in Norvell, "Supreme Court of Texas under the Confederacy," 50. For the next century, Texas historians unable to shake off the thrall of the Old South struggled to explain so many Texans' dogged devotion to the Union. Norvell attributed Houston's election to the force of his own personality ("Supreme Court of Texas under the Confederacy," 49). But even Rupert Richardson acknowledged that the ordinance's failure in Angelina County, in the heart of East Texas, was "not easily explained" (*The Lone Star State*, 200).

7. Norvell, "Supreme Court of Texas under the Confederacy," 50.

8. Quoted in Goldthwaite, "In Memoriam, James H. Bell," in the preface to 85 Tex. xii–xviii (1893).

9. Norvell, "Supreme Court of Texas under the Confederacy," 61.

10. Moore, a prominent Nacogdoches attorney, was a member of the law firm that furnished reporters for the Supreme Court and published volumes 22–24 of *Texas Reports* ("Moore, George Fleming," *Handbook of Texas Online*, http://www.tshaonline.org /handbook/online/articles/fmo28).

11. Nash, "Trial Rights of Blacks," 640; Greenhill, "Supreme Court of Texas during the Civil War," 2.

12. Confederate Conscription Act of April 16, 1862, Public Laws of the Confederate States of America, 1st. Cong., 1st sess., ch. 31, 29–32. For an extensive discussion of the case, which is summarized here, see Norvell, "Supreme Court of Texas under the Confederacy," 53.

13. According to Davenport, Paschal's jailing was symptomatic of the danger of speaking freely in the Confederacy, and caused a rupture in the friendship between Paschal and Wheeler (*Supreme Court of Texas*, 71–72). See also Greenhill, "Supreme Court of Texas during the Civil War," 6.

14. *Ex parte Coupland*, 26 Tex. 386 (1862).

15. Ibid., at 391.

16. Ibid., at 404–406. Paulsen and Hambleton note that *Ex parte Coupland*, which established Texas habeas corpus law, was one of the Texas Civil War cases with precedential value, "cited with approval by the Texas Supreme Court and Court of Criminal Appeals, the Supreme Courts of other states, and even the Supreme Court of the United States" ("Confederates and Carpetbaggers," 916).

17. Story, *Commentaries on the Constitution*, 1:168–169.

18. *Ex parte Coupland*, 26 Tex. 409. The quotation by Calhoun is from his *Discourse on the Constitution and Government of the United States* (1851).

19. *Ex parte Coupland*, 26 Tex. 418.

20. Ibid., at 409, 413.

21. Ibid., at 419.

22. See generally Pickering and Falls, *Brush Men and Vigilantes*; and see more particularly Clark, *Civil War Recollections of Clark*, on the so-called Great Hanging at Gainesville. Houston to Frazier, August 15, 1862, in Williams and Barker, *Writings of Sam Houston*, 8:322.

23. The Civil War divided the German-Texan community, as described in J. L. Haley, *Passionate Nation*, 299–300. Nineteen German Texans were killed and nine executed in one ambush alone by Confederate vigilantes; see Underwood, *Death on the Nueces*.

24. Gilbert, "'Unwhipped of Justice,'" 5.

25. Ibid., 6. Gilbert's paper describes the circumstances of this bizarre episode in great detail.

26. Greenhill, "Supreme Court of Texas during the Civil War," 7–8.

27. *State v. Sparks*, 27 Tex. 627, 633 (1864), cited in Gilbert, "'Unwhipped of Justice,'" 38.

28. *State v. Sparks*, 27 Tex. 631, 632.

29. *State v. Sparks and Magruder*, 27 Tex. 705, 712 (1864).

30. Ibid.; quoted in Greenhill, "Supreme Court of Texas during the Civil War," 9.

31. *Sparks and Magruder*, 27 Tex. 713.

32. Ibid; cited in Norvell, "Supreme Court under the Confederacy," 56.

33. Gilbert, "'Unwhipped of Justice,'" 56.

34. Norvell, "Supreme Court of Texas under the Confederacy," 57.

35. Gammel, *Laws of Texas*, 5:449. The law did not apply to cases already in progress, or to cases in which the parties agreed to proceed to trial.

36. Wooten, *Comprehensive History of Texas*, 2:144.

37. *Ashley Parker v. State*, 26 Tex. 204, 207 (1862), quoted in Greenhill, "Supreme Court of Texas during the Civil War," 5.

38. Paschal, preface to *A Digest of the Laws of Texas*, 28 Tex. at vi–vii (1866). Paschal is also known to Texas history as the author of "Last Years of Sam Houston." Paschal himself led a highly interesting life, a Georgia teacher and bookkeeper who married and had three children with the daughter of Cherokee chief John Ridge. He resigned his post as chief justice of the Arkansas Supreme Court to aid the Cherokees in their legal proceedings against the United States. He was ardently pro-Union, and after his release from jail, he made himself scarce in Texas and relocated to Washington, D.C. See Amelia W. Williams, "Paschal, George Washington" in *Handbook of Texas Online*, http://www.tshaonline.org/handbook/online/articles/fpa46.

39. Davenport, *Supreme Court of Texas*, 81; Norvell, "Supreme Court of Texas under the Confederacy," 48.

40. West, preface to 27 Tex. at v, vi (1881), quoting Supreme Court reporters A. M. Jackson and Charles L. Robards.

41. According to T. R. Phillips, Roberts received 34,127 votes to Bell's 7,228 ("Elections for the Texas Supreme Court," 8).

42. Oddly, neither Lynch (*Bench and Bar of Texas*) nor Davenport (*Supreme Court of Texas*) contains biographical capsules of Reuben Reeves, virtually alone among past justices at having been so ignored. See Georgia Kemp Caraway, "Reeves, Reuben A.," in *Handbook of Texas Online*, http://www.tshaonline.org/handbook/online/articles/fre23.

43. Norvell, "Supreme Court of Texas under the Confederacy," 61; as Norvell noted, "One may speculate as to [Bell's] probable judicial accomplishments had he . . . been allowed to pursue a judicial career following the war. The jurisprudence of Texas has probably been the loser" (60).

44. See Robards, *Synopses of the Decisions of the Supreme Court of the State of Texas* (1865), known informally as *Robards' Conscript Cases*.

45. Norvell, "Supreme Court of Texas under the Confederacy," 57.

46. *Cowan v. Hardeman*, 26 Tex. 217 (1862), cited in *State v. Valmont Plantations*, 346 S.W.2d 853 (Tex. Civ. App.—San Antonio 1961), opinion adopted at 163 Tex. 381, 355 S.W.2d 502 (1962).

47. *City of Galveston v. Menard*, 23 Tex. 349 (1859).

48. *Buffalo Bayou, Brazos & Colorado Railroad Co. v. George A. Ferris*, 26 Tex. 588 (1863), cited in *State v. Carpenter*, 126 Tex. 604, 89 S.W.2d 194 (1936). Norvell lists various other examples of Civil War–era cases being cited with approval ("Supreme Court of Texas under the Confederacy," 58–59).

49. For a good summary of the durability of the decisions of the variously convened courts, see Paulsen and Hambleton, "Confederates and Carpetbaggers."

CHAPTER 7

1. See Waller, *Colossal Hamilton of Texas*; and Lynch, *Bench and Bar of Texas*, 104–109.

2. Baade, "Supreme Court of Texas," 25–26.

3. Quoted in Campbell, *Gone to Texas*, 272.

4. Haynes to Pease, October 4, 1866, quoted in Crouch, "'All the Vile Passions,'" 34. Crouch (14–16) accurately summarizes the wide range of historical assessments of the Black Codes and their intent, nature, and severity.

5. For a particularly frank assessment of Throckmorton as no friend of the freedman despite his famous earlier vote against secession, see Crouch, "'All the Vile Passions,'" 22.

6. Lynch, *Bench and Bar of Texas*, 285–292; Davenport, *Supreme Court of Texas*, 82; John W. Payne, Jr., "Coke, Richard," *Handbook of Texas Online*, http://www.tshaonline.org/handbook/online/articles/fco15. As a moderate, Hamilton would have found Coke more useful than abhorrent.

7. Lynch, *Bench and Bar of Texas*, 148–150; Davenport, *Supreme Court of Texas*, 86–87; H. Allen Anderson, "Donley, Stockton P.," *Handbook of Texas Online*, http://www.tshaonline.org/handbook/online/articles/fdo14.

8. Charles Christopher Jackson, "Smith, George Washington," *Handbook of Texas Online*, http://www.tshaonline.org/handbook/online/articles/fsm17.

9. Baade, "Supreme Court of Texas," 37.

10. Lynch, *Bench and Bar of Texas*, 295–301; Davenport, *Supreme Court of Texas*, 85–86; Thomas W. Cutrer, "Willie, Asa Hoxie," *Handbook of Texas Online*, http://www.tshaonline.org/handbook/online/articles/fwi43.

11. Paulsen and Hambleton, "Confederates and Carpetbaggers," 917, quoting Shelley, "Semicolon Court of Texas" ("No judicial act of this court was ever the subject of merited criticism"). This sentiment was echoed by Judge Joe Greenhill, who wrote that although the Coke Court operated under Presidential Reconstruction, "it acted . . . with the general consent of the people . . . and its decisions, unlike those of the two Courts which succeeded it, are regarded as authoritative today" ("Supreme Court of Texas during the Civil War," 12).

12. *Gabel v. City of Houston*, 29 Tex. 335 (1867).

13. Ibid., at 347, cited in Baade, "Supreme Court of Texas," 44.

14. Ibid., at 344.

15. *Warren v. State*, 29 Tex. 369 (1867), cited in Baade, "Supreme Court of Texas," 48.

16. *Tippett v. Mize*, 30 Tex. 361 (1867), cited in ibid.

17. *Scranton v. Conlie*, 29 Tex. 237, 238 (1867), cited in Baade, "Supreme Court of Texas," 48–49.

18. *Texas v. White*, 74 U.S. 700 (1869). For a discussion of the case's context, see "Texas v. White," in *Handbook of Texas Online*, http://www.tshaonline.org/handbook/online/articles/jrt01; and at http://en.wikipedia.org/wiki/Texas_v._White. Immediately after the war, the Texas Supreme Court, in Chief Justice Moore's decision in *Bishop v. Jones and Patty*, 28 Tex. 294 (1866), reached the opposite conclusion for purposes of deciding whether a prewar debt was collectible.

19. Randolph B. Campbell states that southern hostility toward freedmen "added to the determination of radical Republicans in Congress to block Presidential Reconstruction" (*Southern Community in Crisis*, 266). See also Crouch, "'All the Vile Passions,'" 18.

20. For general background on Reconstruction in Texas, mentioned here and subsequently, see Moneyhon, *Republicanism in Reconstruction Texas*; Ramsdell, *Reconstruction in Texas*; and Nunn, *Texas under the Carpetbaggers*. The most succinct but usable summary is Carl H. Moneyhon, "Reconstruction," in *Handbook of Texas Online*, http://www.tshaonline.org/handbook/online/articles/mzr01.

21. James Alex Baggett and Joseph G. Dawson III, "Griffin, Charles," *Handbook of Texas Online*, http://www.tshaonline. org/handbook/online/articles/fgr60.

22. Baade, "Supreme Court of Texas," 26.

23. Lynch, *Bench and Bar of Texas*, 151–159; Davenport, *Supreme Court of Texas*, 89–90; "Morrill, Amos," *Handbook of Texas Online*, http://www.tshaonline.org/handbook/online/articles/fm054.

24. Louis W. Kemp, "Latimer, Albert Hamilton," *Handbook of Texas Online*, http://www.tshaonline.org/handbook/online/articles/fla44.

25. Davenport, *Supreme Court of Texas*, 90–91; John D. Thompson, "Lindsay, Livingston," *Handbook of Texas Online*, http://www.tshaonline.org/handbook/online/articles/fli06.

26. Wooten, *Comprehensive History of Texas*, 2:176. With the former rebels freed to vote in the election of 1873, Hamilton was vindicated and the Democrats were returned to power (Norvell, "Reconstruction Courts of Texas," 147).

27. Charles Christopher Jackson, "Caldwell, Colbert," *Handbook of Texas Online*, http://www.tshaonline.org/handbook/online/articles/fca10.

28. Norvell, "Roberts and the Semicolon Court," 287; Baade, "Supreme Court of Texas," 71.

29. Baade, "Supreme Court of Texas," 71. Baade discusses the background and output of the Military Court at great length.

30. The 1869 Constitution (art. V, sec. 2) provided that the judge whose term expired the soonest in the initial staggered three-year terms would be designated "presiding judge." Evans drew the shortest lot.

31. Evans quoted in Davenport, *History of the Supreme Court*, 96; biographical information in Lynch, *Bench and Bar of Texas*, 110–113, and Brian Hart, "Evans, Lemuel Dale," *Handbook of Texas Online*, http://www.tshaonline.org/handbook/online/articles/fev07.

32. Randolph B. Campbell, "Ogden, Wesley B.," *Handbook of Texas Online*, http://www.tshaonline.org/handbook/online/articles/fog04.

33. Paulsen and Hambleton, "Confederates and Carpetbaggers," 919–920.

34. Bruce S. Allardice, "McAdoo, John David," *Handbook of Texas Online*, http://www.tshaonline.org/handbook/online/articles/fmc01.

35. A more evenhanded assessment is found in Campbell, *Gone to Texas*, 281–285. Baade found the term "carpetbagger" to be misplaced even in reference to the Military Court, except in the instance of Moses Walker ("Supreme Court of Texas," 55).

36. Among those cases were *Kinney v. Zimpleman*, 36 Tex. 554 (1871); and *Peay v. Talbot and Brothers*, 39 Tex. 335 (1872).

37. *Houston and Great Northern Railway Company v. Jacob Kuechler*, 36 Tex. 425 (1871). Before the outbreak of the war, Governor Sam Houston, hoping to sign up enough pro-Union Texas Rangers to serve as a loyalist cavalry, tapped Kuechler as his recruiter within Texas's sizeable German communities (J. L. Haley, *Passionate Nation*, 291).

38. *Honey v. Graham*, 39 Tex. 1 (1873).

39. "Honey, George W.," *Handbook of Texas Online*, http://www.tshaonline.org/hand book/online/articles/fho48.

40. See Campbell, *Gone to Texas*, 284.

41. *Honey*, 39 Tex. 1. In an earlier case, the Court had declared Graham state treasurer pro tempore and ordered Honey to hand over the keys to the office, but it left open the question whether the governor's appointment was valid (*Honey v. Davis*, 39 Tex. 1 [1873]). The cases are discussed in Baade, "Supreme Court of Texas," 105–107.

42. *Honey*, 39 Tex. 10.

43. For background on the period, see Campbell, *Gone to Texas*, chap. 11; and J. L. Haley, *Passionate Nation*, chap. 45.

44. Act of March 31, 1873, General Laws, 13th Leg.

45. Texas Constitution of 1869, art. III, sec. 6.

46. *Ex parte Rodríguez*, 39 Tex. 705 (1874).

47. Terrell's friendship with Houston is recalled in Terrell, "Recollections of Sam Houston"; see Irby C. Nichols., Jr., "Terrell, Alexander Watkins," in *Handbook of Texas Online*, http://www.tshaonline.org/handbook/online/articles/fte16.

48. *Ex parte Rodríguez*, 39 Tex. 740.

49. Ibid., at 742.

50. Ibid., at 746.

51. Ibid.

52. Davenport, *Supreme Court of Texas*, 97.

53. Paulsen and Hambleton consider their opinions "precedential, but sometimes not respected," and note some "jurists using an apologetic tone" when citing one of their opinions ("Confederates and Carpetbaggers," 920). Norvell shows that the Roberts Court generally followed the precedents of its predecessors ("Roberts and the Semicolon Court," 191–192), and Baade agrees ("Supreme Court of Texas," 130). In addition, Baade points out that the Court's "massive decisional output . . . fills over six volumes of the Texas Reports," but is judged "almost exclusively in the light of its last reported eponymous decision" (91).

54. *Renn v. Samos*, 33 Tex. 760 (1871). It was Roberts himself who helped frame the legend of the Semicolon Court; see Wooten, *Comprehensive History of Texas*, 2:198.

CHAPTER 8

1. *Stroud v. Springfield*, 28 Tex. 649 (1866).

2. The language of the constitutional amendment passed in December 1873 continued to call the members of the Court "judges," but legislation passed in 1874 specified salaries for "associate justices," and subsequent literature has used that term; see Gammel, *Laws of Texas*, vol. 8, chap. 72.

3. Davenport, *History of the Supreme Court*, 111–113; Yancey L. Russell, "Devine, Thomas Jefferson," *Handbook of Texas Online*, http://www.tshaonline.org/handbook/online/articles/fde50.

4. "George Fleming Moore," in "Justices of Texas, 1836–1986," http://tarlton.law.utexas.edu/justices/profile/view/71.

5. "Reuben A. Reeves," in "Justices of Texas, 1836–1986," http://tarlton.law.utexas.edu/justices/profile/view/86.

6. Davenport, *History of the Supreme Court*, 114–115; C. Richard King, "Ballinger, William Pitt," *Handbook of Texas Online*, http://www.tshaonline.org/handbook/online/articles/fba52. See also Curtsinger, "Career of Judge William P. Ballinger," and Moretta, *William Pitt Ballinger*, for more detailed studies.

7. See Curtsinger, "Career of Judge William P. Ballinger," and King, "William Pitt Ballinger." Ballinger's papers, housed at the Dolph Briscoe Center for American History at the University of Texas, are a rich source of documentation for nineteenth-century Texas legal and financial history. Perhaps his most important contribution to Texas history, though, was his daughter Betty, a founder of the Daughters of the Republic of Texas.

8. Davenport, *Supreme Court of Texas*, 115–117; Thomas W. Cutrer, "Gray, Peter W.," *Handbook of Texas Online*, http://www.tshaonline.org/handbook/online/articles/fgr25.

9. Davenport, *Supreme Court of Texas*, 117–119; Fred F. Abbey, "Gould, Robert Simonton," *Handbook of Texas Online*, http://www.tshaonline.org/handbook/online/articles/fgo22.

10. Claude Elliott, "Ireland, John," *Handbook of Texas Online*, http://www.tshaonline.org/handbook/online/articles/fir01.

11. Davenport, *Supreme Court of Texas*, 125.

12. *Horbach v. State*, 43 Tex. 242, 247 (1875).

13. Davenport, *Supreme Court of Texas*, 125–127.

14. These provisions are reflected in the Texas Constitution of 1876, art. V, secs. 2, 7.

15. Quoted in Willis, "Texas Court of Criminal Appeals," 723.

16. Ibid., 723–724; see also Campbell, *Gone to Texas*, 285–286.

17. *Texas Land Company v. Williams*, 48 Tex. 602 (1878).

18. Ibid., at 605, 604.

19. *Murchison v. Holly*, 40 Tex. 465 (1874).

20. Davenport, *Supreme Court of Texas*, 135–136.

21. Willis, "Texas Court of Criminal Appeals," 724.

22. *Taylor v. Murphy*, 50 Tex. 291 (1878). Moore, in enunciating his determination not to take decisions of the Military Court as precedent, almost obscured his meaning with

prevaricating politeness, but it resulted in one of the most elegant dismissals, and most majestic sentences, in Court history: "And while I am as far as any one from desiring to bring in question the validity of its acts in adjudicating the cases which were disposed of by it, or from detracting from the respect properly due to its opinions, by reason of ability and legal learning of the eminent gentlemen who constituted the court, and who were no doubt selected on this account to discharge the important duties entrusted to them by the general under whose direct control all the functions of government with us were then conducted, nevertheless I cannot regard the opinion of this tribunal as authoritative exposition of the law involved in the cases upon which it was called to pass, but merely as conclusive and binding determinations of the particular case in which such opinion was expressed" (ibid.).

23. *Roundtree v. Thomas*, 32 Tex. 286 (1867).

24. *Taylor*, 50 Tex. 295.

25. Baade examines this issue at length and from a variety of angles ("Supreme Court of Texas," 166–168).

26. *City of San Antonio v. Lane*, 32 Tex. 405 (1869); *City of San Antonio v. Gould*, 34 Tex. 49 (1870–1871).

27. *Giddings v. San Antonio*, 47 Tex. 548, 577 (1877).

28. *San Antonio v. Mehaffy*, 312 U.S. (6 Otto) 312 (1878).

29. *Peck v. San Antonio*, 51 Tex. 490, 492 (1879). Greenhill noted the same disclaimer having been made in Texas cases as late as 1945 ("Supreme Court of Texas during the Civil War," 21–22).

30. *Peck*, 51 Tex. 493.

31. J. L. Haley, *Passionate Nation*, 420.

32. T. R. Phillips, "Elections for the Texas Supreme Court," 13.

33. Lynch, *Bench and Bar of Texas*, 116–120.

34. Willis, "Texas Court of Criminal Appeals," 724, 765.

35. Ibid., 765–766.

36. *Henderson v. Beaton*, 52 Tex. 29 (1879).

37. Ibid., at 53.

38. Davenport, *Supreme Court of Texas*, 146–150, quotation at 149n; Lynch, *Bench and Bar of Texas*, 315–318; Craig H. Rowell, "Stayton, John William," *Handbook of Texas Online*, http://www.tshaonline.org/handbook/online/articles/fst23.

39. J. L. Haley, *Texas: An Album of History*, 231–233; Jennett, "State Capitol and Governor's Mansion," 1.

40. *Yancy v. Batte*, 48 Tex. 46 (1877), discussed in Davenport, *Supreme Court of Texas*, 129–132. The case elicited a strong dissent from Justice Moore, who would have held the heirs' interest to be equitable, coming after the executor's payment of debts on the estate.

41. *Ball, Hutchings & Co. v. Lowell*, 56 Tex. 579 (1882).

42. *Milliken v. City Council of Weatherford*, 54 Tex. 388, 393 (1881).

43. Ibid., at 394. Modern requirements for sex-offender registry and proscriptions from residency place the nineteenth century in the unusual posture of having been more compassionate in this regard than the twenty-first.

44. Quoted in William D. Elliot, "State Bar of Texas," *Handbook of Texas Online*, http://www.tshaonline.org/handbook/online/articles/jos02.

CHAPTER 9

1. Texas State Preservation Board, "Supreme Court Courtroom."
2. Clamp, "In Retrospect," 19.
3. Texas State Preservation Board, "Supreme Court Courtroom."
4. Chriss, "Stayton, Gaines, and the Court," 15.
5. Lynch, *Bench and Bar of Texas*, 323–327; Roy L. Swift, "West, Charles Shannon," *Handbook of Texas Online*, http://www.tshaonline.org/handbook/online/articles/fwe29; Davenport, *Supreme Court of Texas*, 153–156.
6. "Robinson, Sawnie," *Handbook of Texas Online*, http://www.tshaonline.org/hand book/online/articles/fro33; Davenport, *Supreme Court of Texas*, 168–170.
7. Davenport, *Supreme Court of Texas*, 170–172; Randolph B. Campbell, "Gaines, Reuben Reid," *Handbook of Texas Online*, http://www.tshaonline.org/handbook/online/ articles/fga06.
8. Lynch, *Bench and Bar of Texas*, 354–355; Davenport, *Supreme Court of Texas*, 183–185; "Walker, Alexander Stuart," *Handbook of Texas Online*, http://www.tshaonline.org/ handbook/online/articles/fwa14.
9. Davenport, *Supreme Court of Texas*, 217–219; David Minor, "Brown, Thomas Jefferson," *Handbook of Texas Online*, http://www.tshaonline.org/handbook/online/articles/ fbr97.
10. Davenport, *Supreme Court of Texas*, 232–233; Leroy G. Denman, "Denman, Leroy Gilbert," *Handbook of Texas Online*, http://www.tshaonline.org/handbook/online/articles/ fde40.
11. See generally Leckie, *Conquest of the South Plains*, and J. L. Haley, *Buffalo War*.
12. These conflicting goals are well summarized in Chriss, "Stayton, Gaines, and the Court," 40–43.
13. *Hall v. Phelps*, Dallam 435–441 (1841). The case is described in Chapter 4 of this book.
14. *Cannon's Administrator v. Vaughn*, 12 Tex. 399 (1854).
15. *Summers v. Davis*, 49 Tex. 541 (1878).
16. Chriss, "Stayton, Gaines, and the Court," 44. Chriss cites Kens, "Wide Open Spaces?"
17. *Gammage v. Powell*, 61 Tex. 629 (1884). A "deed" is what transfers from one owner to another. A "patent" is what an original owner receives from the sovereign entity that disposes of the land for the first time. After the announcement of this doctrine, and with the establishment of the Commission of Appeals, disputes on this point usually ended at that level, reaching the Supreme Court only when further amplification was needed. See *Poston v. Blanks*, 14 S.W. 67 (Tex. Com. App., 1890); and *Swetman v. Sanders*, 20 S.W. 124 (Tex. Com. App., 1892), cited by Chriss, "Stayton, Gaines, and the Court," 44.

18. *Garrett v. Weaver*, 70 Tex. 463; 7 S.W. 766 (1888).

19. In fact, one of the first labor actions in the United States was the Texas Cowboy Strike of 1883; see Robert E. Zeigler, "Cowboy Strike of 1883," *Handbook of Texas Online*, http://www.tshaonline.org/handbook/online/articles/oec02. For an unromanticized look at the cowboy life, see Frantz and Choate, *American Cowboy*.

20. For all its susceptibility to a responsible reinterpretation, the best biography of Goodnight remains J. E. Haley, *Charles Goodnight*; Burton, "History of the JA Ranch," offers a succinct history.

21. Chriss discusses these public land issues in detail ("Stayton, Gaines, and the Court," 50–54), citing Kens, "Wide Open Spaces?" 178–179.

22. *State v. Goodnight*, 70 Tex. 682, 11 S.W. 119 (Tex. 1888).

23. *Day Land and Cattle Co. v. State*, 68 Tex. 526; 4 S.W. 865 (Tex. 1887).

24. *State v. Day Land and Cattle Co.*, 71 Tex. 252; 9 S.W. 130 (1888).

25. *Smisson v. State*, 71 Tex. 222; 9 S.W. 112 (1888).

26. Gen. Laws Tex., chap. 88, sec. 6, 18th Leg. (1883).

27. *State v. Wichita Land and Cattle Company*, 73 Tex. 450, 11 S.W. 488 (1889); cited by Chriss, "Stayton, Gaines, and the Court," 57.

28. *Busk v. Lowrie*, 86 Tex. 128 (1893), cited by Chriss, "Stayton, Gaines, and the Court," 47.

29. *Busk*, 86 Tex. 131. It could not have helped Lowrie's case that he had acted in concert with a friend named Cornelius, who also "constructively" occupied a further 74 acres of the vacant land. The scrap parcel totaled 234 acres, 74 more than Lowrie could claim for himself, which the Court might well have found savory of a conspiracy (Chriss, "Stayton, Gaines, and the Court," 48).

30. *Hogue v. Baker*, 92 Tex. 58; 45 S.W. 1004 (1898).

31. Ibid., at 65–66.

32. Gov. John Ireland, Inaugural Message, quoted in Roberts, *History of Texas*, 2:257; expounded in Chriss, "Stayton, Gaines, and the Court," generally at 60, and in the railroad context at 49–50.

33. Davenport, *Supreme Court of Texas*, 185–186; Cecil Harper, Jr., "Henry, John Lane," *Handbook of Texas Online*, http://www.tshaonline.org/handbook/online/articles/fhe21.

34. *Galveston, Harrisburg, and San Antonio Railway Company v. State*, 77 Tex. 367; 12 S.W. 988 (1889).

35. Chriss, "Stayton, Gaines and the Court," 62, and generally 61–63. On the topic of railroads bilking the public treasury, see White, *Railroaded*, 205–206.

36. *Galveston, Harrisburg and San Antonio Railway Company v. State*, 89 Tex. 340; 34 S.W. 746 (1896).

37. *Houston and Central Texas Railway Company v. State*, 90 Tex. 607; 40 S.W. 402 (1897). The same railroad had lost another case the year before on a similar issue: whether the company had been organized before the 1869 constitutional bar was passed; see *Quinlan v. Houston and Texas Central Railway Company*, 89 Tex. 356; 34 S.W.738 (1896).

38. *Thompson v. Baker*, 90 Tex. 163; 38 S.W. 21 (1896); discussed in Chriss, "Stayton, Gaines, and the Court," 66–67.

CHAPTER 10

1. Chriss, "In the Arena," 2. This would have been indeed ironic, since Willie took office with the prospect of being a better friend to the railroads than Justice Gould had been. The issue of fortunate or unfortunate collateral name identification was one that would come to the fore a century later. See Chapters 15 and 17 in this book for accounts of Chief Justice Robert Calvert's timely run for office during an advertising campaign by Calvert Whiskey, and Don Yarbrough's election.

2. Fred F. Abbey, "Gould, Robert Simonton," *Handbook of Texas Online*, http://www .tshaonline.org/handbook/online/articles/fgo22. One observer believed that one of Gould's finest expositions was a dissent from Roberts's opinion in *Ex parte Towles*, 48 Tex. 413 (1877). Roberts held that district courts had no power to review contested county court elections; Gould argued that such power was a necessary inference of the constitutional wording (Lynch, *Bench and Bar of Texas*, 312–314). The issue was settled by a more precisely worded amendment in 1891; see Braden et al., *Constitution of Texas*, art. 5.

3. Chriss, "In the Arena," 1.

4. *Queen Insurance Company v. State*, 86 Tex. 250, 24 S.W. 397 (1893); the quotation is at 86 Tex. 266, cited by Chriss, "In the Arena," 14n15.

5. *P. J. Willis Bros. v. McNeil*, 57 Tex. 465, 479 (1882).

6. Chriss, "In the Arena," 13n5.

7. *Texas and St. Louis R.R. Co. v. Young*, 60 Tex. 201 (1883).

8. Ibid., at 203–204.

9. *Texas and Pacific Railway Co. v. De Milley*, 60 Tex. 194, 197 (1883).

10. *Ormond v. Hayes, Receiver*, 60 Tex. 180 (1883).

11. Ibid., at 182.

12. Chriss, "In the Arena," 3.

13. *Houston and Texas Central Railway Co. v. Simpson*, 60 Tex. 103 (1883); cited in Chriss, "In the Arena," 8.

14. *Houston and Texas Central Railway*, 60 Tex. 106.

15. Chriss, "In the Arena," 8.

16. *Texas and Pacific Railway Company v. Gay*, 88 Tex. 111, 30 S.W. 543 (1895).

17. *Texas and Pacific Railway*, 30 S.W. 543.

18. Chriss, "In the Arena," 9; Chriss, "Stayton, Gaines, and the Court," 73.

19. *So Relle v. Western Union Telegraph Company*, 55 Tex. 308 (1881).

20. Ibid., at 312. The scholarly text was Thomas G. Shearman and Amasa A. Redfield's *Treatise on the Law of Negligence* (3rd. ed. with addenda, 1880).

21. *Gulf, Central, and Santa Fe Railway Co. v. Levy*, 59 Tex. 542 (1883); 59 Tex. 563 (1883); cited and discussed in Chriss, "Stayton, Gaines, and the Court," 74–77.

22. *Houck and Dieter v. Anheuser-Busch Brewing Association*, 88 Tex. 184, 30 S.W. 869 (1895); cited and discussed in Chriss, "In the Arena," 6–7, and Chriss, "Stayton, Gaines, and the Court," 95.

23. *Queen Insurance Company*, 86 Tex. 250, 24 S.W. 397 (1893).

24. *Queen Insurance Company*, 24 S.W. 397, 406.

25. *Gulf, Colorado, and Santa Fe Railway Co. v. Eddins*, 26 S.W. 161 (Tex. Civ. App.—Austin 1894).

26. Ibid., at 166.

27. *Railroad Commission of Texas v. Houston and Central Texas Railway Co.*, 90 Tex. 340, 38 S.W. 750, 752 (1897).

28. *Houston and Central Texas Railway*, 38 S.W. 755. Chriss points out the procedural nature of due process in Texas, making it an easier hurdle to cross than if it had been seen as economic or substantive ("In the Arena," 6).

29. Chriss, "In the Arena," 13–14n. The speech was "An Independent Judiciary as the Salvation of the Nation," delivered by Brewer in 1893. Brewer, appointed by the probusiness president Benjamin Harrison, became famous for his leonine defenses of private property rights against anything like regulation.

CHAPTER 11

1. Davenport, *Supreme Court of Texas*, 238–239; F. L. Williams, "Frank A. Williams," 241.

2. Clamp, "In Retrospect," 1. Leavening a study in which much of the source material tends toward the abstract and the cerebral, the typescript memoirs of deputy clerk H. L. Clamp, whose tenure spanned the five decades from 1902 to 1954, and later those of his colleague Carl Lyda, who worked from 1920 to 1965, provide colorful behind-the-scenes insights into the justices.

3. Worthen, "Intermediate Appellate Courts in Texas," 35–36. As the system of civil appeals courts took hold, further appellate districts were established in El Paso and Amarillo (1911), Beaumont (1915), Waco (1923), Eastland (1925), Tyler and Corpus Christi (1963), and finally Houston, coterminous with Galveston (1967).

4. *Choate v. San Antonio and Aransas Pass Railway Co.*, 91 Tex. 406, 44 S.W. 69 (1898); see Ariens, "Storm between the Quiet," 676.

5. Guittard, "Texas Appellate Courts," 317.

6. Brewster, "I Respectfully Dissent," 108–109.

7. *Missouri, Kansas & Texas Railway Co. of Texas v. Freeman*, 97 Tex. 394, 79 S.W. 9, 13 (1904). The Missouri, Kansas & Texas Railway was known as the "Katy" because its earliest stock-exchange symbol was K-T.

8. *Missouri, Kansas & Texas Railway*, 97 Tex. 410.

9. *Autry v. Reasor*, 102 Tex. 127, 108 S.W. 1164 (1908).

10. Brewster, "I Respectfully Dissent," 111.

11. Clamp, "In Retrospect," 2.

12. Ibid., 6. Acousticon hearing aids went on the market in 1905, a kind of miniature personal telephone consisting of a microphone and amplifier placed next to the ear, powered by a three-volt battery. They came in a variety of models, including a "Dining Table" version with three microphones to allow the hearing-impaired person to take part in group conversation. This was apparently not the one used, since Gaines declined to

shout into a microphone. Hearing Aid Museum Online: http://www.hearingaidmuseum
.com/gallery/Carbon/Acousticon/info/acousticonmodela.htm.

13. Clamp, "In Retrospect," 4–5, 6–7. Gaines's camping trips sometimes included
other guests, such men as federal judge and later University of Texas benefactor R. L.
Batts, and Col. A. S. Burleson, a former postmaster general of the Confederacy.

14. Clamp, "In Retrospect," 2.

15. Lyda, "Association with the Supreme Court of Texas," 2–3.

16. Clamp, "In Retrospect," 5.

17. Lyda, "Association with the Supreme Court of Texas," 4.

18. Clamp, "In Retrospect," 6.

19. See generally McKnight, "Texas Community Property Law," and Ariens, "Legal
Status of Women in Texas." For more contemporaneous assessments, see Simkins, "Law
of Community Property in Texas," and Bobbitt, "Married Women in Texas."

20. *Anderson v. Neighbors*, 25 Tex. Civ. App. 504, 61 S.W. 145 (1901).

21. *Flannery v. Chidgey*, 33 Tex. Civ. App. 638, 77 S.W. 1034 (1903).

22. Ariens, "Legal Status of Women in Texas," 2.

23. *Richburg v. Sherwood*, 101 Tex. 10, 102 S.W. 905 (1907).

24. *Edwards v. Annan*, 127 S.W. 299 (Tex. Civ. App., 1910).

25. *Dority v. Dority*, 96 Tex. 215, 71 S.W. 950 (1903).

26. *King v. Sassaman*, 64 S.W. 937 (Tex. Civ. App., 1901).

27. Rev. Stat. 1893, art. 3380.

28. *Wright v. Tipton*, 92 Tex. 168, 46 S.W. 629 (1898); Davenport, *Supreme Court of
Texas*, 238.

29. *Hatcher v. Range*, 98 Tex. 85, 81 S.W. 289, 292 (1904).

30. Ariens, "Legal Status of Women in Texas," 3–4.

31. Texas Revised Civil Statutes, art. 4629a (1911).

32. Ward, *Property Rights of Married Women in Texas* (1912; pamphlet), quoted in *Texas
Almanac* online, www.texasalmanac.com/history/highlights/supreme/.

33. Ariens, "Legal Status of Women in Texas," 5.

34. *State ex rel. Alice Wood v. Daniel Deaton*, 93 Tex. 243, 54 S.W. 901 (1900).

35. *State ex rel. Alice Wood*, 93 Tex. 246, 247.

36. *Higgins v. Bordages*, 88 Tex. 458, 31 S.W. 52 (1895); motion for rehearing at 31 S.W.
803.

37. *Higgins*, 31 S.W. 54.

38. Ibid.

39. *Lufkin v. City of Galveston*, 63 Tex. 437 (1885). The quotation is from *Higgins*, 31
S.W. 805.

40. *Storrie v. Cortes*, 90 Tex. 283, 38 S.W. 154 (1896).

41. *United States Fidelity & Guaranty Co. v. Fossati*, 97 Tex. 497, 80 S.W. 74 (1904).

42. McCormick, "Pioneer Spirit in Texas Procedure," 431–432, 435.

43. *First Baptist Church v. Fort*, 93 Tex. 215, 54 S.W. 892 (1900).

44. *First Baptist Church*, 54 S.W. 896.

45. Ibid., at 895.

46. Ibid. Interestingly, Brown decided the case not on any inherent right of a congregation to change its confession, but on whether the trust created by the original donors, of unknown intentions, could be changed without their consent.

CHAPTER 12

1. *Railroad Commission of Texas v. Houston and Texas Central Railway Co.*, 90 Tex. 340, 38 S.W. 750 (1897), upholding *Gulf, Colorado, and Santa Fe Railway Co. v. Eddins*, 26 S.W. 161 (Tex. Civ. App.–Austin, 1894).

2. *International and Great Northern Railroad Company v. Railroad Commission of Texas*, 99 Tex. 332, 89 S.W. 961 (1905). The Court did limit its approval to the Railroad Commission's righting those wrongs delineated in the bill, and not to other abuses they might encounter—requiring them to partially overrule their previous opinion in *Houston and Texas Central Railway*.

3. *State of Texas v. Galveston, Harrisburg and San Antonio Railway Company*, 100 Tex. 153, 97 S.W. 71 (1907).

4. *Missouri, Kansas and Texas Railway Company v. Shannon, Secretary of State, et al.*, 100 Tex. 379, 100 S.W. 138 (1907).

5. *State of Texas v. Texas and Pacific Railway Company*, 100 Tex. 279, 98 S.W. 834 (1907).

6. *Lively v. Missouri, Kansas and Texas Railway Company of Texas*, 102 Tex. 545, 120 S.W. 852 (1909).

7. Julia Cauble Smith, "Corsicana Oilfield," *Handbook of Texas Online*, http://www.tshaonline.org/handbook/online/articles/doc03.

8. The classic general history of the era is Rister, *Oil!* It has been more recently supplemented by Linsley, Rienstra, and Styles, *Giant under the Hill.*

9. A. W. Walker, "Fee Simple Ownership of Oil," 125. A history of oil and gas law in Texas is beyond the scope of this book, but a reasonably approachable introduction to the field is *Selected Works of A. W. Walker, Jr.*, compiled and published by the Oil, Gas, and Mineral Law Section of the State Bar of Texas (2001).

10. *Medina Oil Development Company v. Murphy*, 233 S.W. 333 (Tex. Civ. App., 1921). Cited in Walker, "Fee Simple Ownership of Oil," 125.

11. Walker, "Fee Simple Ownership of Oil," 125–126.

12. Campbell, "Gaines, Reuben Reid," *Handbook of Texas Online.*

13. See Ariens, "Storm between the Quiet," 642 ff.

14. See generally Campbell, *Gone to Texas*, 341–348, for a discussion of prohibitionism in Texas during this era, or Gould, *Progressives and Prohibitionists*, for a more expansive treatment.

15. The slogan was taken from Colossians 2:21.

16. Gould's map of wet and dry counties is reprinted in Calvert, De León, and Cantrell, *History of Texas*, 276, which also see for a general summary. For Texas prohibitionism's roots in religious fervor, see J. L. Haley, *Passionate Nation*, Chapter 56.

17. Brian Hart, "Ramsey, William Franklin," *Handbook of Texas Online*, http://www.tshaonline.org/handbook/online/articles/fra27.

18. Clamp, "In Retrospect," 7.

19. "Joseph Burton Dibrell," "Justices of Texas, 1836–1986," http://tarlton.law.utexas.edu/justices/profile/view/28; W. W. White, "Dibrell, Joseph Burton," *Handbook of Texas Online*, http://www.tshaonline.org/handbook/online/articles/fdi04. The Dibrells were also instrumental in having obtained the state's commission for Ney to sculpt the famous likenesses of Stephen F. Austin and Sam Houston, now housed in the state Capitol. Ella maintained Ney's house privately for several years before donating it to the Texas Fine Arts Association, which she founded in honor of Ney in 1911.

20. Clamp, "In Retrospect," 8.

21. *Wilson v. Brown*, 154 S.W. 322 (Tex. Civ. App.–Austin, 1913).

22. McKnight, "Texas Community Property Law," 124–126.

23. Clamp, "In Retrospect," 8.

24. Ariens, "Storm between the Quiet," 651–652, 654.

25. "Court Holds Services for Judge Phillips," 203.

26. Angela Box, relative of Nelson Phillips, to Bill Pugsley, July 22, 2010, Texas Supreme Court Historical Society.

27. Clamp, "In Retrospect," 10.

28. Ariens, "Storm between the Quiet," 658–659.

29. Ibid., 663. Under the Terrell primary election law rules, offices need be won only by a plurality, not a majority.

30. The following cases are cited as exemplary in Hill, "Nelson Phillips": on real estate law, *Burnham v. Hardy Oil Co.*, 108 Tex. 555, 195 S.W. 1139 (1917); on fraud, *Hooks v. Bridgewater*, 111 Tex. 122, 229 S.W. 1114 (1921); on mineral law, *Cox v. Robison, Commissioner*, 105 Tex. 426, 150 S.W. 1149 (1912); and *Greene v. Robison, Commissioner*, 109 Tex. 367, 210 S.W. 498 (1919).

31. "Hawkins, William E.," *Handbook of Texas Online*, http://www.tshaonline.org/handbook/online/articles/fhabb.

32. Ariens, "Storm between the Quiet," 660–662. Hawkins was the first primary challenger to a sitting justice.

33. *Dallas Morning News*, October 15, 1911, quoted in Ariens, "Storm between the Quiet," 661.

34. *State v. Texas Brewing Co.*, 106 Tex. 121, 157 S.W. 1166 (1913); described in Ariens, "Storm between the Quiet," 684.

35. Clamp, "In Retrospect," 9.

36. Ibid.

37. Quoted in Ariens, "Storm between the Quiet," 673.

38. Quoted in ibid., 678.

39. Ibid., 680.

40. *Green v. Grand United Order of Odd Fellows*, 106 Tex. 225, 163 S.W. 1071 (1914); quoted in Ariens, "Storm between the Quiet," 685–686.

41. Quoted in Ariens, "Storm between the Quiet," 678.

42. *Dallas County v. Lively*, 106 Tex. 364, 167 S.W. 219 (1914).

43. Ariens also takes Davenport to task for his uniformly uncritical assessments ("Storm between the Quiet," 675). Clamp, at least, was willing to describe Hawkins's election as "very unfortunate" ("In Retrospect," 9).

44. *St. Louis and Southwestern Railway v. Griffin*, 171 S.W. 703 (1914). Hawkins, at 707, notes, as he was wont to do, that he would file his dissent at a later date.

45. *Ex parte Mitchell*, 177 S.W. 953 (1915).

46. *State v. Swisher*, 17 Tex. 441 (1856).

47. Clamp, "In Retrospect," 4.

48. W. St. John Garwood and Virginia Parton, "Greenwood, Thomas Benton," *Handbook of Texas Online*, http://www.tshaonline.org/handbook/online/articles/fgr41; "Thomas Benton Greenwood," "Justices of Texas, 1836–1986," http://tarlton.law.utexas.edu/justices/profile/view/42.

49. Wasson, "Pilgrimage of a Law Suit," 58.

50. F. A. Williams, "To Aid the Supreme Court"; cited in Ariens, "Storm between the Quiet," 693.

51. *San Antonio and Aransas Pass Railway Co. v. Blair*, 108 Tex. 434, 196 S.W. 502 (1917).

52. Act of Apr. 3, 1918, 35th Leg., C.S., ch. 34, 1918 Tex. Gen. Laws 61; Ariens, "Storm between the Quiet," 722 ff.

53. "Committee on Jurisprudence and Law Reform, Report of the Committee," *Proceedings of the Texas Bar Association* 36 (1917): 22, 24; quoted in Ariens, "Storm between the Quiet," 679.

54. "Committee on Legal Ethics and Admission to the Bar, Report of the Committee," *Proceedings of the Texas Bar Association* 36 (1917): 43, 46; quoted in Ariens, "Storm between the Quiet," 679.

CHAPTER 13

1. Lyda, "Association with the Supreme Court of Texas," 5.

2. David Minor, "Pierson, William," *Handbook of Texas Online*, http://www.tshaonline.org/handbook/online/articles/fpi17.

3. Lyda, "Association with the Supreme Court of Texas," 7–8.

4. Clamp, "In Retrospect," 11.

5. Lyda, "Association with the Supreme Court of Texas," 5.

6. William C. Pool, "Cureton, Calvin Maples," *Handbook of Texas Online*, http://www.tshaonline.org/handbook/online/articles/fcu26.

7. Clamp, "In Retrospect," 11.

8. Ibid., 12.

9. The justices were constitutionally required to recuse themselves, and the governor had the power by statute to appoint a temporary court to hear the case (Texas Constitution

of 1876, art. 5, sec. 11; Texas Revised Civil Statutes, art. 1516 [1911]). For a full discussion of the case and the special Court, see Dunn, "Legacy of *Johnson v. Darr*," and McAfee, "All-Woman Supreme Court."

10. Woodmen of the World, "History," http://www.woodmen.org/inside.cfm?main_menu_id=1&sub_menu_id=3&Page_Id=126.

11. Richard Bailey, "Sheppard, John Morris," *Handbook of Texas Online*, http://www.tshaonline.org/handbook/online/articles/SS/fsh24.html; "Sheppard, Morris," *Biographical Directory of the United States Congress*, http://bioguide.congress.gov/scripts/biodisplay.pl?index=S000337.

12. *Johnson v. Darr*, 114 Tex. 516, 272 S.W. 1098 (1925).

13. Brian Hart, "Ramsey, William Franklin," *Handbook of Texas Online*, http://www.tshaonline.org/handbook/online/articles/fra27.

14. As enumerated by Dunn, they were *Hutcherson v. Sovereign Camp, Woodmen of the World*, 112 Tex. 551 (1923); *Sovereign Camp, Woodmen of the World v. Ayres*, 113 Tex. 564 (1924); and *Wirtz v. Sovereign Camp, Woodman [sic] of the World*, 114 Tex. 471 (1925) ("Legacy of *Johnson v. Darr*," 19).

15. *Dallas Morning News*, January 2, 1925; cited in "Texas' All-Woman Supreme Court," *Texas Almanac* online, http://www.texasalmanac.com/topics/history/texas-all-woman-supreme-court.

16. Blodgett, Blodgett, and Scott, *Land, Law, and Lord*, 148.

17. *Koy v. Schneider*, 110 Tex. 369 (1920).

18. *Harper v. State*, 90 Tex. Crim. 252, 234 S.W. 909 (Tex. Crim. App., 1921); discussed in Ariens, "Legal Status of Women in Texas," 9.

19. McKnight, "Texas Community Property Law," 125–126; *Arnold v. Leonard*, 114 Tex. 535, 273 S.W. 799 (1925).

20. *Dickson v. Strickland*, 114 Tex. 176 (1924); discussed in Dunn, "Legacy of *Johnson v. Darr*," 25–26. In considering whether use of the male pronoun was a deliberate exclusion of women from the office or merely a default usage of English language, the Supreme Court reached the opposite result from the Criminal Appeals Court's *Harper* decision.

21. Dunn, "Legacy of *Johnson v. Darr*," 22–23; Blodgett, Blodgett, and Scott, *Land, Law, and Lord*, 144.

22. See Janelle D. Scott, "Ward, Hortense Sparks," *Handbook of Texas Online*, http://www.tshaonline.org/handbook/online/articles/fwa83.

23. Dunn, "Legacy of *Johnson v. Darr*," 4–5.

24. *Dallas Morning News*, January 2, 1925.

25. J. W. Stayton, "First All-Woman Supreme Court," 5; cited in McAfee, "All-Woman Texas Supreme Court," 467.

26. Dunn, "Legacy of *Johnson v. Darr*," 27.

27. Clamp, "In Retrospect," 11–12.

28. *Motl v. Boyd*, 116 Tex. 82, 286 S.W. 458 (1926).

29. *Motl*, 116 Tex. 99.

30. The flaws in Cureton's opinion in *Motl* were revealed in *State of Texas v. Valmont Plantations*, 346 S.W.2d 853 (1961), and subsequently in *Valmont Plantations v. State of*

Texas, 355 S.W.2d 502 (1962). Baade describes in great detail how the "dual system" of water-law rights evolved and how it played out in the *Motl* and *Valmont* cases ("Texas Water Law"). Button offers a sympathetic but critical analysis of Cureton's thinking in the case ("Big Muddy").

31. Sanford, "Texas' Million Dollar Anti-Trust Suit," 187. See also Wallace, "Waters Pierce Oil Company Case," 221. For a different version of the story, see Adams, *The Waters-Pierce Case in Texas*. The best modern treatment of the Waters-Pierce saga is Singer, *Broken Trusts*.

32. *Texas v. Daugherty*, 107 Tex. 226, 176 S.W. 717 (1915).

33. *Bender v. Brooks*, 103 Tex. 329, 127 S.W. 168 (1910).

34. *Grubb v. McAfee*, 109 Tex. 527, 212 S.W. 464 (1919).

35. *Stephens County v. Mid-Kansas Oil and Gas Company*, 113 Tex. 160, 254 S.W. 290 (1923). The quotation is from "Thomas Benton Greenwood," "Justices of Texas, 1836–1986," http://tarlton.law.utexas.edu/justices/profile/view/42, citing Johnston, "Thomas Benton Greenwood," 226.

36. *W. T. Waggoner Estate v. Sigler Oil Co.*, 118 Tex. 509, 19 S.W.2nd 27 (1929).

37. *Sheffield v. Hogg*, 124 Tex. 290, 80 S.W.2nd 741 (1934).

38. Thomas D. Anderson, "Sharp, John Henry," *Handbook of Texas Online*, http://www.tshaonline.org/handbook/online/articles/fsh66.

39. "Bandits Kill Texas Supreme Court Justice and His Wife," *Dallas Morning News*, April 25, 1935.

40. *Austin American-Statesman*, April 25 and 26, 1935. Howard Pierson escaped from mental institutions twice, resulting in some years of freedom before he was recaptured. He was declared sane in September 1963, and put on trial at age forty-nine, but found not guilty by reason of insanity two months later (Vertical File, AF Murders M8900 [27] Pierson Case, Austin History Center).

41. Lyda, "Association with the Supreme Court of Texas," 8.

42. W. St. John Garwood, "Critz, Richard," *Handbook of Texas Online*, http://www.tshaonline.org/handbook/online/articles/fcr22.

CHAPTER 14

1. According to deputy clerk H. L. Clamp, Moore could not afford to make the race ("In Retrospect," 15).

2. "Andrew Houston," *Texas State Cemetery*, http://www.cemetery.state.tx.us/pub/user_form.asp?pers_id=223.

3. "Memorial: James P. Alexander," 197; Folley, "James Patterson Alexander," 1049.

4. Campbell, *Gone to Texas*, 395, 406; J. L. Haley, *Passionate Nation*, 513–514.

5. Davidson and Rutter, "Texas Women Respond," 20–21.

6. Alexander to Greenhill, July 12, 1941, in Greenhill, "War Years," 3.

7. Davidson and Rutter, "Texas Women Respond," 20. The capsule biographies of the female clerks are from the same source.

8. Ibid.

9. *Seay v. Latham,* 143 Tex. 1, 182 S.W.2d 251 (1944).

10. Davidson and Rutter, "Texas Women Respond," 21n11.

11. *Ex parte Thomas,* 141 Tex. 591, 174 S.W.2d 958 (1943); *Thomas v. Collins,* 323 U.S. 516 (1945).

12. Greenhill, "War Years," 54. Davidson and Rutter note that Greenhill's return from the war coincided with that of Ramsey's husband ("Texas Women Respond," 22).

13. This account and the following ones are drawn from Davidson and Rutter, "Colonel and the Judge."

14. "Richard Critz," "Justices of Texas, 1836–1986," http://tarlton.law.utexas.edu/justices/profile/view/19.

15. Davidson and Rutter, "Colonel and the Judge," 148n1. Clamp found Critz friendlier with the Court clerks, in whose office he stopped for a daily visit ("In Retrospect," 15).

16. *Tide Water Oil Co. v. Bean et al.,* 130 Tex. 497; 160 S.W.2d 235 (1942).

17. Davidson and Rutter, "Colonel and the Judge," 144.

18. Ibid., 146.

19. Clamp, "In Retrospect," 16.

20. Greenhill, "War Years," 54.

21. American Judicature Society, "History of Reform Efforts: Texas," http://www.judicialselection.us/judicial_selection/reform_efforts/failed_reform_efforts.cfm?state=TX.

22. *Texas Bar Journal,* "Nine-Judge Supreme Court Amendment," 448.

23. McCormick, "Modernizing the Texas Judicial System," 676–677. McCormick favored a system in which justices would be appointed, but then be regularly subjected to popular referendum, not against an opponent, but only on the question whether they should be continued in office. To do otherwise, he wrote, would subject the judge to "the hotchpot of political rivalry" (678).

24. Ibid., 679.

25. Several of the newly elevated justices served relatively short tenures on the high court. Charles S. Slatton served only two years before leaving to become general counsel to Southwestern Bell Telephone Company. He was a three-term district attorney for the Eighty-First Judicial District before his appointment to the Fourth Court of Appeals by Governor Allred in 1937; he was appointed a commissioner in 1940. He was fifty-five when he was felled by a heart attack in 1951.

Alfred Jennings Folley ("Jack" to his friends) served only three and a half years before leaving for private practice in Amarillo. A Central Texas native, he spent many years as a small-town district attorney before serving eight years as judge of the 110th District Court and then six years on the Seventh Court of Civil Appeals. President of the State Bar in 1959–1960, he practiced law until age eighty-five, retiring in 1980 and dying the following year. A Tennessean born in 1876, William M. Taylor was the oldest of the commissioners to become an associate justice. After a career as a schoolteacher in Denton and Lewisville, he read for the law under a Denton attorney, being one of the last justices not to have a formal law school education. After serving five years as judge of the Fourteenth District

Court, he was a commissioner from 1935, with a previous stint from 1918 to 1921. He was seventy-five when he retired from the Court in 1950. See also individual entries on the website "Justices of Texas, 1836–1986," http://tarlton.law.utexas.edu/justices/.

26. "Graham B. Smedley," "Justices of Texas, 1836–1986," http://tarlton.law.utexas .edu/justices/profile/view/99. See also his memorial in the *Texas Bar Journal* 17 (December 1954).

27. Robert C. Cotner, "Brewster, Few," *Handbook of Texas Online*, http://www.tsha online.org/handbook/online/articles/fbr43. See also "Few Brewster," "Justices of Texas, 1836–1986," http://tarlton.law.utexas.edu/justices/profile/view/10; and his memorial at 156 Tex. 655 (1958).

28. See Brewster, "I Respectfully Dissent."

29. "Hickman, John Edward," *Handbook of Texas Online*, http://www.tshaonline.org/ handbook/online/articles/fhi01; see also "John Edward Hickman," "Justices of Texas, 1836–1986," http://tarlton.law.utexas.edu/justices/profile/view/53.

30. Awbrey, *Legends of Dublin*, 110. The venue to which the class was relocated was the Tower Theater, on the northwest corner of Twenty-Fourth and Guadalupe Streets. Green-hill's memory was generous; portions of the church were being renovated, which necessi-tated moving Hickman's class across the street in any event.

31. This discussion is informed by a paper written by Judge Mark Davidson, "Alex-ander's Waterloo," presented at the 2006 Annual Meeting of the Texas State Historical Association.

32. *State of Texas v. Antonio Balli, et al.*, 144 Tex. 195, 194 S.W.2d 71 (1944).

33. Davidson, "Alexander's Waterloo," 15–16.

34. Ibid., 19–20.

35. Quoted in ibid., 16.

36. *Trapp v. Shell Oil Co.*, 145 Tex. 323, 198 S.W.2d 424 (1946).

37. *Railroad Commission v. Shell Oil Company*, 161 S.W.2d 1022 (1942); discussed in Davidson, "Texas Supreme Court," 8.

38. Davidson, "Texas Supreme Court," 9–10.

39. Ibid., 10.

40. Clamp, "In Retrospect," 15.

CHAPTER 15

1. "Wilmer St. John Garwood," "Justices of Texas, 1836–1986," http://tarlton.law .utexas.edu/justices/profile/view/36. When Garwood first ran for election to keep his seat, his nontraditional name — Wilmer St. John — almost cost him his job. Chief Justice Robert Calvert later recalled that Garwood told him that "next time he ran, he would run as Stonewall Jackson Garwood." Fortunately, he won the next election handily, but the ex-perience led him to advocate strongly for a merit-based judicial selection process ("His-torical Background," in *Guide to the W. St. John Garwood Papers at Tarlton Law Library*, http://www.lib.utexas.edu/taro/utlaw/00028/law-00028.html).

2. "Griffin, Meade Felix," *Handbook of Texas Online*, http://www.tshaonline.org/hand book/online/articles/fgr62; "Meade Felix Griffin," "Justices of Texas, 1836–1936," http://tarl ton.law.utexas.edu/justices/profile/view/43.

3. "Ralph Hicks Harvey," "Justices of Texas, 1836–1936," http://tarlton.law.utexas .edu/justices/profile/view/48.

4. Brands, *Interview with Robert W. Calvert*, 49, 51–52.

5. Calvert was one of the few Texas justices to leave a published memoir: *Here Comes the Judge*. See also "Robert W. Calvert," "Justices of Texas, 1836–1986," http://tarlton.law .utexas.edu/justices/profile/view/12.

6. Jim Wright, "Judicial Selection: The Name Game," *Dallas Morning News*, December 22, 1983.

7. "Clyde Earl Smith," "Justices of Texas, 1836–1936," http://tarlton.law.utexas.edu /justices/profile/view/100; Pope, "Clyde E. Smith."

8. W. Wilson, "Reappraisal of *Motl v. Boyd*"; A. White and W. Wilson, "Flow and Underflow of *Motl v. Boyd*."

9. "Will Reid Wilson, Sr.," "Justices of Texas, 1836–1936," http://tarlton.law.utexas .edu/justices/profile/view/118.

10. "Frank Pugh Culver, Jr.," "Justices of Texas, 1836–1986," http://tarlton.law.utexas .edu/justices/profile/view/21.

11. "Ruel Carlile Walker," "Justices of Texas, 1836–1986," http://tarlton.law.utexas .edu/justices/profile/view/110.

12. "Remarks of Chief Justice Hickman upon the Opening of the Court, June 23, 1954, in recognition of the passing of Associate Justice Graham B. Smedley," 254 S.W.2d (preface), quoted in Bishop, "Texas Supreme Court, 1953–1961," 1.

13. *Harned v. E-Z Finance Co.*, 151 Tex. 641, 254 S.W.2d 81 (1953). The succession of cases (among numerous others) in the following paragraphs was assembled and discussed in Bishop, "Texas Supreme Court, 1953–1961."

14. *Sybert v. Sybert*, 152 Tex. 106, 254 S.W.2d 999 (1953); the quotation is at 152 Tex. 108.

15. *Cox v. Wood*, 152 Tex. 283, 256 S.W.2d 841 (1953); cited in Bishop, "Texas Supreme Court, 1953–1961," 3.

16. *Railroad Commission of Texas v. Rowan Oil Co.*, 152 Tex. 439, 259 S.W.2d 173 (1953); cited in Bishop, "Texas Supreme Court, 1953–1961," 4–5.

17. *Rowan Oil*, 152 Tex. 447.

18. *Norris v. Vaughan*, 152 Tex. 491, 261 S.W.2d 676 (1953).

19. *Pecos Co. Water Control and Improvement Dist. No. 1 v. Williams*, 271 S.W.2d 503 (Tex. Civ. App.—El Paso, 1954, writ ref'd n.r.e. [writ refused, no reversible error]). This case and the following one are discussed in Bishop, "Texas Supreme Court, 1953–1961," 9–10.

20. *City of Corpus Christi v. City of Pleasanton*, 154 Tex. 289, 276 S.W.2d 798 (1955).

21. Bill Neal, interview with author, November 1, 2009, Texas Book Festival, Austin, Texas. Neal was Ruel Walker's briefing attorney.

22. The Gaines Court case was *Houston and Texas Central Railroad Co. v. East*, 98 Tex. 146, 81 S.W. 279 (1904).

23. *City of Corpus Christi*, 154 Tex. 296; cited in Bishop, "Texas Supreme Court, 1953–1961," 14.

24. *Aultman v. Dallas Railway and Terminal Co.*, 260 S.W.2d 596 (Tex. 1953).

25. *Texas Employers Insurance Association v. Haywood*, 266 S.W.2d 856 (1954).

26. Bishop, "Texas Supreme Court, 1953–1961," 6.

27. *Brown v. Board of Education*, 347 U.S. 483 (1954).

28. *Sweatt v. Painter*, 339 U.S. 629 (1950). A prospective law student named Heman Marion Sweatt applied to the University of Texas Law School, was denied admission, and with the Texas NAACP filed suit in state court. The case was continued in order to allow the state to establish an all-black law school, which proved to be inadequate. The suit was refiled, Sweatt lost at trial and on appeal, and the Texas Supreme Court denied a writ of error to consider the case. Sweatt and the NAACP then pursued the matter in federal court. The *Sweatt* case is covered in minute detail in Gary M. Lavergne, *Before Brown: Heman Marion Sweatt, Thurgood Marshall, and the Long Road to Justice*.

29. *McKinney v. Blankenship*, 154 Tex. 632, 282 S.W.2d 691 (1955).

30. S.B. 115, S.B. 116, S.B. 117, 50th Leg. (1949); and see generally Stills, *Gilmer-Aikin Bills*.

31. Brewster, "Prime Obligation," 41.

32. Davidson and Rutter, "Making of a Justice," 962.

33. Brands, *Interview with Joe Greenhill*, 17. Greenhill also paid tribute to his former adversary at the dedication of the Thurgood Marshall School of Law at Texas Southern University (Bubany, "Greenhill and the Judicial Process," 311).

34. Davidson and Rutter, "Making of a Justice," 962, 964.

35. Ibid., 966, 967. Judge Hughes's career became only more lustrous. President John F. Kennedy appointed her U.S. district judge in 1961. In 1963, she administered the presidential oath to Lyndon Johnson following Kennedy's assassination in Dallas; see Robert S. La Forte, "Hughes, Sarah Tilghman," in *Handbook of Texas Online*, http://www.tshaonline.org/handbook/online/articles/fhu68.

36. *Davis v. City of Lubbock*, 160 Tex. 38, 326 S.W.2d 699 (1959).

37. Quoted in Bishop, "Texas Supreme Court, 1953–1961," 23.

38. Ceremonial program, Vertical File AF COURTS—TEXAS C7935 (3) Texas Supreme Court, Austin History Center, Austin Public Library.

39. *Texas Bar Journal*, "Court Building Dedicated," 6.

40. Lyda, "Association with the Supreme Court of Texas," 2.

41. Ken Towery, "When Court Convenes, It's Goodbye Olden Bench," *American Statesman*, August 18, 1959.

42. Richard M. Morehead, "Justices Put On Black Robes, Move to New Supreme Court," *Austin American*, December 4, 1959.

CHAPTER 16

1. "Norvell, James R.," *Handbook of Texas Online*, http://www.tshaonline.org/hand book/online/articles/fnohc; "James Rankin Norvell," "Justices of Texas, 1836–1986," http://tarlton.law.utexas.edu/justices/profile/view/76.

2. McCall, a Baylor Law School graduate, was dean of the law school when appointed to the Court. He later served as president of Baylor for twenty years, followed by four years as chancellor; see "Abner Vernon McCall," "Justices of Texas, 1836–1986," http://tarlton .law.utexas.edu/justices/profile/view/68.

3. "Robert William Hamilton," "Justices of Texas, 1836–1986," http://tarlton.law .utexas.edu/justices/profile/view/44.

4. "John Edward Hickman," "Justices of Texas, 1836–1986," http://tarlton.law.utexas .edu/justices/profile/view/53. Hickman's retirement at age seventy-seven was not to be re-peated by future justices. In 1965, Texas voters amended the constitution to set the manda-tory retirement age for state judges at seventy-five.

5. Calvert, *Here Comes the Judge*, 134–135.

6. "Zollie Coffer Steakley, Jr.," "Justices of Texas, 1836–1986," http://tarlton.law .utexas.edu/justices/profile/view/105; "In Memoriam: Honorable Zollie Steakley; The Supreme Court of Texas, June 11, 1993," 879 S.W.2d 39 (1993).

7. *State of Texas v. Valmont Plantations*, 346 S.W.2d 853 (Tex. Civ. App.–San Antonio, 1961).

8. Ibid., at 879.

9. Ibid., at 883–885. An additional objection, that Pope should have recused himself from the case because he had an undivided interest in a huge family ranch that bordered on the Rio Grande and fell within the class described in the suit, was obviated when Pope divested himself of interest in the land before hearing the case. All attorneys involved were questioned about whether they wished Pope to stand down, but none did, and the other justices on the San Antonio Appeals Court endorsed his participation (*Valmont*, 346 S.W.2d, 885–886).

10. *Valmont Plantations v. State of Texas*, 163 Tex. 381, 355 S.W.2d 502 (1962). For a review of the background and aftermath of the *Valmont* case, see Pope, "Texas Surface Waters." Pope acknowledges the importance of Justice Will Wilson's 1955 water-law con-ference paper in revealing flaws in the case (Wilson, "Reappraisal of *Motl v. Boyd*"). For more about the influence of Spanish law, see Baade, "Texas Water Law," and McKnight, "Spanish Watercourses of Texas."

11. "Andrew Jackson ('Jack') Pope, Jr.," "Justices of Texas, 1836–1986," http://tarlton .law.utexas.edu/justices/profile/view/82. Pope did later espouse the cause of judicial-selection reform.

12. This and the following observations from Pope are from "In Memoriam: Chief Justice Calvert: Simple Rules Made Him Great," quoted in Scott, "Calvert Years," 5 ff.

13. Brands, *Interview with Robert W. Calvert*, 53–54.

14. Scott, "Calvert Years," 3.

15. Neal interview.

16. *Ferguson v. Huggins*, 122 Tex. 95, 52 S.W.2d 904 (1932); see Calvert, *Here Comes the Judge*, Chapter 17. In *Ferguson*, sitting governor Ross Sterling challenged his defeat for renomination by Miriam Ferguson, but the Supreme Court ruled that the executive committee's only function was to tally the vote, not determine any other issues, such as fraud.

17. Jack Pope, interview with the author, November 1, 2009.

18. Greenhill, "Remarks at the Memorial Service for Robert W. Calvert," January 18, 1995, 4; quoted in Scott, "Calvert Years," 13–14.

19. Scott cites the case of Calvert's telling a story that may or may not have been true about a postcard sent from a vacationing Justice Norvell, describing two "meeces" [moose] he had seen at the side of the road ("Calvert Years," 11). The story was repeated in Brands, *Interview with Robert W. Calvert*, 56. Calvert's memoir was titled *Here Comes the Judge*, after a running gag on the popular television show *Rowan and Martin's Laugh-In*.

20. Scott, "Calvert Years," 16–17, enumerates more cases.

21. *Landers v. East Texas Salt Water Disposal Co.*, 151 Tex. 251, 248 S.W.2d 731 (1952).

22. Brands, *Interview with Robert W. Calvert*, 53. This account differs in minor respects from Calvert, *Here Comes the Judge*, 150.

23. Pope, "In Memoriam: Chief Justice Calvert," quoted in Scott, "Calvert Years," 8.

24. Quoted in Scott, "Calvert Years," 17.

25. *Watkins v. Southcrest Baptist Church*, 399 S.W.2d 530 (1966); Brands, *Interview with Joe R. Greenhill, Sr.*, 35; Calvert's dissent (at 399 S.W.2d 536) is quoted in Scott, "Calvert Years," 16n15.

26. McKnight, "Tracings of Texas Legal History," 267.

27. *Humber v. Morton*, 426 S.W.2d 554 (1968).

28. Ibid., at 561–562.

29. Calvert, *Here Comes the Judge*, 149–150.

30. Brands, *Interview with Robert W. Calvert*, 56.

31. "Thomas Morrow Reavley," "Justices of Texas, 1836–1986," http://tarlton.law .utexas.edu/justices/profile/view/85. Reavley's judicial career eventually expanded to include not only nine years on the Supreme Court, but also stints as a special judge on the Court of Criminal Appeals and, since 1979, as a judge and then senior judge of the U.S. Court of Appeals for the Fifth Circuit.

32. "William Sears McGee," "Justices of Texas, 1836–1986," http://tarlton.law.utexas .edu/justices/profile/view/69.

33. Daniel Murph, "Daniel, Marion Price, Sr.," *Handbook of Texas Online*, http://www .tshaonline.org/handbook/online/articles/fda94; "Marion Price Daniel, Sr.," "Justices of Texas, 1836–1936," http://tarlton.law.utexas.edu/justices/profile/view/23.

34. "James Gray Denton," "Justices of Texas, 1836–1986," http://tarlton.law.utexas .edu/justices/profile/view/26.

35. Calvert, *Here Comes the Judge*, 151.

36. Scott, "Calvert Years," 12.

37. Calvert, "Next Hundred Years," 20–22. The quotations in the next two paragraphs come from the same source.

38. American Judicature Society, "History of Reform Efforts: Texas."

39. Ibid.

40. See Jim Wright, "Judicial Selection: The Name Game," *Dallas Morning News*, December 22, 1983.

CHAPTER 17

1. Greenhill kept copious notes throughout his years on the Court. These, along with his correspondence and other materials, make up a 127-volume collection housed in the Tarlton Law Library at the University of Texas. He also published a number of articles on the Court's history; see, e.g., Greenhill, "Early Supreme Court of Texas."

2. *Goldberg v. Kelly*, 397 U.S. 254 (1970); *Board of Regents v. Roth*, 408 U.S. 564 (1972).

3. *Board of Water Engineers v. Colorado River Municipal Water District*, 152 Tex. 177, 254 S.W.2d 369 (1953); Bishop, "Texas Supreme Court, 1953–1961," 3. An amicus curiae, literally "friend of the court," refers to someone who is not a party to the litigation, but who believes the court's decision might affect its interest.

4. Tex. Rev. Civ. Stat. Ann., art. 6252-13a.

5. Eissinger, "Administrative Law under the Greenhill Court," 304; see the cases cited there.

6. *Friendswood Development Company v. Smith-Southwest Industries, Inc.*, 576 S.W.2d 21 (Tex. 1978).

7. Mixon, "Jurisprudence and Greenhill," 356.

8. See, e.g., Greenhill, "Governmental Immunity for Torts."

9. "Barrow, Roberts Lawyer Pick," *Austin American-Statesman*, March 11, 1976.

10. *Beaumont Journal*, April 27, 1976.

11. "Yarbrough Win Causes Uproar," *Austin American-Statesman*, May 6, 1976.

12. "The Gospel According to Don," *Texas Monthly*, August 1976, 12.

13. Maxwell and Crain, *Texas Politics Today*, 91.

14. "Jaworski Brands Yarbrough Unfit," *Houston Post*, December 3, 1976; "Letters to the Editor: Don Yarbrough."

15. "God Did It—Yarbrough," *San Antonio Express*, May 5, 1976; "Yarbrough Gives Creator Credit," *Dallas News*, May 5, 1976.

16. Greenhill Papers, Texas Supreme Court Historical Society Archives.

17. "Donald Burt Yarbrough," "Justices of Texas, 1836–1986," http://tarlton.law.utexas.edu/justices/profile/view/120.

18. Greenhill, "Constitutional Amendment Giving Criminal Jurisdiction," 394.

19. Bubany cites Greenhill's stepping into this issue with approval ("Greenhill and the Judicial Process," 306).

20. Greenhill, "State of the Judiciary Message, April 21, 1981," 4.

21. Ibid., 7–8.

22. Ibid., 8–9. He opened address by remarking on the propriety that he spoke to them

on San Jacinto Day, for one cause of the Texas Revolution was the lack of an efficiently functioning judiciary.

23. "Franklin Scott Spears," "Justices of Texas, 1836–1986," http://tarlton.law.utexas.edu/justices/profile/view/103.

24. "Cread L. Ray, Jr.," "Justices of Texas, 1836–1986," http://tarlton.law.utexas.edu/justices/profile/view/84.

25. Garwood was sidelined only briefly, being appointed by President Ronald Reagan to the U.S. Fifth Circuit Court of Appeals, where he remained, attaining senior status sixteen years later; see "William Lockhart Garwood," "Justices of Texas, 1836–1986," http://tarlton.law.utexas.edu/justices/profile/view/37.

26. Brands, *Interview with Joe R. Greenhill*, 39.

27. "Ruby Kless Sondock," "Justices of Texas, 1836–1986," http://tarlton.law.utexas.edu/justices/profile/view/102.

28. "William Wayne Kilgarlin," "Justices of Texas, 1836–1986," http://tarlton.law.utexas.edu/justices/profile/view/63.

29. Calvert's letter is quoted in Pope, "They May Shoot Me," 36.

30. For a full account of the episode, see Pope, "They May Shoot Me," 36–40.

31. Jack Pope, interview with author, Austin, Texas, October 30, 2009.

32. Pope, "State of the Judiciary Message, January 17, 1983."

33. Senate Bill 179, Appropriations Act, art. 4, Judiciary, May 26, 1983.

34. "Raul A. Gonzalez, Jr.," "Justices of Texas, 1836–1986," http://tarlton.law.utexas.edu/justices/profile/view/38.

35. Pope later said he retired because he would have hit the mandatory retirement age for judges during his next term: "Too young to be a judge in the beginning; too old to comply with the retirement law, at the end. Just about the time I was getting the hang of being a judge, I had to retire"; quoted in "Andrew Pope," *Texas State Cemetery*, http://www.cemetery.state.tx.us/pub/user_form.asp?pers_id=2904.

36. "John L. Hill, Jr.," "Justices of Texas, 1836–1986," http://tarlton.law.utexas.edu/justices/profile/view/54.

37. Hill and Stromberger, "About the Authors," *John Hill for the State of Texas*, http://johnhillfortexas.com/authors.html.

38. Oscar Mauzy," *Texas State Cemetery*, http://www.cemetery.state.tx.us/pub/user_form.asp?pers_id=5978.

39. Ibid. For a detailed story of the Killer Bees episode, see "Flight of the Killer Bees," *Time*, June 4, 1970; online at http://www.time.com/time/magazine/article/0,9171,946253,00.html (subscription required).

40. *Mayes v. Massachusetts Mutual Life Insurance Co.*, 608 S.W.2d 612 (Tex. 1980).

41. Harrist and Kawalek, "Ride the Roller Coaster," 1.

42. Ibid., 2.

43. *Humber v. Morton*, 426 S.W.2d 554 (1968).

44. *G-W-L, Inc. v. Robichaux*, 643 S.W.2d 392 (1982).

45. See Guzzo, "Buying a Home in Texas," 98.

46. *Melody Homes Manufacturing Co. v. Barnes*, 741 S.W.2d 349 (1987).

47. Brown, "Case of the Month," 2.

48. This refers to the "Is Justice for Sale?" episode on CBS's *60 Minutes*, December 6, 1987, which precipitated closer public scrutiny of the Texas Court and the election of three Republicans in 1988.

49. See Appendix B, "Justices of the Texas Supreme Court, 1836–2012, with Appointment/Election Dates" for information on members of the modern Court.

BIBLIOGRAPHY

Adams, Frederick Upham. *The Waters-Pierce Case in Texas.* St. Louis: Skinner and Kennedy, 1908.

Almaráz, Felix D. "Governor Antonio Martínez and Mexican Independence in Texas." *Permian Historical Annual* 15 (1975).

Ariens, Michael. "The Legal Status of Women in Texas, 1900–25." Paper presented at the Annual Meeting of the Texas State Historical Association, Austin, Texas, 2004. Copy in Texas Supreme Court Historical Society files.

———. *Lone Star Law: A Legal History of Texas.* Lubbock: Texas Tech Univ. Press, 2011.

———. "The Storm between the Quiet: Tumult in the Texas Supreme Court, 1911–21." *St. Mary's Law Journal* 38, no. 3 (2007).

Ashford, Gerald. "Jacksonian Liberalism and Spanish Law in Early Texas." *Southwestern Historical Quarterly* 57, no. 1 (July 1953).

Austin, Mattie Alice. "The Municipal Government of San Fernando de Bexar, 1730–1800." *Quarterly of the Texas State Historical Association* 8, no. 4 (April 1905).

Awbrey, Jon A. *Legends of Dublin: Personalities of the Irish Capital of Texas.* Dublin, Tex.: BookSurge Publishing, 2009.

Baade, Hans W. "Chapters in the History of the Supreme Court of Texas: Reconstruction and 'Redemption' (1866–1882)." *St. Mary's Law Journal* 40, no. 1 (2008).

———. "The Historical Background of Texas Water Law: A Tribute to Jack Pope." *St. Mary's Law Journal* 18, no. 1 (1986).

———. "Law and Lawyers in Pre-Independence Texas." In State Bar of Texas, *Centennial History of the Texas Bar, 1882–1982.*

Baker, DeWitt Clinton. *A Texas Scrap Book, Made Up of the History, Biography, and Miscellany of Texas and Its People.* Austin: Steck, 1935.

Bandelier, Adolph Francis, ed. and trans. *The Journey of Álvar-Nuñez Cabeza de Vaca and His Companions from Florida to the Pacific, 1528–1536.* New York: Barnes, 1905.

Barker, Eugene C. *The Life of Stephen F. Austin, Founder of Texas, 1793–1836.* Nashville: Cokesbury Press, 1925. Reprint, Austin: Texas State Historical Association, 1949.

Barker, Nancy Nichols, ed. and trans. *The French Legation in Texas*, Vol. 1: *Recognitions, Rupture, and Reconciliation.* Austin: Texas State Historical Association, 1971.

Bell, Spurgeon E. "A History of the Texas Courts." In State Bar of Texas, *Centennial History of the Texas Bar.*

Biographical Encyclopedia of Texas. New York: Southern Publishing, 1880.

Bishop, Barry. "History of the Texas Supreme Court, 1953–1961." Unpublished draft, 2006. Texas Supreme Court Historical Society History Book Project. Texas Supreme Court Historical Society files.

Blodgett, Dorothy, Terrell Blodgett, and David L. Scott. *The Land, the Law, and the Lord: The Life of Pat Neff.* Austin: Homeplace, 2007.

Bloomfield, Maxwell. "The Texas Bar in the Nineteenth Century." *Vanderbilt Law Review* 32 (1979).

Bobbitt, D. F. "Contractual Power of Married Women in Texas." *Texas Law Review* 1 (1922–23).

Bolton, Herbert E. "Notes and Fragments: The Founding of Mission Rosario." *Southwestern Historical Quarterly* 10, no. 1 (July 1906).

———. *Texas in the Middle Eighteenth Century: Studies in Spanish Colonial History and Administration.* Berkeley and Los Angeles: Univ. of California Press, 1915. Reprint, Austin: Univ. of Texas Press, 1970.

Braden, George D., et al. *The Constitution of Texas: An Annotated Comparative Analysis.* Austin: Texas Advisory Commission on Intergovernmental Relations, 1977. Available at http://www.sll.state.tx.us/const/braden.html.

Bradley, Ed. "Fighting for Texas: Filibuster James Long, the Adams-Onís Treaty, and the Monroe Administration." *Southwestern Historical Quarterly* 102, no. 3 (January 1999).

Brands, H. W., interviewer. *A Texas Supreme Court Trilogy,* Vol. 1: *Oral History Interview with the Honorable Robert W. Calvert.* Austin: Jamail Center for Legal Research, University of Texas School of Law, 1998.

———. *A Texas Supreme Court Trilogy,* Vol. 2: *Oral History Interview with the Honorable Joe R. Greenhill.* Austin: Jamail Center for Legal Research, University of Texas School of Law, 1998.

———. *A Texas Supreme Court Trilogy,* Vol. 3: *Oral History Interview with the Honorable Jack Pope.* Austin: Jamail Center for Legal Research, University of Texas School of Law, 1998.

Brewster, Few. "I Respectfully Dissent." In *The Dallas Bar Speaks,* vol. 11. Dallas: Wilkinson, 1948.

———. "Prime Obligation." *Texas Bar Journal* 17 (1954).

Brown, Richard F. "Case of the Month: *Melody Manufacturing Co. v. Barnes.*" Opinion piece, Brown & Fortunato, PC, Amarillo, Texas. http://www.bf-law.com/dmsdl.php?docid=131.

Bubany, Charles P. "Chief Justice Greenhill and the Judicial Process." *Thurgood Marshall Law Review* 8, no. 2 (Special Issue, 1983).

Buckley, Eleanor C. "The Aguayo Expedition into Texas and Louisiana, 1719–1722." *Southwestern Historical Quarterly* 15, no. 1 (July 1911).

Burton, H. T. "A History of the JA Ranch." *Southwestern Historical Quarterly* 31 (April 1928).

Button, Roger D. "The Big Muddy: Chief Justice Cureton and Texas Water Law, 1921–40." Paper presented at the Annual Meeting of the Texas State Historical Association, Austin, Texas, 2006. Texas Supreme Court Historical Society files.

Calvert, Robert A., Arnoldo De León, and Gregg Cantrell. *The History of Texas.* 4th ed. Wheeling, Ill.: Harlan Davidson, 2007.

Calvert, Robert W. *Here Comes the Judge: From State Home to State House.* Waco, Tex.: Texian Press, 1977.

————. *Judicial System of Texas.* Reprinted from 361–362 S.W.2nd. Saint Paul, Minn.: West, 1963.

————. "The Next Hundred Years." *Houston Bar Journal* (June 1971).

Campbell, Randolph B. *Gone to Texas: A History of the Lone Star State.* New York: Oxford Univ. Press, 2003.

————. *A Southern Community in Crisis.* Austin: Texas State Historical Association, 1983.

————, ed. William S. Pugsley and Marilyn P. Duncan, comps. *The Laws of Slavery in Texas.* Austin: Univ. of Texas Press, 2010.

Cantrell, Gregg. *Stephen F. Austin: Empresario of Texas.* New Haven, Conn.: Yale Univ. Press, 1999.

Casis, Lilia M. "Carta de Don Damian Manzanet á Don Carlos de Siguenza sobre el Descubrimiento de la Bahía del Espíritu Santo" ("Letter of Don Damian Manzanet to Don Carlos de Siguenza Relative to the Discovery of the Bay of Espiritu Santo)." *Quarterly of the Texas State Historical Association* 2, no. 4 (April 1899).

Chambers, William M. *Sketch of the Life of General T. J. Chambers.* Galveston: Galveston News Book and Job Office, 1853.

Chapman, Betty Trapp. *Rough Road to Justice: The Journey of Women Lawyers in Texas.* Austin: Texas Bar Books, 2008.

Childs, William R. *Texas Railroad Commission: Understanding Regulation in America to the Mid-Twentieth Century.* College Station: Texas A&M Univ. Press, 2005.

Chipman, Donald E. *Spanish Texas, 1519–1821.* Austin: Univ. of Texas Press, 1992.

Chriss, William J. "In the Arena: The Texas Supreme Court's Steady Rein on Railroads and Big Business, 1880–1900." Paper presented at the Texas State Historical Association Annual Meeting, Corpus Christi, Texas, March 2008. Available at http://works.bepress.com/william_chriss/3.

————. "Stayton, Gaines, and the Capitol Court, 1882–1900." In *The Selected Works of William J. Chriss.* Available online at http://works.bepress.com/william_chriss/6/.

Clamp, H. L. "In Retrospect." Unpublished memoir, 1956. Texas Supreme Court Historical Society files.

Clark, L. D. *Civil War Recollections of James Lemuel Clark.* College Station: Texas A&M Univ. Press, 2002.

Cobb, Thomas R. R. *An Inquiry into the Law of Negro Slavery in the United States of America.* Philadelphia: Johnson, 1858.

Cohen, J. M., ed. *Christopher Columbus: The Four Voyages; Being His Own Log-Book, Letters, and Dispatches with Connecting Narratives.* New York: Penguin Classics, 1992.

Connor, Seymour V. *The Peters Colony of Texas.* Austin: Texas State Historical Association, 1959. Reprint, 2006.

Crouch, Barry A. "'All the Vile Passions': The Texas Black Code of 1866." *Southwestern Historical Quarterly* 97, no. 1 (July 1993).

Curtsinger, Louise C. "The Career of Judge William P. Ballinger." *West Texas State Historical Association Yearbook* 18 (1942).

Dallam, James Wilmer, comp. *Opinions of the Supreme Court of Texas from 1840 to 1844 Inclusive.* St. Louis: Gilbert, 1883.

Davenport, J. H. *The History of the Supreme Court of the State of Texas, with Biographies of the Chief and Associate Justices.* Austin: Southern Law Book Publishers, 1917.

Davidson, Mark. "Alexander's Waterloo: The Fight for the Texas Supreme Court and Padre Island Intersect." Paper presented at the Annual Meeting of the Texas State Historical Association, Austin, Texas, 2006.

———. "One Woman's Fight for Freedom: *Gess v. Lubbock.*" *Houston Lawyer,* January–February 2008, 10–15. Reprinted in Campbell, *Laws of Slavery in Texas,* 87–93.

———. "Texas Supreme Court, 1945–1954." Unpublished draft, 2005. Texas Supreme Court Historical Society History Book Project. Texas Supreme Court Historical Society files.

Davidson, Mark, and Kent Rutter. "The Making of a Justice: The 1958 Joe Greenhill/Sarah T. Hughes Race for the Supreme Court." *Texas Bar Journal* 63, no. 10 (November 2000).

———. "The Texas Supreme Court Goes to War: Texas Women Respond to the Court's Call to Duty." *Texas Bar Journal* 65, no. 1 (January 2002).

———. "The Texas Supreme Court Goes to War: The Colonel versus The Judge." *Texas Bar Journal* 65, no. 2 (February 2002).

Day, Arthur Grove. *Coronado's Quest: The Discovery of the Southwestern States.* Berkeley and Los Angeles: Univ. of California Press, 1940.

Dixon, Samuel Houston, and Louis Wiltz Kemp. *The Heroes of San Jacinto.* Houston: Anson Jones Press, 1932.

Dunn, Jeffrey C. "The Legacy of *Johnson v. Darr*: The 1925 Decision of the All-Woman Texas Supreme Court." Paper presented at the Annual Meeting of the Texas State Historical Association, Austin, Texas, 2004.

Eissinger, James R. "Developments in Administrative Law under the Greenhill Court, 1972–1982." *Thurgood Marshall Law Review* 8, no. 2 (Special Issue, 1983).

Ely, James W. *Railroads and American Law.* Lawrence: Univ. of Kansas Press, 2001.

Ericson, Joe E. *Judges of the Republic of Texas (1836–1846): A Biographical Directory.* Dallas: Taylor, 1980.

Everett, Dianna. *The Texas Cherokees: A People between Two Fires, 1819–1840.* Norman: Univ. of Oklahoma Press, 1990.

Fisher, John E. "The Legal Status of Free Blacks in Texas, 1836–1861." *Texas Southern University Law Review* 3, no. 1 (Spring 1973).

Folley, A. J. "A Texas Portrait—James Patterson Alexander." *Texas Bar Journal* 24 (Nov. 1961).

Frantz, Joe B., and Julian Ernest Choate. *The American Cowboy: The Myth and the Reality.* Norman: Univ. of Oklahoma Press, 1955.

Friend, Llerena B. *Sam Houston: The Great Designer.* Austin: Univ. of Texas Press, 1954.

Gaines, Reuben Reid. "John Hemphill, 1803–1862." In *Great American Lawyers,* ed. William Draper Lewis. Vol. 4. Philadelphia: Winston, 1908.

Gammel, H. P. N. *The Laws of Texas, 1822–1897.* 10 vols. Austin: Gammel Book Co., 1898. Available at http://texashistory.unt.edu/ark:/67531/metapth5872/.

Gardner, Linda. *The Texas Supreme Court: An Index of Selected Sources on the Court and Its Members, 1836–1981.* Tarlton Legal Bibliography, no. 25. Austin: Tarlton Law Library, Univ. of Texas at Austin, 1983.

Gatschet, Albert S. *The Karankawa Indians: The Coast People of Texas.* Cambridge, Mass.: Peabody Museum of American Archeology and Ethnology, 1891.

Gilbert, Randal. "'Unwhipped of Justice': The Conflict between John Bankhead Magruder and the Texas Supreme Court." Paper presented at the Annual Meeting of the Texas State Historical Association, Austin, Texas, 2009.

Gilmer, Daffan. "Early Courts and Lawyers of Texas." *Texas Law Review* 12 (1934).

Godfrey, Cullen M. "A Brief History of the Oil and Gas Practice in Texas." *Texas Bar Journal* 68, no. 9 (2005).

Gould, Lewis J. *Progressives and Prohibitionists: Texas Democrats in the Wilson Era.* Austin: Univ. of Texas Press, 1973.

Gracy, David B., IV. *Moses Austin: His Life.* San Antonio: Trinity Univ. Press, 1987.

Greenhill, Joe R. "The Constitutional Amendment Giving Criminal Jurisdiction to the Texas Courts of Civil Appeals and Recognizing the Inherent Power of the Texas Supreme Court." *Texas Tech Law Review* 33, no. 2 (2002).

———. "The Early Supreme Court of Texas and Some of Its Justices." *Texas Bar Journal* 62, no. 7 (July 1999).

———. "Should Governmental Immunity for Torts Be Re-examined, and, If So, by Whom?" *Texas Bar Journal* 31, no. 11 (Dec. 1968).

———. "State of the Judiciary Message: Address to the Sixty-Sixth Legislature, January 31, 1979." Texas Supreme Court Historical Society files.

———. "State of the Judiciary Message: Address to the Sixty-Seventh Legislature, April 21, 1981." Texas Supreme Court Historical Society files.

———. "The Supreme Court of Texas during the Civil War and Reconstruction." Unpublished paper, n.d. Texas Supreme Court Historical Society files.

———. "The War Years." Unpublished memoir, 1997. Texas Supreme Court Historical Society files.

Gruben, Karl T., and James E. Hambleton. *A Reference Guide to Texas Law and Legal History: Sources and Documentation.* 2nd ed. Austin: Butterworth, 1987.

Guittard, Clarence A. "Unifying the Texas Appellate Courts." *Texas Bar Journal* 37, no. 4 (April 1974).

Guzzo, Julie. "Buying a Home in Texas: What the Law Implies." *Journal of Consumer and Commercial Law* 6, no. 3 (Spring 2003). Available at https://www.judicialview.com/Law-Articles/Property/Buying-a-Home-in-Texas/What-the-Law-Implies/40/8656.

Haley, J. Evetts. *Charles Goodnight: Cowman and Plainsman*. Boston: Houghton Mifflin, 1936.

Haley, James L. *The Buffalo War: The History of the Red River Indian Uprising of 1874–1875*. Garden City, N.Y.: Doubleday, 1976.

———. *Passionate Nation: The Epic History of Texas*. New York: Free Press, 2006.

———. *Sam Houston*. Norman: Univ. of Oklahoma Press, 2002.

———. *Texas: An Album of History*. Garden City, N.Y.: Doubleday, 1985.

———. *Texas: From the Frontier to Spindletop*. New York: St. Martin's, 1991.

Hall, Dorris Collie, ed. "N. C. Raymond's Report on the Legislature of 1846." *Southwestern Historical Quarterly* 75, no. 1 (July 1971).

Hall, Ford W. "An Account of the Adoption of the Common Law by Texas." *Texas Law Review* 28 (1950).

Hamilton, Jeff. *My Master: The Inside Story of Sam Houston and His Times*. As told to Lenoir Hunt. Dallas: Manfred, Van Nort, 1940.

Harrist, Richard C., and Matthew C. Kawalek. "Trends in the Texas Supreme Court: Ride the Roller Coaster with the Insurance Industry." Paper presented at the 16th Annual Insurance Symposium, Dallas, Texas, 2009.

Hart, Katherine Drake, ed. and trans. *Alphonse in Austin*. Austin: Encino, 1986.

Henson, Margaret Swett. *Juan Davis Bradburn: A Reappraisal of the Mexican Commander at Anahuac*. College Station: Texas A&M Univ. Press, 1982.

Hightower, Jack. "Freemasonry, the Texas Supreme Court, and the Law of Texas: An Examination of the Relevance of Freemasonry to the Development of the Law." Anson Jones Lecture, Texas Lodge of Research, 1999.

Hill, Vernon B. "A Texas Portrait: Nelson Phillips." *Texas Bar Journal* 23, no. 9 (October 22, 1960).

Hogan, William Ransom. *The Texas Republic: A Social and Economic History*. Norman: Univ. of Oklahoma Press, 1946.

Jackson, Jack. *Los Mesteños: Spanish Ranching in Texas, 1721–1821*. College Station: Texas A&M Univ. Press, 2006.

Jacobs, James Ripley. *Tarnished Warrior: Major-General James Wilkinson*. New York: Macmillan, 1938.

Jennett, Elizabeth LeNoir. "Description of the State Capitol and the Governor's Mansion, Austin, Texas, and Brief History of the Various Capitols of the State." October 26, 1943. Legislative Reference Library, Austin, Texas.

Johnston, V. M. "A Texas Portrait: Thomas Benton Greenwood." *Texas Bar Journal* 24 (1961).

Journals of the Convention, assembled at the city of Austin on the Fourth of July, 1845, for the purpose of framing a constitution for the State of Texas. Austin: Miner and Cruger, printers to the Convention, 1845. Available at http://tarlton.law.utexas.edu/constitutions/pdf/images/index1845.html.

Kemp, Louis Wiltz. "The Capitol at Columbia." *Southwestern Historical Quarterly* 48 (July 1944).

Kens, Paul. "Wide Open Spaces? The Texas Supreme Court and the Scramble for the

State's Public Domain, 1876–1898." *Western Legal History* 16, no. 2 (Summer–Fall, 2003).

Kilgarlin, William W. "A Review of a Decade of Change." Paper presented to the St. Mary's Torts Institute, San Antonio, Texas, May 1989.

King, C. Richard. "William Pitt Ballinger: Texas Bibliophile." *Texas Libraries* 31 (Winter 1969).

Kittrell, Norman G. *Governors Who Have Been, and Other Public Men of Texas.* Houston: Dealy-Adey-Elgin, 1921.

Klemme, Chris. "Jacksonian Justice: The Evolution of the Elective Judiciary in Texas, 1836–1850." *Southwestern Historical Quarterly* 105 (2002).

Krieger, Alex D. *We Came Naked and Barefoot: The Journey of Cabeza de Vaca across North America.* Austin: Univ. of Texas Press, 2002.

La Vere, David. *The Texas Indians.* College Station: Texas A&M Univ. Press, 2003.

Lavergne, Gary M. *Before Brown: Heman Marion Sweatt, Thurgood Marshall, and the Long Road to Justice.* Austin: Univ. of Texas Press, 2010.

Laws and Decrees of the State of Coahuila and Texas. Translated by J. P. Kimball; introduced by Joseph W. McKnight. Houston: Telegraph Power Press, 1839. Reprint, Lawbook Exchange, 2010.

Leckie, William. *Military Conquest of the South Plains.* Norman: Univ. of Oklahoma Press, 1963.

Linsley, Judy, Ellen Rienstra, and Jo Ann Styles. *Giant under the Hill: A History of the Spindletop Oil Discovery at Beaumont, Texas, in 1901.* Austin: Texas State Historical Association, 2002.

Locheed, Alicia L. "The Development of the Court of Criminal Appeals." *Texas Bar Journal* 55, no. 10 (November 1992).

Looscan, Adele B. "Life and Service of John Birdsall." *Southwestern Historical Quarterly* 26 (July 1922).

Lubbock, Francis Richard. *Six Decades in Texas.* Austin: Jones, 1900.

Lyda, Carl B. "Forty-five Years' Association with the Supreme Court of Texas." Unpublished memoir, May 1971. Texas Supreme Court Historical Society files.

Lynch, James D. *The Bench and Bar of Texas.* St. Louis: Nixon-Jones, 1885.

Mabry, Robert Smith. "Capitol Context: A History of the Texas Capitol Complex, 1839–1989." Master's thesis, School of Architecture, University of Texas at Austin.

Maher, Edward R. "Sam Houston and Secession," *Southwestern Historical Quarterly* 55, no. 4 (April 1952).

Markham, Edward Lee, Jr. "The Reception of the Common Law of England in Texas and the Judicial Attitude Toward that Reception, 1840–1859." *Texas Law Review* 29 (1951).

Maxwell, William Earl, and Ernest Crain. *Texas Politics Today.* 13th ed. Florence, Ky.: Cengage Learning, 2007.

McAfee, Alice G. "The All-Woman Supreme Court: The History behind a Very Brief Moment on the Bench." *St. Mary's Law Journal* 39, no. 3 (2008).

McClendon, James W. "Development of the Judicial System of Texas." *Texas Bar Journal* 12, no. 2 (February 1949).

McCormick, Andrew Phelps. *Scotch-Irish in Ireland and in America as Shown in Sketches of the Pioneer Scotch-Irish Families Mccormick, Stevenson, Mckenzie, and Bell, in North Carolina, Kentucky, Missouri, and Texas.* New Orleans, 1897.

McCormick, Charles T. "Modernizing the Texas Judicial System." *Texas Law Review* 21, no. 6 (June 1943).

———. "The Revival of the Pioneer Spirit in Texas Procedure." *Texas Law Review* 18 (1939–40).

McGown, Nancy. "The Supreme Court of the Republic of Texas, 1836–1845." Unpublished paper, December 1977. Texas Supreme Court Historical Society files.

McKnight, Joseph W. "Hispanic Legal Antecedents (1716–1836): Law on the Spanish Frontier." Draft chapter, 2007. Texas Supreme Court Historical Society History Book Project. Texas Supreme Court Historical Society files.

———. "Stephen Austin's Legalistic Concerns." *Southwestern Historical Quarterly* 89 (January 1986).

———. "The Spanish Watercourses of Texas." In *Essays in Legal History in Honor of Felix Frankfurter.* Indianapolis: Bobbs Merrill, 1966.

———. "Texas Community Property Law—Its Course of Development and Reform." *California Western Law Review* 8, no. 1 (Fall 1971).

———. "Tracings of Texas Legal History: Breaking Ties and Borrowing Traditions." In State Bar of Texas, *Centennial History of the Texas Bar, 1882–1982.*

Mixon, John. "Jurisprudence and Chief Justice Joe Greenhill: The Influence of the Chief Justice on Texas Real Property Law." *Thurgood Marshall Law Review* 8, no. 2 (Special Issue, 1983).

Moneyhon, Carl H. *Republicanism in Reconstruction Texas.* Austin: Univ. of Texas Press, 1980.

Moretta, John. *William Pitt Ballinger: Texas Lawyer, Southern Statesman.* Austin: Texas State Historical Association, 2000.

Muir, Andrew Forest, ed. *Texas in 1837: An Anonymous, Contemporary Narrative.* Austin: Univ. of Texas Press, 1958.

Nash, A. E. Keir. "The Texas Supreme Court and Trial Rights of Blacks, 1845–1860." *Journal of American History* 58, no. 3 (December 1971). Reprinted in Campbell, *Laws of Slavery in Texas.*

Neu, C. T. "The Case of the Brig *Pocket." Quarterly of the Texas State Historical Association* 12 (April 1909).

Newcomb, William W., Jr. *The Indians of Texas from Prehistoric to Modern Times.* Austin: Univ. of Texas Press, 1961.

Norvell, James R. "Oran M. Roberts and the Semicolon Court." *Texas Law Review* 37 (1959).

———. "The Reconstruction Courts of Texas, 1867–1873." *Southwestern Historical Quarterly* 62, no. 2 (October 1958).

———. "The Supreme Court of Texas under the Confederacy, 1861–1865." *Houston Law Review* 4 (Spring–Summer 1966).

Norvell, James R., and Ronald L. Sutton. "The Original Writ of Mandamus in the Supreme Court of Texas." *St. Mary's Law Journal* 1 (1969).

Nunn, William C., ed. *Ten More Texans in Gray*. Hillsboro, Tex.: Hill Junior College Press, 1980.

———. *Texas under the Carpetbaggers*. Austin: Univ. of Texas Press, 1962.

Ogletree, D. W. "Establishing the Texas Court of Appeals, 1875–1876." *Southwestern Historical Quarterly* 47, no. 1 (July 1943).

Paschal, George W. "Last Years of Sam Houston." *Harper's New Monthly Magazine* 32 (1865–1866).

Paulsen, James W. "Community Property and the Early American Women's Rights Movement: The Texas Connection." *Idaho Law Review* 32 (1996).

———. "The Judges of the Supreme Court of the Republic of Texas." *Texas Law Review* 65, no. 2 (December 1986).

———. "The Missing Cases of the Republic." *Texas Law Review* 65, no. 2 (December 1986).

———. "Sam Houston v. Mirabeau B. Lamar: A Forgotten Frontier Furniture Fracas." *Houston Law Review* 45 (January–February 2008).

———. "A Sesquicentennial Celebration: The Establishment of a Unique Texas Institution." *Texas Bar Journal* 53 (January 1990).

———. "A Short History of the Supreme Court of the Republic of Texas." *Texas Law Review* 65, no. 2 (December 1986).

Paulsen, James W., and James Hambleton. "Confederates and Carpetbaggers: The Precedential Value of Decisions from the Civil War and Reconstruction Era." *Texas Bar Journal* 51, no. 9 (October 1988).

Phillips, Thomas R. "Justice Franklin S. Spears: Unsung Hero of Texas Justice," *St. Mary's Law Journal* 28 (1997).

———. "The Merits of Merit Selection." *Harvard Law Review* 85 (2009).

———. "Popular Elections for the Texas Supreme Court." Draft monograph, December 16, 2010. Austin, Texas.

Phillips, William D., Jr., and Carla Rahn Phillips. *The Worlds of Christopher Columbus*. Cambridge: Cambridge Univ. Press, 1991.

Philquist, S. A. "The Supreme Court of Texas." *Texas Bar Journal* 1 (1938).

Pickering, David, and Judy Falls. *Brush Men and Vigilantes: Civil War Dissent in Texas*. College Station: Texas A&M Univ. Press, 2004.

Pope, Jack. "In Memoriam: Chief Justice Calvert: Simple Rules Made Him Great." *St. Mary's Law Journal* 26 (1995).

———. "Memorial Ceremony, Justice Clyde E. Smith, October 30, 1971." Pope Papers. Abilene Christian University and University of Texas at Austin.

———. "State of the Judiciary Message: Address to the Sixty-Eighth Legislature, January 17, 1983." Texas Supreme Court Historical Society files.

———. "A Story about Texas Surface Waters." Pope Papers, No. 14:02, May 1999. Abilene Christian University and University of Texas at Austin.

———. "They May Shoot Me Down in Flames, But I Will Never Make a Deal." Pope Papers, Abilene Christian University and University of Texas at Austin.

Pugsley, William S. "The Curious Case of the Runaway Slave Who Was Free." Paper presented at the Annual Meeting of the Texas State Historical Association, Dallas, Texas, 2010.

Rackley, J. Caleb. "A Survey of Sea-Change on the Supreme Court of Texas and Its Turbulent Toll on Texas Tort Law." *South Texas Law Review* 48, no. 3 (Spring 2007).

Raines, Cadwell Walton. *Analytical Index to the Laws of Texas, 1823–1905.* Austin: Von Boeckmann-Jones, 1906. Reprint, Littleton, Colo.: Rothman, 1987.

———. "Enduring Laws of the Republic of Texas, I." *Texas Historical Association Quarterly* 1, no. 2 (1897).

Ramsdell, Charles W. *Reconstruction in Texas.* New York: Columbia Univ. Press, 1910. Reprint, Austin: Texas State Historical Association, 1970.

Richardson, Rupert Norval, Adrian Anderson, Cary D. Wintz, and Ernest Wallace. *Texas: The Lone Star State.* 10th ed. Upper Saddle River, N.J.: Prentice Hall, 2010.

Ricklis, Robert A. *The Karankawa Indians of Texas.* Austin: Univ. of Texas Press, 1996.

Rister, Carl Coke. *Oil! Titan of the Southwest.* Norman: Univ. of Oklahoma Press, 1949.

Robards, Charles L. *Synopses of the Decisions of the Supreme Court of the State of Texas.* Austin: Brown and Foster, 1865.

Roberts, Oran. "The Political, Legislative, and Judicial History of Texas for its Fifty Years of Statehood, 1845–1895." In *Comprehensive History of Texas, 1685 to 1897* (1898), ed. Dudley G. Wooten. Dallas: Scarff, 1898.

Robinson, Duncan W. *Judge Robert McAlpin Williamson: Texas' Three-Legged Willie.* Austin: Texas State Historical Association, 1948.

Rowe, Edna. "The Disturbances at Anahuac in 1832." *Quarterly of the Texas State Historical Association* 6, no. 4 (April 1903).

Rubin, Nancy. *Isabella of Castile: The First Renaissance Queen.* New York: St. Martin's, 1992.

Sanford, Allan D. "Texas' Million Dollar Anti-Trust Suit." *Texas Bar Journal* 11 (1948).

Scott, L. Wayne, "In Memoriam: Robert Wilburn Calvert, the Prudentialist." *St. Mary's Law Journal* 26, no. 4 (1995).

———. "The Texas Supreme Court: The Calvert Years (1961–1972)." Draft chapter, 2007. Texas Supreme Court Historical Society History Book Project. Texas Supreme Court Historical Society files.

Shelley, George E. "The Semicolon Court of Texas." *Southwestern Historical Quarterly* 48 (April 1945).

Siegel, Stanley. *A Political History of the Texas Republic, 1836–1845.* Austin: Univ. of Texas Press, 1956.

Simkins, W. S. "Some Phases of the Law of Community Property in Texas." *Texas Law Review* 3 (1924–25).

Sinclair, T. C. "The Supreme Court of Texas." *Houston Law Review* 7, no. 1 (September 1969).

Singer, Jonathan W. *Broken Trusts: The Texas Attorney General versus the Oil Industry, 1889–1909.* College Station: Texas A&M Univ. Press, 2002.

Speer, Ocie. *Texas Jurists*. Austin, 1936.

State Bar of Texas. *Centennial History of the Texas Bar, 1882–1982*. Austin: Committee on History and Tradition of the State Bar of Texas, 1981.

Stayton, John William. "The First All-Woman Supreme Court in the World." *Holland's Magazine*, March 1925.

Stayton, Robert W. "A Prospect of Justice." *Texas Bar Journal*, 6, no. 4 (April 1943).

Stills, Rae File. *The Gilmer-Aikin Bills*. Austin: Steck, 1950.

Story, Joseph. *Commentaries on the Constitution of the United States*. 3 vols. Boston: Hilliard, Gray, 1833.

Supreme Court of Texas. *The Texas Reports*. Vols. 1–163. Galveston: Office of the *Galveston News*, 1847–1962.

Teja, Jesús F. de la. *San Antonio de Béxar: A Community on New Spain's Northern Frontier*. Albuquerque: Univ. of New Mexico Press, 1995.

Terrell, A. W. "Recollections of General Sam Houston." *Southwestern Historical Quarterly* 16 (October 1912).

Texas Bar Journal. "Court Building Dedicated." Vol. 23, no. 1 (January 1960).

———. "Court Holds Services for Judge Phillips." Vol. 2, no. 7 (July 1939).

———. "Justice Phillips Was Picturesque Figure." Vol. 2, no. 5 (May 1939).

———. "Letters to the Editor: Don Yarbrough." Vol. 40, no. 3 (March 1977).

———. "Memorial: James P. Alexander." Vol. 11 (February 1948).

———. "Texas Voters Adopt Nine-Judge Supreme Court Amendment." Vol. 8, no. 9 (October 1945).

Texas Jurisprudence. 45 vols. San Francisco: Bancroft-Whitney, 1929; 2nd ed., 1959; 3rd ed., 1979.

Texas Monthly. "The Gospel According to Don." August 1976.

Townes, John C. "Sketch of the Development of the Judicial System of Texas, I." *Quarterly of the Texas Historical Association Quarterly* 2, no. 1 (July 1898).

Trelease, Frank J. "Coordination of Riparian and Appropriative Rights to the Use of Water." *Texas Law Review* 33 (1954).

Underwood, Rodman L. *Death on the Nueces: German Texans Treue der Union*. Austin: Eakin, 2002.

Vigness, David. *Spanish Texas, 1519–1810*. Boston: American Press, 1983.

Walker, A. W., Jr. "Fee Simple Ownership of Oil and Gas in Texas." *Texas Law Review* 6 (1927–28).

———. *Selected Works of A. W. Walker, Jr*. Austin: Oil, Gas, and Mineral Law Section, State Bar of Texas, 2001.

Walker, Andrew. "Mexican Law and the Texas Courts." *Baylor Law Review* 55 (Winter 2003).

Wallace, Charles B. "Waters Pierce Oil Company Case Revisited." *Texas Bar Journal* 64 (1961).

Wallace, Ernest, David M. Vigness, and George B. Ward, eds. *Documents of Texas History*. Rev. ed. Austin: Texas State Historical Association, 2003.

Waller, John L. *Colossal Hamilton of Texas*. El Paso: Texas Western Press, 1968.

Walsh, William Thomas. *Isabella of Spain: The Last Crusader, 1451–1504*. New York: Mc-Bride, 1930.

Wasson, Alonzo. "Pilgrimage of a Law Suit." *Texas Bar Journal* 3 (1940).

Weddle, Robert S. *The French Thorn: Rival Explorers in the Spanish Sea, 1682–1762*. College Station: Texas A&M Univ. Press, 1991.

———. *The San Saba Mission: Spanish Pivot in Texas*. Austin: Univ. of Texas Press, 1964.

Weeks, William F., reporter. *Debates of the Texas Convention, 1845*. Houston: Cruger, 1846.

———, ed. *Journals of the Convention, assembled at the City of Austin on the Fourth of July, 1845, for the purpose of framing a Constitution for the State of Texas*. Facsimile ed., Austin: Shoal Creek, 1974. Available at http://tarlton.law.utexas.edu/constitutions/pdf/images/00000001.pdf.

Welch, June Rayfield. *The Texas Governor*. Dallas: GLA Press, 1977.

Wharton, Clarence. "Early Judicial History of Texas." *Texas Law Review* 12 (1934).

White, A. A., and Will Wilson. "The Flow and Underflow of *Motl v. Boyd*: The Problem." *Southwestern Law Journal* 9, no. 1 (1955).

White, Richard. *Railroaded: The Transcontinentals and the Making of Modern America*. New York: Norton, 2011.

White, William W. "The Texas Slave Insurrection of 1860." *Southwestern Historical Quarterly* 52 (January 1949).

Widener, Michael. "Foreign Law Books on the Texas Frontier: The Civil Law Collection of the Texas Supreme Court." Paper presented at the Annual Meeting of the Roman Law Society, University of Kansas School of Law, August 26, 2000.

Williams, Amelia W., and Eugene C. Barker, eds. *The Writings of Sam Houston 1813–1863*. 8 vols. Austin: Univ. of Texas Press, 1938–1943.

Williams, F. A. "What Can Be Done to Aid the Supreme Court." *Proceedings of the Texas Bar Association* 35, no. 14 (1916).

Williams, Fred L. "A Texas Portrait: Frank A. Williams." *Texas Bar Journal* 27 (1969).

Williams, Michael L. "Can Oil and Water Mix?" *Texas Bar Journal* 68, no. 9 (2005).

Willis, William L. "The Evolution of the Court of Criminal Appeals." *Texas Bar Journal* 29 (1966).

Wilson, Maurine T., and Jack Jackson. *Philip Nolan and Texas: Expeditions to the Unknown Land*. Waco, Tex.: Texian Press, 1987.

Wilson, Will. "Reappraisal of *Motl v. Boyd*." *Proceedings, Water Law Conferences, 1952 and 1954*. Austin: Univ. of Texas School of Law, 1955.

Winfrey, Dorman H. *Capitols of Texas*. Waco: Texian Press, 1970.

Woodard, Calvin. "Common Law and Common-Law Legal Systems." In *Encyclopedia of the American Judicial System* 2:500–16. Chicago: Scribner's, 1987.

Woods, J. M. "Pioneer Jurists of Texas." *Texas Bar Journal* 4, nos. 1 and 2 (January–February 1941).

Wooten, Dudley G., ed. *Comprehensive History of Texas, 1685 to 1897*. 2 vols. Dallas: Scarff, 1898.

Worthen, James T. "The Organizational and Structural Development of Intermediate Appellate Courts in Texas, 1892–2003." *South Texas Law Review* 46, no. 1 (Fall 2004).

Wynn, Leila Clark. "A History of the Civil Courts in Texas." *Southwestern Historical Quarterly* 60, no. 1 (July 1956).

Yoakum, Henderson K. *History of Texas from Its First Settlement in 1685 to Its Annexation to the United States in 1846*. New York: Redfield, 1856.

ONLINE RESOURCES

American Judicature Society. "History of Reform Efforts: Texas." http://www.judicial selection.us/judicial_selection/reform_efforts/failed_reform_efforts.cfm?state=TX.

State Bar of Texas. *Texas Bar Journal* archive. Journal issues from 1938 to the present are available from the state bar's website via Hein Online. http://www.texasbar.com.

Supreme Court of Texas. "Court History." http://www.supreme.courts.state.tx.us/court /history.asp.

Texas Courts Online. http://supreme.courts.state.tx.us/court/.

Texas State Cemetery. *Database of Biographies, Texas Public Officials*. http://www.cemetery .state.tx.us/database.asp.

Texas State Historical Association. *Handbook of Texas Online*. http://www.tshaonline.org /handbook.

University of North Texas. *Nineteenth-Century Texas Online: Gammel's The Laws of Texas, 1822–1897*. http://texinfo.library.unt.edu/lawsoftexas/.

———. *Portal to Texas History*. "Explore Texas Reports; Texas Supreme Court Reports Online." http://texashistory.unt.edu/explore/collections/TXRPT/browse/.

University of Texas at Austin, Tarlton Law Library. "Justices of Texas, 1836–1986." http:// tarlton.law.utexas.edu/justices/.

———. "Timeline of the Texas Supreme Court and Court of Criminal Appeals." http:// tarlton.law.utexas.edu/justices/texas_courts/timeline.

MANUSCRIPTS

Austin History Center, Austin Public Library, Vertical Files
    John Hemphill
    AF Murders M8900 (27) Pierson Case
    Supreme Court
Dolph Briscoe Center for American History, University of Texas at Austin, Vertical Files
    Moses and Stephen F. Austin Papers
Catholic Archives of Texas
    Sam Houston Papers
Texas State Preservation Board
    "Supreme Court Courtroom: Adaptive Historical Room Treatment, Interpretive Date: c. 1905." Unpublished manuscript.

INDEX

Note: Italic page numbers refer to photographs.

Granger, Gordon, 75
Grant, Ulysses S., 79, 86, 119
Grass Lease Fight, 123
Grassmeyer v. Beeson (1855), 37
Gray, Peter W., 90
Gray, William Fairfax, 90
Greenback faction, 95
"Green Flag" rebellion of 1812, 9
Greenhill, Joe Robert: and amicus curiae, 206; as associate justice of Texas Supreme Court, 192–193, 195, 202; as briefing attorney, 174, 175, 177, 183–184, 206, 284n12; on Robert W. Calvert, 201; as chief justice, 206–207, 209, 210–212; on Richard Critz, 178; on John E. Hickman, 181, 285n30; on history of Texas Supreme Court, 206, 213, 269n11, 273n29, 290n1; and Thurgood Marshall, 192, 287n33; portrait of, *224*; resignation of, 212, 213, 234
Greenwood, Thomas B., 160–161, 164–165, 169–170
Griffin, Charles, 79
Griffin, Meade F., *113*, 185, 197, 200, 202, 203
Group of Fourteen, 212
Grubbs, Virginia, 175
Grubb v. McAfee (1919), 170
Guess v. Lubbock (1851), 61–62, 265n31
Guittard, Clarence, 174
Gulf, Central, and Santa Fe Railway Co. v. Levy (1883), 135
G-W-L, Inc. v. Robichaux (1982), 216

Hall, Warren D. C., 45, 121
Hall v. Phelps (1841), 44–45, 121
Hambleton, James, 267n16, 271n53
Hamilton, Andrew Jackson: as associate justice of Texas Supreme Court, 80; and Richard Coke, 77; and election of 1869, 81, 85; and election of 1873, 270n26; and Lemuel Evans, 80–81, 82; as provisional governor, 75–76, 77,

81; and Joseph Rodríguez, 84, 85; as Unionist, 61, 76
Hamilton, Jeff, 263n23
Hamilton, Robert William, 196–197, 204
Hamilton v. Blank (1844), 37
Hammett, J. V., 174
Hansford, John M., 30
Harned v. E-Z Finance Co. (1953), 188
Harvey, Ralph Hicks, 185–186
Harvey v. Patterson (1840), 34–35
Hatcher v. Range (1904), 146
Hawkins, William E., 157–162, 163, 281n43
Haynie v. Republic (Tex. 1845), 24
Hemphill, Henrietta, 59
Hemphill, John: as associate judge of Republic of Texas Supreme Court, 34, 35, 36; background of, 20–21; as chief justice of Republic of Texas Supreme Court, 20, 21, 27, 34, 36, 37–38, 39, 40–41, 51, 121; as chief justice of Texas Supreme Court, 21, 54, 56–57, 58, 73, 103, 173, 190, 264n12; and Council House Fight, 26–27; on election of Texas judiciary, 73, 158; and equity jurisprudence, 41–42, 57, 129; and hybridized system of pleading, 264n19; portrait of, *103*, 117, 194, *219*; salary of, 32; and Spanish civil law, 21, 36, 38–42, 43, 54, 56, 57, 58–59, 170, 264n12; and Texas Constitution, 56; as U.S. Senate replacement for Houston, 61, 67; Royall Wheeler on, 39, 40–41, 261n38, 261n43; will of, 59, 264n23; and women's rights, 58, 59
Hemphill, Sabina, 59
Hemphill, Theodora, 59, 264n23
Henderson, James Pinckney, 31, 95
Henenberg, Hattie, *110*, 167
Henry, John Lane, 119, 127, 128
Herbert, P. W., 47–49
Hickman, John Edward: as chief justice of Texas Supreme Court, 111, 185,

struction, 79–87, 88, 270n19; and
Andrew Hamilton, 75–76; Presiden-
tial Reconstruction, 75–76, 79, 88, 129,
269n11, 270n19; and Texas Supreme
Court, 76–87, 93, 229
Red River War of 1874, 119
Red Rolls, Lewis John, 62–64, 65
Reeves, Reuben A., 73, 74, 89, 92, 105, *105*,
268n42
Regulator-Moderator War, 25, 29, 30
religion, freedom of, 78, 149–150, 279n46
Renn v. Samos (1871), 87
Republican Party: and elections, 86, 115,
207, 208, 209, 210, 211, 214, 233, 234;
and Reconstruction, 80, 81, 83, 84, 86
Republic of Texas: capital of, 17–18; and
Chambers, 16; constitution of, 18, 19;
election of 1841, 45–46; judiciary of,
18; and public domain, 119; Spanish
law's legacy in, 16, 21, 33, 36; and U.S.
annexation of Texas, 53
Republic of Texas Constitution: adoption of, 19, 21; and judiciary, 18, 32–33,
34, 37, 259n26; and Spanish civil law,
38–39
Republic of Texas Supreme Court: and
appellate courts of Anglo-American
settlers, 256n25; caseload of, 33; chief
justices of, 18, 19–21, 29, 32, 34, 235;
conservatism of, 36; district judges as
associate judges, 18, 22, 33, 39, 101; and
free blacks, 49–50; and Indian tribes,
47–49; and judicial regularity, 43–44;
jurisdiction of, 32, 33, 35; justices of,
18, 235–236; and land disputes, 44–45;
moral tone of, 46–47; organization of,
227–228; president nominating judicial candidates, 17; sessions of, 18, 34;
term of, 33, 34. *See also specific justices*
Republic of Texas Supreme Court,
cases: *Benton v. Williams* (1843),
49–50; *Board of Land Commissioners of Milam County v. Bell* (1840),

35–36; *Cavenah v. Somervill* (1843),
46; *Donald McDonald v. Lewis Hancock* (1846), 49, 263n22; *Duggan v.
Cole* (Tex. 1845), 22; *Fowler v. Poor*
(1841), 37; *Grassmeyer v. Beeson* (1855),
37; *Hall v. Phelps* (1841), 44–45, 121;
Hamilton v. Blank (1844), 37; *Harvey v.
Patterson* (1840), 34–35; *Haynie v. Republic* (Tex. 1845), 24; *Jones v. Nowland*
(1842), 43; *Lamar v. Houston* (1845),
50–51; *Mitchell v. Barton* (1842), 44;
Saddler v. The Republic (1843), 46–47;
Scott and Solomon v. Maynard et uxor.
(1843), 37–38; *Whiting v. Turley* (1842),
39–40
Revised Statutes of Texas, 118
Richburg v. Sherwood (1907), 144–145
Roberts, Oran Milo: as associate justice
of Texas Supreme Court, 60, 64, 72;
and Black Codes, 76; as chief justice,
73, 74, 87, 88–89, 91, 92–93, 94, 95,
98, 105, 271n53, 271n54; and election
of 1878, 95; and Robert Gould, 129,
276n2; as governor, 95–96, 120; on
Andrew Hamilton, 81; on John Hemphill, 39; and Sam Houston, 31, 60,
265n24; as law faculty at University of
Texas, 130; portrait of, *105*, *220*; and
public lands, 120, 127; and railroads,
126–127, 128; resignation of, 67; and
Secession Convention, 66; and John
Stayton, 96, 97, 118; as U.S. Senator,
77, 88; and Alexander Walker, 118
Robertson, Nellie, 167
Robertson, Sawnie, 118
Robinson, James W., 26–27, 34
Rodríguez, Joseph, 84–86
Rule in Shelley's Case, 188
rule-making power, 231
Rules of Civil Procedure, Texas, 174, 204,
231
Runnels, Hardin, 77
Rusk, Thomas Jefferson: as chief justice

of Republic of Texas Supreme Court, 20, 34–36, 54–55, 102, 138, 258n13; on election of Texas judiciary, 73, 158; as general of militia, 262n16; and Lamar's war to expel Cherokees, 20, 47; portrait of, *102, 219*; resignation of, 21, 32; and siege of Bexar, 258n12
Rust, Richard, 59

Saddler v. The Republic (1843), 46–47
St. Louis and Southwestern Railway v. Griffin (1914), 160
Sampson and Keene v. Williamson and Wife (1851), 56, 57
Samuels, Sidney, 42
San Antonio, Texas, 6, 7–8, 9, 26, 28, 94, 260n36
San Antonio v. Mehaffy (1878), 94
San Jacinto, Battle of, 19, 23, 26, 28, 30
Santa Anna, Antonio López de, 13, 16, 23, 28, 260n36
Sayers, Joe, 139
school lands, Texas, 120, 122–123, 125, 126, 127, 144
Scott, John, 24
Scott and Solomon v. Maynard et uxor. (1843), 37–38
Scrap Law of 1887, 125–126
Scurry, Richardson, 29–30
Seabury, Francis, 182
Seay v. Latham (1944), 176
Secession Convention (1861), 66–67, 77, 84, 88, 90, 91, 265n24
Semicolon Case (*Ex parte Rodriguez*), 86
Semicolon Court, 83–86, 87, *104*, 271n53, 271n54
sex-offender registry, 273n43
Sharp, John Henry, *111*, 170–171, 172, 174, 183
Sheffield v. Hogg (1934), 170
Shelby, Anthony, 22, 34
Shepherd v. Cassiday (1857), 56–57
Sheridan, Philip, 79, 80, 84, 93

Shivers, Allan, *112*, 186, 191, 192, 196, 199, 203–204
Shivers, Robert, 186
Simpson, Gordon, 177–179, 183, 185
Slatton, Charles S., 183, 184, 284n25
slaves and slavery: and Anahuac Disturbances, 13, 50; and brutality against black residents, 49; and German settlers, 60, 70, 265n28, 267n23; and John Hemphill, 59; and Sam Houston, 49, 61, 66, 263n23; and Reconstruction, 75, 76; in Republic of Texas, 61; and Texas Supreme Court, 60, 61–64, 65, 78–79, 81, 265n25. *See also* free blacks
"Smallpox Case," 140–141
Smedley, George B.: as associate justice of Texas Supreme Court, 180, 181, 183, 187, 188, 200, 201; death of, 180, 187, 204; and Nelson Phillips, 157
Smisson v. State (1888), 124
Smith, Clyde Earl, 186–187, 199, 200, 204
Smith, George Washington, 77
Smith v. Smith (1847), 58
Snoddy v. Cage (1849), 57–58
Sondock, Ruby Kless, *115*, 212, 216
So Relle v. Western Union Telegraph Company (1881), 134–135, 188
Spanish Constitution, 9, 10
Spanish law: and adoption, 2; civil law, 7–8, 11, 14, 21, 33, 36, 38–42, 43, 58–59, 169; and criminal justice, 42; and debt, 2, 56; and land disputes, 44, 74; legacy of, 16, 21, 33, 36; and water rights, 2, 169, 187, 190, 198–199, 288n10; and women's rights, 2, 3, 38, 56, 58–59
Spanish missions, 5–6, 7
Sparks, J. H., 71
Spears, Franklin, 211
Speer, Ocie, 157
Spencer, Frank, 84
Spindletop Hill, 152, 169
Spraberry Field, 189

271n53, 271n54; and slaves and slavery, 60, 61–64, 65, 78–79, 81, 265n25; structure and organization of, 227–234; and "substantial evidence" rule, 177, 184; in temporary Capitol, *107, 108*; terms of, 54, 91; Wartime Court, 174–184; and water law, 168–169, 189–190, 197–199, 282–283n30, 288n10; and women's rights, 58, 98, 143–147, 148, 155, 167, 202, 282n20; writ of error system, 178. *See also* Republic of Texas Supreme Court

Texas Supreme Court Historical Society, 112, 213, 234

"Texas Troubles," 266n49

Texas Urban Renewal Statute, 193

Texas (U.S. state): and annexation, 17, 25, 51, 53–54; antipathy toward slavery in, 60–61; antisecession sentiment in, 61, 66, 76, 80, 266n2; public lands of, 119–128; refugees from other Confederate states in, 95, 118; secessionist sentiment in, 65, 66–67, 73, 89, 103, 265n24, 266n2; Spanish law's legacy in, 16; Unionism in, 69, 70, 80

Texas v. Daugherty (1915), 170

Texas v. White (1869), 79, 269n18

Texas Woman's University, 163

Thomas, R. J., 176

Thomas v. Collins (1945), 176

"Three-Legged Willie" (Robert M. Williamson), 24–25, 29, *101*

Throckmorton, James W., 61, 77, 79, 80, 95, 119

Tidelands case, 187

Tide Water Oil Co. v. Bean et al. (1942), 177

tort law: and attractive nuisance doctrine, 133; and charitable immunity doctrine, 202; and Joe Greenhill, 211; joint tortfeasors, 201; and Oscar Mauzy, 215; and telegraph companies, 134

Townes, John C., 157

Trapp v. Shell Oil Co. (1946), 184

Travieso, Vicente Álvarez, 7

Trespalacios, Felix, 256n18

United States: annexation of Texas, 17, 25, 51, 53–54; English common law in, 41; and Indian tribes, 47, 48, 262n18; observations of Texas jurisprudence, 32, 40

United States Fidelity & Guaranty Co. v. Fossati (1904), 149

United States Supreme Court: and corporate influence, 137; and due process in administrative hearings, 206; and Hortense Sparks Ward, 167; and oil and gas law, 170; and Texas bonds, 79, 94

United States Supreme Court, cases of: *Board of Regents v. Roth* (1972), 206; *Brown v. Board of Education* (1954), 191, 192; *Bush v. Gore* (2000), 176; *Cherokee Nation v. Georgia* (1831), 48, 262n18; *Dred Scott* decision (1857), 60; *Goldberg v. Kelly* (1970), 206; *San Antonio v. Mehaffy* (1878), 94; *Sweatt v. Painter* (1950), 191, 192, 287n28; *Texas v. White* (1869), 79, 269n18; *Thomas v. Collins* (1945), 176; *Tidelands* case, 187

University of San Augustine, 60

University of Texas School of Law, 130, 175, 179, 191, 192, 287n28

Valmont Plantations v. State of Texas (1962), 199, 282–283n30

Vermont, 188

Waco tribe, 47

Walker, Alexander Stuart, *107*, 118–119

Walker, A. W., Jr., 152–153

Walker, Moses B., 81, 82, 83, 104, *104*, 270n35

Walker, Richard S., 89

CPSIA information can be obtained at www.ICGtesting.com
Printed in the USA
BVOW08s1634130913

331119BV00004B/14/P